Packet Video Communications over ATM Networks

K. R. Rao
University of Texas at Arlington

Z. S. Bojkovic
University of Belgrade, Yugoslavia

ISBN 0-13-011518-5

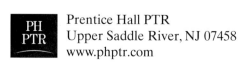

PH PTR
Prentice Hall PTR
Upper Saddle River, NJ 07458
www.phptr.com

Library of Congress Cataloging-in-Publication Data

Rao, K. R. (Kamisetty R.)
  Packet video communications over ATM networks / K. R. Rao, Z. S. Bojkovic.
    p. cm.
  Includes bibliographic references.
  ISBN 0-13-011518-5 (hc)
  1. Asynchronous transfer mode. 2. Digital video. 3. MPEG (Video coding standard)
  I. Bojkovic, Z. S. II. Title.
  TK5105.35.R36 1999
  621.382'16--dc21   99-44156
                                                        CIP

Editorial/Production Supervision: Benchmark Productions, Inc.
Acquisitions Editor: *Bernard Goodwin*
Cover Design Director: *Jerry Votta*
Cover Design: *Talar Agasyan*
Manufacturing Manager: *Alexis R. Heydt*
Editorial Assistant: *Diane Spina*
Marketing Manager: *Lisa Konzelmann*
Project Coordinator: *Anne Trowbridge*

© 2000 Prentice Hall PTR
Prentice-Hall, Inc.
Upper Saddle River, NJ 07458

Prentice Hall books are widely used by corporations and government agencies for training, marketing, and resale.

The publisher offers discounts on this book when ordered in bulk quantities. For more information, contact: Corporate Sales Department, Phone: 800-382-3419; Fax: 201-236-7141; E-mail: corpsales@prenhall.com; or write: Prentice Hall PTR, Corp. Sales Dept., One Lake Street, Upper Saddle River, NJ 07458.

Printed in the United States of America

10 9 8 7 6 5 4 3 2 1

ISBN 0-13-011518-5

Prentice-Hall International (UK) Limited, *London*
Prentice-Hall of Australia Pty. Limited, *Sydney*
Prentice-Hall Canada Inc., *Toronto*
Prentice-Hall Hispanoamericana, S.A., *Mexico*
Prentice-Hall of India Private Limited, *New Delhi*
Prentice-Hall of Japan, Inc., *Tokyo*
Pearson Education Asia Pte. Ltd., *Singapore*
Editora Prentice-Hall do Brasil, Ltda., *Rio de Janeiro*

Contents

Preface

Five broad aspects characterize a modern communications network:

- **Transmission.** A means of transporting bits across a medium.
- **Switching**, **routing.** Given an "increment of information" (a frame, a cell, a circuit), determine the destination of that increment.
- **Signaling.** Provide a method by which users can describe to the network what they want to do.
- **Services.** Provide "something of value" that the user wants.
- **Management.** Provide for the handling of faults, connections, and traffic flow.

These five terms have existed and have been used for a long time in the communications industry. They have, however, over the years become confused, redefined, misapplied, and indistinct. In the "old" days when there was only circuit switching and the function was performed by mechanical switches, transmission was analog over twisted pair subscriber loops, signaling was by dial tone/pulse dialing, and services included end-to-end telephony/long distance/operator assistance. The terms were fairly obvious.

The ability of Asynchronous Transfer Mode (ATM) networks to combine voice, video, and data communications capabilities in a single network are expected to make ATM the networking method of choice for video delivery in the future. The ATM Forum is currently developing standards to address the issues associated with video delivery. The marriage of communications and computers has opened a new era in interactive audio-visual applications. The Audiovisual Multimedia Services Technical Committee is currently addressing the issues relating to numerous video applications, including broadcast video, videoconferencing, desktop multimedia, video on demand, interactive video, near video on demand, distance learning, and interactive games. Packet video communications over ATM networks is a rapidly evolving field with growing applications in science and industry [1, 257].

Packet Video Communications over ATM Networks provides a comprehensive coverage of various surveys of the current issues relating to video delivery over ATM networks. This book addresses the fundamentals of the major topics of video communications over ATM networks: asynchronous transfer mode technique, scalability, MPEG digital video standards, quality of service, and multimedia communications. We have focused our attention on mature topics with the hope that the level of discussion provided will enable an engineer or a scientist to design a packet video communication system over ATM networks or conduct research on advanced and newly emerging topics. The objective of this book is not only to familiarize the reader with packet video communications over ATM networks, but also to provide the underlying theory, concepts, and principles related to these problems, including the power and the practical utility of the topics. In most cases, the applications are described conceptually, rather than in detail.

A major challenge during the preparation of this book was the rapid pace of development, both in software and hardware related to packet video communications over ATM networks. Many specific applications have been realized in the past few years. We have tried to keep pace by including many of these latest developments. In this way, it is hoped that the book is timely and will appeal to a wide audience in the engineering, scientific, and technical communities.

In addition, we have included more than 180 figures and over 518 references. Although this book is primarily for graduate students, it can be also very useful for academia, researchers, scientists, and engineers dealing with packet video communications over ATM networks.

Acknowledgments

It is a pleasure to acknowledge the help received from colleagues associated with universities, research labs, and industry. This help was in the form of technical papers and reports, valuable discussions, information, brochures, the review of various sections of the manuscript, computer programs, and more. Special thanks are due to the following people:

G. Chenghui	Tsinghua University
R. M. Gray	Stanford University
M. Isnardi	Sarnoff Corporation
J. K. Kim	Korea Advanced Institute of Science and Technology
T. Maldonado	University of Texas at Arlington
J. Nafornita	Politechnica University of Timisoara
S. Panchanathan	Arizona State University
G. Seckin	Arizona State University
G. Sullivan	PictureTel Corporation
C. Zhigang	Tsinghua University

The help of Abrahim Nadimi, Kay Khanthalangsy, Vivian Jeng, Napodon Kaewkamnerd, Rene Elizalde, Saowaluck Areepongsa, Danh Nguyen, Susannah Man, Cindy Smith, Huihui Wang, Mary Jo Handke, Yasser Syed, Chang Kee Choi, Orachat Sukmarg, and Dr. Robert Magnusson is immensely appreciated. Special thanks go to Dragorad Milovanovic, University of Belgrade, Yugoslavia, for improving some of the text in Chapters 5 and 7 (ITU-T, MPEG-4, MPEG-7, Internet standards) and Appendices A, B, and C. He was also instrumental in the formatting of the final manuscript.

Acronyms

2D	Two-Dimensional
3D	Three-Dimensional
AAL	ATM Adaptation Layer
AAP	ATM Access Point
ABR	Available Bit Rate
AC	Arithmetic Coder
ACF	Auto Covariance Function
ACM	Association for Computing Machinery
ACR	Allowed Cell Rate
ADSL	Asymmetric Digital Subscriber Loop (Line)
AFI	Authority and Format Identifier
AL	Adaptation Layer
AP	Access Point
AR	Autoregressive
ARMA	Autoregressive Moving Average
ARPANET	Advanced Research Project Agency Network
ASIC	Application-Specific Integrated Circuit
ASSP	Acoustics, Speech, and Signal Processing
ATDM	Asynchronous Time-Division Multiplexer
ATM	Asynchronous Transfer Mode
ATSC	Advanced Television Systems Committee
AV	Audio-Visual
AVO	Audio-Visual Object
AW	Additional Weighter
BAB	Binary Alpha Block
BAP	Body Animation Parameter
BER	Bit Error Rate
BGP	Border Gateway Protocol
BIFS	Binary Format for Scene Description

BISDN	Broadband ISDN
BMA	Block-Matching Algorithm
bpp	Bits per pixel
BT	Burst Tolerance
CAC	Connection Admission (Acceptance) Control
CAE	Content-based Arithmetic Encoding
CBR	Constant Bit Rate
CCIR	International Radio Consultative Committee
CCITT	International Telephone and Telegraph Consultative Committee
CCR	Current Cell Rate
CD	Compact Disc, Committee Draft
CD-ROM	Compact Disc-Read Only Memory
CDV	Cell Delay Variation
CDVT	Cell Delay Variation Tolerance
CE	Core Experiments
CEC	Commission of the European Communities
CI	Congestion Indicator
CIF	Common Intermediate Format
CLP	Cell Loss Priority
CLR	Cell Loss Rate (Ratio)
CMIP	Common Management Information Protocol
CPCS	Common Part Convergence Sublayer
CPE	Customer Premises Equipment
CPI	Common Part Indication
CPU	Central Processing Unit
CR	Conversion Ratio
CRC	Cyclic Redundancy Check
CS	Convergence Sublayer
CSI	Convergence Sublayer Identifier
CSVT	Circuits and Systems for Video Technology
CTD	Cell Transfer Delay
DAI	DMIF Application Interface
DARPA	Defense Advanced Research Project Agency
DBR	Deterministic Bit Rate
DBS	Direct Broadcast Satellite
DCT	Discrete Cosine Transform
DDL	Description Definition Language
DES	Destination End System

DFT	Discrete Fourier Transform
DIS	Draft International Standard
DLC	Data Link Control
DLL	Data Link Layer
DMIF	Delivery Multimedia Integration Format
DMS	Distributed Multimedia System
DNI	DMIF Network Interface
DNS	Domain Name System
DPCM	Differential Pulse Code Modulation
DS	Description Scheme, DMIF Signaling
DSM	Digital Storage Media
DSP	Digital Signal Processing
DSSSL	Document Style Semantics Specification Language
DVB	Digital Video Broadcasting
DVD	Digital Video Disc
DWT	Discrete Wavelet Transform
EBU	European Broadcasting Union
ECSQ	Entropy-Constrained Scalar Quantizers
ECTCQ	Entropy-Constrained Trellis Coded Quantizer
ECVQ	Entropy-Constrained Vector Quantizer
ELT	Extended Lapped Transform
EOB	End of Block
ER	Explicit Rate
ERM	Explicit Rate Marking
ES	Elementary Stream
ETSI	European Television Standards Institute
FAP	Facial Animation Parameter
FBR	Fixed Bit Rate
FCD	Final Committee Draft
FD	Frame Difference
FDDI	Fiber Distributed Data Interface
FDP	Facial Definition Parameter
FEC	Forward Error Correction
FIFO	First-In First-Out
FlexMux	Flexible Multiplex
fps	Frames per second
FS	Frame Store
FTP	File Transfer Protocol
GA	Grand Alliance

GCRA	Generic Cell Rate Algorithm
GFC	Generic Flow Control
GMC	Global Motion Compensation
GOB	Group of Blocks
GOP	Group of Pictures
GSM	Global System for Mobile Communications
H.261, H.263	ITU-T Recommendations
HBV	High Bit Rate Video
HDTV	High Definition Television
HEC	Header Error Control
HFS	Higher Frequency Subband
HP	High Priority
HPF	High Pass Filter
HPT	High Pass Temporal
HTML	Hypertext Mark-up Language
HTTP	Hypertext Transfer Protocol
HVS	Human Visual System
IBCN	Integrated Broadband Communications Network
ICASSP	IEEE International Conference on Acoustics, Speech, and Signal Processing
ICC	International Color Consortium
ICC	International Conference on Communications
ICIP	IEEE International Conference on Image Processing
ICMP	Internet Control Message Protocol
IDCT	Inverse DCT
IDWT	Inverse DWT
IEC	International Electrotechnical Commission
IEEE	Institute of Electrical and Electronics Engineers
IETF	Internet Engineering Task Force
IFS	Iterated Function Systems
IJG	Independent JPEG Group
IMCP	Interframe Motion Compensated Predictor
IME	Interframe Motion Estimator
IMTC	International Multimedia Teleconferencing Consortium
IN	Intelligent Network
IP	Internet Protocol
IS	Integrated Services
IS	International Standard
ISCAS	International Symposium on Circuits and Systems

ISDN	Integrated Services Digital Network
ISO	International Organization for Standardization
ISOC	Internet Society
ISP	Internet Service Provider
IT	Information Type
ITU	International Telecommunications Union
ITU-R	International Telecommunications Union—Radio comm. sector
ITU-T	ITU Telecommunications Standardization Sector
ITV	Interactive Television
IVS	Integrated Video Services
IWU	Inter Working Unit
IZ	Isolated Zero
J	Journal
JPEG	Joint Photographic Experts Group
JTC	Joint Technical Committee
JURA	JPEG Utilities Registration Authority
Kbps	Kilobits per second
KLT	Karhunen-Loeve Transform
LAN	Local Area Network
LBG	Linde-Buzo-Gray
LFS	Lowest Frequency Subband
LI	Length Indicator
LMC	Local Motion Compensation
LOT	Lapped Orthogonal Transform
LP	Low Priority
LPF	Low Pass Filter
LPT	Low Pass Temporal
LT	Lapped Transform
MAC	Media Access Control
MAL	Media Access Layer
MAN	Metropolitan Area Network
MB	Macroblock
MBONE	Multicast Backbone
Mbps	Megabits per second
MBS	Maximum Burst Size
MC	Motion Compensated
MCR	Minimum Cell Rate
MDCT	Modified Discrete Cosine Transform

ME	Motion Estimation
MIDI	Musical Instrument Digital Interface
MLT	Modulated Lapped Transform
MM	Multimedia
MMR	Modified Modified READ
MOP	Mesh Object Plane
MPEG	Moving Picture Experts Group
MSDL	MPEG-4 Systems Description Language
MSE	Mean Square Error
MTU	Maximum Transfer Unit
MV (mV)	Motion Vector
MVs	Motion Vector of shape
NI	No Increase
NNI	Network to Network Interface
NNTP	Network News Transfer Protocol
NOSSDAV	Network and Operating System Support for Digital Audio and Video
NPC	Network Parameter Control
nrt	Non-real-time
NSAP	Network Service Access Point
NTSC	National Television System Committee
OBMC	Overlapped Block Motion Compensation
OSI	Open System Interconnection
OSPF	Open Shortest Path First
PAL	Phase Alternating Line
PBM	Preventive Bandwidth Management
PBP	Priority Breakpoint
PC	Personal Computer
PCR	Program Clock Reference, or Peak Cell Rate
PCS	Personal Communications Service
PCS	Picture Coding Symposium
PDU	Packet Data Unit
PES	Program Elementary Stream
PHY	Physical Layer
POCS	Projection Onto Convex Sets
PPP	Point-to-Point Protocol
PR	Perfect Reconstruction
PRA	Pel-Recursive Algorithm
PS	Program Stream

PSN	Packet Switched Network
PSTN	Public Switched Telephone Network
PT	Payload Type
PVC	Permanent Virtual Circuit
PVC	Permanent Virtual Connection
Q	Quantization
QBIC	Query By Image Content
QCIF	Quarter CIF
QMF	Quadrature Mirror Filter
QoS	Quality of Service
QP	Quantization Parameter
READ	Relative Element Address Designate
RIP	Routing Information Protocol
RM	Resource Management
ROS	Region Of Summation
RPR	Reference Picture Resampling
RRC	Radio Resource Control
RRU	Reduced-Resolution Update
RSVP	Resource Reservation Protocol
RTP	Real-Time Protocol
RVLC	Reversible Variable Length Code
SAD	Sum of Absolute Difference
SAR	Segmentation And Reassembly
SBC	Subband Coding
SBR	Statistical Bit Rate
SC	Sub Committee
SCR	Sustainable Cell Rate, or Sustained (Average) Cell Rate
SDT	Structured Data Transfer
SDTV	Standard Definition Television
SECAM	Sequential Couleur Avec Memoire
SES	Source End System
SGML	Standardized General Markup Language
SIF	Source Input Format
sL	SubLayer
SLIP	Serial Line Internet Protocol
SMDL	Standardized Music Description Language
SMG	Statistical Multiplexing Gain
SMSL	Standardized Multimedia Scripting Language
SMTP	Simple Mail Transfer Protocol

SN	Sequence Number
SNHC	Synthetic and Natural Hybrid Coding
SNMP	Simple Network Management Protocol
SNP	Sequence Number Protection
SNR	Signal-to-Noise Ratio
SONET	Synchronous Optical NETwork
SPIE	Society of Photooptical and Instrumentation Engineers
SPTS	Single Program Transport Stream
SQ	Scalar Quantization
SSCS	Service Specific Convergence Sublayer
SPDL	Standard Page Description Language
SPIFF	Still Picture Interchange File Format
STB	Set-Top Box
STM	Synchronous Transfer Mode
STT	Set-Top Terminal
SVC	Switched Virtual Circuit
SW	Spatial Weightier
Sys Demux	Systems Demultiplexer
SysMux	Systems Multiplexer
SZ	Stepsize
TCP/IP	Transmission Control Protocol/Internet Protocol
TD	Traffic Descriptor
TDAC	Time-Domain Aliasing Cancellation
TDM	Time Division Multiplexing
ToS	Type of Service
Trans	Transactions
TransMux	Transport Multiplex
TS	Transport Streams
TTS	Text-To-Speech
UBR	Unspecified Bit Rate
UDP	User Datagram Protocol
UDT	Unstructured Data Transfer
UMTS	Universal Mobile Telecommunications System
UNI	User Network Interface
UPC	Usage Parameter Control
UU	User-to-User
VAL	Value
VB	Video Buffer
VBR	Variable Bit Rate

VC	Virtual Connection
VCI	Virtual Call (Channel) Identifier
VLB	Very Low Bit Rate
VLBV	Very Low Bit Rate Video
VLC	Variable Length Coding (Coder)
VLD	Variable Length Decoder
VLE	Variable Length Encoder
VLSI	Very Large Scale Integration
VM	Verification Model
VO	Video Object
VoD	Video on Demand
VoIP	Voice over Internet Protocol
VOL	Video Object Layer
VOP	Video Object Plane
VP	Virtual Path
VPI	Virtual Path Identifier
VSB	Vestigal Sideband
VQ	Vector Quantization
VRML	Virtual Reality Modeling Language
VZTR	Value Zero Tree Root
W3C	World Wide Web Consortium
WAN	Wide Area Network
WATM	Wireless Asynchronous Transfer Mode
WD	Working Draft
WG	Working Group
WSS	Wide Sense Stationarity
WT	Wavelet Transform
WWW	World Wide Web
XML	Extensible Markup Language
ZTR	Zero Tree Root
ZTS	Zero Tree Scanning

CHAPTER 1

Introduction

1.1 OVERVIEW
1.2 ORGANIZATION OF THE BOOK
1.3 APPENDICES
1.4 BIBLIOGRAPHY

SUMMARY

The philosophy behind packet video communications over ATM networks is outlined. This is followed by the description of the chapters. An outline of the appendices and references concludes this introductory chapter.

1.1 OVERVIEW

In recent years, there has been a tremendous interest in the design of algorithms and architectures for Asynchronous Transfer Mode (ATM)-based high-speed networks. ATM has grown out of the need for a worldwide standard to allow interoperability of information, regardless of the "end system" or type of information. By providing connectivity through an ATM switch, several communication benefits such as dedicated bandwidth per connection, higher aggregate bandwidth, well-defined connection procedures, and flexible access speeds can be realized [1, 31, 34, 43].

A group of the world's telecommunication operators and their equipment suppliers is currently standardizing the ATM within the International Telecommunication Union (ITU) as a basis for broadband integrated services digital networks. In parallel with the ITU, the ATM Forum is furthering the development process by including computer communication manufacturers, as well as the users, in the standardization process. Although the representations give different perspectives on the proposed network solutions, the overall goal of building networks capable of transferring multimedia efficiently is shared between the ITU and the ATM Forum [262].

Asynchronous transfer of video, which often is referred to as *packet video*, can be defined as the transfer of video signals over Asynchronously

Time-Division Multiplexed (ATDM) networks. The video may be transferred for instantaneous viewing or for subsequent storage for access later. The former case has requirements on speed so that the received video data can be displayed in a perceptually continuous sequence. The latter case can be seen as a large data transfer with no inherent time constraints. In addition to the requirement on pacing, there may also be bounds on the maximal transfer delay from camera to monitor if the video is part of an interactive conversation or conference. These limits are set by human perception and determine when the delay starts to impede the information exchange. Parts of the signal may be lost or corrupted by errors during the transfer. This will reduce the quality of the reconstructed video and, if the degradation is serious enough, it may cause the viewer to reject the service.

Thus, the general topic of packet video is to code and asynchronously transfer video signals under quality constraints. The research field is active with its own set of workshops: the International Workshops on Packet Video, the first one held at Columbia University in 1987. There is also the more general International Workshop on Network and Operating System Support for Digital Audio and Video (NOSSDAV) [2, 3]. In addition, there are sessions on the topic held at many of the international signal and image processing, and communications conferences.

One of the challenges in the design of ATM networks is to protect them from irrecoverable congestion while realizing high network utilization. A network is said to be congested when increasing the load on a network does not result in an improvement in the network's performance. The problem assumes special significance in ATM networks due to the highly bursty nature of the traffic and the increased mismatches in bandwidth. A congestion control strategy should have the following design objectives: minimized cell loss, maintenance of the agreed quality of service, fairness for all sources, simplicity in implementation without overloading the already congested network, and checking to limit the spread of congestion to other parts of the network.

Broadband Integrated Services Digital Networks (BISDN) utilizing ATM are expected to provide the transport infrastructure for broadband multiservice applications. Video services are expected to share a large portion of the traffic handled by ATM networks. Videoconferencing, image retrieval, and High Definition Television (HDTV) are part of the new services that are to be provided in the access to customer premises.

Variable Bit Rate (VBR) video coding achieves high utilization of the channel bandwidth through statistical multiplexing, leading to constant picture quality during scene cuts and reduction of the end-to-end transmission delay.

In general, modeling of video traffic is carried out either analytically or by simulation. Unlike analytical models, which often require many assumptions and are too restrictive, simulation modeling techniques require fewer restrictions. The majority of the VBR video models based on simulation techniques suffer from a severe disadvantage in that the modeling process is based on statistics carried out from the picture frame because the coded video signals are normally produced by interframe coding methods. This necessitates that the encoder uses at least one-frame smoothing buffer, which is too large for performance analysis. One of the common methods to evaluate the accuracy of traffic model is to exhibit the standard statistical measures such as mean, variance, or other goodness-of-fit tests. However, these methods are inadequate to exploit the impact of video traffic characteristics on the resource allocation and inappropriate to predict the performance of a video source that may occur in an ATM network.

As a cell-switching technology based on small, fixed-length cells, ATM has the capability to support any type of traffic video, voice, and data that has been adapted to ATM with the appropriate ATM Adaptation Layer (AAL). All of these cells of various types of traffic are switched along virtual connections through an ATM network.

1.2 ORGANIZATION OF THE BOOK

This book is organized into the following chapters:

Chapter 2 describes packet video integration in the network architecture from a system point of view. In addition, some benefits and shortcomings of packet video are recalled. This is followed by some issues in packet video such as layered source coding and error recovery, as well as statistical behavior of video signals. A brief description of a packet switched network for real-time video transport is also presented.

Chapter 3 concentrates on video communication using ATM. The concepts of packetization and buffering for ATM networks are presented and illustrated through some examples. This chapter also covers an overview of video coding techniques for ATM systems as well as MPEG video coding. The emphasis is on motion compensation and motion estimation techniques.

Chapter 4 is devoted to scalability techniques. In this chapter, the various types of scalability are presented, analyzed, and compared. A number of applications for different types of scalability are pointed out.

Chapter 5 deals with MPEG-2 as well as MPEG-4 video standardization processes. The scope and potential of the MPEG-4 standard is discussed in the context of the future multimedia communications environments. It is shown that MPEG-4 standard provides tools and algorithms for coding both natural and synthetic video, as well as provisions to represent the video data at the user terminal in a highly flexible way.

Chapter 6 focuses on some issues involved in ATM. Overviews of rate control, multiplexing, delay, errors, and loss control are given.

In Chapter 7, the concept of asynchronous transfer of video in the Internet is introduced. The emphasis is on Internet network architecture, protocols, and ATM. Finally, this is extended to Internet integrated services.

In Chapter 8, the issues concerning Quality of Service (QoS) for packet video over ATM networks are outlined. After presenting QoS parameters, QoS requirements are discussed. In addition, management functions are presented as well as perceptual quality of the received video.

Chapter 9 includes many issues relating to video delivery over ATM: interactive television, video on demand, scalability with respect to multimedia, routing, and pricing. These topics will be of great interest in the near future.

1.3 APPENDICES

Appendix A contains useful information available online on the Internet (documents sources, software/hardware references, FTP sites, as well as a list of products, manufacturers, and vendors). No software is provided, as this can be downloaded from the Web sites. In Appendix B, ATSC digital TV system transport packet stream is described. Multimedia and standardization are discussed in Appendix C, including a summary of present and emerging standards for coding and representation of visual information.

1.4 BIBLIOGRAPHY

The bibliographic references are grouped according to the various chapters and appendices. Special efforts have been taken to make this list as up-to-date and exhaustive as possible. Some of the latest references are listed under "Late Additions" at the end of the section.

Packet Video in the Network Environment

2.1 INTRODUCTION
2.2 BENEFITS AND SHORTCOMINGS OF PACKET VIDEO
2.3 SOME ISSUES IN PACKET VIDEO
2.4 PACKET VIDEO NETWORK ARCHITECTURE MODEL
2.5 PACKET SWITCHED NETWORK FOR REAL-TIME VIDEO TRANSPORT
2.6 VIDEO COMPRESSION IN A PACKET NETWORK ENVIRONMENT

SUMMARY

Packet video integration in the telecommunications network architecture is investigated from a system point of view. Benefits and shortcomings of packet video are recalled. This is followed by some issues in packet video such as layered source coding and error recovery, as well as statistical behavior of video signals. The packet video network architecture model is then reviewed. A brief description of a packet switched network for real-time video transport is presented. Video compression in a packet network environment (compression schemes and digital video compression) concludes this chapter.

2.1 INTRODUCTION

In recent years, significant progress has been made in the digital representation of visual information. The increase in communication of visual information over the past several decades has resulted in many new image processing and video communication systems being put into service. The growing availability of optical fiber links and rapid progress in VLSI circuits and systems have fostered a tremendous interest in developing sophisticated video services with an acceptable cost [1]. Today's fiber technology offers a transmission capacity that can easily handle high bit rates like those required for video transmission. This leads to the development of networks, which integrate all types of information services. By basing such a network on packet switching, the services (video, voice, and data) can be dealt with in a common format.

5

Packet switching is more flexible than circuit switching in that it can emulate the latter while vastly different bit rates can be multiplexed together. In addition, the network's statistical multiplexing of variable rate sources may yield a higher utilization of the channel capacity than what is obtainable with fixed capacity allocation. Many years ago, most of these arguments were verified in a number of projects [2, 3, 4, 5, 6].

2.2 BENEFITS AND SHORTCOMINGS OF PACKET VIDEO

Potential benefits of packet video are

- Integration of video with voice and data in a common packet switched system, which offers some cost savings through sharing of switching and transmission resources.
- Packet internetworking techniques can be applied to provide intercommunication among video users on different types of networks.
- Significant advantages in channel utilization for video services by allowing convenient accommodation of video terminals with different bit rates and data formats.
- Nodal processors use sophisticated error control and packet accounting techniques enabling unsophisticated video terminals to be used in more advanced applications.

It is important to stress that packet networks are not without shortcomings for video communication, some of which are

- Most packet switched networks are designed for time-sharing applications, typically involving slow terminal speeds, asynchronous operation, and relatively short messages. However, video applications have a somewhat different set of requirements; for example, high data rates, long messages, short end-to-end delay, and full duplex real-time mode of operation (video teleconferencing).
- Large end-to-end delay in packet networks; it is a serious problem for real-time applications such as video and voice applications.

In order to realize the benefits of packetized video, a number of problems and issues need to be researched. Some major problems can be summarized as follows:

- Development of packet protocols for call setup and video transport.
- Strategies for reconstruction of video from packets arriving at nonuniform intervals.

- Statistical analysis of different types of video sequences to understand the characteristics of video data to be transmitted over Packet Switched Networks (PSNs).
- Development of efficient packet video multiplexing techniques in order to exploit the uncorrelated time variant characteristics of multiple video sources.
- Strategies to handle packet loss, packet jitter, and channel errors.
- Strategies that will minimize packet overhead and strategies for effective packet control to enable network links to be heavily loaded without congestion.
- Optimal size of video packets that will minimize both end-to-end delay and the effect of packet defects and random bit errors on reconstructed image quality.
- Optimal packet switching strategies to reduce both the packetization delay at each node and the overhead due to a header.

2.3   SOME ISSUES IN PACKET VIDEO

Compared to circuit switching, packet switching offers dynamic allocation of bandwidths and switching resources as well as the elimination of channel structure. Packet networks allow integrated services transport: They can carry voice, video, and data using the same hardware protocols. Furthermore, packet communication does not require users to allocate a fixed channel or bandwidth before data transmission. Since users send packets only when necessary, and since many users can send packets over the same shared channel, resources in packet networks are utilized more efficiently than in circuit switched networks. Video signals are especially well suited for packet transmission. Images usually contain regions of high detail and low detail as well as periods of rapid motion and little motion. Thus, effective video coders should be able to produce data streams with variable bit rates that change with local characteristics [7, 8]. Packet networks can carry Variable Bit Rate (VBR) signals directly. No buffering or rate control feedback is necessary at the transmitter. If a video coder can specify the order in which a network discards data in case of network congestion, then the decoder can often suffer less degradation in picture quality when packet loss occurs. Packet networks that offer prioritization of packets give video coders the ability to protect especially critical information. However, packet networks also provide some difficulties for video coders; namely, when a packet is lost, usually not more than 100 bits are available at the video decoder.

A number of issues in packet video call for signal processing solutions. These issues include layered source coding and error recovery, as well as the statistical behavior of video signals.

2.3.1 Layered Source Coding

The first step in the layered video coding is to classify picture information in terms of its importance, and then assign the most important class the highest priority. After the separation, information is layered into a pyramid form and compressed by various bit rate coding schemes. In the decoder, these layered signals are decoded and combined to reconstruct the original signal subject to a certain distortion. The separation/combination process should be distortionless [9].

Layered coding is a technique first developed for packet voice transmission [10, 11]. One example of a layered coding system is shown in Figure 2.1. The signal is separated into subsignals of various importances that may be coded and transmitted independently of one another. When received and decoded, the subsignals are recombined to form the output signal. The general technique may be advantageously extended to video coding and transmission. In this way, the coding of a subsignal can be tailored to the information it carries, while the subsignal can be transmitted with a priority reflecting its importance. Network congestion, where buffer overflow leads to packet discard, will affect mainly the subsignals of low importance. Thus, layered coding offers a way of achieving error control by preventing loss of perceptually important information. Yet another reason is the possibility of cost/quality tuning. This refers to the fact that high video quality can be traded for reduced transmission cost. A potential problem with layered coding appears if some of the compressed subsignals yield low output rates. The packetization delay may

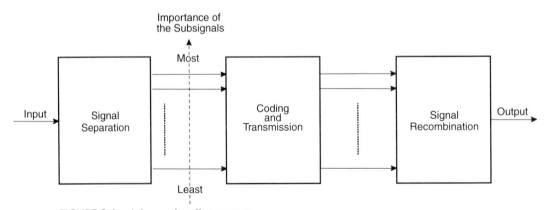

FIGURE 2.1   A layered coding system.

become intolerable for fixed-length packets. The solution would be to multi-plex the low bit rate subsignals.

Consider the basic principle of two-layer coding (see Figure 2.2). The first part, or the first layer of coding, generates the high-priority packets. The information contained in these packets is mainly vital information such as synchronization pulses and change addresses, together with some basic video data. Including video data in this layer is essential—reconstruction of the picture at the receiver based primarily on these packets. In addition, the coder uses this layer for motion detection. The second part of the coder, or second layer, generates enhancement packets. This layer codes the difference between the input and the decoded output of the first layer. Loss of this "add-on" information should not affect the tracking of the reconstructed pictures. For this reason, packets containing the information for this layer, labeled "low priority," should be derived either from an open-loop coder or from an independent closed loop [1, 4, 9].

From the total generated bit rate of B bits/frame, B_g is allocated to the first-layer coder, while $B_e=B-B_g$ is allocated to the second layer. Division of the bit stream B between B_g and B_e is subject to two constraints:

Minimizing the total bit rate B: Since there is no guarantee that "enhancement packets" will be received, the first-layer coder is incorporated in the motion detector. Poor picture quality due to the constraint on the bit rate of this layer, B_g, will cause more blocks to be coded in the second layer. Hence, the total bit rate will be increased. It is desirable to

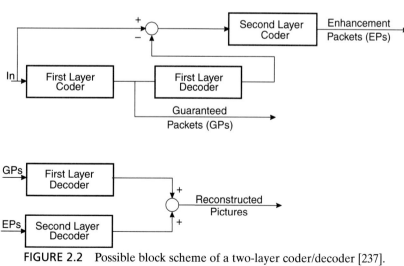

FIGURE 2.2   Possible block scheme of a two-layer coder/decoder [237].
©1989 IEEE.

increase B_g to improve picture quality in order to eliminate retransmission of false moving blocks by the second layer.

Channel-sharing ability: Since the bit rate B_g bits/frame allocated to the first layer is almost guaranteed, only the portion of the total bit rate $B_e=B-B_g$ can be shared in a VBR system. It is desirable to reduce B_g in order to increase the channel-sharing ability of the VBR channel for a fixed total bit rate B.

The preceding two conditions imply that the first-layer coder should be a very sophisticated coding scheme, such that it can produce a good picture quality with minimum bandwidth.

2.3.2 Error Recovery

Along with the advantages of packet transmission inevitably comes the problem of lost packets. Packet loss is caused by bit errors in the packet's address field, leading the packet astray in the network as well as the network congestion, leading to discarding of packets due to filled buffers. Statistical properties differ for two cases. First, bit error can realistically be modeled as an uncorrelated process, which results from noise in the transmission channel [12]. Second, packet loss due to network congestion is not so straightforward. Namely, it depends on the transmission rate in relation to the total network capacity and the source allocation and the sizes of the network buffers.

Generally speaking, there are two approaches to error recovery: first, the use of error control codes, and second, error concealment by use of visual redundancy. The former offers perfect recovery from error until the number of errors exceeds the limit of the used code. In contrast, the latter method never gives perfect recovery, but it can be engineered to be nearly imperceptible. Its advantage, however, is that it works, although with decreasing effectiveness, regardless of the number of errors experienced during transmission.

2.3.3 Statistical Behavior of Video Signals

Knowledge of the statistical behavior of variable-rate coded video will be necessary for network design. The interaction between signal processing and packet transmission is presented in Figure 2.3.

The behavior of variable-rate coded video will affect decisions on resource allocation. In turn, this will influence the network's behavior in terms of packet loss and delay variations, which has to be remedied at the receiver by error recovery and resynchronization.

Variable-rate coded video signals are problematic to describe since they are highly varying, with a burst behavior. The bursts correspond to activity in the

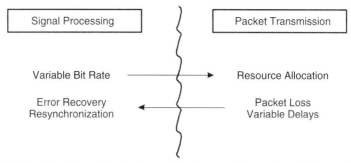

FIGURE 2.3   The interaction between signal processing and packet transmission.

captured scene and they may therefore last several seconds. Consequently, the varying rate cannot be sufficiently smoothed out through buffering because it would introduce unacceptable delays. However, when the rates of all video sessions are summed in the channel, the total rate exhibits less burstiness because of the statistical multiplexing that takes place [13, 14]. As the number of sources increases, the ratio of the standard deviation to mean of the summed rate goes toward zero. Hence, statistical multiplexing may yield a higher utilization than what is possible in circuit switching.

As for voice signals, they have been successfully modeled by a two-state (voice/silence) Markov chain. For video, there is no direct analogy such as motion/no motion. However, there has been a model derived from the voice model, in which the total output rate from N video sources is taken as the aggregate rate from several (>>N) independent on-off sources [13]. Thus, the rate variations are modeled as discrete steps. Each step corresponds to the output from an on-off source, where only one such source may change state at a time (birth-death process). While the model does not capture features of the video rate of a single source, such as its burstiness, the model may serve well for statistically multiplexed sources.

2.4 PACKET VIDEO NETWORK ARCHITECTURE MODEL

The packet video network architecture model is illustrated in Figure 2.4. The starting point for discussion is the Open Systems Interconnection (OSI) model of the International Organization for Standardization (ISO) [15]. The arrows indicate signal flows.

The Lower Network Layers.   The lower network layers comprise the physical link layer, the data link control layer, and the network layer. The lower layers have to be as simple as possible without any processing of information.

FIGURE 2.4   An example of the packet video network architecture model [15].
©1989 IEEE.

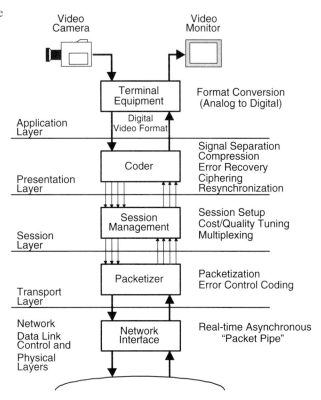

Any sophisticated signal handling is better performed at the higher layers where the signal's format and importance are known. Thus, the networks may be described as a real-time asynchronous "packet pipe" where packets inserted at one end come out orderly at the other end, although some will contain errors and others might be lost. The requirements for the physical link are adequate capacity and low bit error rate. These parameters are determined by the physical limits of the state-of-the-art technology.

Most of the tasks commonly associated with data link control for data transmission are incompatible with real-time services. Although the propagation and processing delays may be short, retransmission will introduce delay variations, which are to be avoided. The data link control is reduced to deal only with the link management issues.

The network layer provides end-to-end communication and shields the transport layer from any physical aspects of the transfer medium [12, 34, 38]. The functions associated with the network layer during a data transfer phase include routing, switching, congestion control, as well as packet duplication for broad and multicast sessions. The necessity to keep end-to-end delays and packet delay jitter under control requires video transmission to be conducted over a fixed route, a virtual circuit, which also guarantees that packets are delivered in order. The logical channel number should be protected in order to avoid packet loss or the delivery of unwanted packets due to bit error in the address field. Since the delivery of video packets cannot be warranted by retransmission, the network layer should maximize the probability of successful and timely delivery through the use of congestion control. In order to perform such a control in a sensible manner, the layer should provide transmission priorities. Priorities may not be necessary if capacity reservations are available. Lower transmission quality due to congestion can be avoided by allocating generous amounts of capacity to important signals.

The lower network layers are not video specific; rather, they provide general real-time service that can serve voice as well as video. Each of these layers shields the layer above from some of the physical structure of the link, so that at the network layer the notation of a virtual network is created whose physical implementation is irrelevant.

The Higher Network Layers.   The higher layers are presented top-down in order to illustrate how the format dependence is incrementally reduced. In these layers, we place functions for those specific video issues that come into consideration. While the lower layers are resident in the network nodes, the upper four—application, presentation, session, and transport—are at the customer's premises. In that sense, a packet video coder is seen as being the set of functions associated with the upper four layers. In a network that provides real-time transmission, the user's choice of video format compression methods and encryption can be made independently of the network. Hence, the network does not restrict the introduction of new signal formats or more advanced compression methods.

> **Application layer:** This layer forms the boundary between the user and the network. For the signal, it provides analog inputs and outputs, which adhere to the standard of the user's choice and the analog-to-digital and digital-to-analog conversions. Thus, this layer is dependent on both the analog and digital video formats.

> **Presentation layer:** This layer holds functions that perform some type of signal compression. Both the signal separation and the compression of hierarchical source coding are performed within the context of the presentation layer. Other functions include ciphering, error concealment by use of visual redundancy, and video resynchronization. Owing to the reduced number of digital video formats stemming from the application

layer, presentation layer implementations can be restricted to one class for each format. Limited error propagation has to be achieved locally at the presentation layer by adding control information to the bit stream. A feasible way of doing this is to insert synchronization flags after every i-th sample in a subsignal [15]. The distance between flags should be chosen so that the values may be concealed reasonably well if lost, while adding little overhead. The flags have to consist of a unique identifier followed by a sequence number to indicate location and, in case of error, the number of erased segments. The flag's uniqueness has to be guaranteed by bit stuffing or reserved codewords. The latter appears advantageous if variable-length codewords are used. Namely, the flags are inserted before the variable-length coding and they are transformed, as any other value, into their reserved codeword.

Session layer: This layer is mainly responsible for session setup and teardown. Additionally, the session layer implements the functions that would be invoked only a limited number of times over an entire session. These functions are in contrast to continuously invoked functions, such as the compression. The session layer should provide not only different types of sessions, but also flexibility in the quality of the sessions. The functions of the session layer are completely forced from the format of the video signal. The layer receives a set of subsignals belonging to a single session and, owing to the format independence, some of these may carry sound information. Hence, at the session layer a complete session of integrated real-time services is created.

Transport layer: Functions associated with this layer are the segmentation of a data stream into packets, the reassembly of the stream at the receiver, and error control coding. The transport layer serves all subsignals emanating from the hierarchical coding at the presentation layer and other associated signals, such as sound that has been added to the session at the session layer. Each such signal would be independently segmented, but the packetized signals would be multiplexed onto the same route at the network layer. Sound and video information will thereby follow a single path so that the delay difference between the two is minimized. Note that the segmentation process does not have information about the video format. The bit stream may therefore be cut at any point. The transport layer at the destination node has to detect lost packets and replace them with dummy packets so that synchronization can be maintained. Orderly delivery is guaranteed, and end-to-end sequence numbers may suffice for this purpose. A detected gap in the sequence indicates the loss of one or more packets. The necessary range of the sequence numbers has to be determined in relation to the channel code used, so that all gap lengths can be detected and corrected by the code. Delays introduced by the channel coding depend on the code length n and the packet size. Long packets and codewords give longer delays but fewer overheads. This tradeoff can be resolved without affecting the functions in the layers above, which are independent of packet format. Consequently, the choice between the use of variable- or fixed-length packets can be made locally. While fixed-length packets simplify segmentation and packet handling along the transmission path, variable-length packets can be used to keep the packetization delay constant.

EXAMPLE 2.1

To give a sense of the needs involved in a general network carrying video, consider transmitting 30 channels with broadcast video quality at 45 Mbits/s. This requires a link with a capacity in excess of 1.35 Gbits/s. An average of no more than one bit error for video frame for each of these sessions (for example, 900 errors per second) would correspond to a bit-error probability of less than 7×10^{-7} for the 1.35 Gbits/s link.

2.5   PACKET SWITCHED NETWORK FOR REAL-TIME VIDEO TRANSPORT

Since Packet Switched Networks (PSNs) are likely to dominate the communication world, the need arises to provide real-time services over such networks. Strong arguments exist to justify the use of packet switching for the transmission of variable-rate, real-time signals. First, signals with varying rates are hard to accommodate in circuit switched channels, resulting in wasted capacity. The integration of services in a network will be greatly facilitated if all of them are dealt with in a common format [16, 26, 31]. This is the strongest point in favor of packet transmission of voice and video. Of course, a price has to be paid for this advantage. The problems are related to a fundamental characteristic of packet networks taking into account that the timely guaranteed delivery of a packet is difficult to obtain.

The timing problems of packet video are twofold. First, there are variations in transmission delays, referred to as *packet delay jitter*. Analogous to packet loss, these variations are an inherent problem with packet transmission. Packet delay jitter can be removed by buffering the packets at the receiver, whereby the delay becomes fixed and equal to the maximal value. This is illustrated in Figure 2.5. As you can see, the delays in a PSN are composed of a fixed part due to the propagation delay and a variable (jitter) part due to waiting time in buffers.

FIGURE 2.5   The delays in a PSN.

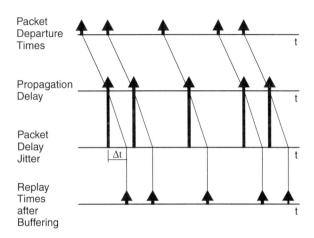

In what follows, video transmission over PSN is briefly presented as well as packet video coding, which is well suited for a packet switched environment. Next, video data scrambling is described.

2.5.1   Video Transmission Over Packet Switched Networks

As image information representing detail, motion, and so forth varies, VBR coding tailored for packet switched networks can be utilized to maintain constant image quality. In addition, by channel sharing among multiple video sources, transmission efficiency can be improved. The problems inherent in this scenario, however, are packet loss and packet delay.

The bit error rate p_e is a crucial descriptor of communication channel quality. In a good model for packet networks, p_e tends toward zero. The probability of an incorrectly received packet header is also consequently negligible. Packet loss due to network congestion and packet discarding become predominant sources of network imperfection. Even if the probability of packet loss p_L is very small, there is no way in general to guarantee a specified p_L for a given user in a given session.

As for packet delay, there are at least two sources. One is the propagation delay in long distance communication. For example, in a high-speed optical network, the direct round-trip delay between New York and San Francisco is about 45 ms. A second source of delay has to do with queuing of packets at given nodes. This kind of switching delay is expected to be relatively minor in a high-speed network, and it can also be traded off against the probability of packet loss. Discarded packets lead to shorter queues. The impact of discarded packet loss can be minimized by introducing a priority in two networks in combination with the layered structure [17]. By classifying the packets into high and low priorities, a high loss rate for low-priority packets can be toler-ated while preserving a low loss rate for high-priority packets. Thus, the packet loss protection recovery is an integral part of VBR coding. Holding the pack-ets at any of the switching nodes until a slot is open, resulting in a differential transmission delay between packets causes packet delay. Buffer design must consider this factor.

From a networking point of view, delivery of packets within a bounded time delay—thus providing real-time service—represents a difficult resource allocation and control problem, especially when the users provide high but varying rates [3]. Fixed allocation of resources, which could eliminate packet loss, would waste channel capacity. On the other hand, packet switching can-not guarantee the absence of packet loss, which depends on the load of the network. However, by not allocating fixed channels, packet switching may yield a higher initialization of the total channel capacity.

A user (video coder) will require various amounts of capacity over time, but the service provider (the packet network) will provide a channel whose capacity changes depending on the total load of the network. Therefore, the separation between source, channel, and receiver of classical communication theory does not hold anymore [18]. An optimal solution to the transmission of variable-rate signals over a variable-capacity channel requires an interaction, or information exchange between the parties involved. Figure 2.6 depicts sche-matically this aspect in the case of the transmission of variable-rate signals over a PSN.

In the represented global system, the information of the required and available capacity is exchanged. The classical separation of coder and channel is not allowed [19, 22].

2.5.2 Packet Video Coding

Taking into account the network aspects and the complexity of implementa-tion we can redefine the goal of image coding as follows: "Minimize the cost of transmitting image data while maintaining the desired image quality." This definition is different from that of Jain in two ways [19]. First, minimizing the

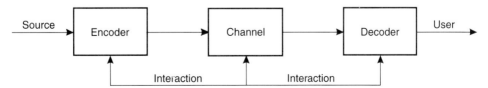

FIGURE 2.6   Interaction of the transmission of variable-rate signals.

bit rate is replaced by a more generalized goal of minimizing the cost. Bit rate alone constitutes only part of the cost in the packet video. Second, the requirement for faithful reconstruction of the original is replaced by the requirement for reconstructing the desired image quality. This provides the users with the flexibility of specifying an acceptable image quality, thus providing a trade-off between cost and quality.

To state the generalized goal more precisely, the goal of packet video coding can be formulated as a minimization problem. For example,

$$\min COST(R_1, ..., R_N, C_L, H) = \sum_{n=1}^{N} a_n R_n + b D(R_1, ..., R_N, C_L) + cH \quad (2.1)$$

subject to

$$\sum_{n=1}^{N} R_n \leq R_{\max} \quad (2.2)$$

D is a measure of the image distortion and is a function of the bit rate for each class of image data, where $D(R_1, ..., R_N, C_L)$ is less than or equal to a specified distortion. All processing must be done in real time. Here, R_n is the bit rate for encoding the nth image class; C_L is the level of spatial complexity and temporal activity in the image sequence, while H is the initial value, which primarily includes the hardware cost. On the other hand, N is the total number of classes of image data, a_n is the transmission cost associated with the nth image class in terms of dollars, b is the weighting factor that converts the image degradation or image quality into a cost in terms of dollars, and c represents a weighting factor that converts the initial installation cost to the same basis as the transmission cost. R_{max} is the maximum allowable bit rate for the image codec. This value will vary depending on the network traffic conditions.

A set of requirements is used as guidelines in the design of an efficient image codec.

- Adaptability of the coding scheme
- Robustness to packet loss
- Control of the coding rate
- Interaction with the protocols
- Parallel architecture

The signals we are dealing with have changing amounts of information over time. It is expected that the coder will take variations into account, which, through the redundancy reduction, will give a varying output rate. Typically, when there is no motion in a video sequence, the output rate should go to zero or a small residual rate.

Packet loss is unavoidable in a packet switched environment. Thus, the coding scheme has to be robust so that when packets are lost, the video session never needs to be seriously disrupted. Hence, suitable error recovery schemes must exist, and redundancy should be built in to minimize the quality degradation of the reconstructed image sequences from incomplete data.

When we extend the notation of flow control to the entire system (the coder and the network), a mechanism for flow control is incorporated in the coder. In the case of a congested network, flow control has to be enforced at the coder in a graceful manner in terms of image quality. The coding scheme should allow for various degrees of quality as required by the user, both in normal operation and in a congested network. A lower Quality of Service (QoS) would mean a higher probability of packet loss in a congested network.

The coder should be implemented in parallel because of the high data rate. This will enable the encoding, packetization, and protocols to run at the lowest possible rate, which simplifies their implementation. Protocols that are often implemented in software may not be able to execute at the speed necessary to handle encoded video as a single bit stream.

2.5.3 Video Data Scrambling and Interleaving

Scrambling is a method of pseudo-randomly scanning through image data in a known, reproducible manner [20]. The result is a sequence of data whose adjacent elements are from spatially disjointed locations in the original data. We scramble by first generating a sequence of pseudo-random numbers using maximum length sequence [21]. The length of the sequence is equal to the size of the region over which we wish to randomize the data. A maximum length sequence is implemented with a shift register and adder with feedback. The contents of the shift register produce a sequence of numbers that cycles through each number between 1 and 2^m-1, where m is the length of the shift register. Randomization is accomplished by using these numbers as an index into the image data and writing the data sequentially. Reversing the process retrieves the original order of data.

Interleaving is a way to combine several data streams, while *deinterleaving* separates one data stream into several streams by extracting the data in a periodic fashion. On the other hand, deinterleaving allows for better prediction of the lost data when reconstructing the sequence at the receiver. In addition, the errors due to lost data spread out over a large area by scrambling. When the inverse at the deinterleaving process is performed at the receiver, excellent error concealment can be achieved [22].

Unfortunately, two drawbacks to deinterleaving exist. First, because we have separated the original frame into subframes by a subsampling process, a loss of coding efficiency results. This means that a higher data rate will result for a given picture quality if we apply deinterleaving. Second, each subframe will also have more high frequencies because of the aliasing that is introduced by the subsampling process. No prefiltering is done when separating the original into the subframes.

2.6   VIDEO COMPRESSION IN A PACKET NETWORK ENVIRONMENT

Video compression, under development for the last 30 years, has recently emerged as the core enabling technology for video via packet networks [23]. The objective of compression technology is to reduce the amount of data necessary to reproduce the original data, while maintaining required levels of coded signal quality, processing delay, and implementation complexity [24].

Digitized video signals contain a significant amount of statistical redundancy. That is, samples are similar to one another, so a sample can be predicted fairly accurately from the neighborhood samples. Removing the predictable or similarity component from a stream of samples can reduce the data rate. Such statistical redundancy can be removed without destroying any information. That is, the original uncompressed video data can be received exactly by various inverse operations. Unfortunately, the techniques for accomplishing this depend on the probabilistic characterization of the signal. Although many excellent probabilistic models of video signals have been proposed, serious limitations continue to exist because of the nonstationarity of the signal statistics. In addition, statistics may vary widely from application to application [25]. The second type of superfluous video data is the information that a human visual system cannot observe. We call this *perceptual redundancy*. Unlike statistical redundancy, the removal of information based on the limitations of the human perception is irreversible. The original video data cannot be recovered following such a removal. Human perception is very complex, varies from person to person, and depends on the context and the application.

The biggest advantage of compression is in data rate reduction [26]. Data rate reduction reduces transmission costs, and when a fixed transmission capacity is available, this results in a better quality of multimedia presentation. Compression not only reduces the storage requirement, but also makes stored multimedia programs portable in inexpensive packages. In addition, the reduction of data rate allows processing of video rate data without choking various resources of either a personal computer or a workstation.

Packetization of digitized video and the reduction of packet rate due to compression are important in sharing a transmission channel with other signals, as well as maintaining consistency with telecom/computing infrastructure (the desire to share transmission and switching has created a new evolving standard, Asynchronous Transfer Mode [ATM], which uses packets of small size, or *cells*).

The quality of presentation that can be derived by decoding the compressed multimedia signal is the most important consideration in the choice of the compression algorithm. The goal is to provide near-transparent coding for the class of multimedia signals that are used in a particular service. The two most important aspects of video quality are *spatial resolution* and *temporal resolution*. Spatial resolution describes the clarity of lack of blurring in the displayed image. Temporal resolution describes the smoothness of motion.

Motion video consists of a certain number of frames per second to adequately represent motion in the scene. The first step in digitizing video is to partition each frame into a large number of picture elements (pels). The larger the number of pels, the higher the spatial resolution. Similarly, the more frames per second, the higher the temporal resolution. As for pels, they are usually arranged in rows and columns as shown in Figure 2.7.

The next step is to measure the brightness of the red, green, and blue color components within each pel. Three binary numbers then represent these three color brightnesses. Some examples for uncompressed and compressed bit rates are listed in Table 2.1.

It can be seen that uncompressed bit rates are all very high and are not economical in many applications. With a compression algorithm, these bit rates can be considerably reduced. Without compression, existing computer platforms, storage devices and networks are unable to meet the requirements

FIGURE 2.7   Pels arranged in rows and columns.

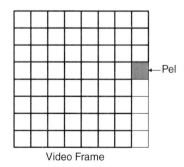

Video Frame

TABLE 2.1 Some Examples for Uncompressed and Compressed Bit Rates

	Video Resolution [pels × lines × frames/s]	Uncompressed Bit Rate (RGB)	Compressed Bit Rate
Film (U.S. and Japan)	480 × 480 × 24 Hz	133 Mbits/s	3–6 Mbits/s
NTSC video	480 × 480 × 29.97 Hz	168 Mbits/s	4–8 Mbits/s
PAL video	576 × 576 × 25 Hz	199 Mbits/s	4–9 Mbits/s
HDTV video	1920 × 1080 × 30 Hz	1493 Mbits/s	10–30 Mbits/s
ISDN videophone (CIF)	352 × 288 × 29.97 Hz	73 Mbits/s	64–1920 Kbits/s
PSTN videophone (QCIF)	176 × 144 × 29.97 Hz	18 Mbits/s	10–30 Kbits/s

of the massive storage space, high data transfer rate, and huge transmission bandwidth typical for multimedia data.

EXAMPLE 2.2

The transmission bandwidth requirement for digital video with a resolution of 640 × 480, 24-b colors, and 30 fps is 640 × 480 × 24 = 7.4 Mb/f and 7.4 Mb/f × 30 fps = 222 Mb/s. The bandwidth currently available is much smaller.

EXAMPLE 2.3

CD-ROM drives require 1.2–4.8 Mb/s of bandwidth, T1 lines 1.5 Mb/s, T3 lines around 45 Mb/s, coaxial cables around 40 Mb/s per 6 Mhz channel, and OC-3 optical fibers 155 Mb/s.

Without data compression, current technologies are inadequate for supporting SDTV, and certainly inadequate for the HDTV.

2.6.1 Compression Schemes

Compression schemes exploit and eliminate any redundancies within each frame (spatial redundancy) and between sequential frames (temporal redundancy), resulting in the reduction of video data being stored and transmitted. The former is called *intraframe* compression, and the latter *interframe* compression. Compression techniques can be categorized based on the following considerations:

- Lossless or lossy
- Entropy encoding or source encoding
- Symmetrical or asymmetrical
- Realtime or nonrealtime
- Software or hardware

If the decompressed data is identical to the original, it is referred to as *lossless* compression [96]; otherwise, we have *lossy* compression. Lossy compression schemes usually have higher compression ratios, but may introduce some artifacts such as blurring, loss of detail, edge distortion, and so forth. The human eye decides the baseline of lossy compression.

Entropy coding does not differentiate the types of data, but analyzes the statistical properties of data to reduce size. Source coding deals with the contents of the source material and makes use of their semantic and special characteristics to achieve data reduction. Entropy coding is usually lossless (run-length coding, Huffman coding), while source coding is usually lossy such as Discrete Cosine Transform (DCT) [27].

If the time required to compress and decompress is roughly the same, it is referred to as *symmetrical* compression. In *asymmetrical* compression, the time taken for compression is usually much longer than decompression. Symmetrical schemes are usually adopted in applications that must digitize and compress data in real time. On the other hand, asymmetrical schemes are often used when the data are compressed once and decompressed many times, such as in most interactive TV applications.

Software and hardware may perform the compression. Hardware codecs (COder and DECoder) are faster and are suitable for Central Processing Unit (CPU) intensive processing. Existing hardware codecs often offer better quality and performance. However, they are available only on platforms with costly extended hardware. Software codecs are suitable for less CPU-intensive processes and are limited to those processes capable of decoding an image within a frame period.

2.6.2 Digital Video Compression

Digital video compression may either apply intraframe coding to each individual frame of the video or combine both intraframe and interframe coding. The former scheme yields a lower compression ratio than the latter because it does not exploit temporal redundancy. Frame differential encoding (that is, Differential Pulse Code Modulation [DPCM]) is one approach to squeeze out temporal redundancy. It encodes and sends the differences in the adjacent frames. Motion compensation is another technique for interframe compression. It compares the current frame with the previous one and encodes the motion vectors; in other words, the change in coordinate values due to the motion and pixel differences after motion, as shown in Figure 2.8 [28].

FIGURE 2.8 Motion compensation [28].
©1997 IEEE.

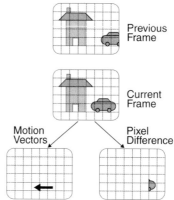

The algorithms used in a compression system depend on the available bandwidth or storage capacity, the features required by the application, and the affordability of the hardware required for implementation of the compression algorithm (encoder as well as decoder).

CHAPTER 3

Video Communication Using Asynchronous Transfer Mode Technique

SUMMARY

This chapter concentrates on video communication using Asynchronous Transfer Mode (ATM). Among various components of the Broadband Integrated Services Digital Network (BISDN), the cell-based ATM multiplexing technique is a powerful tool for providing integrated services effectively. Unlike the conventional packet switching, ATM uses a fixed-length packet so that it is suitable for high-speed applications. The concepts of packetization and buffering for ATM networks are presented and illustrated with examples. We also include video source model description and a brief description of video coding techniques for ATM systems. Finally, an overview of MPEG video coding is given. The emphasis is on motion compensation as well as motion estimation techniques.

3.1 INTRODUCTION

With the information explosion, new ways of transmitting information have been developed. One of the most efficient ways of transferring information among a large number of users is the use of Asynchronous Transfer Mode

(ATM) technology. In the past, communication usually took place over dedicated channels. In order to communicate between two points, a channel was dedicated only for transferring information between those two points. Even if there was no information transfer going on during a particular period, the channel could not be used by anyone else. Because of the inefficiency in this approach, there is an increasing movement away from it. In an ATM network, users divide their information into packets that are transmitted over channels that can be used by more than one user [29].

Historically, 1988 may well be remembered as the year when the former International Telephone and Telegraph Consultative Committee (CCITT) (now called ITU-T) decided on ATM as the target switching and multiplexing technique for the Broadband ISDN (BISDN). ATM carries all types of information—voice, data, and video—in a common cell (packet). Up to then, deployment of narrowband ISDN had been very limited.

During the past few years, the data communication industry has taken the lead in driving ATM development. ATM is becoming an established technology for campus and Local Area Networks (LANs). ATM is also seeing deployment for wide area data communications. Several public carriers have announced ATM services. Since 1992, ATM has been demonstrated and studied in several gigabit network test beds in the United States. For example, North Carolina and other states are planning statewide ATM "information highways." In Europe, 18 network operators have agreed to interconnect their national ATM trials into a virtual path-based pan-European ATM pilot network. The Commission of the European Communities (CEC) defined a 4 billion ECU (U.S. 4.7 billion dollars) research program for 1994–1998 toward the Integrated Broadband Communication Network (IBCN) [30].

The ATM Forum, a consortium of users and equipment vendors that began with only six members in 1991, has grown beyond 700 from different businesses, including office automation, LANs, computer systems, software, microelectronics, and Wide Area Network (WAN) service providers.

In BISDN, the ATM technique is regarded as a desirable transfer mode that can generate heterogeneous types of traffic with different characteristics (mean bit rate, peak bit rate, burstiness) [31]. ATM is a switching and multiplexing technique that uses constant-length packet cells as the basic data units. An ATM cell as defined by the International Telecommunications Union (ITU), formerly CCITT Recommendation I.361, contains 48 bytes of user information and 5 bytes of control information. This technique, based on fixed-length cells, enables very high transmission rates and enhances statistical multiplexing because of its flexible bandwidth allocation capabilities.

The merits of packet video coding and of transmitting video packets through ATM networks are many. The first advantage of video packet coding is that improved and consistent picture quality is obtained using a variable bit rate. When video signals are transmitted through fixed bit rate circuits, there is a need to control the coded bit rate by keeping it constant, resulting in a large decrease in picture quality during rapid motion. The second advantage is multimedia integration. Using unified protocols provides integrated broadband services. The third merit is improved transmission efficiency using channel sharing among multiple video sources. The coding bit rate of a video channel usually changes according to the motion in its scenes. In the case of fixed bit rate coding, the quality of scenes with rapid motion is decreased. Using variable bit rate coding and channel sharing among multiple video sources, these scenes can be transmitted without distortion if other video channels at the same time have little motion.

Broadband networks based on ATM will support, among others, traffic coming from VBR codecs, which are capable of maintaining a constant picture quality of the decoded image [32]. The characterization of such VBR video sources becomes important in the analysis and design of BISDN. The network architecture and its characteristics such as cell loss probabilities, transmission delay, high-speed statistical multiplexing gain, buffering, and so forth, are strongly related to the statistical properties of the sources and the coding schemes involved [33].

ATM-based networks are expected to accommodate a wide range of users, including some whose applications require guarantees on minimum cell loss and/or delay. In order to obtain these guarantees from the network, users have to describe their traffic inputs by specifying values from the network; in other words, define traffic descriptors such as Peak Cell Rate (PCR) or Sustainable Cell Rate (SCR) [34]. However, some users may not be able to describe their traffic accurately, because

- Their application cannot be sufficiently well characterized by the given traffic descriptors.
- Their actual traffic inputs depend on factors outside their control (such as the number of applications competing for shared resources) [35].

In ATM, networks allocate bandwidth differently. Video data are bursty and are coded with VBR, so ATM networks can obtain a statistical multiplexing gain. ATM networks can be easily congested because the bandwidth requirement of VBR traffic is not fixed. Therefore, reliable computation of the effective bandwidth of VBR video traffic is desirable. For computation of the effective bandwidth of video traffic, a reliable video traffic model is needed [36].

Generally speaking, ATM is flexible enough to transport constant bit rate voice and video traffic at the same time as variable bit rate bursty data such as LAN traffic and compression video. It does this by using a different ATM adaptation layer for each service being carried. On the other hand, the ATM layer is the heart of the BISDN protocol model; in other words, a model with some resemblance to the Open Systems Interconnection (OSI) model promulgated by the International Organization for Standardization (ISO). The adaptation layer has the job of adapting layer-level data into the format needed by the ATM layer. The beauty of ATM is that, when the necessary adaptation layers have been defined and implemented, many kinds of traffic can be mixed together to form an aggregate traffic to cut costs while being flexible about service provisioning [37].

Multiplexing shows up in many places in ATM systems. At the lowest level, it appears in the physical transmission systems that carry the cells. It may also appear elsewhere: at the ATM cell level, with cells from many different sources mingled together, or at higher service layers with mixtures of data protocols combined within a single ATM virtual channel—a defined connection through a network in which bandwidth is only allocated when a user's cells require transport. It is also possible for traffic to multiple destinations to be mixed within one protocol.

One of the most important performance parameters of ATM equipment is the *overhead* associated with switched virtual circuits, which assumes even greater significance in applications such as the World Wide Web (WWW), distributed computing, command/control, and modeling/simulation, which create and discard short-lived connections at a significant rate. In an effort to enhance the adoption of ATM technology and equipment, the ATM Forum has identified certain goals for benchmarks. They include metrics that help compare ATM equipment from different vendors; metrics that help predict the performance of an application or design a network configuration to meet specific performance objectives; and metrics to measure the performance of network management, connection setup, and normal data transfer. While the intentions of the ATM Forum are clear, the benchmarking specifications are still in an early phase [38, 39].

The term "benchmark" generally refers to a set of experiments that can be used to evaluate the performance of particular equipment against a standard. The tests making up the benchmark must be specific enough to stress the abilities of the equipment in various ways, but general enough to be applicable to equipment from a variety of manufacturers. The rationale for each test in the benchmark is equally important because it provides a basis for interpretation of the results and integration with the results of other tests. Individual vendors test their own equipment and software, but there is little motivation for a single company to expend time, effort, and resources required to produce general, portable, and objective evaluation tools only to place them in the public domain for the benefit of their competitors. Furthermore, a comprehensive benchmark ought to reflect the contributions and consensus of the ATM community as a whole, rather than the perspective of a single company.

3.2   ATM FOR THE FUTURE BROADBAND ISDN

The BISDN is a new concept for exchange area communications. Based on high-speed circuit and packet switching, BISDN will integrate services such as voice, data, and video on LAN and Metropolitan Area Network (MAN). Among various components of the BISDN, the cell-based ATM multiplexing technique is a powerful tool for providing integrated services effectively. The ATM technique has some desired attributes of both circuit switching and packet switching. Unlike the conventional packet switching, ATM uses a *fixed-length* packet so that it is suitable for high-speed applications. Each cell contains a header and an information field. The header allows easy multiplexing of user data and also allows dynamic bandwidth allocation to accommodate users' needs [34]. It typically includes the routing information in addition to some other fields, while the adaptation header in the information field carries the service- and/or technique-dependent information end to end. Generally speaking, ATM is a *connection-oriented* transfer technique, where fixed-size ATM cells from different sources are asynchronously multiplexed in a communication channel. On the other hand, a Synchronous Transfer Mode (STM) is a transfer mode that is based on Time Division Multiplexing (TDM), where connections use predefined channels or time slots within the 125 µs frame. Among them, ATM is defined to be the transfer mode solution for implementing a BISDN.

Major characteristics of an ATM-based BISDN include:

- High flexibility of network access
- Dynamic bandwidth allocation on demand
- Flexible bearer capacity allocation
- Independence of the means of transmission at the physical layer
- Multimedia integration (data, voice, image, video) [40, 45]

From a user's point of view, the advantages of ATM include:

- Format-independent, rate-free, and time-transparent transmission
- Reduction of end-to-end delay
- Constant video quality, even for active motion area/frames
- Quality control by the user instead of rate control by the channel

A concept of broadband communication networks is shown in Figure 3.1. Since ATM networks organize information into cells to which are attached short flow-identification labels, and the cells are transported to their destination according to their labels, ATM-based networks provide a high degree of flexibility to the User-Network Interface (UNI). The realization of an ATM-based BISDN will allow many services, such as telephone, video, and data communication, to be offered through a universal cell-based UNI [40].

Video services and related studies so far have been carried out with the assumption that individual networks or transmission facilities will provide signal transmission. For example, TV program broadcasting to end users has been supported to dedicate terrestrial or satellite transmission links.

BISDN based on ATM technology can make the integration of video services possible. Via BISDN, one terminal will be able to access various types of video sources, including TV program and motion or still picture databases, as well as communicating with other terminals. The maximum service bit rate of BISDN will be sufficient to support video signal transport up to High Definition Television (HDTV) level.

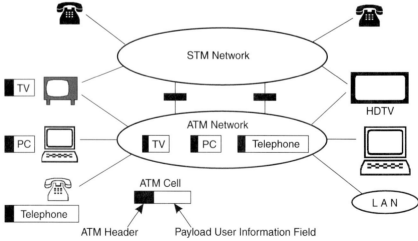

FIGURE 3.1   An example of a broadband communication networks concept [40].
©1989 IEEE.

The need for integration of video services was identified during BISDN standardization activities [41]. Integrated Video Services (IVS) represent a concept wherein maximum integration of video services is achieved through harmonization of terminal and network capabilities in BISDN. Video services in BISDN to be considered for IVS are

- Distributed services, including TV program and entertainment
- Conversational services, including videophone and video conferencing
- Messaging services, including moving-picture mail
- Retrieval services, including film libraries and high-resolution images

Examples of IVS showing how video data will be utilized among various types of communication services provided by BISDN are illustrated in Figure 3.2. A TV program can be transferred to film libraries via BISDN messaging services as well as to TV viewers via distribution services. On the other hand, users can retrieve programs stored in film libraries after video editing if necessary. Retrieved video data may be exchanged between users in BISDN conversational services like videophone and videoconferencing. Processing video data in film libraries may generate video data with different resolutions, that is reduction of resolution from HDTV level to normal TV level, in order to meet the requirements of terminals at retrieving services [42]. As for retrieved video data, they may be processed by terminals to produce still lower resolution data, which may be exchanged between terminals.

3.3 MAIN ATM FEATURES

Due to the limited bandwidth capabilities of the narrowband ISDN, the broadband ISDN utilizing the ATM technique has been realized and developed for the future transmission of different video sources. As previously stated, the main advantage of this packet transmission system is the possibility for high-speed and variable bit rate transmissions, resulting in virtually constant quality of services.

An ATM fast switching transfer mode has been chosen as a specific way of transmitting and switching information in the future BISDN. It is a variable-rate, source-independent transport mechanism in which video data from a large number of statistical independent variable-rate sources are packetized into fixed-length cells and multiplexed over a common ATM channel.

ATM uses short, fixed-length cells with minimal headers to allow cells to be routed at high speed by means of hardware-implemented routing tables at each switch. International agreement has resulted in the header of each cell consisting of 5 bytes followed by the cell information field of 48 bytes, making

FIGURE 3.2   Example of integrated video services provided by BISDN [40].
©1989 IEEE.

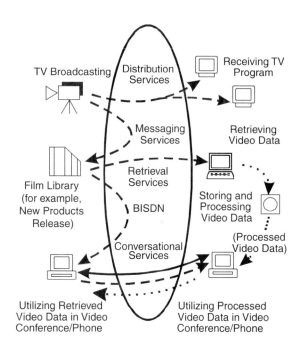

a total cell length of 53 bytes. The basic unit is called a "cell" to avoid confusion with "packets" of lower bit rates. The header consists of bits to provide two main routing functions:

- **Virtual Path Identifier (VPI).** A path is the equivalent of a route in a circuit-based environment, permanently connecting two points together. In an ATM environment, the path would not have a fixed capacity. The virtual tag indicates that cells would be routed from node to node based on the VPI, the route being established at the beginning of each call based on signaling messages.
- **Virtual Call Identifier (VCI).** These calls would be set up as required over the virtual path indicated by the VPI.

The structure of the header at the user-network interface is shown in Figure 3.3. It has the following subfields:

- Generic Flow Control (GFC) field (4 bits).
- Routing field (VPI, VCI) with 24 bits available.
- Payload type (PT) field (2 bits).
- Reserved field (1 bit).
- Cell Loss Priority (CLP) indicates whether the cell has a lower priority and can therefore be discarded during overload conditions.
- Header Error Control (HEC) field (8 bits) [43].

FIGURE 3.3   The structure of
the ATM header [34].
©1991 Addison Wesley.
(Reprinted by permission of
Pearson Education Limited.)

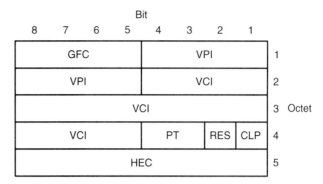

At a call setup, a reservation of the network resources is made based on some predefined traffic parameters, which include the peak cell rate, the average rate, burstiness, and peak duration. If no sufficient resources are available, the connection for the requested terminal is refused. During the call, the Usage Parameter Control (UPC) provides some actions taken by the network to monitor and control the traffic flow, making sure that the traffic agreement initiated at the cell setup is not violated. The resources are released when the information transfer is completed.

Generally speaking, the information field is available to the user, while the header field carries information that belongs to the ATM layer functionality itself. Like packet switching techniques, ATM can provide a communication with a bit rate that is individually tailored to the actual need, including time-varying bit rates [43].

In the synchronous transfer mode, a data unit associated with a given channel is identified by its position in the transmission frame. In asynchronous transfer mode, a data unit or a cell associated with a specific virtual channel may occur at essentially any position.

In ATM-based networks, the multiplexing and switching of cells are independent of the actual application. In principle, the same module of equipment can handle a low bit rate connection as well as a high bit rate connection. On the other hand, the flexibility of the ATM-based BISDN network access due to the cell transport concept supports the idea of a unique interface that can be employed by a variety of customers with quite different service needs. ATM has the capability to multiplex and switch on the cell level and support flexible bit rate allocation, as is known from packet networks. The strategy in which generated cells from a source follow the same route is required in order to minimize transmission delay variation, which is vital for delay-sensitive sources such as speech and video [44].

The fixed cell length simplifies hardware processing and complexity of buffer and queue management compared to traditional packet switching networks with varying packet lengths. ATM requires only a minimal functionality in the switching nodes and thus facilitates high-speed switching with low delay and small jitter. This is of importance for real-time service (voice, video) and constant bit rate applications.

The services do not have to produce information at a constant rate either, which is more efficient when transmitting interactive data or using video coding techniques where only changes in picture content have to be transmitted. It is for these reasons that ATM is seen as an ideal candidate for integrated broadband networks.

3.4 ATM LAYERS

To illustrate the relationship of the ATM layer with the physical layer and upper layers, it is convenient to use the BISDN protocol reference model, which is analogous to the Open Systems Interconnection (OSI) model of the International Organization for Standardization (ISO). The latter has been widely used to model a variety of communication systems. The model also uses the concept of separated planes for the segregation of user, control, and management functions.

The various planes and layers in the BISDN protocol reference model are illustrated in Figure 3.4 [34]. This model consists of a user plane, control plane, and a management plane. The user plane, with its layered structure, provides for user information flow along with associated controls—flow control and recovery from errors. The control plane, also with a layered structure, comprises the call control and connection control functions. The management plane provides two types of functions: the plane management and layer management functions (that is, supervision functions). The user plane and control plane each has a layered structure as an OSI to describe the functions associated with each layer. The layers are the physical layer, the ATM layer, the ATM Adaptation Layer (AAL), and the layers above the AAL.

The physical layer is based on the Synchronous Optical NETwork (SONET) transmission standards and is equivalent to layer 1 (physical layer) of the OSI model. This layer is meant mainly for transport information.

The ATM layer and the AAL together are roughly equivalent to layer 2 of the OSI model, although the routing function belongs to layer 3 of the OSI model. The role of the ATM layer is to transport the ATM cells, and it is common to all services. Its main functions are switching/routing and multiplexing

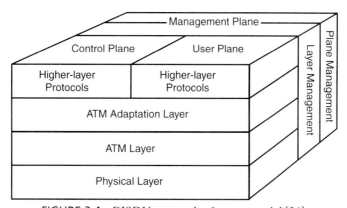

FIGURE 3.4   BISDN protocol reference model [34].
©1991 Addison Wesley. (Reprinted by permission of Pearson Education Limited.)

cells of different connections into a single cell stream. The cell headers are added/extracted to/from the cell here.

Since ATM supports many kinds of services with different traffic characteristics and system requirements, it is necessary to adopt the different classes of applications to the ATM layer. This function is performed by the AAL, which is service dependent. Its functions as described in ITU-T Rec. I.362, include [34]:

- Error control of transmission errors in the information field
- Segmentation and reassembly of higher-layer information into ATM cells
- Handling of cell loss and misinserted cells in the ATM layer
- Handling of cell delay jitter
- Transfer of timing information

The two AALs presently used for transfer of digital video are AAL-1 and AAL-5. AAL-1 has a range of capabilities that allow it to "emulate" a constant bit rate connection. This is useful because many technologies, including video codecs, have been designed based on (or adopted to) the characteristics of the existing network. The MPEG-2 transport stream, for example, works under the assumption that there is a fixed constant delay between transmitter and receiver. As ATM is asynchronous, AAL-1 is equipped with additional information, such as time stamps and sequence numbers, to perform the adaptation. Hence, the effects of cell delay variation, cell misinsertion, cell loss, and other ATM layer-caused impairments can be dealt with.

AAL-1 can handle transfer of data in two modes: Unstructured Data Transfer (UDT), or Structured Data Transfer (SDT). When UDT is used, the

AAL expects the data flow to be a beat stream with associated clock synchronization. Using STD, the data flow is expected to be structured in octet "blocks" such as time division multiplexed signals with n channels of 64 Kbps.

Like all other AALs, AAL-1 is split into two sublayers: the Segmentation and Reassemble (SAR) sublayer and the Convergence Sublayer (CS). The function of the CS covers the generation and recovery of timing information. It can compensate for the effects of cell delay variation. It also takes care of cell misinsertion, cell loss, and cell missequencing and it flags possible error conditions to the management plane.

The structure of AAL-5 sublayers is shown in Figure 3.5. AAL-5 is divided in two major parts: the CS and SAR. CS consists of the Service-Specific Convergence Sublayer (SSCS) that can be null, and the Common Part Convergence Sublayer (CPCS). The services layer enters the AAL, SSCS, and/or CPCS and control information is added. At the receiving side, the user data is reassembled to its original form, and the CPCS control information is removed and dealt with. The CPCS payload containing the service layer is of variable size up to 65,536 bytes.

The layers above the AAL in the control plane provide call control and connection control.

3.5   PACKETIZATION FOR ATM NETWORKS

The packetizer's task is to assemble video information, coding mode information and synchronization information into cells for transmission over ATM networks. The way information is packetized influences the propagation of errors caused by cell loss and the complexity of synchronization of the decoder side. It also determines packetization delay, especially for Variable Bit Rate (VBR) coding [14].

FIGURE 3.5   Structure of AAL-5 sublayers [34].
©1991 Addison Wesley. (Reprinted by permission of Pearson Education Limited.)

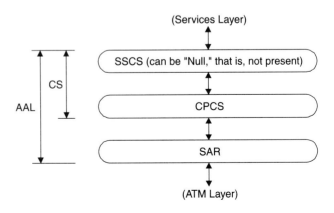

In the VBR encoder, the data for one horizontal strip of blocks are assembled into a single self-contained unit that is transmitted by means of multiple ATM cells. The unit is called the *video packet*. Errors propagated due to the loss of a cell are in this way limited to a single strip. A video packet consists of a varying number of cells, depending on the coding mode of the blocks in the strip and on the variable-length codes used. If no blocks are updated in the strip, the video packet is not transmitted. Because of this and vertical blankings, successive video packets may be separated by relatively long pauses. To limit the packetization delay, it is therefore necessary to stuff the last cell of a video packet with dummy bits when the cell is not completely full. This ensures that a video packet starts at the beginning of a cell, which simplifies the detection of the start of a video packet at the decoder side.

The layout of a video packet is presented in Figure 3.6. It starts with a flag of 14 ones that identifies the beginning of the video packets. It is immediately followed by the vertical address of the strip in the frame. This address provides a time reference for decoder synchronization. The next field signals the current grid offset in the block dithering process followed by the coding modes for the 28 blocks of the strip. Thereafter, the quantization set is indicated, followed by the variable-length coded quantized prediction errors. The last cell is stuffed with zeros.

The packetization scheme introduces minimal delay as all information is packetized in the sequence in which it is generated. The total delay, including encoding, packetization, dejittering, depacketization, and decoding, is well below 1 ms. Thus, it is not necessary to introduce delay in the accompanying audio path, which is important for video communication applications.

It is very important to clarify the generation interval distribution of packetized variable-rate video coding data streams in order to effectively transmit these streams by statistically multiplexing them in an ATM network. There are three outputs of the variable-rate video coding based on motion compensated adaptive intra/interframe prediction coding: prediction error information, motion vector information, and quantizer selection information. In an ATM network, it is very important to give the priority to the most important information and transmit it to compensate for its packet losses. The above variable-rate video coder outputs are each packetized separately. Since among these three outputs, the quantizer selection information's entropy is constant in one picture frame, and fixed-length coding is applied to its entropy, the generation interval of the packetized data is constant.

For transmission over ATM networks, the video stream is split into fixed-length cells. Figure 3.7 shows one method for packing the encoded

FIGURE 3.6 Layout of a video packet [33].

©1989 IEEE.

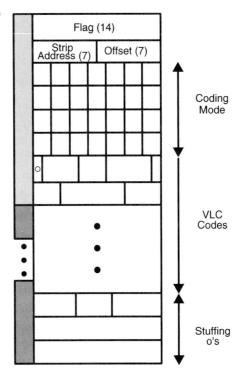

The information field of a cell is made up of blocks and headers. When the number of bits left in the cell is less than that required for an entire block

video information into an AAL information field [46]. There are 48 bytes in the information field of an ATM cell. Excluding the overhead information for maintaining cell sequence, error detection, and locating the beginning of the encoded data, there are 43 bytes left for the encoded video information in each ATM cell.

The information field of a cell is made up of blocks and headers. When the number of bits left in the cell is less than that required for an entire block

FIGURE 3.7 Information field of an ATM cell [34].

©1991 Addison Wesley. (Reprinted by permission of Pearson Education Limited.)

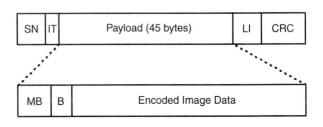

SN – Sequence Number (6 bits)
IT – Information Type (2 bits)
LI – Length Indicator (6 bits)
CRC – Cyclic Redundancy Check (10 bits)
MB – Address of the Beginning Macroblock (12 bits)
B – Address of the Beginning Block (3 bits)

or header, the bits are left blank (putting zero on them). The use of overhead bits for representation of the starting macroblock's absolute address in the picture is to minimize the error propagation due to loss of synchronization in the slice layer. Without this overhead information, we cannot locate where the received macroblocks should be placed using the relative address in the macroblock header if the slice header is lost or corrupted.

With the block-address information, the codewords in each received packet are directly decodable, except for those in the beginning of the packet left from a block contained in a lost packet, unless backward decoding is performed [47].

EXAMPLE 3.1

The specific packetization format is shown in Figure 3.8. In the 48-byte payload field of each cell, the first 3 bits specify the band (2 bits) and odd/even index (1 bit) information. The following few bits describe the spatial location of the first block included in the packet.

Band Index (2 bits)	Odd / Even Index (1 bit)	Address of 1st Block (10 bits)	Codewords Left from the Last Block in the Previous Packet	Codewords from the 1st Block, 2nd Block, ..., Last Block	Null Bits

FIGURE 3.8   Contents of the payload field of a cell carrying the coded bit stream [34]. ©1991 Addison Wesley. (Reprinted by permission of Pearson Education Limited.)

For images in the Source Input Format (SIF) with 352×240 active pixels or 44×30 blocks of 8×8 samples, 10 bits are sufficient to specify the block address, together with the previous odd/even bit. The rest of the packet is then filled with the code words left from the best block in the previous packet, followed by the code words of the remaining blocks in this band, with possible insertion of null bits at the end.

3.6   BUFFERING IN THE ATM ENVIRONMENT

In a synchronous transfer mode network, plus bits are inserted into the buffer memory of codecs when the amount of video information is small. However, when the information amount is large, a quantizer whose quantization steps are large (coarse) is selected, so that the codec's bit rate is constant. Therefore, the picture quality of codecs changes from hour to hour, and in the worst case, there is degradation in quality. In fixed-rate transmission, a buffer is necessary to keep the transmission rate constant. In addition, the coder has to be controlled to prevent buffer overflow. The "rate buffer" and "rate control" cause delay and quality degradation during active motion. On the other hand, variable-rate transmission does not require a "rate buffer" due to the variable-rate channels offered by the network, while "quality control" can be introduced instead of "rate control." There are some advantages in variable bit rate transmission of video signals: reduced delay, constant video quality, user's control of video quality, simple implementation of the video codec, and adaptability to changing traffic.

ATM-based networks are subject to congestion that could introduce random delay and cell losses. A challenging problem is how to maintain the advantage of constant video quality offered by VBR source coding in the face of delay and cell losses caused by an imperfect system. The problem may be alleviated by using layered source coding to generate a high-priority layer or base layer, which contains the most important video information and whose transport should be guaranteed to ensure the delivery of an acceptable video quality. The difference between the High Priority (HP) layer and the original video sequence is encoded and transmitted as a Low Priority (LP) layer or enhancement layer. The LP layer can exploit the characteristics of statistical multiplexing, as loss of video information at this level is not so critical.

Previous studies on layered source coding assumed that HP video data will be delivered by the underlying network. However, in an ATM-based network, a Usage Parameter Control (UPC) function (such as the leaky bucket) enforces bandwidth utilization (at the receiver-to-network interface) [31]. In the leaky bucket control policy, the transmitter agrees to a peak transmission rate and a burst interval. The burst interval specifies the maximum time that the transmitter can stay at the peak transmission rate. Even if an HP layer carries high video quality, it still cannot be guaranteed if its traffic characteristics do not comply with the UPC algorithm. On the other hand, the HP video data stream could meet the traffic characteristic requirement and still not be acceptable if the HP layer does not carry enough video data, thereby compromising quality.

For a high-end, real-time video service, the performance of a layered source coding scheme can be measured by two criteria: whether the HP layer constitutes a high enough visual image quality, and whether the transmission of the HP layer can be guaranteed by a UPC function in a simple and efficient manner such as the leaky bucket control function. Here, by efficient manner, we mean that bandwidth allocation should be close to the average source rate and that the token bucket (pool) size should not be too large.

A key issue in video transmission design is to find an efficient transmission bandwidth for guaranteed quality of services (QoS). By stochastic modeling, video traffic can be represented by a stationary random process. The notation of effective bandwidth, measured in *cells per unit time*, is then equivalent to the minimum transmission bandwidth allocated to the input traffic subject to QoS constraints. Limited analytical solutions are available on transmission bandwidth evaluation, usually with simplified input traffic models and under the asymptotic assumption of large buffer size and small loss rate [48]. Based on the traffic descriptor, Reibman and Haskell [49] derive a set of constraints on the encoded bit rate of a video signal that is imposed by the ATM channel and codec buffers. They present a rate control algorithm for transmitting compressed video over the VBR channel, which ensures absence of buffer underflows and overflows. The subject of matching compressed video to ATM networks is discussed in [50].

3.6.1 Leaky Bucket

Since video sources are located remotely on the network, open-loop flow control uses certain models—traffic descriptors—to describe source traffic. Such a model has to be simple enough to involve only a few parameters, since parameters of one source will be transmitted to other switches on the network. The parameters also have to be accurate enough to describe traffic characteristics and to allow correct bandwidth allocation and management.

Leaky bucket is one of the descriptors. It is specified by three parameters: the peak rate R_p, the sustainable rate R_s in bits per frame period, and the size of the leaky bucket N in bits. The three parameters specification is sometimes called *dual leaky bucket*, where (R_s, N_{max}) are parameters of a leaky bucket and the peak rate R_p is enforced by another leaky bucket with parameters $(R_p,1)$. The three parameters are multiples of the packet size 48 bytes, and so is the channel transmission rate R_i. These parameters are usually given in packets [51]. The peak rate R_p is the maximum rate with which a source can transmit packets onto a network at any instance. N_{max} is the maximum size of a counter. When a packet arrives and the counter is less than N_{max}, the packet can be sent immediately to the network; the counter is then incremented by the packet size. When the counter is equal to N_{max}, any arriving packet is either dropped or marked as a low-priority packet. It can be noted that a larger N_{max} allows more bursty traffic to pass. The leaky bucket parameters are negotiated and agreed upon by both the video source and network.

3.6.2   Transmission of High-Priority Video Data

Lossless transmission of HP video data is one of the basic assumptions of layered source coding and can be achieved by choosing an appropriate combination of the corresponding leaky bucket parameters. In the leaky bucket scheme, a certain bandwidth is allocated for the transmission in terms of a token generation rate γ. There is also a token bucket to hold the residual tokens when the source has fewer cells to send. For each cell generated by the encoder, if there is no token in the token bucket, the cell is tagged and in times of congestion in the network, the tagged cells are discarded. On the other hand, if there are tokens in the token bucket, the cell is not tagged and its delivery is guaranteed. The maximum token bucket size is B, as shown in Figure 3.9, which represents the leaky bucket control diagram [52]. For the leaky bucket control, bandwidth efficiency can be defined as $\Theta = \frac{\gamma}{\alpha}$, where α is the average video source rate. A large Θ indicates that the network bandwidth is under utilized since the token arrival rate is larger than the average source rate. For a given γ, B can always be increased so that the token bucket has enough tokens to hold the longest burst period. Given a B, it is always possible to increase γ up to the peak rate to transmit all the cells without being tagged.

3.7   VIDEO SOURCES MODEL DESCRIPTION

It is expected that video will be a major source on ATM networks, which will place a very large bit rate requirement on the network. Therefore, it is very necessary to analyze and assess the performance of an ATM network supporting VBR video traffic, and to determine appropriate mechanisms for the traffic control. For these reasons, an accurate modeling is needed to describe the process of emission of a VBR video codec. Several Markov chain models have been proposed to model multiplexed video sources [54–57], while the Autoregressive

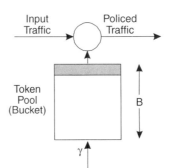

FIGURE 3.9   Leaky bucket control diagram [52]. ©1995 IEEE.

EXAMPLE 3.2

Consider $N+1$ consecutive pictures at one time, say pictures n-N to n. Suppose picture n-N is encoded with $b(n)$ bits and the encoder buffer releases $t(n)$ bits to the channel during this time. We may then advance by one picture and consider the next $N+1$ pictures: pictures n-$N+1$ to $n+1$. Generally speaking, we may advance by k pictures, where $1 < k \leq N + 1$. Assume delayed coding with delay equal to N pictures. Let E_{bs} denote the encoder buffer size, while $e(n)$ represents the encoder buffer level after the n-N th picture has been coded [53]. Then,

$$e(n) = e(n - 1) + b(n) - t(n) \tag{3.1}$$

In order to avoid the encoder buffer under and overflows, we need

$$0 \leq e(n - 1) + b(n) - t(n) \leq E_{bs} \tag{3.2}$$

The constraints on the cumulative sums of encoded bits for the n-N th to the nth pictures are

$$\sum_{k=n}^{n+l} t(k) - e(n - 1) \leq \sum_{k=n}^{n+l} b(k) \leq \sum_{k=n}^{n+l} t(k) + s E_{bs} - e(n - 1) \tag{3.3}$$

where $l = 0,1,...,N$. Here, the factor s is invoked for an additional control on buffer fullness. A numerical choice is $s = 1$ for $l \leq N - 1$, and $s<1$ for $l = N$.

For the best video quality, we should maximize $\sum_{k=n}^{n+l} b(k)$. This in turn calls for maximization of $\sum_{k=n}^{n+N} t(k)$. On the other hand, this quality is bounded due to the finite decoder buffer size and the ATM policing function.

EXAMPLE 3.3

Let D_{bs} and d denote the decoder buffer size and the total coding and decoding buffer delay in number of pictures, respectively. The decoder buffer level after extraction of data for the n-d-N th picture for decoding is

$$r(n) = r(n - 1) + t(n) - b(n - d) \tag{3.4}$$

To avoid decoder buffer underflow and overflow, we have

$$0 \leq r(n - 1) + t(n) - b(n - d) \leq D_{bs} \tag{3.5}$$

Thus, we can write

$$\sum_{k=n-d}^{n-d+l} b(k) - r(n - 1) \leq \sum_{k=n}^{n+l} t(k) \leq \sum_{k=n-d}^{n-d+l} b(k) + D_{bs} - r(n - 1) = U_D^{l(n)} \tag{3.6}$$

where $l = 0,1,...,N$.

EXAMPLE 3.4

Consider now leaky bucket policing function. Let $L(n)$ denote bucket fullness and R_c the average leak rate. Then,

$$L(n) = \max\{0, L(n-1) + t(n) - R_c\} \tag{3.7}$$

To ensure the absence of bucket overflow, we need

$$t(n) \leq L_{max} - L(n-1) + R_c \tag{3.8}$$

where L_{max} is the bucket size.

Taking into account (3.7) and (3.8), the constraint from leaky bucket policing on the transmission rate becomes

$$\sum_{k=n}^{n+l} t(k) \leq s L_{max} - L(n-1) + (l+1)R_c = U_L^{l(n)} \tag{3.9}$$

where $l = 0,1,...,N$.

From (3.9) and (3.6), it can be seen that

$$\max \sum_{k=n}^{n+N} t(k) = \min\{U_L^{N(n)}, U_D^{N(n)}\} \tag{3.10}$$

Hence, the rate budget is

$$R = \sum_{k=n}^{n+N} t(k) = \min\{U_L^{N(n)}, U_D^{N(n)}\} + \frac{1}{2}E_{bs} - e(n-1) \tag{3.11}$$

The rate budget can be applied in the optimal bit allocation problem for independently coded pictures.

(AR) model has been proposed to approximate a single video source [58]. The AR model is suitable for simulating the output bit rate of a VBR video source to a certain extent. Video sources are significantly characterized by the statistics of scene changes, which determine the activity exhibited by the pictures. However, traditional AR models and Markov chain models do not clearly describe these scene change effects so that it is not suitable to the real application. The model proposed in [59] resolves these problems with two complementary processes of the three-state Markov chain process satisfactorily. In the proposed model, the first is to capture the autocorrelation function of the bit rate accurately. The second is to show that a simple path from the model fits the empirical data reasonably, especially to account for the peaks observed during scene changes. The first objective is met by modeling the bits from the two first-order autoregressive processes. With a suitable choice of parameters, one can mimic the behavior of the autocorrelation function obtained from empirical data [60]. Taking into account that the autocorrelation function of empirical data shows a sharp drop at low values of lag and a slow decay at higher values, at least two AR models must be used. The second objective is met by the introduction of an additional process that determines extra bits generated at scene changes [61]. Generally speaking, these models have an exponential shape for autocorrelation function and Gaussian shape for the bit rate distribution.

EXAMPLE 3.5

Since the AR process exhibits an exponential autocovariance function, it is desirable to model real sources using this AR process, especially for low-activity scenes. The AR process has the property that the bit rate required to encode a frame, $X(n)$, is proportional to the output bit rate of a previous frame, $X(n-1)$. The first-order AR process is represented by

$$X(n) = aX(n-1) + b\omega(n) \tag{3.12}$$

where a and b are coefficients that determine the AR process, while $\omega(n)$ is a Gaussian noise process.

The bit rate distribution gives no information about the temporal behavior of the stochastic process. To obtain the bit rate fluctuations over time, it is necessary to determine the pattern of scene change intervals. Since the complementary process is used only to represent scene change effects, it is important to determine the mean and variance of the complementary process compatible to the bit rate in scene changes.

3.8 VIDEO CODING TECHNIQUES

The objective of video coding is representing a video signal with as few bits as possible while maintaining a high quality of the video signal. Because rate distortion performance and complexity are both important issues in developing any practical video coding techniques, the objective of video coding should be stated as achieving the best rate distortion performance under a complexity constraint. Within such a framework, coding efficiency is scalable according to the capability of encoder and decoder in terms of computing power and memory size.

It is widely accepted that second- and third-generation video coding techniques can provide key technologies for efficient compression of video [61–63]. However, since these techniques usually employ advanced image analysis

---

EXAMPLE 3.6

The AR process mentioned in Example 3.5 has such characteristics that the distribution of the bit rate per frame can be approximated with a normal distribution, while the autocovariance function can be approximated with exponential function. This model is good for the short-term phase of the autocorrelation function of the real source within only 7–8 frame lags, but is not good for the long-term phase beyond these frame lags. In order to compensate for this undesirable long-term effect, one more AR process was suggested in [60], so that two AR processes create the bits of the n th frame. This is called the *2-AR process* and is represented by

$$X(n) = \sum_{i=1}^{2} X_i(n) \tag{3.13}$$

where $X_i(n) = a_i X_i(n-1) + b_i \omega_i(n)$.

The 2-AR process has the characteristic that the steady state distribution of $X(n)$ is a normal distribution with mean $E(X)$ and variance σ^2, that is,

$$E(X) = \sum_{i=1}^{2} \frac{b_i}{(1-a_i)} \mu_i \tag{3.14}$$

$$\sigma^2 = \sum_{i=1}^{2} \frac{b_i^2}{(1-a_i^2)} \tag{3.15}$$

where μ_i is the mean of the normal random noise process $\omega_i(n)$.

The autocovariance has an exponential distribution and is represented by

$$C_r(m) = \sum_{i=1}^{2} C_r(m) = \sum_{i=1}^{2} \frac{a_i^m b_i^2}{(1-a_i^2)} \tag{3.16}$$

Now, we have to determine the coefficients a_i, b_i by which the 2-AR process may approach the real source as closely as possible. The determination of these coefficients is accomplished through the following steps:

STEP 1. The initial value σ^2 is the sum of the variances σ_1^2, and σ_2^2 of each AR process.

STEP 2. Define Z_1 equal to $C_r(m_1)/2$. Since the short-term property of the 2-AR process is satisfied with that of a real source up to 7–8 frame lags, we take m_1 as the 8th frame lag.

STEP 3. Define Z_2 equal to $C_r(m_2)$. The value of m_2 is set as a sufficiently large value so that the value of $C_1(m_1)$ is close to 0.

From these steps, the coefficient values are determined as follows:

$$a_2 = (Z_1/Z_2)^{1/(m_1 - m_2)}$$

$$b_2 = [Z_2(1 - a_2^2)/a_2^{m_2}]^{1/2}$$

$$a_1 = \left[Z_1 / \left\{ \sigma^2 - b_2^2 / (1 - a_2^2) \right\} \right]^{1/m_1}$$

$$b_1 = [Z_1(1 - a_2^2)/a_1^{m_1}]^{1/2} \tag{3.17}$$

The mean of the normal random noise process is determined for (3.14), where the mean value $E(X)$ is given as a user parameter. Also, we assume that the mean of each random noise process in the 2-AR process has the same value. For low-motion video such as in a videophone or videoconference, we may choose the Rayleigh distribution instead of the normal distribution.

EXAMPLE 3.7

In the case of an AR process, the distribution of the bit rate is considered a normal distribution with mean μ and variance σ^2. Therefore, the total bit rate distribution of the 2-AR process created by two AR processes can be represented by the convolution of the bit rate distribution of the two AR processes. The bit rate distribution per frame, $f(x)$, is approximated as

$$f(x) = 1/(\sigma\sqrt{2\pi})e^{-(x-\eta)^2/2\sigma^2} \tag{3.18}$$

with mean η and variance σ^2.
The characteristic function of $f(x)$ is

$$F(s) = e^{s\eta}e^{[(s\sigma)^2/2]} \tag{3.19}$$

By the convolution theorem, the characteristic function of the bit rate distribution for the 2-AR process excluding the complementary process is given by

$$F_{AR}(s) = F_1(s)F_2(s) = e^{s(\eta_1 + \eta_2)}e^{s^2(\sigma_1^2 + \sigma_2^2)/2} \tag{3.20}$$

where $F_1(s)$ and $F_2(s)$ are characteristic functions of the two AR processes with means η_1 and η_2 and variances σ_1^2 and σ_2^2, respectively.

From (3.20), we can calculate the mean and variance of the 2-AR process as follows:

$$E(X) = \eta_{AR} = \eta_1 + \eta_2 \qquad \sigma_{AR}^2 = \sigma_1^2 + \sigma_2^2 \tag{3.21}$$

EXAMPLE 3.8

In order to obtain the steady state probability of a video source model represented by a three-state Markov chain, consider the model of the video source shown in Figure 3.10.

FIGURE 3.10   Three-state Markov model of the video source [59].
©1994 IEEE.

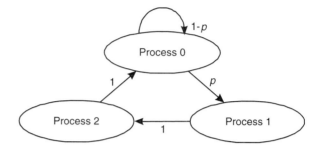

Process 0: 2-AR Process (Normal Condition)
Process 1: Complementary Process I
           (Scene – Change Condition)
Process 2: Complementary Process II
           (Scene – Change Condition)

First, we define the state transition probability matrix T (p_{ij} = probability of transition from the state i to the state j), from the state diagram of Figure 3.10 as follows

$$T = \begin{bmatrix} 1-p & p & 0 \\ 0 & 0 & 1 \\ 1 & 0 & 0 \end{bmatrix}$$

In the normal case, the state of three-state Markov chains is in the state corresponding to Process 0 where only two AR processes (2-AR process) exist. A transition to Process 1 represents a scene change with probability p, by which the state goes to the Complementary Process I. Since the effect of the scene change lasts for two frame lags, the probability of the next transition to Process 2 (which is the Complementary Process II) is always 1. Π_0, Π_1, and Π_2 are assumed to be the steady state probabilities of each process state. Therefore, at steady state, the following equation is satisfied:

$$\overline{\Pi} = \overline{\Pi}T \qquad \sum_{all\ i} \Pi_i = 1 \tag{3.22}$$

where $\overline{\Pi}$ is a row vector of Π_0, Π_1, and Π_2.
From these two equations, we can obtain the following:

$$\Pi_0 = \frac{1}{(1+2p)}, \qquad \Pi_1 = \Pi_2 = \frac{p}{(1+2p)} \tag{3.23}$$

prior to coding (segmentation of video into separate objects and the description of an object by few object-related parameters), this advanced knowledge about the content of video can also be used to increase the functionality for the user. We refer to this attribute as "functional" video coding. Functional coding of video relates to the desire to exploit the capabilities of the next-generation video coding schemes with the aim to achieve more than just efficient compression of video. The ultimate goal is to provide the user with an increased flexibility for generation, coding, transmission, manipulations, and assessment of video content [64–67].

ATM introduces rather different sets of requirements on video coding, some of which are

- Flexibility to specify video quality and average bit rate
- Adaptability so that the output bit rate varies as a function of the changes in the information content of the video frames
- Controllability of the coding rate to enforce flow control
- Robustness to packet defects, such as lost packets, packet jitter, and random bit errors

The functional blocks of a video coding algorithms are energy compaction, quantization, and representation. A full video coding algorithm takes the input signal and applies one or more forms of energy compaction, quantizes the resultant values and gives them a representation that aims at assigning a minimum number of bits per value.

The three most common techniques for energy compaction are prediction, subband analysis [68], and orthogonal transformation. Orthogonal transforms are basically a subset of the subband analysis systems, but are usually treated separately.

Sample values of the input signal can be limited to, say, half or a quarter of the number of values in the original signal. This is done before the change of representation. Such quantization, when a value is rounded to its nearest permissible output value, distorts the signal. Figure 3.11 shows a symmetric quantizer that is specified by three parameters: the width of zero level called the *dead zone*, the step size, and number of steps. Namely, a quantizer is specified by an inner zone given by threshold T where all values are truncated to zero, by a quantization step size Q and by the number of steps.

With higher degrees of quantization (small number of quantization levels), the error becomes visible as artificial contours between intensity levels. It is especially noticeable in areas with smoothly varying shading. At this point, it is important to recognize that the original signal may not be well suited for coarse quantization; rather, the signal should undergo an energy compaction before being quantized. The compacted signal form is often such that many values get coarsely quantized. Hence, a coarser quantization can be applied while still yielding a perceptually unobjectionable distortion. Quantization can

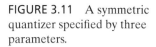
FIGURE 3.11   A symmetric quantizer specified by three parameters.

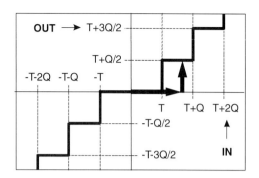

be done one value at a time, denoted by scalar quantization, or a group at a time, called *vector quantization*.

Assume now a digital video signal with a fixed number of bits per sample. This means that all sample values are represented by the same number of bits even though the values may have different likelihoods of appearing in the signal. Figure 3.12 shows an illustration of intensity values from 0 to 255 in a video sequence.

Hence, a new representation that assigns shorter codewords using fewer bits to frequent sample values and longer codewords with more bits to infrequent values may actually represent the signal more efficiently. A concise representation may lower the bit rate a few times depending on the distribution of the sample values.

3.8.1   Fixed Bit Rate and Variable Bit Rate Coder

Figure 3.13 compares a Variable Bit Rate (VBR) coder with a Fixed Bit Rate (FBR) coder. An FBR coder typically has an output rate buffer to smooth out variations in the compressed bit rate. Buffer occupancy rate is controlled by varying the quantization resolution so that the coded video quality is varied in order to maintain a fixed bit rate at the channel. By contrast, in a VBR coder, a rate buffer is not needed because of variable bit rate channels offered by the

FIGURE 3.12   A distribution of intensity values in a video sequence.

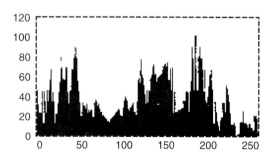

EXAMPLE 3.9

The concept of variable-length coding to reduce the average bit rate is presented in Table 3.1 (Huffman coding).

TABLE 3.1   An Example of Huffman Coding

Quantization Level	Input Codeword	Frequency (Probability)	Output Codeword
0	00	0.6	0
1	01	0.15	100
2	10	0.2	11
3	11	0.05	101

ATM system, thus maintaining a fixed video quality. Nevertheless, in extreme conditions, congestion and flow control are invoked by introducing quality control.

3.8.2   Layered Coding Models in ATM

The concept of layered video coding (Section 2.3) was first introduced in the context of ATM networks in [69, 70]. The video information is divided into several layers, with lower layers containing low-resolution information and higher layers containing the fine information. Such a model enables integration of video telephony and broadcast video services. In the former case,

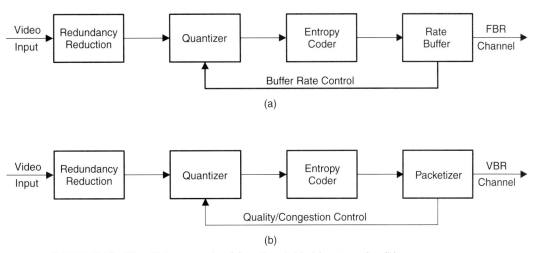

FIGURE 3.13   Fixed bit rate coder (a) and variable bit rate coder (b).

where bandwidth is at a premium, lower layers can provide the desired quality. In broadcast applications, a variable number of higher layers can be integrated with the lower ones to provide the quality and the bit rate that is compatible with the receiver.

Layered coding models in ATM offer a number of advantages:

- User selectable quality level
- User selectable average bit rate
- Flexible traffic structure
- Error concealment capability
- The ability to adopt to the available network bandwidth
- Flow control

It is the general consensus that the VBR coding model for the ATM should be layered. The proposed techniques can be classified into frequency domain techniques (subband coding, discrete cosine transform, lapped orthogonal transform, and so forth) and spatial/temporal domain techniques. For example, in spatial domain, DPCM and vector quantization have been implemented [65, 69, 88, 138, 139, 145, 151]. Frequency domain techniques have been shown to possess the properties suitable for ATM, whereas the spatial/temporal techniques lack the layered structure offering tolerance to packet loss and packet jitter. Next, we briefly review the basic principles concerning some advanced video coding techniques for ATM systems.

3.8.3 Subband Coding

Subband coding is a viable alternative for video transmission over ATM networks because the subband system can be efficiently split into a base layer and an enhancement layer without incurring any overhead [92]. The base layer can be a standardized coding algorithm and is intended to provide reduced, but acceptable, resolution video for given parameters such as image size, frame rate, and nominal bandwidth. The enhancement layer is devised to increase the image quality if sufficient bandwidth is available. During times of network congestion, the enhancement information can be discarded.

The Subband Coding (SBC) technique was initially proposed for speech coding [72] and has since proved to be a powerful technique for both speech and image compression. The extension of the subband coding to multidimensional signal processing was introduced in [73], and the application to image and video compression has been extended with much success [74–76]. The subband decomposition is accomplished by passing the image data through a bank of analysis filters. Since the bandwidth of each filtered subband image is reduced, each subband image can be subsampled at its new Nyquist rate, resulting in a series of reduced-size subband images. These subbands are more tractable than the original signal in that each subband image may be coded separately, transmitted, and decoded at the destination. These received subband images are then upsampled to form images of original size and passed through the corresponding bank of synthesis filters, where they are interpolated and added to obtain the reconstructed image.

Various coding methods have been examined to code the higher-frequency subbands in order to retain the edge information but still using a low average bit rate. Johnsen et al. [77] defined an activity index based on amplitude changes in the Lowest Frequency Subband (LFS) and used this to select a set of quantizers for the Higher Frequency Subbands (HFS). Podilchuk et al. [78, 79] generated a large dimension (81) sparse codebook for coding the HFS, where the code vectors are based on geometric considerations. This approach eliminates the need for a training sequence. Mohsenian and Nasrabadi [80] used an edge detection operator on the baseband to determine the location of important high-frequency information.

Entropy-constrained quantization provides a powerful, information-theoretic approach for coding the higher-frequency subbands. Tanabe and Farvardin used [81] Entropy-Constrained Scalar Quantizers (ECSQ) for the subband coding of still images [82]. Kim and Modestino [83] extended this work to the vector case and used Entropy-Constrained Vector Quantizers (ECVQ) to code the still image subbands [84]. Marcellin et al. used Entropy-Constrained Trellis Coded Quantization (ECTCQ) to code full-band images [85]. Sriram and Marcellin extended this to subband coding of images [86]. The work described in [87] generalizes these ideas for subband video coding. For the intraframe case, both ECVQ and ECTCQ are examined.

The SBC technique is used to decorrelate a signal [88]; in other words, to minimize some types of source redundancies. In the case of video, two types of redundancy have to be reduced:

- Intraframe redundancy in spatial domain
- Interframe redundancy in temporal domain

A signal is passed through band-pass filters, the analysis filters. Due to the reduced bandwidth, each resolution component may be subsampled to its new Nyquist rate, thus yielding the channel signals. Following that, each subband is encoded, transmitted, and, at the destination, decoded. To finally reconstruct the signal, each frequency band is upsampled to the sampling rate

---

EXAMPLE 3.10

The technique of SBC can be easily explained using a two-band SBC system shown in Figure 3.14.

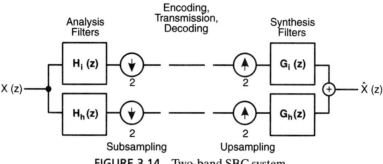

FIGURE 3.14   Two-band SBC system.

---

of the input. All upsampled components are passed through the synthesis filter bank, where they are interpolated, and added to form the reconstructed signal. In the case of a division into two bands only, a low-pass and a high-pass filter are used in the analysis bank and their modulated versions are used as, respectively, high- and low-pass filters in the synthesis bank. Le Gall has found pairs of perfect reconstruction filters that are well suited for image processing. These filters have linear phase, low computational complexity, and relatively good characteristics for frequency selection and interpolation [89].

The most important aspect of an SBC encoder is the correct choice of the filter banks performing the signal analysis and synthesis. Some of the properties to be taken into consideration are the linear phase character of the filters, perfect reconstruction capability of the overall system, and alias suppression in the subsampled frequency components. Two different filter bank approaches can be recommended in advanced packet video coding based on SBC technique:

- Quadrature Mirror Filters (QMFs) arranged as cascade structures of two band systems [90].
- Parallel filter banks based on a Time-Domain Aliasing Cancellation (TDAC) [91].

QMFs are generally linear-phase filters. Higher-order filters produce good results, but perfect reconstruction is only obtained in the case of length-2 filters, which exhibit very smooth frequency roll-off and cause bad alias suppression in the particular subbands. On the other hand, TDAC is an N-band parallel filter bank implementation of a subband system that may be interpreted as a critically sampled single-sideband modulation system with perfect aliasing cancellation at the synthesis stage [92]. A two-dimensional 2D TDAC can be realized efficiently via a 2D DCT algorithm [27].

The advantages of a subband coding scheme are

- Bit rate reduction by utilizing energy concentration in the lower bands.
- Control of the quantization noise ratio among subbands.
- Hierarchical coding that is robust to cell loss can be realized.
- Parallel processing can be applied to each band at a reduced clock rate.
- A coding gain can be exploited by optimal bit allocation procedure matched to the statistical characteristics of each subband and by shaping the noise spectrum according to the subjective noise perception of the human visual system [93].
- Image distortion looks more natural than the blocking effects of DCT-based image coding schemes and is therefore less annoying.
- A reduction in the data rate may be achieved through the application of the proper coding method to each subband [94].
- Subband decomposition provides many possible architectural trade-offs to achieve a low-power implementation.

3.8.4 Three-Dimensional Subband Spatio-Temporal Decomposition

Three-Dimensional (3D) subband coding was originally proposed in [95] as a promising technique for video compression. The video signal is decomposed into temporal and spatial frequency subbands using temporal and spatial analysis filter banks. To recognize the difference between the temporal frequency response and spatial frequency response of the Human Visual System (HVS), the filter banks used for temporal decomposition are often different from those for spatial decomposition. After subband decomposition, each subband exhibits certain distinct features corresponding to the characteristics of the filter banks. These features are utilized in the design of compression strategies to fully exploit the redundancy in the decomposed subbands.

To minimize the computation of the temporal filtering in decomposing the video signal, temporal decomposition is based on the two-tap Haar filter bank [79]. This also minimizes the number of frames that need to be stored and the delay caused by the analysis and synthesis procedures. The temporal decomposition results in two subbands: the High Pass Temporal (HPT) band (that is, frame difference [FD]), and the Low Pass Temporal (LPT) band.

EXAMPLE 3.11

Four levels of subband decomposition are shown in Figure 3.15. Here, LL represents the filtered output of the low-pass vertical and low-pass horizontal filters; LH, the output of the low-pass vertical and high-pass horizontal filters; HL, the output of the high-pass vertical and low-pass horizontal filters; and HH, the output of the high-pass vertical and high-pass horizontal filters. Because each subband has a reduced frequency content, it is downsampled by a factor of 2 in each dimension. The LL subband can be recursively filtered creating four levels of 13 subbands. For decoding, the four level subbands are each upsampled and filtered, then summed together to form a reconstructed LL subband. This process is repeated through all four levels until the final image is formed.

FIGURE 3.15   Four levels of subband decomposition.

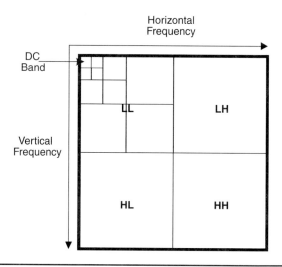

Spatial decomposition, both horizontal and vertical, is often based on multitap filter banks. With separable filters, multidimensional analysis and synthesis can be carried out in stages of directional filtering. Figure 3.16 shows an 11-band tree-structured decomposition scheme for video signals. The template for displaying the decomposed 11-band subband images is shown in Figure 3.17. To achieve high compression, the lowest-frequency band can be further decomposed in a tree structure fashion. The high-frequency subbands contain structures approximately aligned along horizontal, vertical, or diagonal directions. For the 11-band decomposition of the video signal, band 1 is the low-resolution representation of the original image and has similar histogram characteristics, but with much smoother spatial distribution. It can be efficiently coded using DPCM. Bands 2–7 contain spatial high-frequency components of the LPT band. They consist of different amounts of "edges" and "impulses" corresponding to different directions and resolution levels. Since the signal energy and the

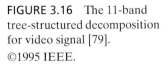

FIGURE 3.16 The 11-band tree-structured decomposition for video signal [79]. ©1995 IEEE.

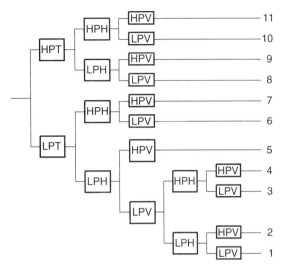

perceptual importance in general decreases as the resolution level increases, the bit allocation should be adjusted accordingly. Band 8 is the low-pass spatial band of the HPT band and contains the most motion energy. It needs more bits or finer quantization when the motion activity is high. Bands 9–11 represent spatial high-frequency components of the FD. They usually contain very low signal energy and are of low perceptual sensitivity.

The quantization and coding algorithm should be developed based on these characteristics. In general, subbands at the lower-resolution levels contain the most signal energy, and are of higher visual significance. They require higher-quality coding and, hence, finer quantization. On the other hand, subbands at the higher levels can be quantized coarsely or may even be discarded without significant loss in visual quality. The 3D spatio-temporal subbands decomposition is followed by the appropriate redundancy reduction techniques [96].

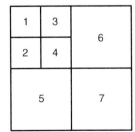
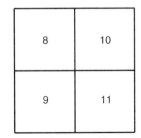

FIGURE 3.17   Template for displaying the 11-band decomposition scheme [79].
©1995 IEEE.

3.8.5 Discrete Cosine Transform

The discovery of the Discrete Cosine Transform (DCT) has had a significant impact in the Digital Signal Processing (DSP) field [27, 303]. The objective is very simple: how an image (spatial domain) or sequence of images (spatial-temporal domains) can be mapped into the transform domain, so that the bandwidth for transmission or the memory for storage can be reduced, with subsequent recovery of the image or image sequence by inverse transformation with negligible distortion. Minimizing the distortion provides a preliminary, but partial, insight into the efficiency and effectiveness of transform coding. However, the human viewer is the ultimate judge regarding the quality of the processed images.

A major objective of transform coding is to make as many transform coefficients as possible of small magnitudes so that they are insignificant in terms of statistical and subjective measures, and therefore need not be coded for transmission. At the same time, it is desirable to minimize statistical dependencies between coefficients with the aim to reduce the number of bits needed to encode the remaining coefficients. The variance (energy) distribution of intraframe DCT coefficients is presented in Figure 3.18. This variance distribution is calculated based on a large number of image blocks. Here, u and v describe the horizontal and vertical image transform domain variables within the 8×8 block. Most of the total variance is concentrated around the dc coefficient (u=0, v=0). Coefficients with small variances are less significant for the reconstruction of the image blocks than coefficients with large variances. On average, only a small number of DCT coefficients need to be transmitted to the receiver to obtain an approximate reconstruction of the image blocks. Moreover, the most significant DCT coefficients are concentrated around the upper-left corner (low-frequency DCT coefficients), and the significance of the coefficients decays with increased distance. This implies that higher-frequency DCT coefficients are less important for reconstruction than lower-frequency coefficients.

The properties of the DCT can be summarized as follows [96]:

- The energy of the signal/picture is packed in a few coefficients.
- It has fast implementation, forward and inverse.
- It has a recursive structure (easier to implement multiple size transforms).
- It uses real arithmetic, orthogonal and separable: extension to multiple dimensions is simple.

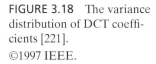

FIGURE 3.18   The variance distribution of DCT coefficients [221].
©1997 IEEE.

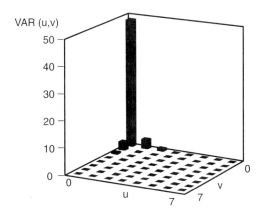

- It is close to statistically optimal Karhunen-Loeve Transform (KLT). KLT is infrequently used because it is not a fixed transform (statistical dependence) and has no fast algorithm. It is, however, used as a benchmark in comparing the discrete transforms.
- There is minimal residual correlation.
- There is minimal Mean Square Error (MSE).
- Application-Specific Integrated Circuits (ASIC) DCT chips are available. A number of functions such as on-chip addition/subtraction, zigzag scan, besides DCT, are integrated into a single chip.
- It has been adopted for different applications by ITU-T, ISO, and IEC (that is, JPEG, MPEG, HDTV, H.261, H.263, and so on).
- There is minimal rate distortion and maximum (transform/DPCM) coding gain.
- It has decimation and filtering properties in the DCT domain.
- Modified DCT (MDCT) is utilized to decompose a signal into equal sub-bands.
- DCT is used for Vector Quantization (VQ).

In the case of adaptive DCT coding, the image is divided into blocks of fixed size (typically 8×8 pixels). Each block is then transformed into a frequency space. The transform most commonly used for this operation is the 2D DCT.

The DCT is closely related to the Discrete Fourier Transform (DFT). It is of some importance to realize that the DCT coefficients can be given a frequency interpretation close to the DFT. The DCT transforms a block of image data to the same number of coefficients where to each coefficient is assigned a basis image with different frequency contents. Coefficients with high index numbers are assigned to basis images with high frequencies.

From a visual perception viewpoint, the low-frequency coefficients are much more sensitive than the high-frequency coefficients. By incorporating HVS weighting in the DCT coefficients, a number of high-frequency coefficients can be coarsely quantized [96].

3.8.6   Adaptive Subband Discrete Cosine Transform Coding

Classical orthogonal block transform like the DCT can also be interpreted in terms of a subband system. The basis functions of the transform are the impulse responses of the analysis and synthesis filters. The impulse response length is restricted to the block length and does not allow block overlaps, which causes the well-known blocking artifacts. The adaptive SBC/DCT coding in an ATM-based network is shown in Figure 3.19. The QMFs decompose the input signal into two bands in horizontal directions, while the second stage filters decompose two bands into four bands (LL, LH, HL, HH) in a vertical direction.

Here, the LH band means, for example, the lower band in the horizontal direction and the higher signal in the vertical direction. Among the four bands, the LL band has the largest amount of signal energy and the highest pixel-to-pixel correlation. To maximize the bit rate reduction efficiency in LL band signal, an adaptive selection of the input signal to DCT coding from the intrafield, interfield, and motion compensated interframe signals was proposed in [97].

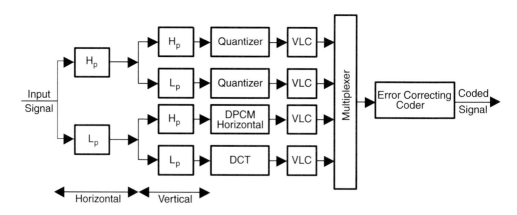

L_p – Low Pass and Downsampling
H_p – High Pass and Downsampling
DCT – Discrete Cosine Transform
VLC – Variable Length Coding

FIGURE 3.19   Adaptive SBC/DCT video coding scheme [97].

3.8.7 Lapped Orthogonal Transform

The main motivation behind the development of Lapped Transform (LT) is the removal of the major artifacts generated by the block transform coding technique; in other words, the blocking effects. These are discontinuities in the reconstructed signal in the vicinity of the block boundaries. Transform coding based on LT is essentially free from blocking effects, with the added bonus of slightly higher coding gains [98].

The driving force behind the development of the Lapped Orthogonal Transform (LOT) is the reduction of blocking effects in transform coding. However, the term "LOT" has been used for a lapped transform whose basis functions have even or odd symmetry and lengths equal to L=2M, where M is the transform size or the number of subbands. An LOT is a special case of an LT, with L=2M (see Figure 3.20).

In the LOT coding, an image is divided into overlapping blocks of 2L×2L pixels and each block is overlapped with its neighboring blocks by L pixels on each side [99]. The 2D LOT is defined by an L×2L matrix T, where

$$T = [X_u|X_l|Y_u|Y_l] \tag{3.24}$$

while X_u, X_l, Y_u, and Y_l are L×L/2 matrices. Let $b_{k,l}$ be a 2L×2L matrix representing the pixel values of the (k,l)-th block of the image. The corresponding 2D LOT coefficients $B_{k,l}$ can be calculated from

$$B_{k,l} = Tb_{k,l}T^t \tag{3.25}$$

where the coefficient block $B_{k,l}$ is of size L×L. The LOT reconstruction of a block requires information from its neighboring coefficient blocks:

$$\hat{b}_{k,l} = \begin{bmatrix} Y_l^t & X_l^t & 0 \\ 0 & Y_u^t & X_u^t \end{bmatrix} \begin{bmatrix} B_{k-1,l-1} & B_{k,l-1} & B_{k+1,l-1} \\ B_{k-1,l} & B_{k,l} & B_{k+1,l} \\ B_{k-1,l+1} & B_{k,l+1} & B_{k+1,l+1} \end{bmatrix} \begin{bmatrix} Y_l & 0 \\ X_l & Y_u \\ 0 & X_u \end{bmatrix} \tag{3.26}$$

The reconstructed block $\hat{b}_{k,l}$ has L×L pixels as opposed to the original block, $b_{k,l}$, which has 2L×2L pixels. From the preceding equation, we can observe that if the coefficient block at (k,l) is missing, all the blocks surrounding it will be affected as well.

LOT represents an elegant technique for reducing the aliasing of the block DCT [100]. This is an orthogonal transformation on the block DCT coefficients that combines coefficients computed from adjacent blocks. As for the LOT of the images, the basis functions from adjacent blocks overlap one another and their impulse responses are tapered at the edges.

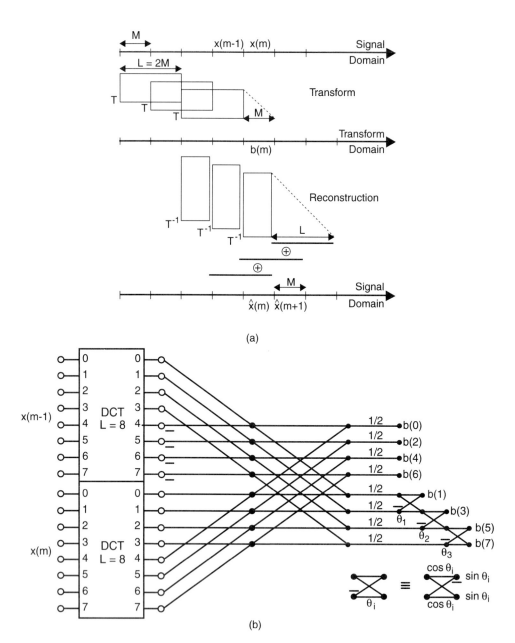

FIGURE 3.20 Lapped orthogonal transform/reconstruction with L=2M. (a) The forward LOT is obtained by processing the data from left to right, and the inverse LOT from right to left. (b) A flow graph of the fast LOT for a single block, for M=8 [101].

©1989 IEEE.

An efficient version of the LOT in which the additional orthogonal transformation is computed using a butterfly network of simple rotation transformation is known as the *fast LOT* [101].

With the introduction of the LOT in which the basis functions have lengths given by L=2M, a new alternative in transform coding is available. For a given transform length, the LOT has a higher coding gain than the usual DCT and, as we pointed out, is free from blocking effects. The LOT basis functions also correspond to filters with much better bandpass responses than those of the DCT [102].

Another lapped transform with L=2M is the Modulated Lapped Transform (MLT), first developed in [103]. The MLT is similar to the LOT. The main differences are that the MLT basis functions are not symmetrical, and the MLT is actually a cosine-modulated filter bank, which has slightly better bandpass responses than the LOT.

The family of lapped orthogonal transforms can be extended to include basis functions of arbitrary length. Within this new family, the Extended Lapped Transform (ELT) is introduced as a generalization of the previously reported modulated lapped transform. Design techniques and fast algorithms for ELT are presented in [104], while the perfect reconstruction conditions for time-varying lapped transform are analyzed in [105].

The ELT is a promising substitute for the traditional block transform in the transform coding systems, and also is a good substitute for less-efficient filter banks in subband coding systems. Namely, ELT can replace the DCT in transform coding systems with higher coding gains and absence of blocking effects. In subband coding, the ELT can replace filter banks, since the ELT is the perfect reconstruction filter bank with the lowest computational complexity.

3.8.8   Wavelet Transform Coding

Wavelet Transform (WT) coding is a variant from DCT-based transform coding that reduces or eliminates some of its limitations. The name "wavelet" comes from the special localized basis functions used to break down an image (or other data) into its essential details. By using bursts of short-duration waves, rather than the continuous sinusoids used by the DCT, wavelet coding can more efficiently represent small features in an image such as the rapid transitions that occur at object edges. Another advantage is that rather than working with 8×8 blocks of pixels, as do JPEG [96] and other block-based DCT techniques, wavelet coding can simultaneously compress the entire image. Thus, a wavelet-compressed image never suffers from the blocking artifacts that are visible when block-based DCT techniques are pushed to high compression ratios. Taken in combination, these factors allow wavelet coding to offer high compression ratios for a given image quality level [106]. In some image coding applications, compression ratios as high as 300:1 are possible—several times greater than for JPEG and other DCT-based algorithms. One of the advantages of wavelet coding is that it quite naturally supports progressive transmission and decomposition of images. That is, by simply ordering the compressed image file, an image can first be displayed at low resolution and fine detail can be added as more image subbands are transmitted. The multi-resolution characteristics of wavelet-compressed images can also be used to advantage for wavelet-compressed video. When storage or transmission limits are encountered, image resolution can be temporally reduced to produce slightly "softer" images. This is easily accomplished by dropping one of more of the subband images. In contrast, under the same conditions, those DCT-based compression techniques that do not use progressive transmission may deliver images with block artifacts or must resort to more drastic measures such as frame dropping.

Wavelet transform is a solution to avoid the blocking effect that occurs in any DCT-based coding scheme widely used currently for data compression [107–110]. The wavelet-transformed image has certain geometric similarity among the frequency bands having the same orientation in the spatial two dimensions. This similarity can be represented by various tree structures. Some years ago, several coding schemes in cascade with adaptive arithmetic coders were developed using various tree structures [111–113]. The main limiting factors of these algorithms are the requirement of multiple scans for a given transformed image and multiple arithmetic coders each using different numbers of symbols.

Wavelet transform is the decomposition of a signal into expansions and translations of a mother function $\Psi(t)$. It has become very popular for image and video coding applications [108, 114]. It provides a tool for image data decorrelation, resulting in a set of coefficients that can be coded more efficiently than the original pixel values. Despite the low correlation among the bands, there exists a strong structural similarity among the bands of same orientation [115]. This implies that the zero-valued coefficients of the bands of the same orientation tend to be in the same corresponding positions.

The property that the wavelet transform performs analysis of a signal in the frequency domain can be exploited in image coding, so that bit allocation among the wavelet coefficients can be implemented according to the HVS sensitivity to each of the frequency bands, known as *noise shaping* [116]. Therefore, in order for a wavelet coder to achieve this bit allocation, it is convenient that an arbitrary level of distortion can be set for each band. Another important issue in the design of a coder for wavelet coefficients is the level of quantization error introduced to each individual coefficient. The overall picture quality can be significantly affected by a poorly quantized coefficient, because the wavelet synthesis process spreads this error over an area of the image [117, 118].

Wavelet image transform is based on a decomposition of the image space into a subspace and its complement. The projection onto the subspace gives a lower approximation of the original image, while missing details are present in the projection onto the complementary subspace. This process can be iterated by decomposing the approximation subspace into two terms: a lower-resolution subspace and its complement. Orthogonal bases for all involved subspaces are obtained from one single function through scaling and shifting [119].

The multiresolution or multiscale view of signal analysis is the essence of the wavelet transform [120]. During the last few years, wavelet analysis has emerged as a very powerful tool in multiresolution image coding. For image coding, the decomposition (wavelet) coefficients are quantized using various techniques. The high-efficiency image coding is achieved by the quantization of the wavelet coefficients, which use the properties of human visual perception. From a coding point of view, it is equivalent to the analysis of a signal into several frequency bands, each one representing a trade-off between time and frequency resolution.

Wavelet transform can be written as inner products of $f(t)$ and a family of functions as in the case of windowed Fourier transform [121]. The family of functions is defined by

$$\Psi_{a,b}(t) = \frac{1}{\sqrt{|a|}} \Psi\left(\frac{t-b}{a}\right), \qquad a, b \in R, \qquad a \neq 0 \tag{3.27}$$

where a is dilation parameter and b is a translation parameter. The wavelet transform can be written in the form

$$W\{f(a, b)\} = \left[\frac{1}{\sqrt{|a|}} \Psi\left(\frac{t-b}{a}\right), f(t)\right] = \frac{1}{\sqrt{|a|}} \int_{-\infty}^{+\infty} \Psi\left(\frac{t-b}{a}\right) f(t) dt, f(t) \in L^2(R) \ space \tag{3.28}$$

The wavelet representation provides a multiresolution/multifrequency expression of a signal with localization in both time and frequency. A WT decomposes a nonstationary image into set of multiscaled wavelets where each component becomes relatively more stationary and hence easier to code. Coding schemes and parameters can be adapted to the statistical properties of each wavelet. Hence, coding each stationary component is more efficient than coding the entire nonstationary image. One nice feature about using wavelets is that one has the ability to "zoom in" on singularities. For example, a rough approximation of the signal might look stationary, while at a more detailed level (that is, at a finer scale), a different behavior can be observed.

With WT, a signal can be decomposed into many different time and frequency scales so that both low-frequency, long-duration phenomena and high-frequency, short-duration features can be studied within the same transform. That is, a WT can be interpreted as a decomposition into a set of frequency channels having the same bandwidth on the logarithmic scale [116]. The multiresolution of signal analysis has become a desired feature for many signal decomposition techniques [122]. An important application to video coding is closely related both to subband coding and wavelets.

3.8.9 Wavelets and Scaling Functions

A wavelet is a signal or a waveform having desirable characteristics such as localization in time and frequency, and orthogonality across scale and translation [109, 134]. Because of these properties, wavelets appear to be promising waveforms in communications. Motivation for the use of wavelets for waveform coding stems from the fact that the two ideal waveforms often used to benchmark analog pulse shaping performance (namely, the time-limited rectangular pulse and band-limited sinc pulse) are the so-called scaling functions and have corresponding wavelets [135].

Let $\Psi(t)$ be a mother wavelet. A dilated or scaled and translated wavelet $\Psi_{j,k}(t)$ is given by

$$\Psi_{j,k}(t) = 2^{-\frac{j}{2}}\Psi[2^{-j}(t - 2^{j}k)] \tag{3.29}$$

where 2^{j} and $2^{j}k$ indicate the amount of dilation and translation for some integers j and k. It can be shown that inner product between $\Psi_{j,k}(t)$ and $\Psi_{m,n}(t)$ for some integers j, k, m, n is given by

$$[\Psi_{j,k}(t)\Psi_{m,n}(t)] = \int_{-\infty}^{+\infty} \Psi_{j,k}(t)\Psi_{m,n}(t)dt = \delta_{j-m}\delta_{k-n} \tag{3.30}$$

which implies that dilated and translated wavelets $\Psi_{j,k}(t)$ for different (j, k) values are orthogonal to one another. Wavelets are unit-energy bandpass functions. There also exist corresponding unit-energy low-pass functions, called *scaling functions* $\Phi_{j,k}(t)$, which are generated from a mother function $\Phi(t)$. Orthogonality relations

$$[\Phi_{j,\,k}(t)\Phi_{m,\,n}(t)] = \delta_{k-n}, \qquad [\Psi_{j,\,k}(t)\Phi_{m,\,n}(t)] = 0, \qquad j \le n \qquad (3.31)$$

imply that scaling functions, for a given dilation, are orthogonal across translation, whereas wavelets and scaling functions are orthogonal at certain dilations and arbitrary translations [136].

There exist many families of wavelets and scaling functions. For example, the Haar [110] wavelet is given by $\Psi(t) = \frac{1}{2}$ for $0 \le t \le \frac{1}{2}$ and $\Psi(t) = -\frac{1}{2}$ for $\frac{1}{2} \le t \le 1$ and has the corresponding scaling function $\Phi(t) = 1$ for $0 \le t \le 1$. Both the Haar wavelet and the corresponding scaling function are commonly used to represent digital information in communication systems. The Haar scaling function is generally referred to as the *full-width rectangular pulse*, and the Haar wavelet as the *biphase pulse*.

3.8.10   Filter Banks and Wavelets

Mallat used the concept of the multiresolution analysis to define wavelets [109, 116], while Daubechies constructed compactly supported orthonormal wavelets based on iterations of the discrete filters [123]. Corresponding to each orthonormal basis, there exists a subband decomposition filter bank realizing the multiresolution signal representation.

Filter bank is a signal processing device that produces M signals from a signal by means of filtering by M multiresolution filters. While this device performs an analysis of the input signal, a filter bank can also be used to synthesize a signal from the M decomposed signals. Orthogonal filter banks were first derived by Smith and Barnwell [124] as well as Mintzer [125], and were systematically studied by Vaidyanathan [126, 127].

Continuous wavelets can be obtained from tree-structured quadrature mirror filter banks, with the same filters on each level [123]. In fact, the Discrete Wavelet Transform (DWT) was recognized to be equivalent to an octave-band filter bank allowing perfect reconstruction, which was successfully applied for some time in subband coding of images [74, 92].

3.8.11   Discrete Wavelet Transform

The discrete wavelet transform has recently emerged as a powerful technique for image compression because of its flexibility in representing images and its ability in adapting to the human visual system characteristics. The DWT decomposes an image into various multiresolution approximations, which are accomplished by iteratively applying high- and low-pass filters to the image. The advantage of using the DWT over the Discrete Cosine Transform (DCT) is that the DWT projects high-detail image components onto shorter basis functions, with higher resolution, while lower-detail components are projected onto larger basis functions, which correspond to narrower subbands, establishing a trade-off between time and frequency resolutions [120]. In addition, the wavelet transform coding provides a superior image quality at low bit rates, since it is free from both blocking effects and mosquito noise [128]. However, there are still significant amounts of redundancies among the subbands. That is, most coding techniques using the DWT disregard cross-correlation among the various scale and orientation bands. Hence, the performance of the wavelet transform coding can be improved if the cross-correlation among these subbands is exploited in the encoding process.

Figure 3.21 represents the image decomposition and reconstruction scheme using the 1D DWT [129]. Figure 3.21(a) shows the analysis section of a 2D separable filter bank, where first the image rows are passed through the two-channel filter bank and then the columns are processed: wavelet coefficients of the image are computed, as in the one-dimensional case, using subband coding algorithm. Figure 3.21(b) shows the synthesis section to reconstruct the signal from the subband signals. The filters are one dimensional. The analysis section can be viewed as a 2×2 transform applied to image. Note that each subband has one-fourth of the samples of the original signal. The synthesis section can be viewed as a 2×2 inverse transform. Figure 3.21(c) shows the scheme, which is composed of a succession of three stages of 2×2 transforms. Only the low-pass subband is connected to the next stage. The inverse transform is, of course, accomplished by reversing the paths and the transforms.

Using these schemes, the decomposition of the Lena image is shown in Figure 3.22. To reconstruct the image from the subbands, one may choose the set of Low Pass (LPF) and High Pass (HPF) Filters, so as to provide Perfect Reconstruction (PR).

The discretization of wavelet transform [123] can be written as follows: $a = a_0^m$, $b = nb_0 a_0$, m, n = integers, $a_0 > 1$, $b_0 \neq 0$

$$W_d\{f(m, n)\} = a_0^{-\frac{m}{2}} \int_{-\infty}^{+\infty} f(t)\Psi(a_0^m t - nb_0)dt \qquad (3.32)$$

If $a_0 = 2$ and $b_0 = 1$, then it can be shown that there is an orthogonal basis of the space $L^2(R)$ [121]. The choice of $a_0 = 2$ is advantageous because the decomposition algorithm is simpler than in other cases.

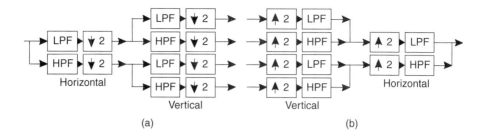

(a)   (b)

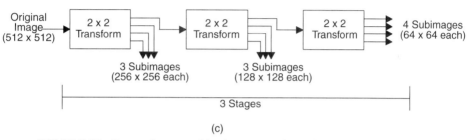

(c)

FIGURE 3.21   Image decomposition/reconstruction scheme using DWT [129].
©1994 SPIE.

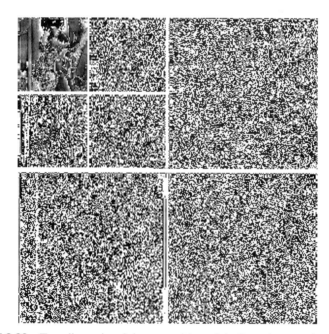

FIGURE 3.22   Two-dimensional decomposition of the Lena image using DWT in
two stages.

For the two dimensions in an image, the 2D wavelet transform is implemented independently, first in the horizontal direction and then in the vertical direction. This method of applying the DWT on a two-dimensional signal that is sampled on a rectangular lattice is called the *dyadic 2D DWT*. The word "dyadic" means the scale factor in both directions. The dyadic 2D DWT has two advantages. First, it is easy to implement—the separate processing of rows and columns requires the same computational complexity and hardware realization as needed for the processing of the 1D signals. Second, the transform has the property that it emphasizes the directions along the axes in comparison to all other directions in the plane. As HVS is more sensitive to the horizontal and vertical directions than any other directions, the dyadic 2D DWT is suitable for most image coding applications.

A 2D spatial DWT is used for coding video (as a sequence of images). As shown in Figure 3.23, the first step for compression is to process the entire image with a bank of filters. The wavelet filters separate the image into a series of subbands of logarithmically increasing spatial frequency. The filter outputs create a set of transformed images at different resolutions that can be efficiently coded. The lowest-frequency subband contains a reduced-resolution, blurred copy of the original image. The higher-frequency subbands contain edge information needed to reproduce the fine detail of the original image at successively larger resolutions. Because of the way humans perceive spatial detail, the wavelet coefficients for consecutively higher-frequency subbands can be quantized more coarsely [130, 131]. Either scalar or vector quantization can be used [132, 133]. The final step is to combine the quantized coefficients from all subbands and then entropy code them with run-length and Huffman or arithmetic coding. By reversing the encoding operations, the wavelet decoder produces an approximate representation of the input image.

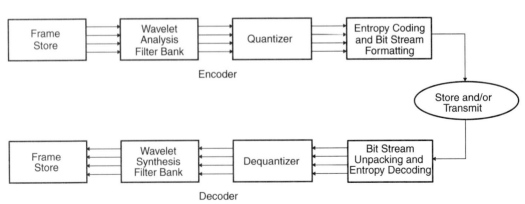

FIGURE 3.23   Wavelet encoding and decoding [106].
©1997 Chapman and Hall.

3.8.12 Predictive Encoding

Predictive encoding exploits the redundancy from sample to sample and derives the upcoming sample from the previous sample(s), where the sample may be a pixel, line, audio sample, or video frame. It encodes, stores, and transmits the differences between the prediction and the input sample value. The decoder produces the prediction from the previous sample(s) and reproduces the sample from both the prediction and the difference value. Since the entropy of the difference between samples is usually smaller than that of the original sample, the file size may be reduced. However, its success highly depends on the prediction function and the ability to anticipate the changing signal [137].

In the case of video signal, the underlying philosophy is that if the current pixel (*pixel* or *pel* means "picture element") can be predicted reasonably well, based on the previous neighborhood pixels, then the prediction error has a smaller entropy than the original sampled signal [96]. Hence, the prediction error can be quantized with fewer quantization levels than can the sampled video signal. The prediction can be based on the statistical distribution of the video signal [88, 138].

The most common approach to predictive coding is DPCM (Differential Pulse Code Modulation) [139]. It is a simple and popular predictive encoding method that exploits the property that the values of adjacent pixels in an image are often similar and highly correlated. A general block diagram of DPCM is illustrated in Figure 3.24. Suppose an original image has M rows and N columns. Let $X(m,n)$ denote the pixel value at the m-th row and n-th column from the origin located at the top-left corner. An image is typically encoded one pixel at a time across a raster scan line, from left to right for two consecutive raster lines.

The value of a pixel is predicted as a linear combination of a few neighboring pixel values that have been previously reconstructed. The predicted value of a pixel, $x_{est}(m,n)$, is

$$x_{est} = \sum_{[i,j] \in ROS} \sum \alpha(i,j) x_r(m-i, n-j) \tag{3.33}$$

where $\alpha(i,j)$ are known as the prediction coefficients or weighting factors specified by the user. For the purpose of coding, the Region of Summation (ROS) is chosen so that the set $\{x_r(i,j)\}$ includes only those pixels whose values have been already decoded or reconstructed at the receiver.

With predictive coding, the redundancy in video is determined from the neighboring pixels within frames or between frames. This concept is promising

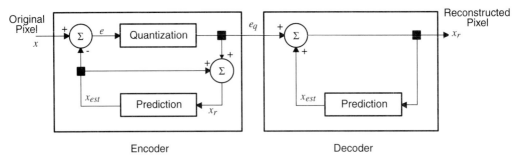

Encoder   Decoder

FIGURE 3.24   DPCM encoder/decoder.

EXAMPLE 3.12

The predicted value of the pixel, $x(m, n)$, can be written using three adjacent pels in the form

$$x_{est}(m, n) = \alpha(0, 1)x_r(m, n-1) + \alpha(1, 0)x_r(m-1, n) + \alpha(1, 1)x_r(m-1, n-1) \quad (3.34)$$

Then, the prediction error given by $e(m, n) = x(m, n) - x_{est}(m, n)$ is quantized, entropy coded, and transmitted to the decoder. The motivation for this is that the differential image typically has a much reduced variance and can thus be encoded more efficiently. From the quantized prediction error $e_q(m, n)$, the decoder reconstructs the pixels as

$$x_r(m, n) = x_{est}(m, n) + e_q(m, n) \quad (3.35)$$

It is easy to show that the reconstruction error $r(m, n) = x(m, n) - x_r(m, n)$ is the same as the quantization error, $e(m, n) - e_q(m, n)$.

---

if the correlation among adjacent pixels that are spatially as well as temporally close to one another is strong [19].

The performance of the predictive coding method is strongly dependent on the actual predictors used to decorrelate the data. Figure 3.25 outlines possible locations of pixels used for intraframe and interfield prediction in some of the standard coding schemes. Location of the predicted pixel x and already coded pixels (A, B, C, D, or E, F) used for prediction in two separate scenarios, are shown. The prediction is calculated as a weighted linear combination of the previously coded pixels. The first scenario on the left side uses predictor geometry with intraframe coding, while the second scenario represents prediction between fields for coding of interlaced pixels in odd fields. The prediction is based on pixels already coded in even fields; in other words, interfield coding.

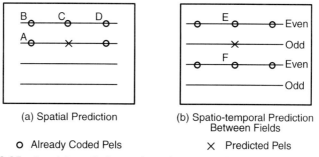

(a) Spatial Prediction   (b) Spatio-temporal Prediction
                                           Between Fields

o   Already Coded Pels   ×   Predicted Pels

FIGURE 3.25   Spatial prediction and spatio-temporal prediction between fields.

The concept of layered coding for ATM by employing DPCM and intrafield/interfield transform coding on a video sequence was first proposed in [140, 141]. To transmit this single sequence, a bit rate of 67 Mbits/s, which accommodates the peak bit rate, is needed, whereas the mean bit rate is only 14 Mbits/s. When 16 of these independent video sequences are multiplexed, the required bit rate drops to 28 Mbits/s per channel without the need of an output buffer or a feedback mechanism [142]. Problems of packet defects—packet loss, packet inconsistency, packetization delay, and packet jitter—are addressed by a number of remedial approaches; for example, substitution of lost information by dummy information or by information of the lower layer to compensate for lost packets, to preserve packet consistency, and inclusion of an input buffer at the decoder to remove the effects of packet jitter.

3.8.13   DPCM and Subband Coding Techniques

Consider a coder using both DPCM and subband coding techniques. At each time, the prediction error signal, decomposed into subbands, can be considered as divided into two different types of areas:

- Homogenous areas where the pixel values are quite constant. We will call them "background."

- Transitions areas where the pixel values describe, somehow, very rough regions. We will call them "active areas."

This decomposition stems from the use of DPCM in conjunction with subband coding. By taking the difference between two consecutive images, if the video signal is "quite stationary" in time (there are no scene changes or camera movements), several regions of the resulting frame will have pixel values very close to zero. By applying high-pass filtering, which differentiates the signal, active areas are extracted. On the other hand, low-pass filtering will integrate the signal, and this enhances the background. An active area consists of a signal having a large variance, so it is important to quantize accurately these regions. In comparison, background has, by definition, a very low variance, and a small number of quantization levels can be sufficient to code this kind of area. The algorithm used to separate active regions and background is very close to activity detection algorithms used in motion compensation mechanisms. Subbands are therefore divided into fixed-size blocks. If tree subband decomposition (see Figure 3.16) is applied, higher and lower subbands do not have the same size. Therefore, if N×N blocks are used for lower subbands, 2N×2N blocks must be taken for higher subbands. A block is said to be active if it contains at least T_2 active pixels. A pixel is said to be active if the absolute value is greater than a given threshold T_1. These thresholds are set empirically. By the use of this algorithm each subband is split into active and background blocks.

3.8.14 Hybrid DCT/DPCM Coding

The hybrid image coding technique refers to mixed techniques such as transform and predictive coding. The advantages of the hardware simplicity of DPCM and the robust performance of transform coding are combined. The transform is taken along every row of an image, while DPCM is performed on the transform coefficients along each column [143]. DCT is one of the most attractive unitary transforms from the standpoint of coding performance and implementation simplicity. This transform possesses a high entropy compaction property that is superior to any known transform with a fast computational algorithm [27]. On the other hand, the ease of design as well as the speed of the operation have made the use of DPCM possible in real-time coding of image. However, there are two limitations, the sensitivity to image statistics and the propagation of channel error on the transmitted image [144].

It is well known that the 2D transform coding technique requires the large number of operations needed for coding image data, while the equipment is complex. This limitation becomes less significant when the picture is divided into smaller block sizes and then encoded. This also limits the efficiency of the system since the elements of various blocks remain correlated in the transformed domain. A coding system using 2D transformation and a bank of DPCM systems would exploit this correlation, thereby improving the coding efficiency of the system.

A block transform hybrid image coding and decoding DCT/DPCM system is shown in Figure 3.26. The image array is segmented into blocks of size M×M. Two-dimensional transforms are taken separately and independently in each block to form the sequence of transform blocks. After a 2D unitary transformation of each block of image is obtained, it is ordered to form a 1D array $S_i i = 1,2,...,M^2$, where S_i refers to the i-th number of the image array. The elements of S_i arrays for various values of i are correlated, and thus could be coded by DPCM systems. The sequence $\{X(u, v)\}$ represents the transmitted 2D sequence whose values assume one of possible output levels of the $n(u, v)$-bit DPCM quantizer. The uniform quantizer is designed to minimize the mean square reconstruction error. The algorithm assigns $n(u, v)$ bits proportional to variance $\sigma^2(u, v)$ of the corresponding spectral element.

The use of 2D block transform image coding using the DCT in hybrid image coding has proved an efficient source coding technique in the absence of channel errors. However, in the presence of channel error, the performance degrades rapidly, thereby requiring some error control protection if high-quality image reconstruction is to be achieved. By providing selective error control protection to those bits that contribute most significantly to image reconstruction, it is possible to improve significantly the reconstructed image quality without sacrificing transmission bandwidth.

A common approach in hybrid DCT/DPCM video coding is to combine a temporal DPCM technique with the DCT method into a hybrid coding scheme to efficiently explore spatial as well as temporal redundancies in video scenes (see Figure 3.27). Temporal correlation is reduced first from the video scene, possibly using motion compensated prediction. In the second step, the DCT method is applied to the DPCM prediction error images to explore the remaining spatial redundancies. Finally, the DCT coefficients are quantized and entropy coded. Hybrid DCT/DPCM coding has become the coding method for all recent video coding standards [303].

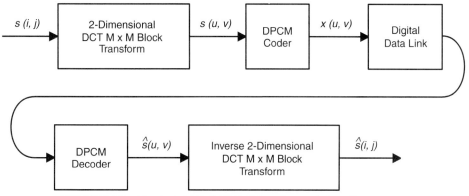

FIGURE 3.26   The hybrid DCT/DPCM coding and decoding system.

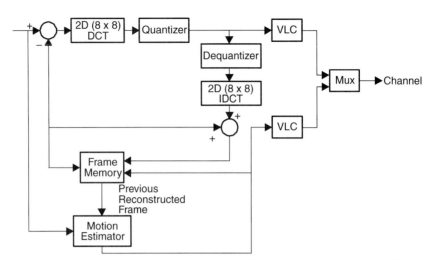

FIGURE 3.27   The hybrid DCT/DPCM coder with motion-compensated prediction.

3.8.15   Vector Quantization

The concept of Vector Quantization (VQ) is simple. Namely, it is based on identifying or representing an input vector with a member of the codebook (assuming this has already been designed and stored) based on some valid criterion like best match, least distortion, and so forth. A block diagram of a simple vector quantization is shown in Figure 3.28 [96]. Of course, there are several ways of choosing the representative code vector. An index, not the code vector, is sent to the receiver where an exact replica of codebook (lookup table) is stored. Using this index, the decoder retrieves the code vector from the lookup table and outputs it as the reconstructed vector. VQ is ideal in a single-encoder/multiple-decoder scenario.

VQ is a well-known method used for data compression. In the case of image compression [145], the image is divided into blocks of size $K = P \times Q$

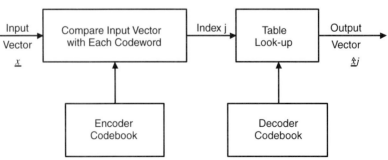

FIGURE 3.28   A block diagram of a simple vector quantizer [96].
©1996 Prentice-Hall.

(P,Q=3,4 usually). These blocks are then approximated by the closest (in the sense of a given distortion measure) block taken from a codebook. Since the aim of the method is to exploit correlation between the pixels of the blocks, the codebook is adapted to the image statistics by means of the codebook design algorithms, like the well-known LBG algorithm [146] or splitting procedures like the MD algorithm [147].

The result of Shannon's rate distortion theory is that for a given rate R (measured in bits per pixel, or bpp), the distortion of the vector quantized image decreases with growing block dimension K [148]. For a given rate R, the number of codebook vectors grows exponentially with K. This results not only in an exponentially increasing storage complexity, but also in an exponentially growing nearest-neighbor search complexity. A reliable codebook design becomes computationally unfeasible, since large training sequences are necessary to represent the statistics of the signal blocks. As can be seen, the use of large block dimensions is restricted by these technical bounds.

Theoretically, we can consider a video signal to be a set of highly correlated random variables, with each pixel being a random variable. The most efficient coding method is to jointly code all these random variables together. Because they are highly dependent on one another, the joint entropy of these random variables is much less than the number of bits used in the original video signal. Therefore, joint entropy coding would result in a very high coding efficiency without any loss of video quality. However, in reality, the complexity of joint entropy coding of a few pixels is already too high. To lower the entropy and consequently reduce the complexity of joint entropy coding, quantization can be used. According to the rate-distortion theory, vector quantization is always better than Scalar Quantization (SQ). However, the complexity of VQ is higher than the complexity of SQ. The question that often arises is, what technique provides the best rate-distortion performance under a given complexity constraint? An important task to make VQ-based techniques competitive in terms of rate-distortion performance, under a complexity constraint, is to develop vector-based signal processing techniques.

The main practical concerns about using a codebook in VQ are how to generate the codebook, how to scale the codebook for various rate-distortion requirements, and how much storage space is reasonable for storing the codebook. A problem of these techniques is scalability according to rate-distortion requirements. For example, a codebook generated using training vectors from one format of video sequences may not be suitable for VQ of a different format. Even within the same spatial resolution, different bit rates would require different codebooks. Another problem with these techniques is that

---

EXAMPLE 3.13

An 8×8 image block is to be coded. The best rate-distortion performance can be achieved by VQ of the 8×8 block as one vector and entropy coding the 8×8 VQ index. However, the complexity of such a method may be too high. Therefore, we may have to use VQ of 4×4 blocks four times in order to bring the complexity down, at the expense of coding efficiency. On the other hand, an 8×8 2D DCT can be applied to the 8×8 block, followed by SQ of the DCT coefficients, zigzag ordering of the quantized DCT coefficients, and joint (runlength, level) entropy coding. After quantization and zigzag ordering (see Figure 3.37), joint entropy coding is equivalent to jointly coding a group of DCT coefficients at a reasonable complexity. The point to be made in this example is that the rate-distortion performance of VQ is lost because only a small size VQ is possible under the complexity constraint, while the DCT and SQ help reduce the complexity of joint entropy coding so that total coding efficiency can be higher.

---

the codebook is not well structured so it has to be specified by a table. The complexity of searching the table and storing the table is too high to have a very large codebook.

Much work has been done in the past to overcome the complexity problems by imposing certain structural constraints on the codebook. By means of these structures, the number of codewords to be stored can be reduced and/or the nearest neighbor search can be accelerated. In this sense, the product code method [149]; lattice vector quantization [150]; tree structured VQ [151], classified VQ [139], and several other VQ schemes [152, 153]; have been proposed to counteract the complexity problems. For equal block size, the performance of the alternative methods is generally inferior to that of the classical VQ. This is due to the observation that the structural constraints imposed on the codebook are usually not verified by the probability density function of the signal blocks. Therefore, we apply only constraints that are apparent in the signal statistics in order to minimize the suboptimality.

The codebook for lattice VQ is simply a collection of lattice points uniformly distributed over the vector space. Scalability can be achieved by scaling the cell size associated with every lattice point. This is similar to uniform scalar quantization where the codewords are uniformly distributed over the one-dimensional (1D) space and the scalability is achieved by scaling the quantization step size. However, there are other problems associated with lattice VQ. One of them is that uniformly distributed lattice points may not match the input vector distribution. Similar to the case of uniform scalar quantization, this problem can be solved by using entropy coding after quantization. Another problem is how to assign indexes to the lattice points within a finite boundary. Since one of the advantages of lattice VQ is that no storage of code vectors is needed due to the regular structure of code vectors (lattice points), index assignment should be based on an algorithm instead of a lookup table. Therefore, a key to using lattice VQ is to have an efficient lattice labeling algorithm. Using a labeling algorithm for lattice VQ at the encoding end, the closest lattice point to an input vector can be obtained by calculation, while an index can be calculated for lattice point. At the decoding end, a lattice point can be calculated from an index and the lattice points become an approximation of the original vector.

Vector quantization offers several advantages. The obvious one is that decoding is extremely simple, requiring only a table lookup operation. This makes VQ a favorite technique for software decoding and all applications where limited resources and time are available for decoding. Another advantage of VQ is that the quantization operation is more efficient than scalar quantization. VQ groups several components and encodes them as a single block. The illustration of vector quantization encoding and decoding in Figure 3.29 indicates that it operates directly on the pixels. To compress the image, the encoder cycles through the codebook and finds the stored codewords or code vector that best approximates each input block. The elements of this code vector are the quantized values of pixels. When the match is found, the encoder transmits the corresponding index-codebook address to the decoder. To decompress the image, the decoder maintains an identical codebook. The decoder reconstructs the image by looking up each index in its codebook and outputting the corresponding codeword. Because the compressed image is represented by indices, the compressed representation requires fewer bits.

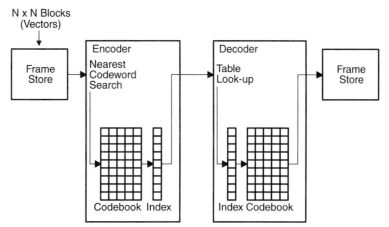

FIGURE 3.29   Vector quantization encoding and decoding [106].
©1997 Chapman and Hall.

EXAMPLE 3.14

Assume each input block contains 4×4, 8-bit pixels and there are 16 codewords in the codebook. Because each codeword requires a 4-bit index, the compression ratio is 32:1. In most VQ applications, the compression ratio is further increased by applying entropy coding to the codewords before transmission. In general, the number of codewords would be much larger than 16, say 128 or 256.

VQ can be combined with other signal processing techniques. For example, one could use DCT or another form of transform coding and then code the transform coefficients more efficiently with vector quantization. The result is better picture quality at lower bit rates. Another example is applying vector quantization for efficient video compression, a technique applied in several PC software video compression algorithms. When interframe coding is required, it is possible to develop vector quantizers that can be applied to interframe pels.

3.8.16   Fractal Coding

Fractal coding [154] provides an alternative to DCT-based transform coding. It can provide resolution-independent decoding and higher compression ratios at the expense of far more complex encoding. The term "fractal" comes from a Latin word meaning "broken or irregular fragments." Fractals are shapes or pieces of images that can be described by mathematical formulae. Fractals were first used to generate natural-looking images, having the interesting property that they can be shrunk or magnified without loss of detail. Fractal coding is a block-based technique, and although fractal-coded images may display blocking artifacts, in practice the compression ratio can be pushed to higher values than for images coded with block-based DCT coding. Results on real-world images suggest it is about three times more efficient than traditional block-based DCT or VQ algorithms at comparable quality levels [154, 155]. Fractal coding promises the unlimited compression ratio for images with marked fractal features, but one also has huge computational complexity [156].

The basic idea of fractal image compression is to exploit the self-similarity in an image by modeling a picture as several smaller pictures of itself. Block-based fractal image coding is shown in Figure 3.30. It compresses an image in the following manner: First, a pool of domain (D) blocks is created. These blocks act as prototypes to represent the entire image. Then the image is broken into a set of nonoverlapping range (R) blocks. Typically, domain block sizes are 16×16 pixels and range blocks are 8×8 pixels. The block sizes are chosen to efficiently combine large, smoothly varying regions of the image. Each range block may be split into up to four nonoverlapping subblocks to capture

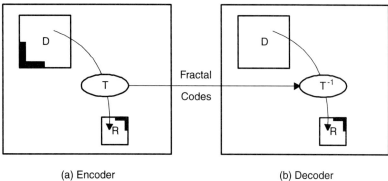

(a) Encoder   (b) Decoder

FIGURE 3.30   Fractal coding and decoding [106].
©1997 Chapman and Hall.

fine detail in complex areas such as object edges. For each range block, one by one, domain blocks are selected from the pool, and through a series of transformations, known as *affine* transformations, are mapped to the range block. These transformations scale, translate, and transform pixels within the domain block. This process continues until a transformed domain block is found that closely approximates the range block. The list of block transformation parameters, known as *fractal code*, is then transmitted to the decoder. Decoding is accomplished by iteratively applying inverse transformations. The domain blocks need not be transmitted because any arbitrary image can be used to start the reconstruction process. The first application to the transformations generates an image containing rough approximations of the range blocks. Then the transformations are applied to that image to better approximate the range block, and so on. Usually, only a few iterations are required to create an image that closely resembles the original [157].

The mathematical theories of Iterated Function Systems (IFS) and Recurrent Iterated Function Systems [158], along with the important Collage Theorem, constitute the broad foundations of fractal image compression. IFS uses affine transformations to express between parts of an image. Affine transformation can be described as combinations of rotations, scalings, and translations. Collage Theorem [156] helps to find a systematic method for searching the affine transformations that will produce an IFS encoding of a desired image. It states that the more accurately the image is described in this way, the more accurately the transformations provide an IFS encoding of it.

The main characteristics of IFS fractal block coding are [159]

- It relies on the assumption that image redundancy can be efficiently captured and exploited through piecewise self-transformability on a block-wise basis.

- It approximates an original image by a fractal image, obtained from a finite number of iterations of an image transformation called *fractal code*. Fractal code consists of a description of both an image partition and a contractive image transmission, each specified by a small set of quantized parameters.

A block IFS image coding system consists of the following steps:

1. Partition the image into a set of nonoverlapping square range blocks R_i.
2. Search for an appropriate larger domain (codebook) block D_i of the same image that is to be used to approximate range block.
3. Find the transformation which, when applied to the domain block, produces the best approximation to the range block.

Only the transformation of each range block has to be transmitted to the decoder. The set of all transformations is the fractal code of original image. This code, iteratively applied to any initial image, generates the reconstructed image (see Figure 3.31).

The limitation of fractal coding is that it is highly asymmetric because the process of searching for the best matching domain blocks is computationally intensive. Smart encoding strategies can reduce the workload, as there are classes of blocks whose similarity can be recognized before applying the transformations. Most often, the best matching domain block is found near the range block being coded. Decoding is far less complex, even less complex than DCT technique and most current implementations for both image and video coding are in software.

FIGURE 3.31   Original test image Lena (a) and IFS decoded (b) with compression ratio 26:1.

It is possible to extend the IFS techniques of image coding to code a video sequence [154]. The most straightforward approach would be to partition a video sequence into nonoverlapping 3D range sequences as is done for a single image. Then, for each 3D range block, a search would be performed over a region extending in space and time for the best domain block that would be mapped, by an IFS, to the given range block. The second approach is to view the video sequence as a sequence of independent frames and to apply an IFS coding algorithm to each frame separately.

The third approach is to partition the video sequence into 3D range blocks, each consisting of a variable number of rectangular blocks that belong to consecutive frames along the same motion trajectory. The variability of the depth in the range block is introduced to take into account the effect of occlusion. This approach exploits the correlation that exists between successive blocks along the direction of motion by predicting the IFS maps of a given range block with those of a range block along motion trajectory. Since, frame-to-frame motion is relatively limited in space, it is computationally much more efficient to perform motion estimation for a matching range block in the previous frame, followed by a refinement of the predicted map in the current frame. IFS video coders are only in the preliminary stage, and preliminary results of this technique are quite promising.

3.9   MPEG VIDEO CODING

The MPEG coding scheme uses two forms of energy compaction: prediction is used to exploit temporal redundancy, while DCT is applied spatially [160]. There are two types of prediction, both of which are motion compensated. The first type of prediction, denoted P, is unidirectional. It is illustrated in Figure 3.32.

FIGURE 3.32   Motion-compensated unidirectional prediction.

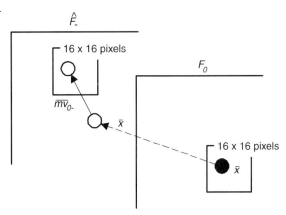

The location $\bar{x}$ refers to a pixel within a block of 16×16 pixels. An area around the same location $\bar{x}$ in a prior encoded and decoded frame $\hat{F}_-$ is searched to find the block that best matches the given block in frame F_0. A common measure for matching that can be easily determined is the sum of the absolute values of the pixel differences in the two blocks. The block motion compensation works well for translational motion; for example, resulting from camera pans. It does, however, approximate other types of motion reasonably well if the block size is small compared to the moving area, and if the movement is minimal. For instance, a zoom can locally be seen as a radial translation of a block, and a rotation as a translation along a tangent.

The second type of prediction is bidirectional (B frame) and consequently is not causal. A block in the frame is estimated, using a frame in the past and one in the future. Motion-compensated, bidirectional prediction is shown in Figure 3.33. The prediction is delayed until the future frame is coded. The bidirectional prediction is more accurate than what is possible for P frames. For example, uncovered areas that are not visible in the past frame can be properly predicted from the future frame. The bidirectional prediction consequently gives a very high degree of compaction. Following the prediction, the prediction error is transformed into blocks of 8×8 pixels to compact the signal spatially. The prediction can be based on previous I or P frame (forward MC), future I or P frame (backward MC), or both (bidirectional MC). This prediction may be bypassed so that the frame is only transformed (I frame). This selection is on an MB-by-MB basis—in this case, a bias of 128 is subtracted. The energy compaction system is shown in Figure 3.34, and an illustration of the periodic interleaving of the I, P, and B frames is presented in Figure 3.35. A period is called a Group of Pictures (GOP). There is usually only one I frame per GOP, but the number of P and B frames can be chosen freely. I stands for "intraframe coded" (DCT only), P for "predicted," and B for "bidirectionally predicted frames" (motion-compensated prediction and DCT).

The transform coefficients are quantized block by block by one of two possible staircase functions: one for blocks from I frames, and the other for blocks from P and B frames. The MPEG quantizers are shown in Figure 3.36. This is motivated by the differing statistical characteristics of the transformed values. A large number of the values are truncated to zero, which constitutes a large percentage of the compression.

The quantized coefficients of each block are scanned in zigzag order and run-length coded (see Figure 3.37). The run length of zero coefficients and the level of the following nonzero coefficient along the zigzag scan is variable-length coded (2D VLC). As the coefficients along this scan represent high spatial

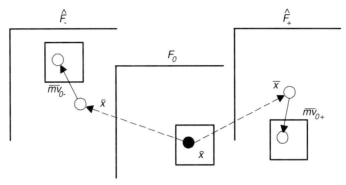

FIGURE 3.33   Motion-compensated bidirectional prediction.

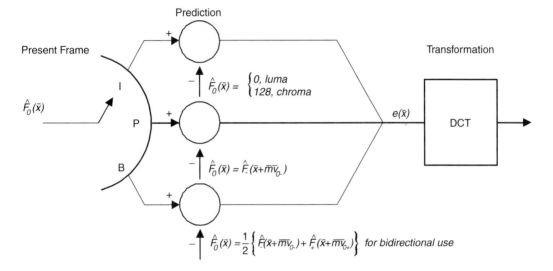

FIGURE 3.34   The MPEG energy compaction.

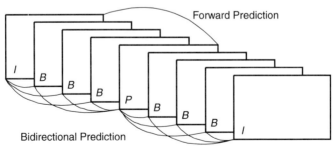

FIGURE 3.35   MPEG's GOP format.

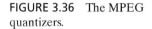

FIGURE 3.36   The MPEG quantizers.

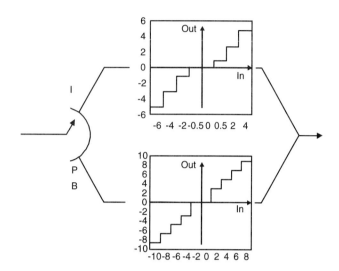

frequencies, many of them tend to be zero. Hence, the zigzag scan and the 2D VLC contribute to the compression ratio.

3.9.1   Motion Compensation

Motion-compensated prediction plays a very important role in the efficient coding of video sequences. ISO/IEC 11172 (MPEG-1) and ISO/IEC 13818 (MPEG-2) [26] adopted Motion Compensation (MC) with half-pixel accuracy and bidirectional MC (B picture), which significantly improves prediction performance. The H.263 uses Overlapped Block Motion Compensation (OBMC) and 8×8 block MC in its advanced prediction mode [161]. All these techniques can be categorized as Local Motion Compensation (LMC), since they are used for prediction of small blocks. Video scenes contain global motion such as panning, scrolling, and zooming, which are mainly caused by camera motion. Therefore, an MC method for predicting global motion is needed to provide further improvements in prediction performance. For this reason, Global

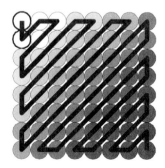

FIGURE 3.37   The (8×8) block of DCT coefficients scanned in zigzag order and run-length coded.

Motion Compensation (GMC) schemes have been proposed and their performance has been confirmed [162, 163]. However, GMC cannot predict all regions in a frame. It does not apply well when there is no global motion and when global motion estimation fails. Therefore, adaptive selection of GMC is required.

Conventional MC methods use traditional motion models to describe the horizontal and vertical motion of objects. However, moving objects have more complex motion, such as rotation, scaling, and deformation. To solve this problem, MC methods using first-order motion models (for example, affine transformation have been examined) [164, 165]. Perspective models and second-order motion models such as quadratic models have also been studied [166, 167]. To improve prediction performance based on H.263, a combination of an affine motion model and overlapped MC should be considered.

The effectiveness of motion compensation in a bit rate reduction scheme depends critically on the statistics of the input image sequence and the accuracy of the motion estimation algorithm. In [168], a model for the motion compensated coder is derived. The pixel-to-pixel correlation of motion compensated frame difference signals was found to reduce to about half the original value. It was also shown that the gain as a result of motion compensation depends critically on the accuracy of motion estimation.

3.9.2 Motion Estimation

Motion Estimation (ME) techniques for video coding have been explored by many researchers for the past 30 years [169]. In general, ME can improve the prediction accuracy between adjacent frames/pictures [170–172]. This technique falls into two categories [96]:

- Pel-by-pel ME, called "Pel Recursive Algorithms" (PRA)
- Block-by-block ME, called "Block Matching Algorithms" (BMA)

PRAs are rarely used because they are complex, and the ME algorithms sometimes run into convergence problems. Nevertheless, a class of motion estimation techniques is represented by pel-recursive algorithms [173–175]. Pel-recursive methods allow the motion vectors to be determined at the receiver as well as at the transmitter. Hence, no motion vectors need to be transmitted. In addition they provide directly, that is without the need of spatial interpolation, motion vectors with sub-pel accuracy.

In BMA, motion of a block of pels, say (M×N), within a frame/field interval is estimated [176, 177]. The range of the motion vector is constrained by the search window and the block size. BMA also ignores rotational motion and assumes all pels within the (M×N) block have the same uniform motion.

Under these limitations, the goal is to find the best match, or the least distortion, between the (M×N) block in the present frame/field and a corresponding block in the previous frame/field within a search window say of size $[(M+2m_2)\times(N+2n_1)]$, as in Figure 3.38 [96]. Here, the Motion Vector (MV) range is $\pm n_1$ pels and $\pm m_2$ lines. In case of fast motion or scene change, ME may not be effective. The pels in the (M×N) block can be moving in different directions. A control mechanism such as the absolute sum of the MC prediction errors of the (M×N) block can be introduced to investigate the effectiveness of BMA. When the BMA is no longer useful in the ME process, one can switch to intraframe coding; in other words, no prediction, just a 2D transform of the (M×N) block.

The adaptive mode (interframe MC prediction or intraframe) requires overhead as the decoder has to track the exact mode of operation. ME of a small block size is much more meaningful than a large block size ME. The penalty is the increased number of bits needed to represent the large number of motion vectors.

Motion estimation of video sequences finds a wide variety of applications ranging from object tracking to spatio-temporal motion-compensated image sequence filtering. In the area of image sequence coding, in particular with applications such as digital TV, videoconferencing, and videophone, bandwidth reduction can be achieved by utilizing the interframe redundancy, which can be characterized by the motion field [178]. A motion estimate, indicating

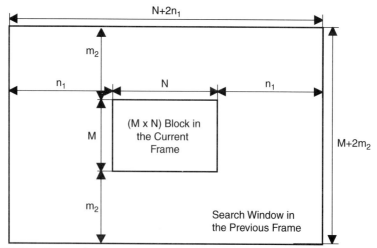

FIGURE 3.38   Motion estimation of an (M×N) block in the previous frame [96].
©1996 Prentice-Hall.

the motion trajectory, can be used to compensate for movement, thereby reducing the prediction error and, consequently, the number of bits needed for transmission or storage of the image sequence.

In many videoconferencing scenes, motion can be modeled to be primarily translational in nature. One popular procedure to estimate this type of motion is the block-matching technique. Here, the motion of a group of pels (block) is represented by a single displacement vector, which is found by a matching technique. The so-called block motion-compensated coding schemes estimate the displacement of moving objects and only encode the block differences in the moving areas between the current frame and the translated previous frame. A complete block motion-compensated coding system consists of three stages:

1. A motion detector that detects the moving blocks.
2. A displacement estimator that estimates the displacement vectors of moving blocks.
3. A data compression algorithm that encodes the differences after motion compensation.

Often, the interframe techniques rely on the compensation for object motion present in image sequences. Prior to this compensation, the motion has to be estimated from the consecutive frames and, besides a motion estimation procedure, a motion detection procedure is involved [96]. If one or more original frames are involved in the estimation procedure, the estimated motion information needs to be transmitted. The need to transmit as efficiently as possible the prediction errors as well as the motion information, consists of obviously conflicting goals and leads to a combined optimization problem. Moreover, the transmission of the motion information limits the data reduction achievable, since for a given sequence, a lower bound on the bit rate is determined by the bit rate required for the transmission of the motion information.

3.9.3 Comments

The structure of MPEG implies that if an error occurs within an I-picture data, it will propagate through all frames in the GOP. Similarly, an error in a P picture will affect the related P and B pictures, while B-picture errors will be isolated. Therefore, effective concealment of lost data in I pictures and P pictures to avoid error propagation effects is of critical importance in MPEG.

MPEG video can offer a further regulation mode of the compression ratio if the GOP format is relaxed. Namely, a lower bit rate can be achieved by increasing the number of B frames in relation to P frames, and P frames in relation to I frames.

MPEG video as described is poorly suited for asynchronous transfer: the B frames cause long delay and the GOP concept introduces highly variable bit rate with strong periodicity [179–182]. Modifications to the scheme are discussed in [183–185]. In simulations, one scheme with only one B frame between any P frames and another with P' frames (predicted from a past frame but not used to code future frames) instead of B frames are found to yield a reasonably good trade-off in encoding delay and compression. The periodicity of the I frames is avoided by replacing them with an intraframe coded column in each frame of the GOP.

CHAPTER 4

Scalability Techniques

SUMMARY

Scalability of video means the same video at different resolutions or qualities simultaneously. A more efficient way to achieve scalability of video is by scalable video coding, which is also referred to as *layered video coding*. In this chapter, the various types of scalabilities are presented, analyzed, and compared: data partitioning, SNR scalability (coding issues, frequency scalability, chroma simulcast), spatial scalability (progressive-progressive spatial scalability, progressive-interlace spatial scalability, interlace-interlace spatial scalability, interlace-progressive spatial scalability), temporal scalability, and hybrid scalability (including spatial and temporal hybrid scalability). A number of applications for different types of scalabilities are discussed.

4.1 INTRODUCTION TO SCALABILITY

Scalability essentially means that the compressed bit stream can be manipulated in a simple manner in order to satisfy constraints on such parameters as bit rates, display resolutions and frame rates, or decompression hardware complexity. Generally speaking, this manipulation consists of the extraction of relevant subsets from the compressed bit stream, each of which should represent an efficient compression of the video sequence, at the same resolution and distortion [25]. In rate scalability, appropriate subsets are extracted in order to trade distortion for bit rate at some fixed display resolution. On the other hand, resolution scalability means that subsets may be extracted that represent the video sequence at a variety of different resolutions. Rate and resolution scalability usually also provide a means of scaling the decompression algorithm's computational requirements. In order for the complete scalable bit stream to also represent an efficient compression of the video sequence at maximum resolution and bit rate, these subsets must be embedded within one another, rather than coexisting independently as they would in a simulcast [186].

Scalable video coding is useful for a number of applications in which video needs to be decoded and displayed at a variety of resolutions (temporal or spatial) and quality levels. One of the advantages of a scalable encoded bit stream is that the encoder can make optimal use of the varying channel bandwidth by extracting a subset of the bit stream to match the available channel bandwidth. In a multicast environment, scalability is a useful property. If communication channels of widely varying bandwidths connect the different receivers, the encoder can achieve efficient transmission from the same coded bit stream without the need for reencoding at different rates. Hence, another functionality support is scalability.

The major applications of scalability include Internet video, wireless video, multiquality video services, video database browsing, and others. In some of these applications, either normal scalabilities on a picture basis such as that in MPEG-2 may be employed, or object-based scalabilities may be necessary. Both categories of scalability are enabled by this specification [187].

The value of scalable compression lies in the fact that the bit stream may be manipulated at any point after the compressed bit stream has been generated. This is significant because in many important applications, advance knowledge of constraints on resolutions, bit rates, or decoding complexities may not be available during compression. Rate scalability is a highly desirable property. Scalability is also a very important property for video database, multicast, and broadcast applications with heterogeneous distribution and/or display requirements.

A number of researchers proposed image or video compression algorithms that offer some degree of scalability. With a specific view toward video applications, scalable video intraframe compression schemes were proposed [188, 189]. Various proposals [190–193] have been advanced for achieving limited scalability within a motion compensated predictive framework. Such approaches generally suffer from rapidly escalating complexity and significant loss in compression performance as the number of available scales increases. A number of researchers have proposed three-dimensional (3D) multiresolution transforms as a vehicle for exploiting temporal redundancy without resorting to nonscalable predictive coding techniques [194, 195]. Such transforms are inherently much more suited to highly scalable compression than techniques based on motion compensated prediction. It should be noted that highly scalable video compression also depends upon efficient layered quantization and coding strategies.

The advantages of scalable compression are primarily realized by allowing such equipment to interact with the compressed bit stream via scaling operations. Previous work [193, 194] focused on tailoring compression schemes to the limited scaling potential afforded by the two priority levels offered by ATM networks.

Besides the outlined major applications of scalability, here is a list of a general set of applications where scalability is useful:

- Error resilience on noisy channels
- Multipoint videoconferencing
- Multiquality video services on ATM and other networks
- Windowed video on computer workstations
- Compatibility with existing standards and equipment
- Compatible digital HDTV and digital TV
- Migration to high temporal resolution progressive HDTV
- Video on computer workstations and LANs

4.2   BASIC APPROACHES TO ACHIEVE SCALABILITY

There are two basic approaches to achieve scalability: *simulcast* and *scalable video* coding. The simulcast technique is based on transmitting a set of various contents of the encoded video sequence simultaneously [196]. In this case, channel bandwidth is not used efficiently, since the bandwidth should be shared among various resolutions. In simulcast coding, each layer of video representing a resolution or quality is coded *independently*. Thus, a single layer (nonscalable) decoder can decode any layer. In simulcast coding, total available bandwidth is simply partitioned depending on the quality desired for each independent layer that needs to be coded. It is assumed that independent decoders would be used to decode each layer [197–200].

Although a simple solution to scalable video is the simulcast technique, which is based on transmission/storage of multiple independently coded reproductions of video, a more efficient alternative is scalable video coding, in which the bandwidth allocated to a given reproduction of video can be partially reutilized in coding of the next reproduction of video. In scalable video coding, one layer (base layer) of video is coded independently whereas other layers (enhancement layers) are coded *dependently*, each following layer coded with respect to the previous layer. Single-layer decoders can decode the independently coded layer. If this layer is coded with another video coding standard, compatibility is said to be achieved. Generally, scalable coding is more efficient than simulcast coding. Except for the independently coded layer, each layer is able to reuse some of the bandwidth assigned to the previous layer. The exact amount of increased efficiency is dependent on the specific technique used, the number of layers, and the bandwidth partitioning used. Also, this increase in efficiency comes at the expense of some increase in complexity compared to simulcast coding. Multiuse of the bandwidth is a condition for scalable video coders. Actually, the enhancement layer is coded by utilizing the information from the base-layer encoder. Scalable video coding can be achieved in spatial, temporal, and frequency domains. We are now ready to briefly introduce various types of scalabilities.

4.3   TYPES OF SCALABILITIES

After clarifying the significance of scalability, we can now list the various types of scalable coding techniques, provide a very short explanation of each technique, and try to determine which type of scalable coding can be used for which applications, as shown in Table 4.1.

Data partitioning is actually a way of partitioning a coded single-layer bit stream into two or more layers so that error resilience transmission or storage can be accomplished. *Hybrid scalability* is a combination of SNR, spatial, and temporal scalabilities. In the case of basic scalability, two layers of video referred to as the lower layer and the enhancement layer are allowed, whereas in hybrid scalability, more layers are supported.

TABLE 4.1   Comparison among Scalable Coding Techniques [201]

Scalable Coding Techniques	Explanation of the Technique	Applications
Data partitioning	Single coded video bit stream is artificially partitioned into two or more layers	Error-resilient video over ATM and other networks
Signal-to-Noise Ratio (SNR) scalability	More than one layer; each layer is at a different quality, but at the same spatial resolution	—Digital broadcast TV (or HDTV) with two quality layers —Error-resilient video over ATM and other networks —Multiquality video-on-demand services

TABLE 4.1   Comparison among Scalable Coding Techniques [201] *(Continued)*

Scalable Coding Techniques	Explanation of the Technique	Applications
Spatial scalability	More than one layer; each layer has the same or different spatial resolution	—Interworking between two different video standards —Digital HDTV with compatible digital TV as a two-layer broadcast system —Video on LANs and computer networks for computer workstations —Error-resilient video over ATM and other networks
Temporal scalability	More than one layer; each layer has the same or different temporal resolution but is at the same spatial resolution	—Progressive digital HDTV —Services requiring progressive video format and interworking with existing equipment —Video on LANs and computer networks —Error-resilient video over ATM and other networks

©1997 Chapman and Hall.

4.4   DATA PARTITIONING

In data partitioning, video bit stream is partitioned into two layers, so that the base layer (partition 0 with high priority) has address and control information as well as low-frequency transform coefficients, while the enhancement layer (partition 1 with low priority) contains high-frequency coefficients. The syntax elements included in partition 0 are indicated by Priority Breakpoint (PBP). Some syntax elements belonging to partition 0 are redundantly included in partition 1 to facilitate error recovery. This type of scalability is useful for data transmission in channels that have different channel error probabilities (ATM networks).

Figure 4.1 illustrates a data partitioning codec with the MC-DCT, data partitioner, and the system multiplexer at the encoder and the corresponding inverse operations at the decoder.

The video bit stream demultiplexer in the data partitioner (see Figure 4.2) has two inputs: a) bit stream of coded video input, and b) same bit stream decoded by VLD. It has also two outputs, base and enhancement partition bit streams "b" and "e," respectively. Depending on the overall bit rate target for each partition, the value of PBP can be adjusted in the priority bit rate controller at every picture slice. In the data combiner (see Figure 4.3) the bit streams "b" and "e" are variable length decoded along with the length of each

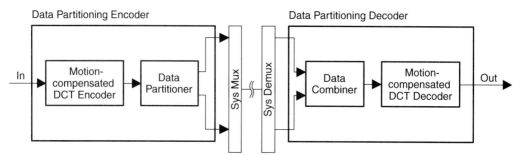

FIGURE 4.1   Data partitioning codec [201].
©1997 Chapman and Hall.

of the VLCs in each bit stream. The actual bit streams and information about the length of each VLC are provided to the bit stream loss concealer, whose function is to regenerate syntactically correct bit streams from bit streams that have undergone losses due to errors. A simple way to filter these losses involves replacing errored parts of bit streams by codes that correspond to zeros for lost DCT coefficients. Unlike the other scalable coding approaches, data partitioning can be implemented outside the encoder and decoder by pre- and postprocessing of nonlayered bit streams.

Figure 4.4 shows block diagrams of systems for data partitioning and merging [202]. At the transmitter, the data demultiplexer receives from the VLD the number of bits used for each VLC and separates the bit stream accordingly based on the PBP value. The PBPs can be changed at each slice based on the rate partitioning logic used. At the receiving end, two VLDs are used to process the base-layer and the enhancement-layer streams and output the number of bits used in each VLC. If losses have occurred, the loss conceal- ment logic generates an appropriate "filter code" to create a syntactically correct

FIGURE 4.2   Data partitioner used in data partitioning encoder [201].
©1997 Chapman and Hall.

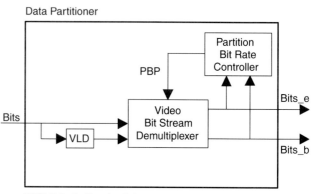

PBP: Priority Breakpoint

FIGURE 4.3 Functional
block diagram of a data
combiner [201].
©1997 Chapman and Hall.

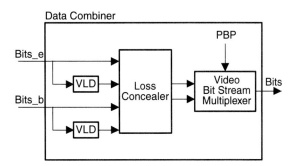

nonlayered bit stream. The simplest filter code is one that corresponds to zeros for the lost coefficients.

Two difficulties of data partitioning are *drift* and the *restricted range of rate partitioning*. Drift is caused when only partial information is used to create the predicted image for the current frame. As a result, the prediction of the included coefficients will not be identical to the prediction if complete information had been available. One way to view this is that the MVs are not correct, since they do not generate a correct prediction block. Therefore, by not incorporating high-frequency coefficients in the reconstruction of the prediction image, errors can result in the low-frequency coefficients. These errors accumulate and they are particularly noticeable when long prediction sequences are used and when the video sequence has panning motion. However, using fragment intracoded frames can reduce drift [203].

The restricted range of rate partitioning stems from the unavoidable use of the same quantization levels for both layers. In data partitioning, increasing the overall bit rate increases the number of bits used to code the low-frequency coefficients included in the base layer, which increases the base-layer bits for

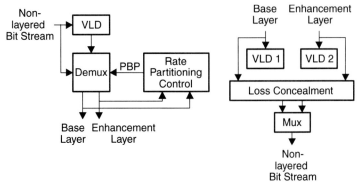

FIGURE 4.4   Data partitioning and merging [202].
©1996 IEEE.

the same PBP. Therefore, the effect of changing the PBP on rate partitioning changes as a function of the overall bit rate. This restriction may be significant for cases where base-layer video needs to be used independently and its rate must be a small percentage of the overall bit rate.

EXAMPLE 4.1

Figure 4.5 shows data partitioning with PBP 64, which means that all headers, the DC, and the first AC coefficient belong to partition 0. In the second block, which has only two nonzero coefficients, only the end of block (EOB) signal belongs to partition 1. Therefore, the base layer can be reconstructed with lower quality, even when data in partition 1 cannot be recovered due to channel errors.

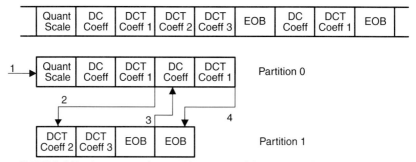

FIGURE 4.5   A segment from a bit stream with two partitions with priority breakpoint set to 64 [204].

©1993 ITU-T.

4.5   SNR SCALABILITY

SNR scalability provides two or more video layers of the same spatial resolution but of different qualities. The enhancement layers contain only coded refinement data for the DCT coefficients of the base layer [96]. The codec (see Figure 4.6) consists of an SNR scalability encoder, systems multiplexer (SysMux), and systems demultiplexer (SysDemux), as well as the decoder. SysMux packetizes video bit streams representing various layers to generate a single stream of packets for transmission, whereas SysDemux implements the inverse operations.

A two-layer SNR scalability encoder consists of base and enhancement encoders. Similarly, an SNR scalability decoder consists of corresponding decoders. Considering two-layer SNR scalability, the base encoder/decoder is an MC DCT encoder/decoder. On the other hand, the SNR enhancement encoder/decoder is a DCT coefficient requantization encoder/decoder. The

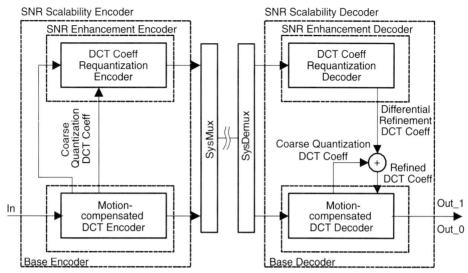

FIGURE 4.6   SNR scalability codec [201].
©1997 Chapman and Hall.

unquantized and coarsely quantized DCT coefficients are input to the DCT coefficients requantization encoder, which quantizes them finely and produces an enhancement-layer bit stream that along with the base-layer bit stream is multiplexed by SysMux. SysDemux separates the two bit streams and inputs the one corresponding to the enhancement layer to the DCT coefficients requantization decoder, which decodes differential refinement coefficients, to which are added coarse quantized DCT coefficients decoded in the base decoder. The resulting refined coefficients are fed back to the base decoder. In SNR scalability, there is very tight coupling between the two layers. Both base- and enhancement-layer outputs can appear at the same output, although not simultaneously. If the enhancement layer is temporally unavailable as a result of channel errors or has incurred packet losses, the base layer is decoded and displayed by itself. This codec suffers from drift problems since differential refinement coefficients do not feed back into the lower-layer MC prediction loop at the encoder, whereas they do so at the decoder. However, if there are channel errors or packet losses and only the base layer is to be decoded and displayed, no drift is expected [201].

The improved codec structure (see Figure 4.7) prevents drift in the enhancement layer by feeding back the differential refinement DCT coefficients to the lower layer via an adder. At the other input of an adder there are coarse quantized DCT coefficients. As long as there are no channel errors or packet losses, no drift is expected in the enhancement layer. However, if there

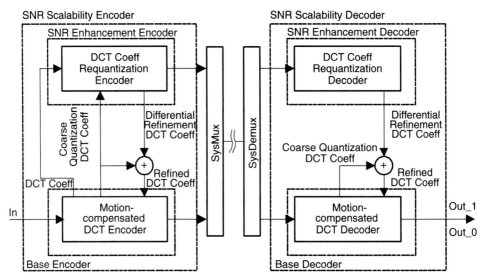

FIGURE 4.7   SNR scalability codec without drift in the enhancement layer [201].
©1997 Chapman and Hall.

are channel errors or packet losses, drift will appear as the MC loops at the encoder and decoder again become unsynchronized owing to the decoder using only lower-layer DCT coefficients in its prediction loop.

In the SNR scalable encoder (see Figure 4.8), the base-layer encoding process is identical to that for a nonlayered encoder. The quantized DCT coefficients from the base layer, after being dequantized, are subtracted from the input DCT block [202]. The resulting quantization error from each block is next requantized and encoded to form the enhancement-layer bit stream.

The standardized decoder for SNR scalability is shown in Figure 4.9. The dequantized base- and enhancement-layer DCT coefficients are first obtained by independently processing the respective bit streams.

At this point, the two sets of coefficients are summed blockwise, and the IDCT is applied to this sum. To this result is added the temporal prediction signal to produce the output pels, which are also fed back into the MC loop. With this encoder configuration, drift occurs only when the base-layer bit stream is decoded. Regarding the DCT coefficients, there is a complete freedom in selecting the quantization parameters for each layer. If a low bit rate is desired for the base layer, a step quantization matrix is appropriate. On the other hand, the enhancement layer can employ a flat matrix so that all coefficients are evenly quantized in the second stage. The base-layer bit stream contains all the MV and MC mode information in addition to the

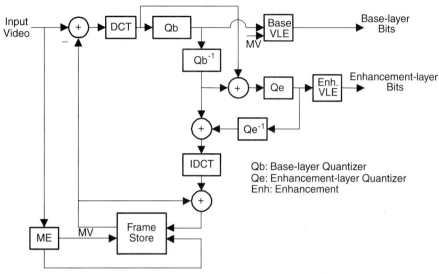

FIGURE 4.8   SNR scalable encoder [202].
©1996 IEEE.

first-stage quantized DCT coefficients. The enhancement layer combines the second-stage quantized coefficient data with a small overhead such as quantizer step sizes that are unique to this layer. Macroblocks (MBs) that are coded in the base layer may or may not be coded in the enhancement layer, and vice versa. Slices are coincident in each layer [199]. The rate-control algorithm uses perceptual quantization only for the base layer and not for the enhancement layer. Perceptual quantization significantly improves the visual quality of nearly smooth blocks. However, once these are finally quantized, additional selection of the quantization step size based on block activity is no longer necessary.

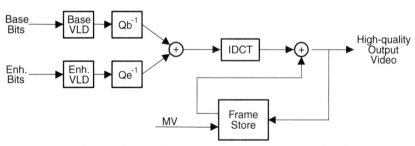

FIGURE 4.9   Standardized SNR scalable decoder [202].
©1996 IEEE.

4.5.1 Coding Issues

In SNR scalability encoding, the base-layer bit stream carries, besides quantization indices for coarse quantized DCT coefficients, all motion compensation and macroblock type information. The enhancement-layer bit stream carries quantization indices representing quantized DCT refinement coefficients and a small amount of overhead. The MPEG-2 standard allows for use of different quantization matrices in the enhancement layer, if needed. Also, the slice structure is required to be the same for both layers. The base layer carries all motion vectors and other overhead. There is an implicit constraint on the lowest bit rate that can be used for the base layer. The actual lowest bit rate that can be achieved depends on the resolution employed and the amount of motion activity in a scene.

EXAMPLE 4.2

Example of coding results of the base layer in SNR scalability to that of single-layer nonscalable coding, each using 2.25 Mbits/s, is shown in Table 4.2. Three sequences of CCIR 601 4:2:0 resolution are coded. The results show that in terms of SNR values, with the bit rate used for the base layer the picture quality achieved in the base layer using SNR scalability is only slightly lower, by about 0.5 to 1.0 dB, than that using non-scalable coding. This is also confirmed by visual comparison on subjective quality.

TABLE 4.2   SNR [dB] Comparison of the Base Layer in SNR Scalability with Single-Layer Coding [201]

Sequence	Nonscalable	2.25 Mbits/s SNR Scalability Base 2.25 Mbits/s
Mobile	26.07	25.50 (-0.57)
Cheerleaders	26.41	25.43 (-0.98)
Bus	27.65	26.92 (-0.73)

©1997 Chapman and Hall.

4.5.2 Frequency Scalability

SNR scalability can also be used as a frequency domain method to achieve scalability in spatial resolution. In this variation of SNR scalability (called *frequency scalability*), lower-layer video is intended for display at reduced spatial resolution [185, 202, 203]. This may be useful if the display is incapable of showing full resolution or in software decoding where owing to lack of sufficient processing resources, only reduced spatial resolution can be decoded for display. To extract reduced signal resolution directly from an SNR scalability

EXAMPLE 4.3

Table 4.3 compares results of nonscalable coding at 4.5 Mbits/s to that of SNR scalability with base and enhancement layers combined. The results show that with base and enhancement layers combined with chosen bits partitioning, the performance of SNR scalability is lower by 0.5 to 1.0 dB, as compared to nonscalable coding.

TABLE 4.3   SNR [dB] Comparison of Base Layer + Enhancement Layer
Coded by SNR Scalability with Single-Layer Coding [201]

Sequence	Nonscalable	4.5 Mbits/s SNR Scalability enh 2.25 Mbits/s Base 2.25 Mbits/s
	30.54	29.59 (-0.95)
	30.10	29.62 (-0.48)
	32.12	31.39 (-0.83)

©1997 Chapman and Hall.

bit stream, SNR scalability syntax without any changes can be used. The only modifications required are those in decoding semantics. However, these do not need to be standardized. The lower-layer decoding can be performed separately and its decoding loop can employ an IDCT of reduced size along with reduced-size frame memory. If only a single MC loop is used at the encoder as is normal for SNR scalability, the lower-layer video would incur drift. This drift can be reduced to some extent by various means such as more frequent I pictures and better interpolation filters.

4.5.3 Chroma Simulcast

The chroma simulcast process is analogous to that of SNR scalability. It can be explained as a kind of SNR scalability. For example, chroma simulcast is used to enhance a 4:2:0 signal after processing the enhancement-layer data. The DC chrominance coefficient of the lower layer is used as a prediction of DC coefficient in the enhancement layer, but the AC chrominance coefficients of the lower layer are discarded and replaced by the AC coefficients of the enhancement layer, which have a higher chrominance resolution [96].

4.6 SPATIAL SCALABILITY

Spatial scalability refers to layered coding in the spatial domain. In this type of coding, a lower layer uses spatial resolution equal to or less than the spatial resolution of the next higher layer. As for the layers, they are coupled, allowing considerable freedom in resolutions and video formats to be used for each layer. A higher layer uses interlayer spatial prediction with respect to decoded pictures of its lower layer. Owing to the flexibility it offers in choice of resolution and formats for each layer, spatial scalability allows interoperability among different video formats. The lower layer may also be coded using a different standard, providing interoperability between standards [204–206].

Some important steps for the implementation of the spatial scalable extensions are [96]

- Generate two spatial-resolution layers from a single video source.
- Code the base layer by itself to provide base (lower) spatial resolution.
- Code the enhancement layer using the spatially interpolated base layer, leading to full spatial resolution.
- Multiplex the two-layer bit streams.
- Use the decoded base layer for decoding the enhancement layer.

Spatial scalability can be considered related to and built on the framework of layered video coding approaches commonly referred to as *pyramid coding*. Spatial scalability clearly extends the pyramid coding, resulting in higher coding efficiency and a higher degree of flexibility. By *higher flexibility* we mean the ability to deal with different picture formats in each layer. Spatial scalability supports interoperability among applications using different video formats, interworking with other standards, interworking among broadcast and computer applications, interworking among various telecommunication applications, a two-layer system consisting of HDTV and TV, video database browsing, error resilience on ATM and other networks, Internet video, and wireless video—in other words, video systems with the primary common feature that a minimum of two layers of spatial resolution is necessary [210]. Error resilience is the ability of spatial scalability to provide resilience to transmission errors as the more important data of the lower layer can be sent over a channel with better error performance, while the less critical enhancement-layer data can be sent over a channel with poor error performance [212]. Object-based spatial scalability can allow better bit budgeting, complexity capability, and ease of decoding [213].

Two-layer codec structure for spatial scalability is shown in Figure 4.10 [201]. Video input is spatially downsampled using a spatial decimator and applied to a base encoder, which produces an encoded bit stream that is fed to a system multiplexer. Base-layer video signal is also input to a spatial upsampler, called a *spatial interpolator*. It provides a spatial interpolated signal to a spatial enhancement encoder. The coded bit stream produced by the spatial enhancement encoder is also fed to SysMux. Here, both the base-layer and enhancement-layer bit streams are packetized. A stream of packets is readied for transport to a network or a storage medium. At the receiving end (decoder), SysDemux separates packets of base and enhancement layers and regenerates base-layer and enhancement-layer bit streams by unpacketizing, and inputs them to corresponding decoders. The base decoder decodes the base-layer bit stream, resulting in decoded video. This is also input to the spatial interpolator, which feeds the spatially interpolated signal to be used for prediction by the spatial enhancement decoder depending on the actual coding mode when decoding the spatial enhancement bit stream. The decoded enhancement-layer video is the output from the spatial-enhancement decoder.

The detailed version of spatial scalable encoder is shown in Figure 4.11 [202]. The base-layer encoder encodes an image, possibly of low resolution [214]. The enhancement-layer codec is similar to a nonlayered encoder with an Additional Weighter (AW, weighting parameter w). It is independent of the base-layer encoder, but can make use of the decoded base-layer images. The enhancement layer encodes the difference between the original signal and the prediction formed by the weighter, which is a weighted average of the previous enhancement-layer image and the base-layer image.

The standardized spatial scalable decoder is shown in Figure 4.12. The enhancement-layer decoder is similar to a nonlayered decoder. The only exception is for the weighter, which uses the spatio-temporal weighting

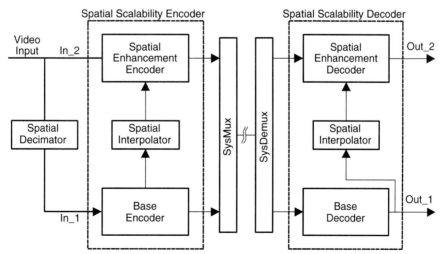

FIGURE 4.10   Two-layer codec structure for spatial scalability [201].
©1997 Chapman and Hall.

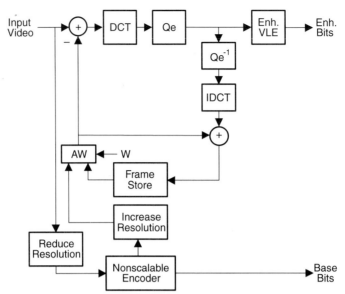

FIGURE 4.11   Spatial scalable encoder (AW: additional weighter) [202].
©1996 IEEE.

parameter *w* to combine the spatial prediction from the base layer with temporal motion compensated prediction from the enhancement layer. The spatio-temporal weighting parameter *w* determines whether the enhancement-layer encoding algorithm uses spatial prediction from the base-layer image in the current frame, temporal prediction from the enhancement-layer image from the previous frame, or a combination of both.

For some applications, such as workstation video, it is advantageous to use a base layer that has reduced resolution. However, for cell loss resilience,

FIGURE 4.12   Spatial scalable decoder [202].
©1996 IEEE.

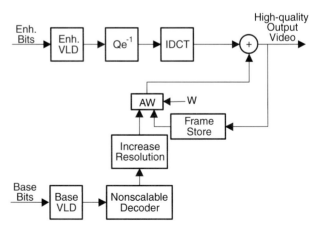

better visual performance can be obtained when the base layer has the same resolution as the enhancement layer.

Now, it will be interesting to compare the coding algorithms for spatial scalability when both layers have the same resolution to other well-known coding algorithms. For example, the predominant difference between spatial and SNR scalabilities is that the standardized decoder for SNR scalability must use one feedback loop, while the standardized decoder for spatial scalability must use two feedback loops (the block nonscalable decoder has a feedback loop), as shown in Figure 4.12. Therefore, if only the base layer of a spatial scalable bit stream is decoded, no error propagation will occur. Depending on the selection of the spatio-temporal weighting parameter w, drift may occur if parts of the enhancement layer are also decoded. It is interesting to note that the algorithm for two-layer coding presented in [215] is identical to the coding algorithm used for spatial scalability when both layers have the same resolution. The spatio-temporal weighting parameter w is selected to preclude temporal resolution.

An additional advantage that spatial scalability has over the other two-layered coding approaches is that the slice length may be different in both layers. Thus, short slices may be used in the enhancement layer to protect against frequent errors without sacrificing the quality of the base layer because of additional overhead.

There are four basic types of spatial scalabilities [199, 209]:

- Progressive-progressive spatial scalability
- Progressive-interlace spatial scalability
- Interlace-interlace spatial scalability
- Interlace-progressive spatial scalability

4.6.1 Progressive-Progressive Spatial Scalability

In progressive-progressive spatial scalability, both the lower layer and the enhancement layer use a progressive video format. The lower layer may use lower or the same spatial resolution as compared to the enhancement layer. One potential application of this type of scalability is in a two-layer system, allowing interoperability among different standards. Other potential applications are in scalable multimedia, allowing windowing on the computer workstations and multiquality service in telecommunication applications.

4.6.2 Progressive-Interlace Spatial Scalability

In this type of spatial scalability, the lower layer uses a progressive video format, while the enhancement layer uses an interlaced video format. The lower

EXAMPLE 4.4

Assume that the base layer uses a picture resolution at one-quarter the size of input picture (or enhancement-layer pictures). Then the spatial decimator (see Figure 4.13a) downsamples both the horizontal and vertical resolutions by a factor of 2 in each direction. The filters used prior to downsampling are not specified because spatial decimation is not standardized. The spatial interpolator (see Figure 4.13b) performs the inverse function by upsampling the decoded base layer by a factor of 2, both horizontally and vertically.

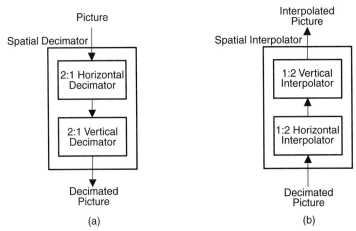

FIGURE 4.13   Spatial decimator and interpolator examples for a progressive base layer [201].

©1997 Chapman and Hall.

layer may use a lower or the same spatial resolution as compared to the enhancement layer. One potential application of this type of scalability is in a two-layer system, allowing interoperability among different standards. Another potential application is in scalable multimedia, which can be simultaneously delivered as high-quality broadcast entertainment and as a window on computer workstations.

4.6.3   Interlace-Interlace Spatial Scalability

In interlace-interlace spatial scalability, the lower layer uses the interlaced video format. The enhancement layer also uses the interlaced video format. The lower layer may use a lower or the same spatial resolution as compared to the enhancement layer. One of the potential applications of this type of scalability is two-layer scalable interlaced HDTV with normal interlaced TV as the base layer [216]. The following example explains the decimation and interpolation operations.

EXAMPLE 4.5

Assume that the base layer uses a picture resolution of one-quarter the size of input pictures or enhancement-layer picture. In the case of progressive-interlace spatial scalability, the spatial decimator simply performs horizontal decimation consisting of filtering and subsampling by a factor of 2. As for vertical decimation, it is performed by simply retaining one field per frame—either the first (odd) field in every frame or the second (even) field of every frame. The spatial decimator downsamples both the horizontal and vertical resolutions by a factor of 2 in each direction. The spatial interpolator performs the upsampling of the decoded base layer by a factor of 2 both horizontally and vertically. Corresponding block diagrams of the spatial decimator and spatial interpolator are basically the same as shown in Figure 4.13.

EXAMPLE 4.6

Assume that the base layer is required to have one-quarter the spatial resolution of the enhancement layer. The spatial decimation consists of deinterlacing, followed by horizontal decimation by a factor of 2 and vertical decimation by a factor of 4. The inverse (spatial interpolation) consists of deinterlacing, followed by horizontal upsampling by a factor of 2, and followed by either outputting a field as is or resampling that field and then outputting. The block diagrams of a spatial decimator and spatial interpolator are shown in Figure 4.14.

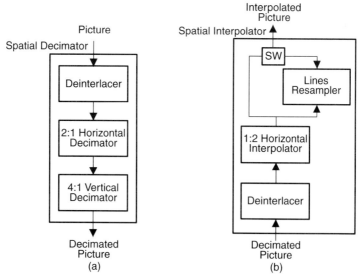

FIGURE 4.14   Examples for spatial decimator and interpolator in interlace-interlace spatial scalability [201].

©1997 Chapman and Hall.

EXAMPLE 4.7

Figure 4.15 explains the spatial decimation and spatial interpolation operations for the luminance signal. In interlace-interlace spatial decimation, interlaced input frames comprising a pair of fields of 704×240 for an NTSC system or 704×288 for a PAL system, undergo downsampling to produce pairs of video fields of 352×120 size (or 352×144) resolution. The process of spatial interpolation is the inverse of decimation and consists of upsampling pairs of video fields of 352×120 (or 352×144) resolution to pairs of video fields of 704×240 (or 704×288) resolution. The decoding process, which uses spatial interpolation, uses exactly the same steps as shown here using a linear interpolation filter to perform upsampling or resampling when required. Since spatial decimation does not need to be standardized, there is freedom in choosing filters for decimation.

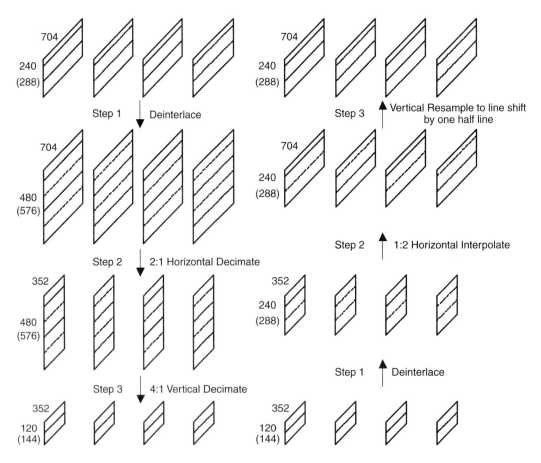

(a) Steps in Decimation   (b) Steps in Interpolation

FIGURE 4.15   Steps in spatial decimation and interpolation in interlace-interlace spatial scalability [201].

©1997 Chapman and Hall.

EXAMPLE 4.8

Table 4.4 shows a comparison of interlaced CCIR-601 4:2:0 resolution coded at a total of 4 Mbits/s, as a single layer, as an enhancement layer using simulcast, and as an enhancement layer using interlace-interlace spatial scalability [212, 213]. The bit rate for the interlaced enhancement layer is 2.5 Mbits/s, using 1.5 Mbits/s for the interlaced base layer.

TABLE 4.4   SNR [dB] Comparison of Interlace-Interlace Spatial Scalability with Simulcast and Single-Layer Coding [201]

	Interl - Interl; 4 Mbits/s Interl;		4 Mbits/s
Sequence	Simulcast Enh 2.50 Mbits/s; Base 1.50 Mbits/s	Spatial scalability Enh 2.50 Mbits/s; Base 1.50 Mbits/s	Nonscalable
Mobile	27.18	27.87 (+0.69)	30.10 (+2.92)
Cheerleaders	26.85	28.00 (+1.15)	29.12 (+2.27)
Bus	29.25	30.47 (+1.22)	31.43 (+2.18)

©1997 Chapman and Hall.

4.6.4   Interlace-Progressive Spatial Scalability

In interlace-progressive spatial scalability, the lower layer uses an interlaced video format, while the enhancement layer uses a progressive video format. The lower layer may use a lower or the same spatial resolution as compared to the enhancement layer. One potential application of this type of scalability is in two-layer scalable progressive HDTV with normal interlaced TV as the base layer.

As in the case of other spatial scalability types, the spatial decimation operation does not need to be standardized. On the other hand, the spatial interpolation operation that takes place at both the encoder and the decoder does need to be standardized in MPEG-2 standard in order to eliminate drift. There are various ways of decimating a progressive video to achieve an interlaced video of the same or lower spatial resolution and include simply line subsampling or prefiltering followed by line subsampling. In interlace progressive scalability, the first two steps are identical. Thus, deinterlacing followed by upsampling as well as the last step involving vertical resampling is not needed.

Besides HDTV, other applications of interlace-progressive spatial scalability are somewhat limited. Its performance is expected to be quite similar to that of interlace-interlace spatial scalability. Figure 4.16 shows interlaced and progressive prediction from the base layer in a spatially scalable coder. For

FIGURE 4.16 Interlaced and progressive prediction from the base layer in a spatially scalable coder [96].
©1996 Prentice-Hall.

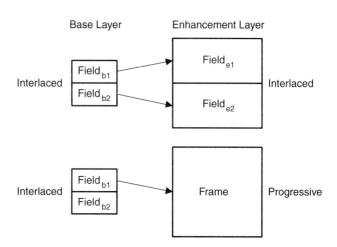

interlaced-to-progressive scalability, the deinterlacing and resampling proce-dure of base-layer fields is similar to interlaced-to-interlaced scalability. Since the two fields belong to one frame in the enhancement layer, only one field is selected by the designer [96]. The two base-layer fields are first deinterlaced to produce two progressive fields. Here, a field in the enhancement layer is regarded as a progressive version of a field in the base layer. Then the two fields in the base layer are resampled vertically and horizontally to fit the size of the enhancement layer. The deinterlacing procedure involves filling the same num-ber of zeros as the number of lines and filtering vertically and temporally.

4.7 TEMPORAL SCALABILITY

Temporal scalability is a tool intended for use in a range of diverse video appli-cations, from video databases, Internet video, wireless video, and multiview/ stereoscopic coding of video. There are also other applications such as a new generation of conversational services using TV resolution video but with a progressive format at twice the frame rate that would require interoperability with existing TV displays. Temporal scalability is also useful in a software encoding environment where the decoding process may not be powerful enough to decode video at the full frame rate, or may be sharing its processing power among a number of different tasks. Furthermore, a temporal demulti-plexer splits up input video sequence frames into two video sequences, one of which is applied to the base encoder and the other to the enhancement encoder. The enhancement encoder is also an MC DCT encoder similar to the base encoder and, moreover, it can also exploit additional redundancies by using interlayer MC with respect to locally decoded frames generated by the base encoder. Temporal scalability is quite flexible to allow different frame rates in each layer [219, 220].

The encoded bit streams generated by the base and the enhancement encoders are multiplexed by the system's multiplexer into a single stream of packets allowing identification of the source of their origination. This stream can be transmitted or stored and is eventually an input to a system's demultiplexer, which performs the complementary function of separating them back into two streams. Namely, the bit streams generated by the base and enhancement encoders are inputs to the corresponding decoders. The base decoder is complementary to the base encoder, depending on the encoder chosen. The enhancement decoder is complementary to the enhancement encoder and can exploit interlayer MC. This decoder is referred to as the *temporal enhancement* decoder. The base decoder to produce decoded frames can decode the base-layer bit stream. The enhancement-layer bit stream is decoded by the enhancement decoder, which also uses base-layer decoded frames. Being decoded, it may also provide a migration path from current lower temporal resolution video systems to higher temporal resolution systems of the future [187].

Temporal scalability refers to layered coding that produces two or more layers, each with either the same or different temporal resolutions, which when combined provide full temporal resolution as available in the input video. Each layer is encoded to generate separate bit streams that are multiplexed, transmitted or stored, demultiplexed, and decoded to generate a separate layer of frames to be recombined for display. Since the input frame rate is simply partitioned between the base layer and the enhancement layer, the temporal scalability decoder does not need to be much more complex than a single-layer decoder [218].

The main use of temporal scalability is expected to be for HDTV applications where migration to high temporal resolution progressive HDTV may be possible from the first-generation interlaced HDTV in a compatible manner [210].

A two-layer temporal scalability codec structure is shown in Figure 4.17. Consider input video sequence frames fed to the base encoder. The frames at the output of the base decoder can be shown by themselves at half the frame rate of the input video. They can also be temporally multiplexed in the temporal remultiplexer with the output of the enhancement decoder to provide full frame rate that is the same as that of the video input.

In order to make the codec structure of Figure 4.17 more precise, consider a specific class of the codec shown in Figure 4.18. The temporal enhancement-layer encoder/decoder is a modified MC encoder/decoder that uses interlayer MC and primarily codes B pictures. The temporal enhancement encoder

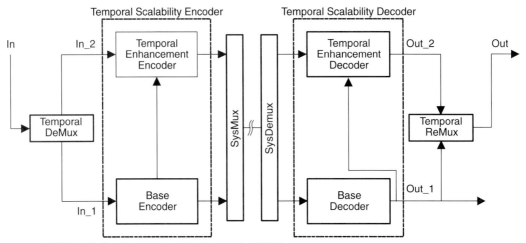

FIGURE 4.17   Temporal scalability codec [201].
©1997 Chapman and Hall.

includes an MC encoder like that used for the base layer, an Interlayer Motion Estimator (IME), and a corresponding Interlayer MC Predictor (IMCP). IME computes MVs between blocks of enhancement-layer pictures with respect to base-layer pictures. These MVs are used by IMCP to perform MC and are also included in the enhancement-layer bit stream, depending on the mode selected on an MB basis. The temporal enhancement decoder consists of an MC decoder and an IMCP. From enhancement-layer bit stream, depending on the mode of a coded MB, when available, interlayer MVs are

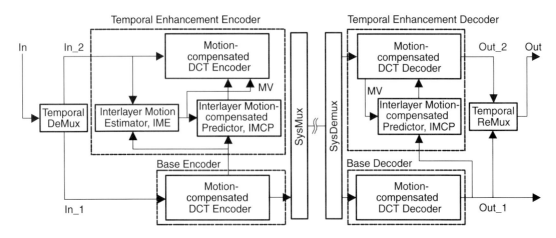

FIGURE 4.18   Temporal scalability codec with details [201].
©1997 Chapman and Hall.

extracted to perform MC prediction in IMCP. The IMCP at the enhancement encoder and enhancement decoder perform identically. The remaining operations in Figure 4.18 are identical to those in Figure 4.17.

When the most recent frame in the lower layer is used as the reference, the frame is temporally coincident with the frame or the first field in the enhancement layer [96]. The predicted pictures are interleaved with the relevant filtering in order to generate higher-temporal resolution video in the enhancement-layer output, where the lower layer is decoded independently.

EXAMPLE 4.9

In P pictures the reference can be selected from: (a) the most recent decoded enhancement picture, (b) the most recent lower-layer picture, or (c) the next lower-layer picture as shown in Figure 4.19. The lower-layer pictures are in the display order.

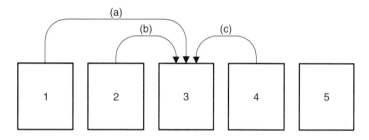

1, 3, 5, ...: Pictures from Enhancement Layer
2, 4, ...: Pictures from Lower Layer

FIGURE 4.19   Prediction selection for the temporally scalable enhancement layer in P pictures [96].
©1996 Prentice-Hall.

4.8   HYBRID SCALABILITY

There are a number of applications where neither the temporal scalability nor the spatial scalability may offer the necessary flexibility and control. This may necessitate the use of temporal and spatial scalabilities simultaneously and is referred to as the *hybrid scalability*. Among the applications of hybrid scalability are wireless video, Internet video, multiview point/stereoscopic coding, and others [187].

Two scalabilities can be combined to form hybrid scalability, resulting in three layers. These are called the *base layer*, *enhancement layer 1*, and *enhancement layer 2*. Here, enhancement layer 1 is the lower layer for enhancement layer 2.

Considering hybrid scalability with three layers employing two different scalabilities at a time, three scalability pairs result and, depending on the order in which these scalabilities are applied, a total of six scalability combinations are possible. In what follows, we discuss high-level codec structure for three scalability combinations.

4.8.1   Spatial and Temporal Hybrid Scalability

In a three-layer hybrid codec employing spatial scalability and temporal scalability, spatial scalability is used between the base layer and enhancement layer 1, while temporal scalability is used between enhancement layer 1 and enhancement layer 2 (see Figure 4.20). The video sequence at "in" is temporally partitioned by temporal DeMux into two sequences that appear at "in_1" and "in_2." The video sequence "in_1" is spatially downsampled in the spatial decimator to yield "in_0." The sequence "in_0" is fed to the base layer of the spatial scalability encoder. The sequence at "in_1" is fed to the enhancement layer, which in the context of hybrid scalability is known as *enhancement layer 1*. The locally decoded enhancement layer from the spatial scalability encoder is used to form interlayer MC prediction in the temporal enhancement encoder, which uses the second sequence from the temporal demultiplexer as its input "in_2." The spatial scalability encoder generates two coded bit streams representing two spatial layers, and the temporal enhancement encoder generates the third coded bit stream representing the third layer. The three coded bit streams are packetized in the system multiplexer and are ready for transmission or storage.

The system demultiplexer unpacks packetized data and forwards coded bit streams for decoding to one of the three decoders: the base decoder, or the

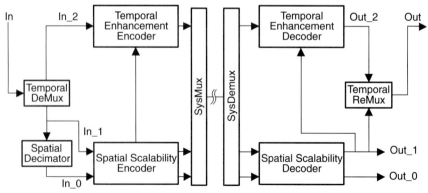

FIGURE 4.20   Spatial and temporal hybrid scalability codec [201].
©1997 Chapman and Hall.

enhancement decoder of spatial scalability, or the temporal enhancement decoder, as appropriate. The spatial scalability decoder performs a function complementary to that of the spatial scalability encoder, decoding coded bit streams to produce a base-layer video sequence at "out_0," a spatial enhancement layer at "out_1." The decoded video sequence at "out_1" is used to generate MC prediction as needed by the temporal enhancement encoder while decoding the corresponding bit stream. The highest-layer output is generated by temporally combining decoded video sequences at "out_1" and "out_2" in temporal ReMux, which produces the multiplexed video sequence at "out."

4.8.2 SNR and Spatial Hybrid Scalability

Figure 4.21 shows a three-layer hybrid codec employing SNR and spatial scalabilities. SNR scalability is used between the base layer and enhancement layer 1, while spatial scalability is used between enhancement layer 1 and enhancement layer 2. The video sequence at "in" is spatially decimated to a lower resolution and is available at "in_1" for input to the SNR scalability encoder. The locally decoded higher-quality video from the SNR scalability encoder is upsampled to full resolution in the spatial interpolator and is used by the spatial enhancement encoder, which encodes full spatial resolution video at "in_2." The SNR scalability encoder generates two coded bit streams representing two SNR layers. The spatial enhancement encoder generates the third coded bit stream representing the spatial layer. The three coded bit streams are packetized in the systems multiplexer and are ready for transmission or storage.

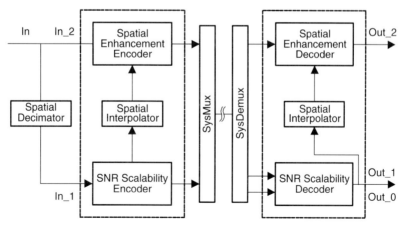

FIGURE 4.21   SNR and spatial hybrid scalability codec [201].
©1997 Chapman and Hall.

The system's demultiplexer unpacks packetized data and forwards coded bit streams for decoding to one of the three decoders: the base decoder, the enhancement decoder of SNR scalability, or the spatial enhancement decoder. The SNR scalability decoder performs a function complementary to that of the SNR scalability encoder, decoding coded bit streams to produce either a base-layer video sequence at "out_0" or an SNR enhancement layer at "out_1." Both "out_0" and "out_1" appear on the same line, but not simultaneously. The highest-layer output at "out_2" is generated by a spatial enhancement decoder that decodes the highest-layer bit stream and utilizes spatial prediction consisting of lower-layer pictures interpolated by the spatial interpolator.

4.8.3   SNR and Temporal Hybrid Scalability

Temporal and SNR hybrid scalability codec (see Figure 4.22) employs SNR scalability as well as temporal scalability. SNR scalability is used between the base layer and enhancement layer 1, while temporal scalability is used between enhancement layer 1 and enhancement layer 2. The video sequence at "in" is temporally partitioned by the temporal Demux into two sequences that appear at "in_1" and "in_2." The sequence at "in_1" is fed to the SNR scalability encoder. The temporal enhancement encoder to form MC interlayer prediction uses the locally decoded higher-quality video from the SNR scalability encoder. The SNR scalability encoder generates two coded bit streams representing two SNR layers. The temporal enhancement encoder generates the third coded bit stream representing the temporal layer. The three coded bit streams are packetized in the systems multiplexer and are ready for transmission or storage. The systems demultiplexer unpacks packetized data and forwards coded bit streams for decoding to one of the three decoders: the base decoder, the enhancement decoder of SNR scalability, or the temporal enhancement decoder. The SNR scalability decoder performs a function complementary to that of the SNR scalability encoder, decoding coded bit streams to produce either base-layer video sequence at "out_0" or SNR enhancement layer at "out_1." Both "out_0" and "out_1" appear on the same line, but not simultaneously. The highest-layer output at "out_2" is generated by the temporal enhancement decoder, which decodes the highest-layer bit stream and utilizes lower-layer video for MC prediction as needed. The decoded lower-layer video at "out_0" or "out_1" is multiplexed with the decoded higher-layer video in temporal remux and outputs "out" as the full temporal resolution signal.

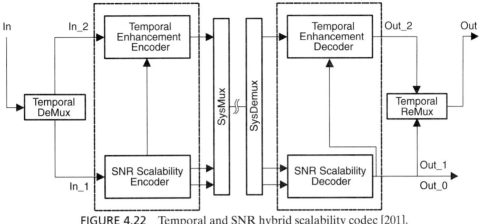

FIGURE 4.22   Temporal and SNR hybrid scalability codec [201].
©1997 Chapman and Hall.

EXAMPLE 4.10

Consider the case of digital HDTV and TV. From the aspect of efficient usage of available spectrum and integration of services, TV should migrate to digital format, allowing digital TV to be a lower layer of HDTV. On the other hand, HDTV itself has challenges to overcome owing to bandwidth constraints and receiver costs in the short term, which appear to favor use of interlaced video format or progressive video format with lower spatial resolution. In nonbroadcast applications, higher spatial resolution progressive video formats would be used to provide high-quality HDTV. Such HDTV services would have to interoperate with less expensive HDTV receivers. Spatial and temporal hybrid scalabilities offer a solution that would be far more meaningful than simulcasting the three layers.

EXAMPLE 4.11

Assume that digital TV of two qualities is required, implying that consumers can receive either standard-quality TV or high-quality TV, depending on the type of receivers and bandwidth they can afford. Consider that there is yet another class of consumers who can afford HDTV receivers. The question is, how can a three-layer service offering TV at two qualities and HDTV at one quality be possible? The answer is SNR and spatial hybrid scalability. Simulcasting three layers would not make a lot of sense from the bandwidth efficiency standpoint. There are too many potential factors that may or may not allow such a service, not only for terrestrial broadcast, but also by cable, satellite, or other means.

EXAMPLE 4.12

In designing a digital TV service, it is not difficult to anticipate the need for three layers. These three layers could very well be normal-quality TV, enhanced-quality TV, and progressive TV, and there would be corresponding TV receivers. Viewers could then choose the quality of receiver and cost of service they can afford. Now, the question is, how can such a three-layer service be possible in a bandwidth-efficient manner? The answer is SNR and temporal hybrid scalability. Simulcasting the three layers would not be efficient compared to scalable coding. This scenario applies equally well to digital HDTV where three layers may be used.

C H A P T E R   5

MPEG and ITU-T Video Standards

SUMMARY

Video standards have to rely on compromises between what is theoretically possible and what is technologically feasible. Standards can only be successful in the marketplace if the cost performance ratio is well balanced. This is specifically true in the field of video coding where a large variety of innovative coding algorithms exist, but may be too complex for implementation with state-of-the-art VLSI technology.

In this chapter we discuss MPEG-2, ITU-T H.263, MPEG-4, AND MPEG-7 video standardization processes. The MPEG-2 standard is highly successful because there is a strong commitment from industry, cable and satellite operators, and broadcasters to use these standards. The H.263 was developed for video compression at rates below 64 Kbps. H.263+ is a revision of the original version. It contains approximately 12 new features. The H.263++ development effort is intended for near-term standardization of enhancement to produce a third version of the H.263 video codec for real-time telecommunications and related nonconversational services. The H.26L is aimed at developing new video coding technology beyond the capabilities of incremental enhancements to H.263 for long-term standardization.

The scope and potential of the emerging MPEG-4 standard is discussed in the context of future visual multimedia communications environments. It is shown that MPEG-4 standard provides tools and algorithms for coding both natural and synthetic video, as well as provisions to represent the video data at the user terminal in a highly flexible way.

The objective of the MPEG-7 standardization process is to facilitate the browsing and retrieval of multimedia (audio, speech, images, video, text, and combinations thereof).

5.1 INTRODUCTION

Modern video compression techniques offer the possibility to store or transmit the vast amount of data necessary to represent digital video in an efficient and robust way [63, 222]. New audiovisual applications in the fields of communication, multimedia, and broadcasting became possible based on digital video technology. With the advances in VLSI technology, it has become possible to open more applications fields to a larger number of users, and therefore the necessity for digital video standards has risen. Commercially, international standardization of video communication systems and protocols aims to serve two important purposes: interoperability and economy of scale. Interworking between video communication equipment from different vendors is a desirable feature for users and equipment manufacturers. It enables large-scale international video data exchange via storage media or communication networks. An increased demand leads to economy of scale; in other words, the mass production of VLSI systems and devices. This in turn makes video equipment more affordable for a wide field of applications and users [221].

From the beginning of 1980, a number of international video standardization activities have started with CCITT (now ITU-T), followed by working to develop international standards for digital audio and video transmission and storage. Unlike H.261, which is optimized for teleconferencing where motion is naturally limited, the ISO/IEC MPEG video standard is devised for a wide range of video and motion pictures. The goal of MPEG is to define a standard for coded representation of moving pictures, associated audio, and the systems [222–224]. It defines the structure of coded video bit streams transmitted to the decoder and the decoder architecture, but leaves the encoder architecture undefined, so that some encoders may produce higher-quality compression, some will be real time, and some will require manual intervention. MPEG compression is lossy and asymmetric, with the encoding more complex than the decoding.

There are different versions of MPEG, denoted by MPEG-x. The first version, MPEG-1, was targeted at CD-ROM with applications at a bit rate of about 1.5 Mbits/s [221]. MPEG-1 has also proved useful in other applications, such as for early Direct Broadcast Satellite (DBS) transmission and for computer-generated video, where transmission bandwidth and storage capacity are limited or expensive. The video is strictly progressive; in other words, non-interlaced. MPEG-2 addresses high-quality coding for all digital transmission of broadcast-TV-quality video at data rates of 2–50 Mbits/s. The major applications include digital storage media; digital television (including HDTV); broadcasting over cable, satellite, and other broadcast channels; and other communication applications [198]. MPEG-2 is intended for both playback and videoconferencing, providing considerable flexibility in the choice of interframe processing and the use of much higher resolution pictures—at higher data rates. MPEG-2 can produce the video quality needed for multimedia entertainment piped to the home and for more demanding business and scientific applications. The MPEG-2 video compression techniques standardized by the MPEG group have also become important and successful video coding standards worldwide, with an increasing number of MPEG-1 and MPEG-2 VLSI chipsets and products available. One key factor for the success is the generic structure of the MPEG standards, supporting a wide range of applications and application-specific parameters. To support the wide range of application profiles, a diversity of input parameters including flexible picture size and frame rate can be specified by the user. Another important factor is the fact that the MPEG group has standardized only the decoder structures and the bit stream formats. This allows a large degree of freedom for manufacturers to optimize the coding efficiency (that is, the video quality at a given bit rate) by developing innovative encoder algorithms even after the standards were finalized. MPEG-4 has a different set of objectives to provide video on low-bandwidth transmission lines or for low-capacity storage devices where no existing standardized video compression algorithm has proved satisfactory. Besides traditional block-based coding (as in MPEG-1, MPEG-2, H.261, H.263, and so on), MPEG-4 addresses object-based and content-based coding with composition, manipulation, interactivity, and so on. It also extends to both synthetic and natural video/audio, layered coding (scalabilities), multiview (stereoscopic video), shape/texture/motion coding of objects, animation, and all possible combinations of these features. Its role extends to the Internet, WebTV, large databases (storage, retrieval, and transmission), mobile networks, multimedia, electronic games, education, training, entertainment, defense, medicine, and others. MPEG-4 version 1 became an international standard in February 1999, and version 2 is scheduled for November 1999. Version 2 with extended functionalities will be backward compatible with version 1 [221, 242].

Multimedia databases on the market today allow searching for pictures using characteristics such as color, texture, and information about the shape of objects in the picture. MPEG started a new work item to provide a solution to the problem described earlier. The new member of the MPEG family (called "Multimedia Content Description Interface") is MPEG-7 [225–227]. It extends the limited current search capabilities to include more information types, such as video, image, audio, graphics, and animation. In other words, MPEG-7 specifies a standardized description of various types of multimedia information. This description is associated with the content itself, to allow fast and efficient searching for multimedia that is of interest to users. The description can be attached to any kind of multimedia material, no matter what the format of the representation is. Stored material that has this information attached to it can be indexed, searched, and retrieved.

5.2 CHARACTERISTICS OF MPEG VIDEO COMPRESSION

It is well known that video sequences contain significant amounts of statistical and subjective redundancies within and between frames. Thus, the goal of video source coding is the bit rate reduction for storage and transmission by exploring both statistical and subjective redundancies and to encode a "minimum set" of information using entropy coding techniques. This results in a compression of the coded video data compared to the original source data. The performance of video compression techniques depends on the amount of redundancy contained in the image data as well as on the actual compression techniques used for coding. It is well known that depending on the applications requirements, we may envisage "lossless" and "lossy" coding of video data. The aim of "lossless" coding is to reduce image or video data for storage and transmission, while retaining the quality of the original images. Namely, the decoded image quality is required to be identical to the image quality prior to encoding. On the other hand, the ultimate aim of lossy coding techniques is to optimize image quality for a given target bit rate subject to "objective" or "subjective" optimization criteria. The degree of image degradation depends on the complexity of the image or video scene as much as on the sophistication of the compression technique. For simple texture in images and low video activity, a good image reconstruction with no visible artifacts may be achieved even with simple compression techniques.

MPEG uses both intraframe and interframe techniques for video compression (see Figure 5.1).

There are three types of encoded frames (Section 3.9), as shown in Figure 5.2.

An I frame contains all of the necessary information to reproduce a complete frame and thus is independent of any other frames in the video sequence. It applies the intraframe compression of the basic JPEG DCT algorithm [96].

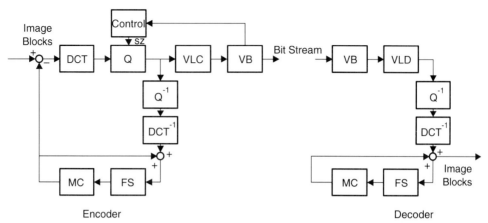

FIGURE 5.1   Block diagram of an MPEG hybrid DCT/DPCM encoder and decoder
structure [221].
©1997 IEEE.

It is used as a reference point for other pictures in a GOP (Section 3.9), and is
an access point to the coded sequence where decoding can begin. It is coded
with only moderate compression.

A P frame is predicted from the previous I or P frame in the sequence. B
frames are allowed to have forward-only or backward-only or bidirectionally
interpolated prediction and can have intramacroblock coding. ME and MC
are based on 16×16 Y blocks whereas 2D DCT is applied to 8×8 blocks. Even
in P and B frames, INTRA coding can be applied on an MB basis.

A B frame is bidirectionally interpolated by the preceding and the subsequent I or P frames. A current P frame can be decoded only if the preceding I or P
frame has been decoded. Similarly, without both the preceding and subsequent

FIGURE 5.2   Different types
of MPEG frames [221].
©1997 IEEE.

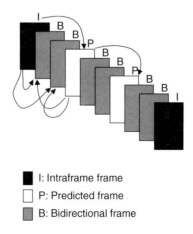

■ I: Intraframe frame
□ P: Predicted frame
■ B: Bidirectional frame

I or P frames in the decoder, it is impossible to generate a B frame. This frame is not used as the reference frame for other frames.

The basic compression steps are

1. Preprocess and color subsample (I and Q or C_B and C_R are subsampled). I and Q are hue and saturation. C_B and C_R are color difference signals [96]).

2. For P frame and B frame, do interframe motion compensation.

3. Send 8×8 pixel blocks (either intrablocks or motion compensated blocks) to the DCT engine and quantizer.

4. Apply zigzag ordering (see Figure 3.34) on the 8×8 quantized coefficients.

5. Apply a run-length encoder to the zeros of the zigzag sequence.

6. Apply a variable-length encoder on the run-length coded stream.

7. Code motion vectors.

8. Insert headers.

The MPEG-1 and MPEG-2 compression algorithms employ Discrete Cosine Transform (DCT) coding techniques on image blocks of 8×8 pels to efficiently exploit spatial correlation between nearby pels within the same image (intraframe coding). However, if the correlation between pels in nearby frames is high (that is, in cases where two consecutive frames have similar or identical content), it is desirable to use interframe DPCM coding techniques employing temporal prediction with or without MC. In MPEG video coding schemes, an adaptive combination of both temporal motion compensated prediction followed by transform coding of the remaining spatial information is used to achieve high data compression (hybrid DCT/DPCM coding of video).

For some applications, video is also subsampled in the temporal direction to reduce frame rate prior to coding. At the receiver, the decoded images are interpolated for display. This technique may be considered one of the most elementary compression techniques. It makes use of specific physiological characteristics of the human eye and thus removes subjective redundancy contained in the video data. The human eye is more sensitive to changes in brightness than to chromaticity changes. Therefore, the MPEG coding schemes first divide images into YUV components (one luminance and two chrominance components). Next, the chrominance components are subsampled relative to luminance component with Y:U:V ratio specified to particular applications. For example, with the MPEG-2 standard, a ratio 4:2:0, 4:2:2, or 4:4:4 is used (see Figure 5.4).

Motion-compensated prediction (see Section 3.9) is a powerful tool to reduce temporal redundancies between frames and is used extensively in MPEG-1 and MPEG-2 video standards as a prediction technique for temporal

DPCM coding. If all elements in a video scene are approximately spatially displaced, the motion between frames can be described by a limited number of motion parameters; in other words, by motion vectors for translatory motion of pels [228]. The best prediction of an actual pel is given by a motion-compensated prediction pel from a previously coded frame. Both prediction error and motion vectors are transmitted to the receiver. Since the spatial correlation between motion vectors is often high, it is sometimes assumed that one motion vector is representative for the motion of a block of adjacent pels. To this aim, images are usually separated into disjoint blocks of pels, 16×16 pels in MPEG-1 and (16×16) or (8×8) pels in MPEG-2 standards. For frame-based unidirectional prediction, only one motion vector is estimated, coded, and transmitted for each of these blocks. Figure 5.3 describes the block-matching approach for motion compensation. One motion vector (mv) is estimated for each block in the present frame, N, to be coded. The motion vector points to a reference block of the same size in a previously coded frame, N-1. The motion-compensated prediction error is calculated by subtracting each pel in a block with its motion-shifted counterpart in the reference block of the previous frame.

Transform coding has been studied extensively during the last three decades and has become a very popular compression method for video coding. The purpose of transform coding is to decorrelate the intraimage or interframe error image content and to encode transform coefficients rather than the original pels of the images. Among many possible alternatives, the DCT (Section 3.8) applied to smaller image blocks of usually 8×8 pels has become the most successful transform for video coding [27, 96, 229]. In fact, DCT-based implementations are used in most image and video coding standards because of their high decorrelation performance and the availability of fast DCT algorithms suitable for real-time implementations. VLSI implementations that operate at rates suitable for many video applications are commercially available [96].

FIGURE 5.3   Block-matching approach for motion compensation [221].
©1997 IEEE.

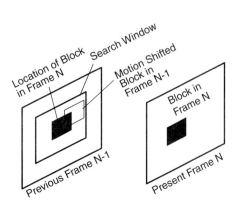

The combination of the two techniques described here (temporal motion-compensated prediction and transform-domain coding) can be seen as the key elements of the MPEG coding standards [230–233]. The third characteristic element of the MPEG algorithms is that these two techniques are processed on small image blocks of typically 16×16 pels for motion compensation and 8×8 pels for DCT coding. For this reason, the MPEG coding algorithms are usually referred to as hybrid block-based DCT/DPCM algorithms.

5.3   MPEG BIT STREAM SYNTAX

The MPEG bit stream syntax shown in Table 5.1 is more flexible than ITU-T Recommendation H.261, reflecting the variety of applications anticipated from MPEG. As can be seen, the MPEG bit stream syntax is constructed in several hierarchical layers with different functions.

The MPEG syntax specifies that the variable-length coding of video may start and end on slice boundaries. This arrangement prevents errors from propagating during the decoding process by forcing the decoder to start processing variable-length video data from a known state at the beginning of every slice.

5.4   MPEG-2 VIDEO STANDARD

Both MPEG-1 and MPEG-2 are the video coding standards for television-based applications in the 1990s and beyond. Since the MPEG-1 standard was intended for audiovisual coding for Digital Storage Media (DSM) applications, and since DSM typically have very low or negligible bit error rates, the MPEG-1 system part was not designed to be highly robust to bit errors. In

TABLE 5.1   MPEG Bit Stream Syntax [106]

Syntax	Function
Video sequence layer	Global context unit: video frame size, frame rate, bit rate, minimum decoder buffer size, constrained parameters information
Group-of-pictures layer	Video coding unit: random access, search, editing
Picture layer	Frame coding unit: type (I, B, P), display-order position
Slice layer	Resynchronization unit: a string of macroblocks in raster-scan order used for resynchronization during decoding
Macroblock layer	Motion compensation unit: a 16×16 block
Block layer	DCT unit: an 8×8 block

addition, the MPEG-1 system was intended for software-oriented processing, and thus large variable-length packets were preferred to minimize software overhead. A key factor for worldwide success of MPEG-1 is the generic structure of the standard, which supports a broad range of applications and application-specific parameters. However, MPEG continued its standardized efforts in 1991 with a second phase (MPEG-2) to provide a video coding solution for applications not originally covered or envisaged by MPEG-1, which is targeted for small picture resolutions (352×240 or 352×288 SIF resolution, with SIF standing for source input format).

Emerging applications, such as digital cable TV distribution, networked database services via ATM, and satellite and terrestrial digital broadcasting distribution were seen to benefit from the increased quality resulting from the MPEG-2 standard. Work was carried out in collaboration with the ITU-T SG 15 Experts Group for ATM video coding, and in 1994 the MPEG-2 Draft International Standard was released. This is also adapted by ITU-T as H.262 Recommendation [208]. The specification of the standard is intended to be generic to facilitate the bit stream interchange among different applications, transmission, and storage media.

5.4.1 MPEG-2 Nonscalable Video Coding

MPEG-2 introduces new coding features not found in MPEG-1 to accommodate the functionality and the quality of an expanded range of applications. Enhancements include the following:

- A choice of picture scanning methods (interlace or progressive scan) to fit television-oriented and computer-oriented applications.
- A choice of chrominance signal encoding methods.
- Two bit streams are defined, transport and program, to support transmission and storage media applications, respectively.
- Spatial and temporal scalabilities are supported.

The macroblock is a basic unit for MPEG-2 encoding. Each frame is composed of nonoverlapping macroblocks. Each macroblock is made up of four 8×8 luminance blocks (Y); one, two, or four 8×8 C_B chrominance blocks; and an equal number of C_R chrominance blocks. The chrominance blocks are formed by subsampling the C_B and C_R pixels related to the corresponding Y pixels. This results in three different MPEG-2 chrominance signal encoding methods, shown in Figure 5.4. The 4:2:0 format provides MPEG-1 and H.261 compatibility. The 4:2:2 and 4:4:4 formats are provided for higher-resolution applications such as studio video coding.

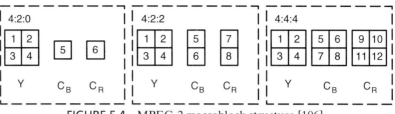

FIGURE 5.4   MPEG-2 macroblock structure [106].

©1997 Chapman and Hall.

Identical to the MPEG-1 standard, the MPEG-2 coding algorithm is based on the general hybrid DCT/DPCM coding scheme presented in Figure 5.1 and incorporates a macroblock structure, motion compensation, and coding modes for conditional replenishment macroblocks. The first frame in a video sequence (I picture) is encoded in intramode without reference to any past or future frames. At the encoder, the DCT is applied to each 8×8 luminance and chrominance block and, after output of the DCT, each of the 64 DCT coefficients is uniformly quantized (Q). The quantizer step size (SZ) used to quantize the DCT coefficient within a macroblock is transmitted to the receiver. After quantization, the DC coefficient is treated differently from the remaining coefficients (AC coefficients). The DC coefficient corresponds to the average intensity of the component block and is encoded using a differential DC prediction method. Because there is usually a strong correlation between the DC values of adjacent 8×8 blocks, the quantized DC coefficient is encoded as the difference between the DC values of the previous block and the current block. The nonzero quantized values of the remaining DCT coefficients and their locations are then zigzag scanned and run-length entropy coded using Variable Length Coding (VLC). The scan attempts to trace the DCT coefficients according to their significance. The low-frequency DCT coefficients contain most of the energy within the 8×8 blocks. The scanning of the quantized coefficients followed by variable-length coding serves as a mapping of the two-dimensional signal into a one-dimensional bit stream. The nonzero AC coefficient quantizer values (length) are detected along the scan line as well as the distance (run) between two consecutive nonzero coefficients. Each consecutive (run, length) pair is encoded by transmitting only one VLC code word. The purpose of zigzag scanning is to trace the low-frequency DCT coefficients, containing the most energy, before tracing the high-frequency coefficients.

The decoder performs the reverse operations, first extracting and decoding (VLD) the variable-length coded words from the bit stream to obtain locations and quantized values of the nonzero DCT coefficients for each block.

With the reconstruction of all nonzero DCT coefficients belonging to one block and subsequent inverse DCT, the decoded block pixel values are obtained. By processing the entire bit stream all image blocks are decoded and reconstructed. The AC coefficients are weighted by an HVS weighting matrix (default).

For coding P pictures, the previously coded I- or P-picture frame N-1 is stored in a Frame Store (FS) in both the encoder and decoder. Motion compensation is performed on a macroblock basis. Only one motion vector is estimated between frame N and frame N-1 for a particular macroblock to be encoded. These motion vectors are coded and transmitted to the receiver. The motion-compensated prediction error is calculated by subtracting each pel in a macroblock with its motion-shifted counterpart in the previous frame. An 8×8 DCT is then applied to each of the 8×8 blocks in the macroblock followed by quantization of the DCT coefficients with subsequent run length coding and entropy coding (VLC). A video buffer (VB) is needed to ensure that a constant target bit rate output is produced by the encoder. As for the quantization step size (SZ), it can be adjusted for each macroblock in a frame to achieve a given target bit rate and to avoid buffer overflow and underflow. The AC coefficients are weighted by a HVS weighting matrix (default).

The decoder uses the reverse process to reproduce a macroblock of frame N at the receiver. After decoding the variable-length words (VLD) contained in the VB, the pixel values of the prediction error are reconstructed including Q^{-1} and DCT^{-1} operations. The motion compensated pixels are added to the prediction error to recover the particular macroblock of frame N.

Figure 5.5 shows a simplified codec for MPEG-2 nonscalable video coding. The MPEG-2 video encoder consists of an interframe/field DCT encoder, a frame/field motion estimator and compensator, and a Variable Length Encoder (VLE). The frame/field DCT encoder exploits spatial redundancies. On the other hand, the frame/field motion compensator exploits temporal redundancies in the video signal. The coded video bit stream is sent to a systems multiplexer, SysMux [234, 235]. The MPEG-2 decoder in this codec consists of a Variable Length Decoder (VLD), interframe/field IDCT, and the frame/field motion compensator. The system demultiplexer (SysDemux) performs the complementary function of SysMux and presents the video bit stream to VLD for decoding of motion vectors and DCT coefficients. The frame/field motion compensator uses a motion vector decoded by VLD to generate motion-compensated prediction that is added back to a decoded prediction error signal to generate decoded video. This type of coding produces video bit streams called *nonscalable*, since normally the full spatial and temporal resolution coded video is the one that is expected to be decoded. If B pictures are used in encoding, because they do not feed back in to the interframe coding loop, it is always possible to discard some or all of them, thus achieving temporal scalability even for nonscalable bit streams. However, by nonscalable coding we usually mean that we have not gone out of our way to facilitate scalability.

5.4.2 MPEG-2 Scalable Video Coding

As we saw in Chapter 4, scalability is the property that allows decoders of various complexities to be able to decode video of resolution/quality commensurate with their complexities from the same bit stream. The intention of scalable coding is to provide interoperability between different services and to flexibly support receivers with different display and processing capabilities. Receivers not either capable or willing to reconstruct the full-resolution video can decode subsets of the layered bit stream to display video at lower spatial or temporal resolution or with lower quality. Another important purpose of scalable coding is to provide a layered video bit stream that is amenable for prioritized transmission. The main challenge is to reliably deliver video signals in the presence of channel errors, such as cell loss in ATM-based transmission networks or cochannel interference in terrestrial digital broadcasting.

In the case of interworking between HDTV and Standard Definition Television (SDTV), it is important that the HDTV receiver be compatible with the SDTV format. Flexibly supporting multiple resolutions is of particular interest. Compatibility can be achieved using scalable coding of the HDTV source, and the wasteful transmission of two independent bit streams to the HDTV and SDTV receivers can be avoided. Interoperability between HDTV

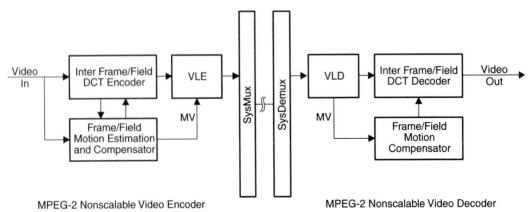

MPEG-2 Nonscalable Video Encoder   MPEG-2 Nonscalable Video Decoder

FIGURE 5.5   Codec for MPEG-2 nonscalable video coding [201].
©1997 Chapman and Hall.

and SDTV services can be provided along with a certain resilience to channel errors by combining the spatial scalability extensions with the SNR scalability tool. The MPEG-2 syntax supports up to three different scalable layers.

Figure 5.6 depicts a multiscale video coding scheme. As can be seen, two layers are provided, each layer supporting video at a different scale. Multi-resolution representation can be achieved by downscaling the input video signal into a lower-resolution video. The downscaled version is encoded into a base-layer bit stream with reduced bit rate. The upscaled reconstructed base-layer video (upsampled spatially or temporally) is used as a prediction for the coding of the original input video signal. The prediction error is encoded into an enhancement-layer bit stream. The display of video at the highest resolution with reduced quality is possible by decoding the lower bit rate base layer. Thus, scalable coding can be used to encode video with a suitable bit rate allocated to each layer in order to meet specific bandwidth requirements of transmission channels or storage media.

The generalized scalable codec structure is shown in Figure 5.7. Input video goes through a preprocessor that produces two video signals, one of which is input to an MPEG-1 or MPEG-2 nonscalable video encoder (base layer) (see Figure 5.1). The other is the input to an MPEG-2 enhancement video encoder (enhancement layer). Some processing of decoded video from MPEG-1 or MPEG-2 nonscalable video encoders may be needed in the midprocessor depending on specific scalability. The two bit streams, one from each encoder, are multiplexed in SysMux along with coded audio and user data. Thus, it becomes possible for two types of decoders to be able to decode a

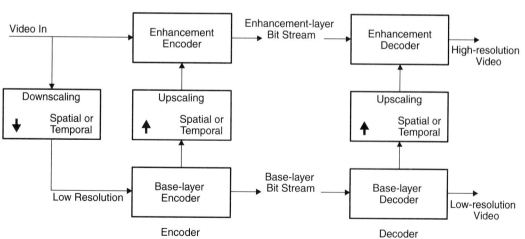

FIGURE 5.6   Block scheme of a multiscale video coding scheme [201].
©1997 Chapman and Hall.

video signal of quality commensurate with their complexity, from the same encoded bit stream. For example, if MPEG-1 or MPEG-2 nonscalable video decoder is employed, a basic video signal can be decoded. If in addition, MPEG-2 enhancement video decoder is employed, an enhancement video signal can be decoded. The two decoded signals may undergo further processing in a postprocessor.

5.4.3   MPEG-2 Video: Discussion

MPEG-2 has been an international standard since November 1994. In fact, it has been adopted for a number of application areas, such as digital TV broadcasting (terrestrial or satellite), pay TV, pay-per-view, video-on-demand, interactive TV, news-on-demand, settop boxes for cable TV, HDTV, DVD, computer games, and others [236]. Implementation of MPEG-2 is possible in several ways: software only, hardware assisted, decoder only, and DSP-based encoder/decoder implementation. Many of the MPEG-2 decoders were commercially available by early 1995. The worldwide acceptance of MPEG-2 in consumer electronics has led to large production scales, making MPEG-2 decoder equipment affordable and therefore also attractive for other related areas such as video communications and storage, and multimedia applications in general. Because MPEG-2 video provides higher quality but is too complex for software-only playback, hardware-assisted codecs provide substantially better image quality and better coding and playback performance than do software-only video codecs. DVD decoders are becoming integral parts of desktop and laptop PCs.

Since July 1990, the ITU-T ATM group has collaborated with MPEG-2. In the beginning of 1994, MPEG-2 was adopted by the Grand Alliance (GA)

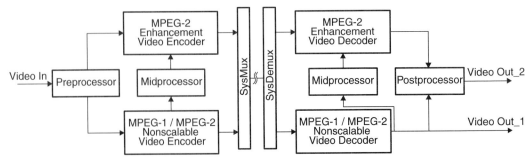

FIGURE 5.7   Codec for MPEG-2 scalable video coding [201].
© 1997 Chapman and Hall.

HDTV system in the United States and Digital Video Broadcasting (DVB) in Europe [96]. U.S. broadcasting and cable TV (video-on-demand) are the first commercial uses of MPEG-2 technology. Thus, MPEG-2 has become the common technology for coding digital video in the spectrum of applications ranging from communication/broadcasting to computers/electronic games. Note that HDTV and DVD have adopted Dolby AC-3 (AC: audio coder) algorithm for audio.

Transmission of compressed video over packet networks with nonreliable transport benefits when packet loss resilience is incorporated into the video coding. One promising approach to packet loss resilience, particularly for transmission over networks offering dual priorities such as ATM networks, is based on layered coding, which uses at least two bit streams to encode video. The base-layer bit stream, which can be decoded independently to produce a lower-quality/resolution video, is transmitted over a high-priority channel. The enhancement-layer bit stream contains less important information, so packet losses are more easily tolerated. The MPEG-2 standard provides four methods to produce a layered video bit stream: data partitioning, SNR scalability, spatial scalability, and temporal scalability (see Chapter 4). Each of these techniques was included in the standard in part for motivation other than loss resilience. Beginning with the pioneering work in [237], dual-priority layered coding has been proposed to combat packet losses in ATM networks [238, 239] and to increase robustness in wireless transmission [240]. Besides packet loss resilience, layered coding can also provide flexibility in traffic shaping. In MPEG-2, layered coding can be accomplished through scalable coding techniques (Section 4.3).

Receiver-based error concealment techniques are essential for many practical video transmission scenarios such as terrestrial HDTV broadcasting, packet network-based multimedia, and digital SDTV/HDTV delivery via ATM. Error concealment is intended to ameliorate the impact of channel impairments by utilizing the available picture redundancy to provide a subjectively acceptable rendition of affected picture regions. The concealment process must be supported by an appropriate transport format that helps to identify image pixel regions that correspond to lost or damaged data. Once the image regions (macroblocks, slices) to be concealed are identified, a combination of spatial and temporal replacement technique may be applied to fill in the lost picture elements. A specific class of spatio-temporal error concealment algorithms for MPEG video is described, and alternative realizations are compared via detailed end-to-end simulations for both one- and two-tier transmission media [23, 241]. Several algorithm enhancements based on directional interpolation (I-picture motion vectors) and use of MPEG-2 scalability features are presented in [202, 242]. The proposed class of error concealment algorithms provides significant robustness for MPEG video delivery in the presence of channel impairments, permitting useful operation at ATM cell-loss rates in the region of 10^{-4} to 10^{-3}, and 10^{-2} to 10^{-1} for one- and two-tier transmission scenarios, respectively.

5.5   ITU-T RECOMMENDATION H.263, H.263+, H.263++, AND H.26L

H.263+ is a revision to the original 1996 version of ITU-T Recommendation H.263 [242]. The original H.263+ was developed for video compression at rates below 64 Kbps and more specifically at rates below 33.4 Kbps (V.34 modem). This was the first international standard for video compression that would permit video communications at such low rates [243, 244]. The key technical features of H.263 are variable block-size motion compensation, overlapped-block motion compensation, pixel-extrapolating motion vectors, three-dimensional run-level-last variable-length coding, median motion vector prediction, and more efficient header information signaling (relative to H.261, arithmetic coding, half-pixel motion estimation, and bidirectional prediction).

In the original ITU-T work plan, the goal was to define a "near-term" recommendation in 1996, followed by a "long-term" recommendation several years later. The near-term recommendation is referred to as H.263. The long-term recommendation H.26L (previously called H.263L) is scheduled for standardization in the year 2002 and may adopt a completely new compression algorithm. After H.263 was completed, it became apparent there were incremental changes that could be made to H.263 that could visibly improve its compression performance. Thus, it was decided in 1996 that a revision to H.263 would be created that incorporated these incremental improvements. This is H.263 "plus" with several new features. Hence, the name H.263+ (now called H.263 version 2).

H.263+ contains approximately 12 new features that do not exist in H.263. These include new coding modes that improve compression efficiency, support for scalable bit streams, several new features to support packet networks and error-prone environments, added functionality, and support for a variety of video formats.

H.263+ falls into the family of video coders commonly referred to as hybrid DPCM/DCT-based video compression algorithms (see Figure 3.27). Other video coders in this family include H.261 [245], MPEG-1, MPEG-2, FCC/HDTV, and MPEG-4 video. These video coders typically employ 16×16 pixel block-based motion estimation and frame differencing to reduce temporal redundancy. Discrete Cosine Transform (DCT) is applied to 8×8 pixel blocks of the resulting residual frame. The transform coefficients are then quantized to reduce spatial redundancy. Lossless coding techniques are applied to the resulting symbols to further reduce statistical redundancies. A frame that has been temporally predicted is referred to as an INTER coded or P frame. The frame used as a basis of prediction, which is usually the decompressed version of the previous frame, is called the *reference* frame. When a frame is coded with no prediction whatsoever from a prior frame, it is referred to as an INTRA coded or I frame. An INTRA coded frame is simply the result of still image compression applied to a frame of video [246]. A B (bidirectionally interpolated) frame is predicted based on motion estimation/compensation of the previous and/or future frame. Various modes for transform (DCT) coding of P and B frames (see Figure 5.2) are adaptively applied on a MB basis; in other words, INTRA, INTER with or without MC (forward and/or backward MC).

Compression Improvements.   The compression performance of INTRA coded frames can generally be improved by exploiting the block-to-block correlation of DC and low-frequency horizontal and vertical transform coefficients. The advanced INTRA coding mode of H.263+ seeks to do just that. Either the INTRA DC or first row or column of DCT coefficients is predicted from neighboring blocks as shown in Figure 5.8.

The selection of DC-only versus DC and AC coefficients and the direction of prediction are indicated on a macroblock basis. When decoding, the prediction is performed after inverse quantization of the coefficient data. Moreover, two new alternate scan patterns are defined to better exploit the bias toward vertical and horizontal frequencies (see Figure 5.9).

A new Variable Length Code (VLC) table is defined to better match the zero-run and amplitude statistics of INTRA coded frames. In H.263, the

FIGURE 5.8 Coefficient prediction in advanced INTRA coding mode [242].
©1997 ITU-T.

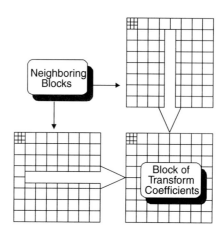

1	2	3	4	11	12	13	14
5	6	9	10	18	17	16	15
7	8	20	19	27	28	29	30
21	22	25	26	31	32	33	34
23	24	35	36	43	44	45	46
37	38	41	42	47	48	49	50
39	40	51	52	57	58	59	60
53	54	55	56	61	62	63	64

a) Alternate-Horizontal Scan

1	5	7	21	23	37	39	53
2	6	8	22	24	38	40	54
3	9	20	25	35	41	51	55
4	10	19	26	36	42	52	56
11	18	27	31	43	47	57	61
12	17	28	32	44	48	58	62
13	16	29	33	45	49	59	63
14	15	30	34	46	50	60	64

b) Alternate-Vertical Scan

FIGURE 5.9 Alternate DCT scanning patterns for advanced INTRA coding [242]. ©1997 ITU-T.

INTER frame VLC table was used for INTRA frames as well. This mode improves compression up to 40 percent in certain INTRA coded frames. "Blockiness" is a common artifact in block-transform-based video compression. It generally results from the lack of AC coefficients, representing high-frequency detail, when decoding a transform block. The results are abrupt transitions at block edges, especially in regions that would normally contain smooth gradations. The deblocking filter (see Figure 5.10) mode reduces these effects by smoothing the transition at block edges. It operates on two pixels on each side of a horizontal or vertical block edge as shown in Figure 5.10. The pixel values A, B, C, and D are replaced with new values according to a set of relations. The amount of smoothing is proportional to the quantization strength and inversely proportional to the pixel gradient at the block edge.

In the original H.263 Recommendation, there is a mode by which a bidirectionally predicted frame or B frame (as in MPEG-2) could be multiplexed with a subsequent P frame in the bit stream, thus saving some of the overhead of having a separate frame in the bit stream. The motion vectors for the B frame

FIGURE 5.10 Illustration of the deblocking filter.

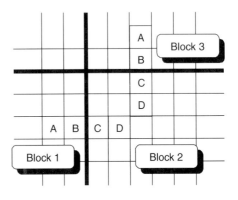

would be interpreted from the P frame motion vectors, and a small offset to the interpolated vectors could be transmitted in the bit stream. Although in most cases, a P-B pair of frames would be more efficient than a pair of P frames, in some situations this arrangement would perform worse. In H.263+ an improvement to the original mode allows a complete motion vector to be transmitted for the MB in the B frame, thus a P-B frame pair can do no worse than a pair of P frames. This is referred to as *improved P-B frames mode*.

H.263+ provides the means by which the reference frame can be resized, translated, or generally warped before being used as prediction for the current frame. This is referred to as Reference Picture Resampling (RPR) mode. Several of the capabilities in RPR mode can positively impact compression performance. For example, it is possible to indicate a global motion parameter. This parameter may be able to describe the global motion, thus allowing most of the block-based motion vectors to be zero. With RPR, an encoder could dynamically switch to quarter-sized video until the large motion subsides, thus avoiding "jerky" video. The display would continue to be full size. However, the video would have to be interpolated back to full size prior to display.

The Reduced-Resolution Update (RRU) mode is a slightly more esoteric technique for employing the extreme rate control measure. In RPR, the reference picture would be reduced to the size of the current picture, the compressed frame would be transmitted at the smaller frame size, and the result would be decoded and interpolated back to the original size prior to display. The visual effect of this operation would be that any high-frequency detail that would have accumulated, say in the background of video, would suddenly disappear when the reference picture is resampled. RRU mode addresses this problem by keeping the reference and current frames at the original size and downsampling the residual frame after motion estimation/frame differencing to produce a valid quarter-size INTER coded frame. In order to do so, macroblocks and blocks are redefined as 32×32 pixels and 16×16 pixels, respectively, so that when the residual frame is downsampled, they return to their original sizes of 16×16 and 8×8 pixels, respectively. With RRU mode, areas of high motion can be accommodated without the side effect of detail loss. The trade-off is the added complexity in implementing this mode of operation.

Block decoding in RRU mode is shown in Figure 5.11. This mode can increase the coding picture rate while maintaining sufficient subjective quality. This mode allows the encoder to send update information for a picture encoded at a lower resolution while preserving detail in a higher resolution reference image to create a final image at a higher resolution.

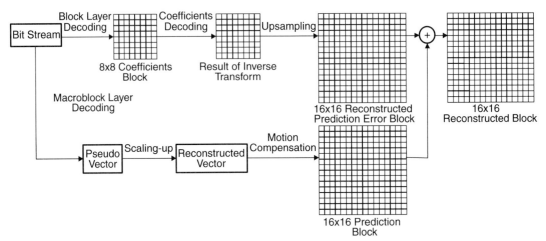

FIGURE 5.11 Block decoding in Reduced-Resolution Update mode [242].
©1997 ITU-T.

New Features of H.263+. Among the new features of H.263+, one of several that correct design inefficiencies of the original H.263 recommendation is Modified Quantization mode. This mode has four key elements:

- Indication for larger quantizer changes from macroblock to macroblock to better react to rate control requirements.
- The ability to use a finer chrominance quantizer to better preserve chrominance fidelity.
- The capability to support the entire range of quantized coefficient values rather than having to clip values greater than 128.
- Explicitly restricting the representation of quantized transform coefficients to those that can reasonably occur.

The second modification of the original H.263 Recommendation is motion vector range, which was for the most part [-16, 15.5]. When H.263+ mode is invoked, the range is generally larger and depends on the frame size (see Table 5.2).

Another modification to the original H.263 Recommendation is the addition of a rounding term to the equation for half-pel interpolation. Without it, there is a positive bias in the half-pel interpolation that can most notably be seen as a pink color drift in the facial flesh tones. The rounding term toggles from frame to frame, thus eliminating this rounding bias and thereby reducing the artifact noticeably.

TABLE 5.2   Motion Vector Ranges in H.263+ [242]

Frame Sizes Up To	Motion Vector Range
352×288	[-32, 31.5]
704×576	[-64, 63.5]
1408×1152	[-128, 127.5]
Widths up to 2048	Hor. range [-256, 255.5]

©1997 ITU-T.

Finally, H.263+ supports a wider variety of input video formats than H.263. In addition to five standard sizes, arbitrary frame sizes in multiples of 4 from (32×32) to (2048×1152) can be supported, as well as other pixel aspect ratios besides 12:11, and other picture clock frequencies (temporal resolution) besides 29.27 Hz.

H.263+ and Packet Video.   In packet-based networks, there is a number of implications on the video. Usually, there is no guarantee of arrival of packets and that packets will arrive in order, and no guarantee that the transmission times will be the same for each packet. For example, packet loss rates over networks such as the Internet can be 10 percent or higher. H.263+ has several new features that improve performance under these conditions. The first is the layered bit stream capability that can be used to prioritize data that, when selectively detected, can reduce network congestion. Second is the improved bit stream fragmentation capability. Third is a more robust mechanism for selecting reference pictures for prediction. Finally, there is the capability to define independent subpictures of a frame.

H.263+ video enhancement layers belong to one of three categories: temporal, SNR, or spatial enhancement. Temporal enhancement is the process by which the frame rate can be increased over the base layer. This is accomplished via disposable bidirectionally predicted (B) frames (see Figure 5.12). Predicting from prior and subsequent frames usually improves compression performance. B frames are not used to predict (with or without MC) the B and P frames. However, when added, they raise the frame rate of the video sequence. Hence, the name "temporal enhancement layer."

SNR enhancement layer is shown in Figure 5.13. It is a refinement to the coded base layer frames. When a video frame is compressed, the decoded version is not an exact replica of the original frame. This is because H.263+ is a lossy compression. It selectively throws away information in order to improve compression performance without excessive degradation of visual quality. If

FIGURE 5.12   Bidirectionally
predicted (B) frames [242].
©1997 ITU-T.

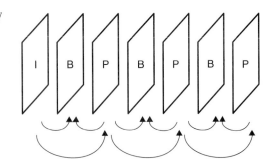

there is enough bandwidth for a decoder to receive the SNR enhancement layer, the visual quality can usually be improved over the base layer. Besides the prediction from the base layer, the H.263+ encoder has the choice of including prediction from the previous frame in the SNR enhancement layer as well. This is a modified form of a bidirectionally predicted frame, called an EP frame. When an SNR enhancement frame is predicted only from the base layer and not from a previous frame, it is called an EI frame.

Spatial enhancement is closely related to SNR enhancement. The only difference is that the enhancement layer is twice the size vertically and horizontally from the base layer. In this case, the input video is first downsized both vertically and horizontally prior to encoding as the base layer. After that, the decompressed base-layer frames are interpolated back to the original size before being used as prediction for the spatial enhancement-layer frames. Different enhancement types can be combined to provide a very flexible layered bit stream architecture.

The Influence of H.263+ on Packetization and Error Resiliency.   Part of the process of transporting a video bit stream over packet networks is the

FIGURE 5.13   SNR enhancement layer [242].
©1997 ITU-T.

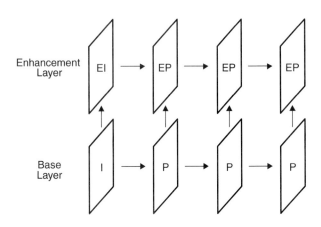

fragmentation of the bit stream before being converted into a packet payload. H.263+ improves support for this fragmentation operation by using arbitrary resynchronization markers. The resynchronization markers are provided by slice headers in a submode of the slice structured mode. Slice headers can be inserted at any MB boundary.

When packet loss becomes substantial, it is possible to define subpictures within each picture that do not depend on any information outside the subpictures' boundaries within the current frame or in any referenced picture. In this way, error due to packet loss can be kept from propagation to other regions. This is referred to as *independent segment decoding mode.*

H.263+ also provides the ability to indicate that a prior frame is suitable to be used as a reference for compression. This is referred to as *reference picture selection.*

To conclude, H.263+ brings numerous new optional features and capabilities to H.263 [247]. These include compression efficiency improvements such as improved INTRA coded frame compression, a deblocking filter, modified quantization, and alternate variable-length code tables. Besides compression improvements, there is support for scalable bit streams, network packetization, the ability to define independent subpictures for error containment, and the capability to acknowledge and identify error-free reference frames. Finally, H.263+ supports a wider variety of input formats compared to H.263 [248, 249].

H.263++ and H.26L Development.   The H.263++ development effort is intended for near-term standardization of enhancements to produce a third version of the H.263 video codec for real-time telecommunications and related nonconversational services. The work plan for H.263++ is shown in Table 5.3.

The H.26L is aimed at developing new video coding technology beyond the capabilities of incremental enhancements to H.263 for long-term standardization. It is aimed at very low bit rates, real-time, low end-to-end delay coding

TABLE 5.3   H.263++ Work Plan [250]

September 1997	Adoption of work plan
November 1998	First formal draft adoptions
February 1999	Last formal draft adoptions
November 1999	Final draft for determination
February 2000	Determination
July 2000	Final draft for decision
November 2000	Decision

©1998 ITU-T.

for a variety of source materials. It is designed to have low complexity permitting software implementation, enhanced error robustness (especially for mobile networks), and adaptable rate control mechanisms. The applications targeted by H.26L include real-time conversational services, Internet video applications, sign language and lip-reading communication, video storage and retrieval service, video store (VoD) and forward services (video mail), and multipoint communication over heterogeneous networks. The IMT-2000, a future mobile communication environment, is a key application area for H.26L. H.26L should provide more error robustness capability and substantially improved compression performance for an application to future mobile multimedia systems. The work plan for H.26L is shown in Table 5.4.

Key technical areas showing potential for performance gain of H.263++ are [252, 253]

- Error resilient data partitioning (creation of a data partitioned and layered protection structure for the coded data, longer resynchronization codeword to improve the detectability and reduce the probability of false detection; Samsung and UCLA scheme [250]).

- 4×4 block-size motion compensation (long-term picture memories, rate-distortion optimization alterations, motion estimation optimization alterations, a new type of deblocking filter, a new type of INTRA spatial prediction, and some VLC alterations for transform coefficients, motion vectors, and coded block pattern; Telenor H.26L proposal [250]).

- Adaptive quantization (rate-distortion optimized quantization; truly optimal rate-distortion trellis encoding for an additive distortion measure; Purdue Univ. and LG Electronics scheme [250]).

- Enhanced reference picture selection (multiframe motion-compensated prediction, modified interframe prediction method; Univ. Erlangen-Nuremberg scheme [250]).

TABLE 5.4   H.26L Work Plan [251]

January 1998	Call for proposals
November 1998	Evaluation of the proposals
April 1999	1st Test Model of H.26L (TML1)
1999–2001	Collaboration phase
October 2001	Determination
July 2002	Decision

©1998 ITU-T.

- Enhanced scalability (new P-picture types in enhancement layers; Ericsson Telecom [250]).
- IDCT mismatch reduction (integer inverse transform; Telenor H.26L proposal [250]).
- Deblocking and deringing filters (directional classifications and identifications of outlying values of block corner pixels for special treatment; UCLA scheme [250]).
- Error concealment (RD optimization coder algorithm; TU Berlin [250]).

The following technical proposals are evaluated in response to the call for proposals for H.26L [254]:

- Modified prediction/transform based method (Telenor [251]).
- SCT Strathclyde Compression Transform: vector quantization with block approximation either by reference to a codebook or by motion compensation from a previous frame (Univ. of Strathclyde [251]).
- Loop-filtering method for reducing the blocking artifacts, corner outliner, and the ringing noise (KAIST and Samsung [251]).
- Adaptive scalar quantizer scheme using nonzero-level codebooks (Purdue Univ. and LG Electronics [251]).
- DCT-based embedded video coder using rearrangement of DCT coefficients (LG Electronics [251]).
- MVC low bit rate video coder: rough segmentation, affine motion compensation scheme, vector quantization, and multishape discrete cosine transform (Nokia [251]).
- Data partitioning method using data reordering algorithm (Samsung [251]).
- Video coding using long-term memory for multiple reference frames and affine motion-compensated prediction (Univ. Erlangen-Nuremberg [251]).

H.263 and MPEG-4 Video Issues. MPEG-4 video decoders that support the features that are similar in the two standards (MPEG-4 and H.263) will be capable of decoding the syntax found in the baseline mode of ITU-T Rec. H.263+ [255]. This commonality of standardization will ensure greater interoperability in video coding and new applications by supporting MPEG-4 in H.324 terminals. ITU-T Rec. H.324 is the videoconferencing system standard that includes H.263 video coding and nonconversational services [256]. For these types of applications, the MPEG-4 features add new types of presentation for H.324 multimedia terminals.

The MPEG-4 video standard has unique functionalities such as multiple arbitrarily shaped video objects, 12-bit video, scalable texture coding, animation, and virtual reality. These functionalities will enhance videoconferencing systems. One example is segmenting the participants of the conferencing system and coding them with an arbitrarily shaped coding strategy.

- In multipoint conferencing systems, it is possible to show the status of participants in a more visible way by enlarging the participants speaking, displaying the silent participants semitransparently, placing the participants on the location of the map where they are speaking, and so on.
- Segmented participants and background images such as documents, maps, and graphs can be coded separately. Users at the decoder sites can select the background image and arrange the segment-based coded participants onto the background at arbitrary positions and sizes.

A simple way to handle MPEG-4 video in the H.324 terminal is described in [257]. In this strategy, existing components of the H.324 (that is, H.223/M and H.245) can be used with only additional codepoints for the MPEG-4 video capability in H.245. Multiple video object bit streams can be transmitted by mapping directly to the logical channels opened individually. A simple composition can be accomplished by the information contained in the MPEG-4 video bit stream such as size and position of the video object, alpha values, and time stamps. This strategy and the additional H.245 code process were proven by the MPEG-4 experts [258].

5.6   MPEG-4 VIDEO STANDARDIZATION PROCESS

New types of networks are carrying audiovisual (AV) information from mobile narrowband to broadband while hardware and software technologies continue to progress. On the other hand, developments taking place in the production and handling of AV data have given use to new demands on AV coding standards. The MPEG-1 and MPEG-2 AV coding standards are successful because they allow digital AV services with high performance, both concerning quality and compression efficiency. However, these standards are limited to a representation of AV information where video is a sequence of frames, each with a certain number of lines. Nevertheless, the MPEG-1 and MPEG-2 are widely adopted in commercial products [250].

After setting the MPEG-1 and MPEG-2 standards, MPEG (Moving Picture Experts Group, ISO/IEC Joint Technical Committee 1, Sub Committee 29, Working Group 11) has developed a new AV standard, MPEG-4. Although at the beginning of the work on MPEG-4 very low bit rates were objective, MPEG adopted changes in the AV environment. This standard addresses the new demands that arise and in which more and more AV material is exchanged in digital form. These needs go much further than achieving more compression and lower bit rates. The MPEG-4 standard is fundamentally different in nature from its predecessors, and it makes the move toward representing the scene as a composition of objects, rather than just the pixels [251, 252, 270].

ISO/IEC MPEG-4 started its standardization in July 1993 with the charter to develop a generic video coding algorithm mainly targeted for a wide range of low bit rate multimedia applications. MPEG-4 version 1 became an IS in February 1999, with version 2 targeted for November 1999. Starting from the original goal of providing an audiovisual coding standard for very low bit rate channels, such as found in mobile applications or today's Internet, MPEG-4 is evaluated as a complex toolkit. The MPEG-4 reference model is represented in Figure 5.14. The MPEG-4 defined composition technology is called Binary Format for Scene Description (BIFS), which achieves the important goal of saving bits for transmitting scan-composition information.

As MPEG-4 deals with objects, it becomes necessary to provide a mechanism enabling the author of a scene to indicate how the different Audio-Visual Objects (AVOs) are composed, and for a user to interact with the scene by changing its original composition (if allowed by the author). The concept of the MPEG-4 "content-based" video functionality is shown in Figure 5.15 as an example of image scene containing a number of video objects. The content-based approach will allow the flexible decoding, representation, and manipulation of video objects in a scene. The attempt is to encode the sequence in a scene in a way that will allow the separate decoding and reconstruction of the

FIGURE 5.14 MPEG-4 reference model [259]. ©1998 IEEE.

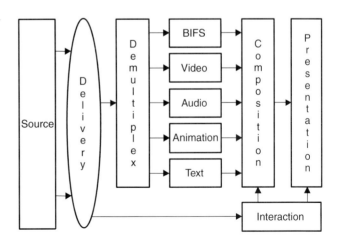

FIGURE 5.15   MPEG-4 content-based video coding flexible decoding, representation, and manipulation of video objects in a scene: a) original, b) manipulated [270]. ©1997 IEEE.

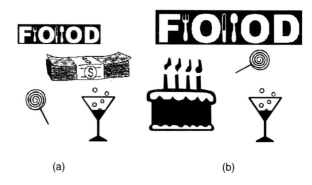

(a)   (b)

object and to allow the manipulation of the original scene by simple operations on the bit stream. The bit stream is "object layered." The shape and transparency of each object, as well as the spatial coordinates and additional parameters describing object scaling, rotation, or related parameters, are described in the bit stream of each object layer.

The receiver can reconstruct the original sequence in its entity by decoding all objects' layers and by displaying the objects at original size and at the original location, as shown in Figure 5.15a. Alternatively, it is possible to manipulate the video by simple operations. For example, in Figure 5.15b, some objects were not decoded and used for reconstruction, while others were decoded and displayed using subsequent scaling or rotation. In addition, new objects were included that did not belong to the original scene. Since the bit stream of the sequence is organized in an object-layered form, the manipulation is performed at the bit stream level, without the need for further transcoding. It is targeted to provide these capabilities for both natural and synthetic AV objects as well as for hybrid representations of natural and synthetic objects. In general, MPEG-4 images and image sequences are considered to be arbitrarily shaped in contrast to the standard MPEG-1 and MPEG-2 definitions.

MPEG-4 defines an AV scene as a coded representation of AV objects that have certain relations in space and time rather than video frames with associated audio. When audio and video objects are associated, an audiovisual object results (for example, the image of a running car together with the sound it makes). This new approach to information representation allows much more interactivity, the reuse of data, intelligent schemes to manage bandwidth, processing resources, and error protection. It also eases the integration of natural and synthetic audio and visual material, as well as text overlays and animation graphics.

The following set of functionalities are defined in MPEG-4 [260]:

- Content-based multimedia data access tools
- Content-based manipulation and bit stream editing

- Hybrid natural and synthetic data, both video and audio coding
- Improved temporal random access
- Improved coding efficiency
- Coding multiple concurrent data streams
- Robustness in error-prone environments
- High content scalability

The objective of MPEG-4 is thus to provide an AV representation that supports new ways of communication, access and manipulation of digital AV data, and a common technological solution to various communication paradigms among which the borders are disappearing. MPEG-4 has responded to the emerging needs of application fields, including interactive AV services, games, AV home editing, advanced AV communication services such as mobile AV terminals, teleshopping, AV on the Internet, and remote monitoring and control [261].

The delivery of multimedia information is changing. New networks carry video and other data, next to the audio information that they were originally intended to transport. Users want to have (when they are traveling) the same possibilities that they enjoy at home or in their offices. This includes access to multimedia information. Even the Global System for Mobile (GSM) communication with data below 10 Kbps is starting to be used for transmission of digitally compressed video [96]. At the same time, high-bandwidth networks are also becoming available. Cable modem and Asymmetric Digital Subscriber Loop (ADSL) technology both promise to deliver several megabits per second to users, without the need to change access network cabling. As a larger variety of networks carry multimedia information, the number of connections that involve more than network type is growing [262].

Another contribution made by MPEG-4 is the Delivery Multimedia Integration Format (DMIF). DMIF's goals are twofold: hide the delivery technology details from the DMIF user and ensure the establishment of end-to-end connections. The former, called the *DMIF application interface*, is a unified interface that allows an application to access AVOs in a way that is transparent to the type of delivery: a local disk, a two-way channel, or even a broadcast channel. The latter is achieved through DMIF signaling messages. Such messages are mapped into native network signaling messages.

In addition to the new or improved functionality, several other important functionalities are needed to support the envisioned AV application. The functionalities listed next may be provided already by existing or other emerging standards [96]:

- Synchronization
- Auxiliary data capability

- Virtual channel allocation flexibility
- Low (end-to-end and/or decoder) delay mode
- User controls
- Transmission media networking
- Interworking with other audiovisual systems
- Security
- Multipoint capability
- Content
- Format
- Quality

MPEG-4 combines some of the typical features of other MPEG standards with the new ones coming from existing or anticipated manifestation of multimedia [260].

- Independence of application from lower-layer details, as in the Internet paradigm
- Technology awareness of lower-layer characteristics (scalability, error robustness)
- Application software downloadability as in the network computer paradigm
- Reusability of encoding tools and data
- Interactivity not just with an integral AV bit stream but with the individual pieces of information (called *AV object*s as in the Web paradigm)
  - Possibility to hyperlink and interact with multiple sources of information simultaneously as in the Web paradigm but at the AV object level
  - Possibility of hyperlinking as in the Web paradigm but at the AV object level
  - Capability to handle natural/synthetic and real-time/nonreal-time information in integrated fashion
  - Capability to composite and present information according to users' needs as in Virtual Reality Modeling Language (VRML) and computer graphics paradigm in general

The structure of MPEG-4 is composed of four different elements: syntax, tools, algorithms, and profiles [263, 264]. The syntax is an extensible description language that allows for selection, description, and downloading of tools, algorithms, and profiles. A tool is a technique (contour representation, motion compensation) that is accessible via syntax. An algorithm is an organized collection of tools that provides one or more functionalities. A profile is a collection of algorithms constrained in a specific way to address a specific application. Hence, MPEG-4 is defined to offer a flexible syntax and an open set of tools supporting a range of both novel and conventional functionalities that extend beyond just better coding efficiency at very low bit rates. MPEG-4 has also developed a flexible and extensible syntactic object-oriented description language called the MPEG-4 Systems Description Language (MSDL) that allows not only for the description of the bit stream structure, but also for configuration and programming of the decoder. MSDL supports the varied set of coding techniques that realize the new functionalities supported by MPEG-4.

MPEG-4 video aims at providing standardized core technologies allowing efficient storage, transmission, and manipulation of video data in multimedia environments. Therefore, video activities aim at providing solutions in the form of tools and algorithms, enabling functionalities such as efficient compression, object scalability, spatial and temporal scalabilities, and error resilience. MPEG-4 video provides a toolbox containing tools and algorithms bringing solutions to the aforementioned functionalities and more. To this end, the approach taken relies on content-based visual data representation. In contrast to the current state-of-the-art techniques, within this approach, a scene is viewed as a composition of Video Objects (VO) with intrinsic properties such as shape, motion, and texture. It is believed that such a content-based representation is a key to enable interactivity with objects for a variety of multimedia applications. In such applications, users can access arbitrarily shaped objects in the scene and manipulate these objects.

The focus of MPEG-4 video is the development of Video Verification Models (VMs) that evolve over time by means of core experiments. The VM is a common platform with a precise definition of encoding and decoding algorithms that can be presented as tools addressing specific functionalities. New algorithms/tools are added to the VM and old algorithms/tools are replaced in the VM by successful core experiments [265].

So far, MPEG-4 video group has focused its efforts on a single VM that has gradually evolved from version 1.0 to version 12.0, and in the process has addressed an increasing number of desired functionalities: content-based object and temporal scalabilities, spatial scalability, error resilience, and compression efficiency. The encoding and decoding process is carried out on the instances of VOs called Video Object Planes (VOPs). The encoding process generates a coded representation of VOP as well as composition information necessary for display. Further, at the decoder a user may interact and modify the composition process as needed. Object-based temporal scalability and spatial scalability can be achieved by means of layers known as Video Object Layers (VOLs), which represent either the base layer or enhancement layer(s) of a VOP. The core experiments in the video group cover the following major classes of tools and algorithms:

Compression efficiency. For most applications involving digital video, such as videoconferencing, Internet video games, or digital TV, coding efficiency is essential. MPEG-4 has evaluated over a dozen methods intended to improve the coding efficiency of the preceding standards.

Error resilience. The ongoing work in error resilience addressed the problem of accessing video information over a vide range of storage and transmission media. In particular, due to a rapid growth of mobile communications, it is extremely important that access is available to video and audio information via wireless networks. This implies a need for useful operation of video and audio compression algorithms in error-prone environments at low bit rates (that is, less than 64 Kbps).

Shape and alpha map coding. Alpha maps describe the shapes of 2D objects. Multilevel alpha maps are frequently used to blend different layers of image sequences for the final film. Other applications that benefit from associating binary alpha maps with images are content-based image representation for image data based, interactive games, surveillance, and animation.

Arbitrarily shaped region texture coding. Coding for texture for arbitrarily shaped regions is required for achieving an efficient texture representation for arbitrarily shaped objects. Hence, these algorithms are used for objects whose shape is described with an alpha map.

Multifunctional tools and algorithms. Multifunctional coding provides tools to support a number of content-based objects as well as other functionalities. For instance, for Internet and database applications, spatial and temporal scalabilities are essential for channel bandwidth scaling for robust delivery. Multifunctional coding also addresses multiview and stereoscopic applications as well as representations that enable simultaneous coding and tracking of objects for surveillance and other applications. Besides the mentioned applications, a number of tools are developed for segmentation of a video scene into objects.

MPEG-4 may be transported over any transport mechanism, such as AAL-5/ATM or transmission coding protocol/Internet protocol. For these reasons, the expected number of MPEG-4 user communities is very large.

- The growing business and audiovisual information over the Internet may benefit from the possibility of sending high-quality audio and video in standardized form on very low bit rate channels such as those provided by the typical telephony modem at 33.6 Kbps.
- Real-time interpersonal communication over low bit rate channels, such as in mobile communications, may benefit from a video coding standard that is robust to error-prone mobile channels.
- Broadcasting may benefit from the ability to download AVOs with rich local interaction capabilities that provide a perceived high level of personalization of the information received.
- Retrieval applications may benefit from the rich audiovisual content, both natural and synthetic.
- Realistic videogames may exploit the mix of synthetic and natural AVOs.
- Educational applications may benefit from the ability to access the individual AVOs.
- Virtual spaces may use realistic synthetic faces and animated bodies.

For the storage and transmission of AVO data, a high coding efficiency, meaning a good quality of the reconstructed data, is required [266]. Improved coding efficiency is particularly necessary for applications such as video transmission over mobile networks or the Internet.

5.6.1 Scope and Features of the MPEG-4 Standard

MPEG-4 standard provides a set of technologies that satisfy the needs of authors, service providers, and end users. For authors, MPEG-4 enables the production of content that has far greater reusability, with greater flexibility than what is possible today with individual technologies such as digital television, animated graphics, World Wide Web (WWW) pages, and their extensions. For network service providers, MPEG-4 offers transparent information that will be interpreted and translated into the appropriate native signaling messages of each network with the help of relevant standards' bodies having the appropriate jurisdiction. As for Quality of Service (QoS) considerations, MPEG-4 provides a generic QoS parameter set for different MPEG-4 media. Signaling of the QoS information end to end will enable transport optimization in heterogeneous networks. For end users, MPEG-4 will enable many functionalities that could potentially be accessed on a single component terminal and higher levels of interaction with content, within the limits set by the author. Among others, end-user applications include real-time communications, surveillance, and mobile multimedia.

MPEG-4 achieves these goals by providing standardized ways to

- Represent units for aural, visual, and audiovisual content called Audio-Visual Objects (AVOs). These AVOs can be of natural or synthetic origin. This means they can be recorded with a camera or a microphone, or generated with a computer.
- Compose these objects together to create compound audiovisual objects that form audiovisual scenes.
- Multiplex and synchronize the data associated with AVOs so that they can be transported over network channels providing QoS appropriate for the nature of the specific AVOs.
- Interact with the audiovisual scene generated at the receiver's end.

Representation of primitive AVOs: Audiovisual scenes are composed of several AVOs, organized in a hierarchical fashion. We find primitive AVOs, such as

- A two-dimensional fixed background
- The picture of a talking person without the background
- The voice associated with the person

MPEG-4 standardizes a number of such primitive AVOs, capable of representing both natural and synthetic content types, which can be either two- or three-dimensional. In addition to the AVOs mentioned previously and shown in Figure 5.16, MPEG-4 defines a coded representation of objects such as

- Text and graphics
- Talking heads and associated text to be used at the receiver and to synthesize the speech and animate the head
- Animated human bodies

In their coded form, these objects are represented as efficiently as possible. This means that the bits used for coding these objects are no longer necessary for the support of desired functionalities. In this coded form, objects (aural or visual) can be represented independent of their surroundings or background.

Composition of AVOs.   Figure 5.16 shows an example that highlights the way in which an audiovisual scene in MPEG-4 is composed of individual objects. This figure contains compound AVOs that group elementary AVOs together. As an example: The visual object corresponding to the talking person and the corresponding voice are tied together to form a new compound AVO, containing both aural and visual components of a talking person. Such grouping allows authors to construct complex scenes and enables consumers to manipulate

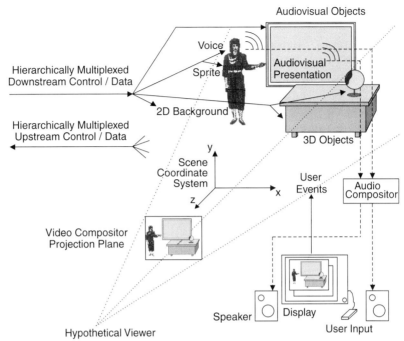

FIGURE 5.16   An example of an MPEG-4 audiovisual scene [267].
©1998 ISO/IEC.

meaningful sets of objects. MPEG-4 provides a standardized way to compose a scene, allowing you to

- Place AVOs anywhere in a given coordinate system.
- Group primitive AVOs in order to form compound AVOs.
- Apply streamed data to AVOs in order to modify their attributes (for example, moving texture belonging to an object).
- Change interactively the user's viewing and listening points anywhere in the scene.

Multiplexing and Synchronization of AVOs.   AV object data is conveyed in one or more Elementary Streams (ESs). The streams are characterized by the Quality of Service (QoS) they request for transmission (for example, maximum bit rate, bit error rate, and so on), as well as other parameters, including stream type information, to determine the required decoder resources and the precision for encoding timing information. How such streaming information is transported in a synchronized manner from source to destination, exploiting different QoS as available from the network, is specified in terms of an access unit layer and a conceptual two-layer multiplexer, as shown in Figure 5.17. The access unit layer allows identification of access units (for example, video or audio frames, scene description commands) in ESs, and recovery of the AV object's or scene description's time base, and enables synchronization among them. The access unit header can be configured in a large number of ways, allowing use in a broad spectrum of systems.

The Flexible Multiplexing (FlexMux) layer is fully specified by MPEG-4. It contains a multiplexing tool that allows grouping of ESs with a low multiplexing overhead. For example, this may be used to group ESs with similar QoS requirements. The Transport Multiplexing (TransMux) layer models the layer that offers transport services matching the requested QoS. Only the interface to this layer is specified by MPEG-4. Any suitable existing transport protocol stack may become a specific TransMux instance. The choice is left to the end user/service provider and allows MPEG-4 to be used in a variety of operational environments.

Use of the FlexMux multiplexing is optional. This layer may be bypassed if the underlay TransMux instance provides equivalent functionality. However, the access unit layer is always present. With regard to the MPEG-4 system layer model, it will be possible to

- Identify access units, transport timestamps and clock reference information, and identify data tools

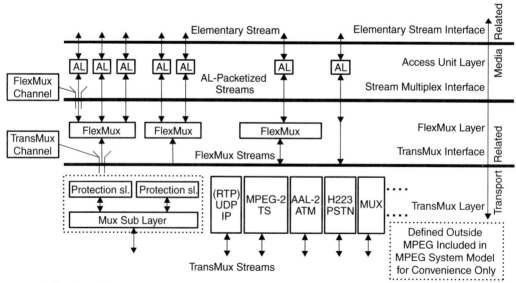

FIGURE 5.17   The MPEG-4 system layer model [267].
©1998 ISO/IEC.

- Optionally interleave data from different ESs into FlexMux streams
- Convey control information

Control information is important to indicate the required QoS for each ES that is mapped into a FlexMux stream, to translate such QoS requirements into actual network resources, and to convey the mapping of ESs associated with AVs to FlexMux and TransMux channels.

Interaction with AVOs.   In general, the user observes a scene that is composed following the design of the scene's author. Depending on the degree of freedom allowed by the author, however, the user has the possibility to interact with the scene. Operations a user may be allowed to perform include:

- Change the viewing/listening point of the scene; that is, by navigation through a scene.
- Drag objects in the scene to different positions.
- Trigger a cascade of events by clicking on a specific object; for example, starting or stopping a video stream.
- Select the desired language when multiple language tracks are available.
- More complex kinds of behavior can also be triggered; for example, a virtual phone rings, the user answers, and a communication link is established.

5.6.2   Overview of the MPEG-4 System

The MPEG committee has set up a process to provide an efficient method to reach adequate standards for AV data communications. The standardization process for the MPEG-1, MPEG-2, and MPEG-4 can be divided into a number of steps: requirements, competitive phase, selection of basic methods, collaborative phase, working draft IS, validation, and finally the IS [268].

Figure 5.18 gives a very general overview of MPEG-4 system. The objects that make up a scene are sent or stored together with information about their spatio-temporal relationships (that is, composition information). The compositor uses this information to reconstruct the complete scene. Composition information is used to synchronize different objects in time and to give them the right position in space. Separating this function from the pure decoding of objects introduces the possibility to influence the presentation of a scene, on a screen or through the loudspeaker. Coding different objects separately makes it possible to change the speed of a moving object in the same scene or make it rotate, to influence which objects are sent and at what quality and error protection. In addition, it permits composing a scene with objects that arrive from different locations.

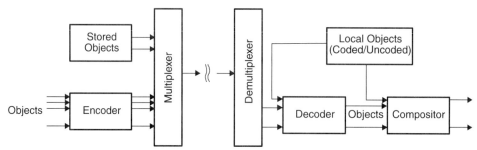

FIGURE 5.18 General overview of the MPEG-4 system.

The MPEG-4 standard does not prescribe how a given scene is to be organized into objects (that is, segmented). The segmentation is usually regarded to take place even before the encoding, as a preprocessor step, which is never a standardization issue. By not specifying preprocessing and encoding, the standard leaves room for systems manufacturers to distinguish themselves from their competitors by providing a better quality or more options. It also allows the use of different encoding strategies for different applications and leaves room for technological progress in analysis and decoding strategies.

MPEG-4 is building on the proven success of three fields: digital television, interactive graphics, and applications/synthetic content of the World Wide Web (distribution of and access to content), and provides the standardized technological elements enabling the integration of the production, distribution, and content access paradigms of the three fields.

5.6.3 Object-Based Coding Syntax

This syntax allows coding of rectangular and arbitrarily shaped video objects in a scene. Furthermore, the syntax supports both nonscalable coding and scalable coding. Thus, it becomes possible to handle normal scalability as well as object-based scalability. The syntax scalability enables reconstruction of useful video from pieces of a total bit stream. This is achieved by structuring the total bit stream in two or more layers, starting from a standalone base layer and adding a number of enhanced layers. For efficient coding of VOPs, both temporal and spatial redundancies are exploited. Thus, a coded representation of VOP includes representation of its shape, motion, and texture. Video objects can be of either natural or synthetic origin.

Natural Textures, Images, and Video. The tools for representing a natural video in MPEG-4 aim at providing standardized core technologies allowing efficient storage, transmission, and manipulation of textures, images, and video data for multimedia environments. These tools allow the decoding and representation of atomic units of image and video content called Video Objects (VOs). An example of a VO could be a talking person (without background) who can then be composed with other audiovisual objects to create a scene. Conventional rectangular imagery is handled as a special case of such objects. In order to achieve this broad goal rather than a solution for a narrow set of applications, functionalities common to several applications are clustered. Therefore, the video part of MPEG-4 provides a solution in the form of tools and algorithms for [270–272]:

- Efficient compression of images and video
- Efficient compression of texture for texture mapping on 2D and 3D meshes
- Efficient compression of implicit 2D meshes
- Efficient compression of time-varying geometry streams that animate meshes
- Efficient random access to all types of video objects
- Extended manipulation of functionalities for images and video sequences
- Content-based coding of images and video
- Content-based scalability of textures, images, and video
- Spatial, temporal, and quality (SNR) scalabilities
- Error robustness and resilience in error-prone environments

Face Object. The face is an object capable of facial geometry ready for rendering and animation. The shape, texture, and expressions of the face are generally controlled by the bit stream containing instances of Facial Definition Parameter (FDP) sets and/or Facial Animation Parameter (FAP) sets. Upon construction, the face object contains a generic face with a natural expression. The face can already be rendered. It is also immediately capable of receiving the FAPs from the bit stream, which will produce the animation of the face: expression, speech, and so forth. If FDPs are received, they are used to transform the generic face into a particular face determined by its shape and (optionally) texture. Optionally, a complete face model can be downloaded via the FDP set as a scene graph for insertion in the face node.

A 3D (or 2D) face object is a representation of the human face that is structured for portraying the visual of speech and facial expressions adequate to achieve visual speech intelligibility and the recognition of the mood of the speaker. A face object is animated by a stream of Face Animation Parameters (FAP) encoded for low-bandwidth transmission in broadcast (one-to-many) or dedicated interactive (point-to-point) communications. The FAPs manipulate key feature control points in a mesh model of the face to produce animation for the mouth (lips, tongue, teeth), as well as animation of the head and facial features like the eyes. FAPs are quantized with careful consideration for the limited movements of facial features, and then prediction errors are calculated followed by arithmetic coding. The remote manipulation of a face model in a terminal with FAP can accomplish lifelike visual scenes of the speaker in real time without sending pictorial or video details of face imagery for every frame.

A simple streaming connection can be made to a decoding terminal that animates a default face model. A more complex session can initialize a custom face in a more capable terminal by downloading FDP from the encoder. The specific background images, facial textures, and head geometry can be portrayed. The FAP stream can be generated by the user's terminal from video/audio, or from text-to-speech. FAPs can be encoded at bit rates up to 2–3 Kbits/s. Optional temporal DCT coding provides further compression efficiency in exchange for delay. Limited scalability is supported. Face animation achieves its efficiency by employing very concise motion animation controls in the channel, while relying on a suitably equipped terminal for rendering of moving 2D/3D faces with nonnormative models held in local memory.

Mesh Object.   A 2D mesh object is a representation of 2D deformable geometric shape, with which synthetic video objects may be created during a composition process at the decoder, by spatially piecewise warping of existing video object planes or still texture objects. The instances of mesh objects at a given time are called Mesh Object Planes (MOPs). The geometry of mesh object planes is coded losslessly. Temporally and spatially predictive techniques and variable-length coding are used to compress 2D mesh geometry. The coded representation of a 2D mesh object includes representation of its geometry and motion.

Object-Based Nonscalable Syntax.   The coded representation defined in the nonscalable syntax achieves a high compression ratio while preserving good image quality. Further, when access to individual objects is desired, the shape of objects also needs to be coded. Depending on the bandwidth available, the shape information can be coded lossy or losslessly.

The compression algorithm employed for texture data is not lossless as the exact sample values are not preserved during coding. Obtaining good image quality at the bit rates of interest demands very high compression, which is not achievable with intracoding alone. The need for random access, however, is best satisfied with pure intracoding. The choice of the techniques is based on the need to balance a high image quality and compression ratio with the requirement to make random access to the coded bit stream. A number of techniques are used to achieve high compression. The algorithm first uses block-based motion compression to reduce the temporal redundancy. Motion compensation is used both for causal prediction of the current VOP from the previous VOP, and for noncausal, interpolative prediction from past and future VOPs. Motion vectors are defined for each 16-pel-by-16-line region of a VOP or 8-pel-by-8-line region of a VOP. The prediction error is further compressed using DCT to remove spatial correlation before it is quantized in an irreversible process that discards the less important information. Finally, the shape information, motion vectors, and the quantized DCT information are encoded using variable-length codes.

Temporal Processing.   Because of the conflicting requirements of random access and highly efficient compression, three main VOP types are defined. Intracoded VOPs (I-VOPs) are coded without references to other frames. They provide access points to the coded sequence where decoding can begin, but are encoded with only moderate compression. Predictive-coded VOPs (P-VOPs) are coded more efficiently using motion-compensated prediction from past intra- or predictive-coded VOPs and are generally used as a reference for further prediction. Bidirectionally predictive-coded VOPs (B-VOPs) provide the highest degree of compression but require both past and future VOPs for motion compensation. Bidirectionally predictive-coded VOPs are never used as a reference for prediction (except in the case that the resulting VOP is used as a reference for a scalable enhancement layer). The organization of the three VOP types in a sequence is very flexible. The choice is left to the encoder and will depend on the requirements of the application.

Shape Coding.   In natural video scenes, VOPs are generated by segmentation of the scene according to some semantic meaning. For such scenes, the shape information is thus binary (binary shape). Shape information is also referred to as the *alpha plane*. The binary alpha plane is coded on a MB basis by a coder that uses context information, motion compensation, and arithmetic coding. For coding the shape of a VOP, a bounding rectangle is first created and is extended to multiples of 16×16 blocks with extended alpha samples to zero. Shape coding is then initiated on a 16×16 block basis. These blocks are also referred to as *binary* alpha blocks. An example showing how it is partitioned into shape blocks as the first step for its encoding process is shown in Figure 5.19. Each shape block is then coded by detecting its color-changing pixels from opaque (255) to transparent (0), and vice versa. Then the distances between successive changing pixels are calculated. If all the pixels in a shape block are of the same color, the coding is not carried out. In this case, only a flag is transmitted to the decoder, informing it that the shape information for that shape block is either all transparent or all opaque.

Motion Representation. The choice of 16×16 blocks (referred to as *macroblocks*) for the motion-compensation unit is a result of the trade-off between the coding gain provided by using motion information and the overhead needed to represent it. Each macroblock can further be subdivided to 8×8 blocks for motion estimation and compensation depending on the overhead that can be afforded. Depending on the type of the macroblock, motion vector information and other side information are encoded. It is the responsibility of the encoder to estimate the appropriate motion vector. The specification does not specify how this should be done.

Spatial Redundancy Reduction. Both source VOPs and VOP prediction errors have significant spatial redundancy. This specification uses a block-based DCT method with optional visually weighted quantization, and run-length coding. After motion-compensated prediction or interpolation, the resulting prediction error is split into 8×8 blocks. These are transformed into the DCT domain where they can be weighted before quantization. After quantization, many of the DCT coefficients are zero in value and so two-dimensional run-length and variable-length coding is used to encode the remaining DCT coefficients efficiently.

Generalized Scalability. The tools in the MPEG-4 specification are designed to support applications beyond those supported by a single-layer video. MPEG-4 allows for object-based temporal spatial and hybrid scalabilities (see Chapter 4 for details). These scalabilities are applied to VOPs.

FIGURE 5.19 Shape coding of a VOP [273]. ©1998 ISO/IEC.

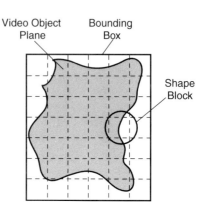

5.6.4 MPEG-4 Terminal

Streams coming from the network or a storage device as TransMux streams are demultiplexed into FlexMux streams and passed to appropriate FlexMux demultiplexers that retrieve elementary streams (ESs) as shown in Figure 5.20. The ESs are parsed and passed to the appropriate decoders. Decoding recovers the data in an AV object from its encoded form and performs the necessary operations to reconstruct the original AV object ready for rendering on the appropriate device. Audio and video objects are represented in their coded form. The reconstructed AV object is made available to the composition layer for potential use during scene rendering. Decoder AVOs, along with scene description information, are used to compose the scene as described by the author. The user can, to the extent allowed by the author, interact with the scene that is eventually rendered and presented.

Individual ESs have to be retrieved from incoming data from network connection or a storage device. Each network connection or file is homogeneously considered a TransMux channel in the MPEG-4 system model. The demultiplexing is partially or completely done by layers (outside the scope of MPEG-4), depending on the application. For integrating MPEG-4 in system environments, the stream multiplex interface (see Figure 5.17) is the reference

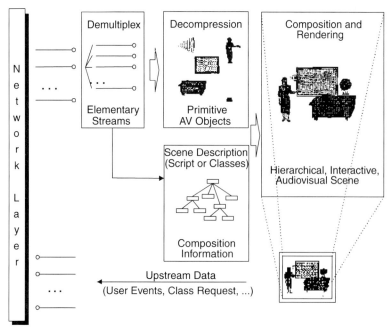

FIGURE 5.20   Major components of an MPEG-4 terminal: receiver side [267].
©1998 ISO/IEC.

point. Adaptation-layer packetized streams are delivered at this interface. The FlexMux layer specifies the optional FlexMux tool. The TransMux interface specifies how either AL-packetized streams (no FlexMux used) or FlexMux streams are to be retrieved from the TransMux layer. This is the interface to the transport functionalities not defined by MPEG-4.

In the same way that MPEG-1 and MPEG-2 described the behavior of an idealized decoding device along with the bit stream syntax and semantics, MPEG-4 defines a system decoder model. This allows the precise definition of the terminal's operation without making unnecessary assumptions about implementation details. This is essential in order to give implementers the freedom to design practical MPEG-4 terminals and decoding devices in a variety of ways. These devices range from television receivers that have no ability to communicate with the sender to computers that are fully enabled with bidirectional communications. Some devices will receive MPEG-4 streams over isochronous networks while others will use nonisochronous means (for example, Internet) to exchange MPEG-4 information. The System Decoder Model provides a common model on which all implementations of MPEG-4 terminals can be based.

5.6.5 Structure of the Tools for Representing Natural Video

The MPEG-4 image and video coding algorithms provide an efficient representation of visual objects of arbitrary shape, with the goal to support so-called content-based functionalities. Next to this, MPEG-4 supports most functionalities already provided by MPEG-1 and MPEG-2, including the provision to efficiently compress standard rectangular-sized video sequences at varying levels of input formats, frame rates, pixel depth, bit rates, and various levels of spatial, temporal, and SNR scalabilities.

A basic classification of the bit rates and functionalities currently provided by the MPEG-4 Visual standard for natural images and video is depicted in Figure 5.21, with the attempt to cluster bit rate levels versus sets of functionalities.

At the left bottom of Figure 5.21, a Very Low Bit Rate Video (VLBV) core provides algorithms and tools for applications operating at bit rates typically between 5–64 Kbits/s, supporting video sequences with low spatial resolution (typically up to CIF resolution) and low frame rates (typically up to 15 Hz). The basic application-specific functionalities supported by the VLBV core include:

- VLBV coding of conventional rectangular size video sequences with high coding efficiency and high error robustness/resilience, low latency and low complexity for real-time multimedia communications applications

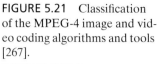

FIGURE 5.21   Classification of the MPEG-4 image and video coding algorithms and tools [267].

©1998 ISO/IEC.

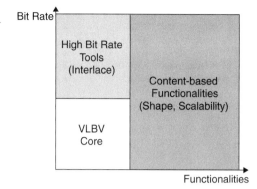

- Provisions for "random access," "fast forward" and "fast reverse" operations for VLB multimedia, database storage, and access applications

The same basic functionalities outlined above are also supported at higher bit rates with a higher range of spatial and temporal input parameters up to ITU-R Rec.601 resolutions—employing identical or similar algorithms and tools as the VLBV core. The bit rates envisioned range typically from 64 Kbits/s up to 4 Mbits/s, and applications envisioned include broadcast or interactive retrieval of video with a quality comparable to digital TV. For these applications at higher bit rates, tools for coding interlaced signals are specified in MPEG-4.

Content-based functionalities support the separate encoding and decoding of content (that is, physical objects in a scene, VOs). This MPEG-4 feature provides the most elementary mechanism for interactivity: flexible representation and manipulation with/of VO content of images or video in the compressed domain, without the need for further segmentation or transcoding at the receiver.

For the hybrid coding natural as well as synthetic visual data (for example, for virtual presence or virtual environments), the content-based coding functionality allows mixing a number of VOs from different sources with synthetic objects, such as a virtual background.

The extended MPEG-4 algorithms and tools for content-based functionalities can be seen as a superset of the VLBV core and high bit rate tools, meaning that the tools provided by the VLBV and High Bit Rate Video (HBV) cores are complemented by additional elements.

Content-based coding (interactivity, manipulation, composition) is illustrated in Figure 5.22. This object-layered coding approach is specified by the MPEG-4 [221, 270]. The coding of video sequences using MPEG-4 VOPs enables basic content-based functionalities at the decoder. Each VOP specifies particular video sequence content and is coded into a separate Video Object Layer (VOL) by coding contour, motion, and texture information. Decoding

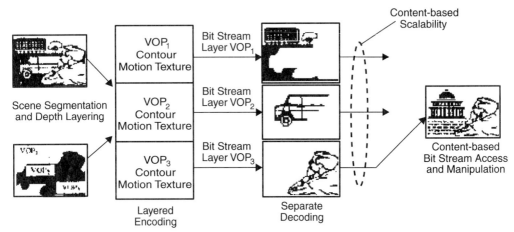

FIGURE 5.22   The object layer coding approach specified by the MPEG-4 video coding standard [221]. ©1997 IEEE.

of all VOP layers reconstructs the original video sequence. Content can be reconstructed by separately decoding a single or a set of VOL layers (content-based scalability/access in the compressed domain). This allows content-based manipulation at the decoder without the need for transcoding.

The input to be coded in Figure 5.22 can be a VOP image region of arbitrary shape. The shape and location of the region can vary from frame to frame. Successive VOPs belonging to the same physical object in a scene are referred to as *video objects*—a sequence of VOPs of possibly arbitrary shape and position. The shape, motion, and texture information of the VOPs belonging to the same VO is encoded and transmitted to be coded into a separate video layer (VOL). Relevant information needed to identify each of the VOLs, as well as how the various VOLs are composed at the receiver to reconstruct the entire original sequence, is also included in the bit stream. This allows the separate decoding of each VOP and the required flexible manipulation of the video sequence. The video source input assumed for the VOL structure either already exists in terms of separate entities or is generated by means of online or offline segmentation algorithms.

As shown in Figure 5.23, the MPEG-4 video standard also supports the coding of rectangular-shape image sequences. This involves motion prediction/compensation followed by DCT-based texture coding. For the content-based functionalities where the image sequence input may be of arbitrary shape and location, this approach is extended by also coding shape and transparency information. Shape may be either represented by an 8-bit transparency component (which allows the description of transparency if one VO is composed

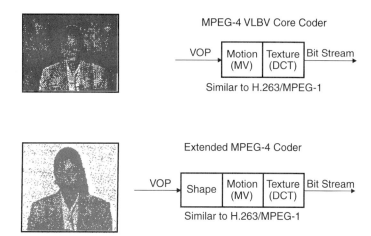

FIGURE 5.23   MPEG-4 VLBV core and the extended core coder [221].
©1997 IEEE.

with other objects) or by a binary mask. The extended MPEG-4 content-based approach can be seen as a logical extension of the conventional MPEG-4 VLBV core or high bit rate tools toward input of arbitrary shape.

Figure 5.24 depicts the MPEG-4 general philosophy of a content-based VOP multiscale video coding scheme. Three layers are provided, each layer supporting a VOP at different spatial resolution scales; in other words, a multi-resolution representation can be achieved by downscaling the input video signal into a lower-resolution video. The downscaled version is encoded into a base-layer bit stream with reduced bit rate. The upscaled reconstructed base-layer video is used as a prediction for the coding of the original input video signal. The prediction error is encoded into an enhancement-layer bit stream. If a receiver is either not capable or not willing to display the full quality VOPs, downscaled VOP signals can be reconstructed by only decoding the lower-layer bit streams. The display of the VOP at higher resolution with reduced quality is also possible by only decoding the lower bit rate base layer(s). Thus, scalable coding can be used to encode content-based video with a suitable bit rate allocated to each layer in order to meet specific bandwidth requirements of transmission channels or storage media.

5.6.6   MPEG-4 Video Verification Model

The MPEG-4 video VM describes a first "common core" video coding algorithm for the collaborative work within the MPEG-4 Video Group. The January 1996 MPEG meeting witnessed the release of the first version of this model. Based on the core algorithm, a number of core experiments are defined

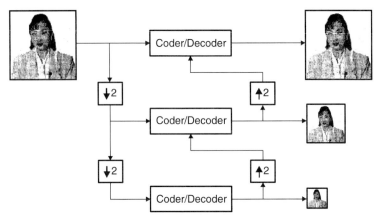

FIGURE 5.24 Content-based VOP multiscale video coding scheme [270].
©1997 IEEE.

with the aim to collaboratively improve the efficiency and functionality of the first VM and to iteratively converge through several versions of the VM toward the final MPEG-4 video coding standard.

The MPEG-4 scenario in terms of standardized components for coding of visual data is summarized in Figure 5.25, which represents a scenario of tools, algorithms, and profiles for the MPEG-4. The MPEG-4 "visual" part of the toolbox contains tools, including fully defined algorithms, for coding both natural pixel-based video and synthetic visual input; in other words, two-dimensional or three-dimensional computer model data sets. The tools can be flexibly combined at the encoder and decoder to enable efficient hybrid natural and synthetic coding video data.

The dynamic coding approach can be fully incorporated within the framework of the VM of MPEG-4 [271]. As illustrated in Figure 5.26, dynamic coding operates along a two-step procedure. The first step defines the set of admissible solutions with respect to the application, whereas the second step

FIGURE 5.25 MPEG-4 scenario of tools, algorithms, and profiles for the MPEG-4 video coding standard [270].
©1997 IEEE.

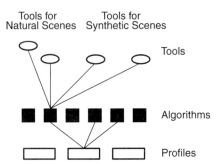

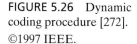

FIGURE 5.26   Dynamic
coding procedure [272].
©1997 IEEE.

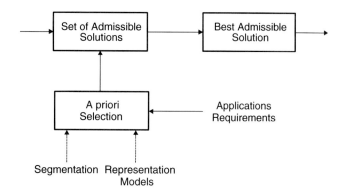

identifies the first admissible strategy. In other words, the first step of a priori
selection defines a set of solutions in which the system is allowed to search for
an appropriate coding scenario. Each coding strategy belonging to the set of
admissible solutions is a very particular way of representing a set of data and
results in different characteristics such as rate, distortion, error signal statistics, number of segmented regions, and so on. Therefore, the second step is
to point out the coding scenario that is optimal with respect to a predefined
criterion. This requires the definition of a criterion together with a procedure
for determining the optimal solution. However, this procedure is transparent
to the decoder.

The general structure of the MPEG-4 VM encoder is shown in
Figure 5.27. The significant feature of this encoder is the representation based
on VO when defining a visual scene. A user, or an intelligent algorithm, may
choose to encode different VOs composing a source data with different
parameters, different encoding methods, or may even choose not to code some
of them. In most applications, each VO represents a semantically meaningful
object in the scene. To maintain a certain compatibility with available video
materials, each uncompressed VO is represented as a set of Y, U, and V components plus information about its shape, stored frame after frame in predefined temporal intervals. Another important feature of the VM is that the
encoder and decoder can therefore function at different frame rates that do
not even need to be constant throughout the video sequence. Interactivity
between the user and the encoder or the decoder can be concluded in different
ways. The user may decide to interact at the encoding level, either in coding
control to distribute the available bit rate among different VOs or to influence
the multiplexing to change parameters such as the composition script at the
encoder. The user can also influence the decoding at the demultiplexer by
requesting the processing of a portion of the bit stream only, such as the shape.

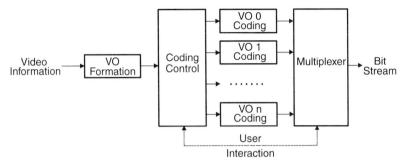

FIGURE 5.27   Block diagram of the encoder in the MPEG-4 video VM [265].
©1998 ISO/IEC.

General structure of the MPEG-4 VM decoder is presented in Figure 5.28. The structure of the decoder is similar to that of the encoder in reverse, except for the composition block. The method of the decomposition of different VOs depends on the applications and the method of multiplexing used at system level. One important issue is that of synchronization among different VOs and other entities such as audio data.

In order to fulfill the required functionalities of the VM, the data structure used in the syntax of encoder/decoder should be designed carefully. The following hierarchy of classes is used in the VM syntax: Video Session, Video Object, Video Object Layer, Video Object Plane.

Video Session is a collection of one or more Video Objects, each of which may consist of one or more layers. Each layer consists of one ordered sequence of snapshots in time. Video Object is a class defining specific objects in a scene. Object scalability is achieved using the Video Object class. Video Object Layer is a class that enhances the temporal or spatial scalabilities (Section 4.7).

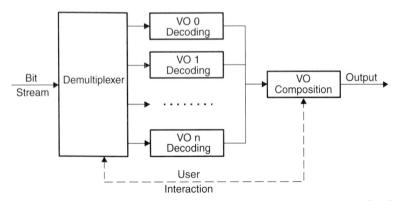

FIGURE 5.28   Block diagram of the decoder in the MPEG-4 video VM [265].
©1998 ISO/IEC.

Video Object Plane (VOP) represents an occurrence of a Video Object (VO) at a given time. Two different VOPs may belong to the same object at two different times. The VO corresponds to entities in the bit stream that the user can access and manipulate (cut, paste, and so on). The encoder sends together with the VOP composition information (using composition-layer syntax) to indicate where and when each VOP is to be displayed. At the decoder side, the user may be allowed to change the composition information. The VOP can be a semantic object in the scene: It is made of Y, U, V (luminance and chrominance) components plus shape information.

5.6.7   Video Coding Algorithms

Video coding algorithms were initially evaluated in January 1996 [274]. There are nine evaluation criteria for these algorithms:

- Functionality addressed.
- Picture quality: frame rate of tape, buffer control, and dominant artifacts.
- Efficiency.
- Adaptability: range of scenes, bit rates, error conditions, resolution, and delay.
- Algorithm characterization: motion estimation, motion compensation, texture coding, shape coding, and syntax.
- Implementation complexity: encoder and decoder.
- Additional advantages.
- Margin and timeframe for improvement.
- List of relevant core experiments.

Picture quality is certainly the most important and most difficult item to evaluate. While frame rate and buffer control algorithms are objective measures, getting an agreement on whether an algorithm introduces a dominant artifact like ringing or blocking is difficult. The viewing conditions, like distance to the monitor and room illumination, were not specified. Figure 5.29 outlines the basic approach of the MPEG-4 video algorithms to encode rectangular as well as arbitrarily shaped input image sequences.

The basic coding structure involves shape coding (for arbitrarily shaped VOs) and motion compensation, as well as DCT-based texture coding (using standard 8×8 DCT or shape adaptive DCT) [273].

An important advantage of the content-based coding approach taken by MPEG-4 is that the compression efficiency can be significantly improved for some video sequences by using appropriate and dedicated object-based motion prediction "tools" for each object in a scene. A number of motion

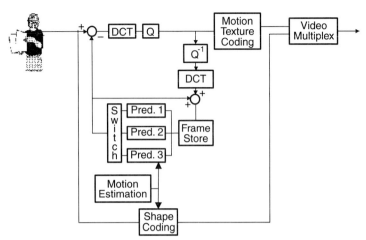

FIGURE 5.29   Basic block diagram of the MPEG-4 video coder [267].
©1998 ISO/IEC.

prediction techniques can be used to allow efficient coding and flexible presentation of the objects.

- Standard 8×8 or 16×16 pixel block-based motion estimation and compensation.
- Global motion compensation using eight motion parameters that describes an affine transformation.
- Global motion compensation based on the transmission of a static "sprite" [273]. A static sprite is a possibly large still image, describing a panoramic background. For each consecutive image in a sequence, only eight global motion parameters describing camera motion are coded to reconstruct the object. These parameters represent the appropriate affine transform of the sprite transmitted in the first frame.
- Global motion compensation based on dynamic sprites. Sprites are not transmitted with the first frame, but are dynamically generated over the scene.

VOP Encoder Structure.   Figure 5.30 presents a general overview of the VOP encoder structure [273]. The same encoding scheme is applied when coding all the VOPs of a given session. The encoder is mainly composed of two parts: the shape coder and the traditional motion and texture coder applied to the same VOP. The VOP is represented by means of a bounding rectangle. The phase between the luminance and chrominance samples of the bounding rectangle has to be correctly set according to 4:2:0 format, as shown in Figure 5.31. Specifically, the top-left coordinate of the bounding rectangle should be

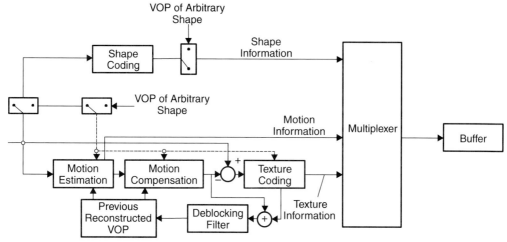

FIGURE 5.30   VOP encoder structure [273].
©1998 ISO/IEC.

rounded to the nearest even number not greater than the top-left coordinates of the tightest rectangle. Accordingly, the top-left coordinate of the bounding rectangle in the chrominance component is that of the luminance divided by 2.

For the purpose of texture padding, motion padding, and composition described further, the chrominance alpha plane is created from the luminance alpha plane by a conservative subsampling process. In the case of a binary alpha plane, this ensures that there is always a chroma sample where there is at least one luma sample inside the VOP.

In grayscale alpha plane for each 2×2 neighborhood of luminance alpha pixels, the associated chroma alpha pixel is set to the rounded average of the four luminance alpha pixels.

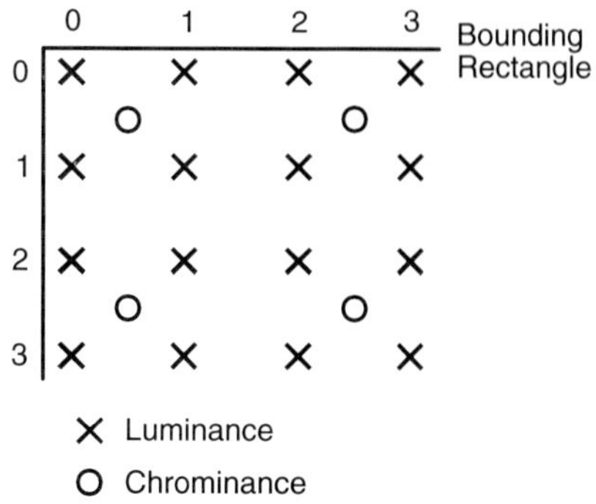

FIGURE 5.31   Luminance versus chrominance bounding box positioning [273].
©1998 ISO/IEC.

Shape Coding.   Shape coding describes the coding methods for binary and grayscale shape information. The shape information is referred to as *alpha planes*. Binary alpha planes are encoded by modified Context-Based Arithmetic Encoding (CAE), while grayscale alpha planes are encoded by motion-compensated DCT similar to texture coding. An alpha plane is bounded by a rectangle that includes the shape of a VOP. The bounding rectangle of the VOP is then extended on the right-bottom side to multiples of 16×16 blocks. The extended alpha samples are set to zero. The extended alpha plane is partitioned into blocks of 16×16 samples (referred to as *alpha blocks*) and the encoding/decoding process is done per alpha block. If the pixels in an MB are all transparent (all zero), the MB is skipped before motion and/or texture coding. No overhead is required to indicate this mode since this transparency information can be obtained from shape coding. This process applies to all I-, P-, and B-VOPs.

A binary alpha plane can be encoded in INTRA mode for I-VOPs and in INTER mode for P-VOPs and B-VOPs. The methods used are based on Binary Alpha Blocks (BABs), while the principal methods are block-based/context-based arithmetic coding and block-based motion compensation.

VOP-level size conversion is carried out before Motion Estimation (ME) and Motion Compensation (MC). MVs (Motion Vector of shape) is used for MC of shape. Overlapped MC [243, 244], half-sample MC, and 8×8 MC are not carried out. In the case that the region outside VOP is referred, the value for it is set to 0. For B-VOPs, forward MC is used and neither backward MC nor interpolated MC is used.

Depending on the value of Conversion Ratio (CR), the Binary Alpha Block (BAB) has the following sizes: (CR=1 BAB size=16×16), (CR=1/2 BAB size=8×8), (CR=1/4 BAB size=4×4).

The pixels in BAB are encoded by context-based arithmetic encoding (CAE). For encoding, the BAB pixels are scanned in raster order. However, the BAB may be transposed before encoding. Furthermore, for P-VOPs, it may be chosen to encode the BAB in INTRA or INTER mode.

Grayscale shape coding is shown in Figure 5.32. Gray-level alpha plane is encoded as its support function and the alpha values on the support. The support function is encoded by binary shape coding, while the alpha values are encoded as texture with arbitrary shape. The support is obtained by thresholding the gray-level alpha plane by 0.

The alpha values are partitioned into 16×16 blocks and encoded the same way as the luminance. The 16×16 blocks of alpha values are referred to as an *alpha macroblock*. The encoded data of an alpha macroblock are appended at

FIGURE 5.32 Grayscale
shape coding [273].
©1998 ISO/IEC.

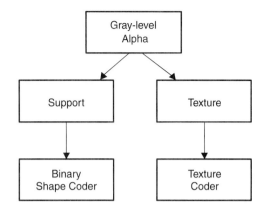

the end of the corresponding (texture) macroblock, or the encoded macro-block texture in the case of separate motion-texture mode.

Motion Estimation and Compensation. In order to perform motion prediction on a per VOP basis, the motion estimation of the blocks on the VOP borders has to be modified from block matching to polygon matching. Furthermore, a spatial padding technique (that is, the macroblock-based repetitive padding) is required for the reference VOP. Since the VOPs have arbitrary shapes rather than rectangular shapes, and the shapes change from time to time, some conventions are necessary to ensure the consistency of the motion compensation in the VM.

The absolute (frame) coordinate system is used for referencing all of the VOPs. At each particular time instance, a bounding rectangle that includes the shape of that VOP is defined. The left and top corners, in their absolute coordinates, of the bounding box are encoded in the VOP spatial reference. Thus, the motion vector for a particular feature inside a VOP (for example, a macroblock) refers to the displacement of the feature in absolute coordinates. No alignment of VOP bounding boxes at different time instances is performed.

In addition to the motion estimation and compensation mode, two additional modes are supported: unrestricted and advanced. In all three modes, the motion vector search range is up to $[-2^{fcode+3}, 2^{fcode+3} - 0.5]$ where $0 \le fcode \le 7$. This mode differs from the unrestricted motion mainly by restricting the motion vectors inside the bounding box of the VOP. The advanced mode allows multiple motion vectors in one macroblock and overlapped motion compensation. In all three modes, macroblock-based padding of the VOP is needed for both motion estimation and compensation.

The padding process defines the values of luminance and chrominance samples outside the VOP for production of arbitrarily shaped objects.

Figure 5.33 shows a simplified diagram of this process. A decimated MB d[y][x] is padded by referring to the corresponding decoded shape blocks [y][x]. The luminance component is padded per 16×16 samples, while the chrominance components are padded per 8×8 samples. A macroblock that lies on the VOP boundary (boundary macroblock) is padded by replicating the boundary samples of the VOP toward the exterior. This process is divided into horizontal repetitive padding and vertical repetitive padding [265]. Extended padding fills the remaining macroblocks that are completely outside the VOP (exterior macroblocks).

Unrestricted Motion Estimation/Compensation.   An unrestricted motion estimation mode is used for VOP motion estimation. The technique is to improve the motion estimation, especially for VOP-based coding schemes. In this technique, the error signal is generated by extending the reference VOP to enough size, padding the extended VOP, applying motion estimation, and taking the difference of the original and the signals. Padding is performed only on the reference VOP. Target VOP remains the same except for extending it to multiples of 16×16 blocks.

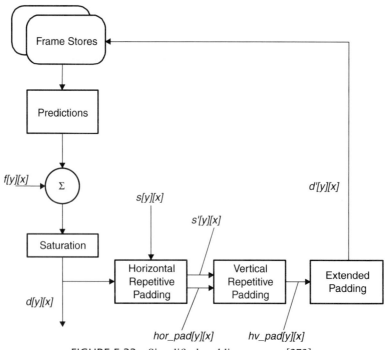

FIGURE 5.33   Simplified padding process [273].
©1998 ISO/IEC.

For the case of a rectangular VOP (nonarbitrary shape), the rectangle is extended in all four directions (left, top, right, and bottom) by $2^{fcode+3}$ pixels by repetitive padding. For arbitrarily shape VOPs, the bounding box is further extended in all four directions (left, top, right, and bottom) by $2^{fcode+3}$ pixels by repetitive padding.

For unrestricted motion compensation, the motion vectors are allowed to point outside the decoded area of a reference VOP. For an arbitrarily shape VOP, the decoded area refers to the area within the bounding box. VOP width and VOP height extended to multiples of 16 define a bounding box. When a sample referenced by a motion vector stays outside the decoded VOP area, an edge pel is used. Limiting the motion vectors to the best full pel position inside the decoded VOP area retrieves this edge pel. Limitation of a motion vector is performed on a pel basis and separately for component of the motion vector.

Modified Block (Polygon) Matching.   The bounding rectangle of the VOP is first extended on the right-bottom side to multiples of macroblock size. Therefore, the size of the bounding rectangle of the luminance VOP is multiples of 16×16, while the size of chrominance plane is multiples of 8×8. The alpha value of the extended pixels is set to be zero. The macroblocks are formed by dividing the extended bounding rectangles into 16×16 blocks. Zero stuffing is used for these extended pixels. Sum of Absolute Difference (SAD) is used as an error measure. The original alpha plane for the VOP is used to exclude the pixels of the macroblocks that are outside the VOP. SAD is computed only for the pixels with nonzero alpha value. This forms a polygon for the macroblock that includes the VOP boundary. Figure 5.34 illustrates an example.

The reference VOP is padded based on its own shape information. For example, when the reference VOP is smaller than the current VOP, the reference is not padded up to the size of the current VOP. In case the 8×8 advanced prediction made is chosen and all of the pixels in an 8×8 block are transparent (completely outside the VOP), no matching needs to be done.

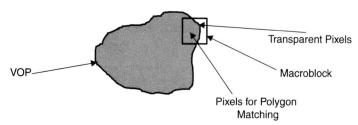

FIGURE 5.34   Polygon matching for an arbitrary shape VOP [273].
©1998 ISO/IEC.

Interlaced Motion Compensation.   When field-based motion compensation is specified (by the field prediction being "1"), two field motion vectors and corresponding reference fields are used to generate the prediction from each reference VOP.

The luminance prediction is generated as follows: The top field motion vector using the reference field specified defines the even lines of the macroblock (0,2,4,...,14). The motion vector is specified in frame coordinates—full sample vertical displacements correspond to even integer values of vertical motion vector coordinate, a half sample vertical displacement is denoted by odd integer values, and a quarter sample displacement by 0.5 values. When a subsample vertical offset is specified, only pixels from lines within the same reference field are combined. The same procedure is used to define the odd luminance lines of the macroblock using the bottom field motion vector and reference field.

Chrominance 4:2:0 motion compensation is done fieldwise. The even lines of a chrominance frame/VOP are derived from the top field chrominance, and the odd lines contain the bottom field chrominance. The top field motion vector and reference field define the even chrominance lines (0,2,4,6), and the bottom field motion vector and reference field define the odd chrominance lines (1,3,5,7). A chrominance motion vector is derived from the (luminance) motion vector by dividing each component by 2 and then rounding as follows:

- Mapping all fractional values into half-pixel offsets rounds the horizontal component.
- The vertical component is an integer and the resulting chrominance motion vector vertical component is rounded to an integer. If the result of dividing by 2 gives a noninteger value, it is rounded to the adjacent odd integer. The odd integer values denote vertical interpolation between lines of the same field.

Texture Coding.   The INTRA VOPs and residual data after motion compensation are coded using the same 8×8 block DCT scheme. DCT is implemented separately for each of the luminance and chrominance planes. Two types of macroblocks belong to an arbitrarily shaped VOP: those that lie completely inside the VOP, and those that lie on the boundary of the VOP. When the shape of the VOP is arbitrary, the macroblocks that belong to the arbitrary shape of the VOP are treated as follows: The former are coded based on the technique used in H.263 [242]. The INTRA 8×8 blocks that belong to the macroblocks lying on the border of the VOP are first padded. For padding of chroma blocks, 16×16 alpha blocks are decimated [265]. For residual blocks, the region outside the VOP within the blocks is padded with zeros. Padding is performed separately for each of the luminance and chrominance 8×8 blocks by using the original alpha values of the luminance or chrominance in this 8×8 block. Transparent blocks are skipped and therefore are not coded. These blocks are then coded in a manner identical to the interior blocks. Blocks that lie outside the original shape are padded using the value (128,128,128) for luminance and chrominance in case of intracoding, and (0,128,128) in case of predictive coding. The blocks that belong neither to the original nor the coded arbitrary shape but to the inside of the bounding box of a VOP are not coded at all.

The still image coding mode enables coding of the still image textures with a high coding efficiency as well as spatial and SNR scalabilities at fine granularity. The granularity of these scalabilities can be selected by the encoder from a wide range of possible levels. Figures 5.35–5.37 show three different examples of such scalabilities. In Figure 5.35, the bit stream has M layers of spatial scalability.

Figure 5.36 shows an example in which the bit stream includes N layers of SNR scalability. Figure 5.37 shows an example of combined spatial-SNR scalabilities. In this example, the bit stream consists of M spatial layers, and each spatial layer includes N layers of SNR scalabilities. The number and the kind of scalability (spatial, SNR) are described in the bit stream by the encoder. The block diagram of the encoder is shown in Figure 5.38.

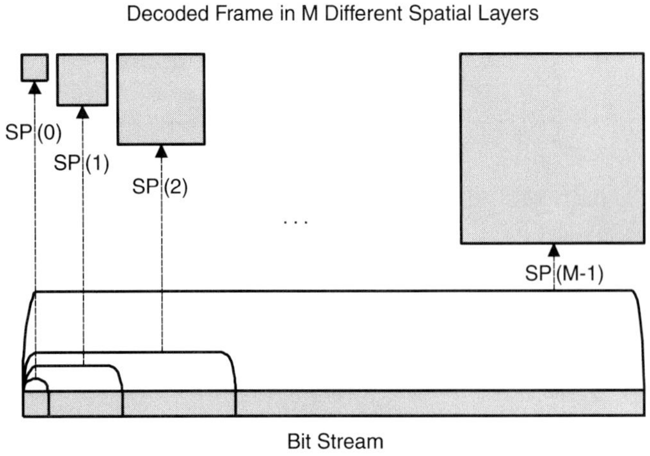

FIGURE 5.35   M layers of spatial scalability [273].
©1998 ISO/IEC.

Decoded Frame in N Different SNR Layers

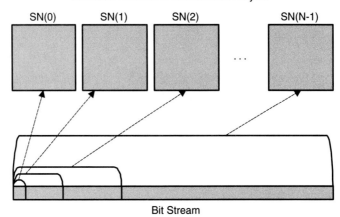

FIGURE 5.36 N layers of SNR scalability [273].
©1998 ISO/IEC.

Decoded Frame in Hybrid Spatial/SNR Layers

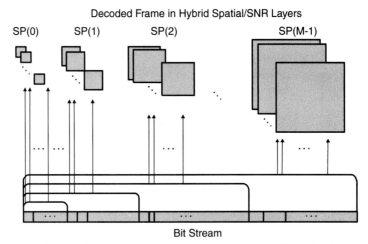

FIGURE 5.37 MxN layers of spatial/SNR scalabilities [273].
©1998 ISO/IEC.

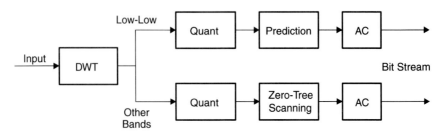

FIGURE 5.38 Block diagram of the still image encoder [273].
©1998 ISO/IEC.

The basic modules of a zero-tree wavelet-based coding scheme (see Figure 5.38) are as follows:

- Decomposition of the texture using discrete wavelet transform (DWT)
- Quantization of the wavelet coefficients
- Coding of the lowest-frequency subband using a predictive scheme
- Zero-Tree Scanning (ZTS) of the higher-order subband wavelet coefficients and the significant map

A two-dimensional separable wavelet decomposition is applied to the still texture to be coded. The wavelet decomposition is performed using a Daubechies (9,3) tap biorthogonal filter, which has been shown to provide good compression performance [273].

The wavelet coefficients of the lowest band are coded independently from the other bands. These coefficients are quantized using a uniform mid-riser quantizer. After quantization of the lowest subband coefficients, a DPCM coding scheme is applied to code the quantized values. Each of the current coefficients w_x is predicted from the three other quantized coefficients in its neighborhood (that is, w_a, w_b, and w_c (see Figure 5.39). The predicted value is subtracted from the current value.

The coefficients after the DPCM are then encoded using an adaptive Arithmetic Coder (AC). This value, "band offset," is subtracted from all the coefficients to limit their lower bound to zero. Next, the maximum value of the coefficients is found ("band max value"). The values "band offset" and "band max value" are put into the bit stream. The arithmetic coder is initialized with a uniform distribution of "band max value" and then the coefficients are scanned and coded using the adaptive arithmetic coder.

In order to achieve a wide range of scalability levels efficiently as needed by the application, a multiscale zero-tree coding scheme is employed. Figure 5.40 shows the concept of this technique. The wavelet coefficients of the first spatial (and/or SNR) layer are quantized with the quantizer Q_0. These

FIGURE 5.39 DPCM coding of lowest band coefficients [273]. ©1998 ISO/IEC.

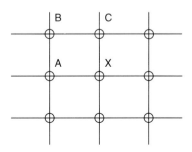

FIGURE 5.40 Multiscale zero-tree coding [265]. ©1998 ISO/IEC.

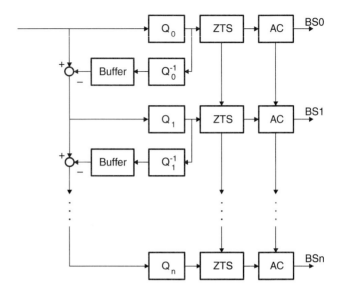

quantized coefficients are scanned using the zero-tree concept and then the significant maps and quantized coefficients are entropy coded. The output of the entropy coder at this level, BSO, is the first portion of the bit stream. The quantized wavelet coefficients of the first layer are also reconstructed and subtracted from the original wavelet coefficients. These residual wavelet coefficients are fed into the second stage of the coder in which the wavelet coefficients are quantized with Q_1, zero-tree scanned, and entropy coded. The quantized coefficients of the second stage are also reconstructed and subtracted from the original coefficients. N+1 stages of the scheme provide N+1 layers of scalability (see Figure 5.40).

In order to achieve a wide range of scalability levels efficiently as needed by the application, a multilevel quantization scheme is employed. The levels of quantization are obtained by the encoder and specified in the bit stream. This multilevel quantization scheme provides a very flexible approach to support the right trade-off between levels and type of scalability, complexity and coding efficiency for any application. After quantization, each wavelet coefficient is either zero or nonzero. Different quantization step sizes (one for luminance and one for chrominance) can be specified for each level of scalability. All the quantizers of the higher bands are uniform midrise quantizers with a dead zone two times the quantization step size. The encoder in the bit stream specifies these quantization step sizes.

In order to achieve the finest granularity of SNR scalability, a bilevel quantization scheme is used for all the multiple quantizers. This quantizer is also a uniform midrise quantizer with a dead zone two times the quantization step size. The coefficents that lie outside the dead zone (in the current and previous pass) are quantized with a 1-bit accuracy. The number of quantizers is equal to the maximum number of bit planes in the wavelet transform representation. In this bilevel case, instead of the quantization step sizes, the maximum number of bit planes is specified in the bit stream.

The zero-tree algorithm is based on the observation that strong correlation exists in the amplitudes of the wavelet coefficients across scales, and on the idea of partial ordering of the coefficients. The coefficients at the coarse scale are called the *parent*, and all coefficients at the same spatial location, and of similar orientation, at the next finer scale are that parent's *children*. Figure 5.41 shows a wavelet tree where the parents and the children are indicated by dots and connected by lines. Since the lowest-frequency subband (shown at the upper left in Figure 5.41) is coded separately using a DPCM scheme, the wavelet trees start from the adjacent higher bands.

In transform coding, it is generally true that a large percentage of the transform coefficients are quantized to zero. A substantial number of bits must be spent either encoding these zero-valued quantized coefficients, or encoding the location of the nonzero-valued quantized coefficients. Zero-tree coding uses a data structure called a *zero-tree* built on the parent-child relationships and used for encoding location of nonzero quantized wavelet coefficients. The zero-tree structure takes advantage of the principle that if a wavelet coefficient at a coarse scale is "insignificant" (quantized to zero), then all wavelet coefficients of the same orientation at the same spatial location at finer wavelet scales are also likely to be "insignificant."

FIGURE 5.41 The parent-child relationship of wavelet coefficients. [273]. ©1998 ISO/IEC.

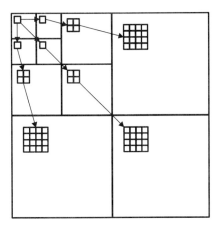

Zero-trees exist at any tree node where the coefficient is zero and all the node's children are zero-trees. The wavelet trees are efficiently represented and coded by scanning each tree from the root in the low-low band through the children, and assigning one of three symbols to each node encountered: zero-tree root, valued zero-tree root, and value. A zero-tree root denotes a coefficient that is the root of a zero-tree. Zero-trees do not need to be scanned further because it is known that all coefficients in such a tree have amplitude zero. A valued zero-tree is a node where the coefficient has a nonzero amplitude, and all four children are zero-tree roots. The scan of this tree can stop at this symbol. A value symbol identifies a coefficient with amplitude either zero or nonzero. The symbols and quantized coefficients are then losslessly encoded using an adaptive arithmetic coder. When bilevel quantization is applied, the significant map is coded with the following symbols: zero-tree root, isolated zero, valued zero-tree root, and value. The coefficients that are already found significant are replaced with zero symbols for zero-tree forming in later scans. In order to achieve both spatial and SNR scalabilities, two different scanning methods are employed in this scheme. For the spatial scalability, the wavelet coefficients are scanned in the subband by subband fashion, from the lowest- to highest-frequency subbands. For the SNR scalability, the wavelet coefficients are scanned in each tree from the top to the bottom.

The zero-tree symbols and the quantized values are coded using an adaptive arithmetic coder. The arithmetic coder adaptively tracks the statistics of the zero-trees. Symbols and quantized coefficient values generated by the zero-tree stage are all encoded using an adaptive arithmetic coder and a three-symbol alphabet. The list of other nonzero quantized coefficients that correspond one-to-one with the valued zero-tree root symbols are encoded using an alphabet that does not include zero. The remaining coefficients, which correspond one-to-one to the value symbols, are encoded using an alphabet that does include zero. For any node reached in a scan that is a leaf with no children, neither root symbol can apply. Therefore, some bits can be saved by not encoding any symbol for this node and encoding the coefficient using the alphabet that includes zero.

5.6.8   Video Decoding Process

The usual decoding process includes several processes such as shape-motion-texture decoding, still texture decoding, mesh decoding, and face decoding. After decoding the coded bit stream, it is sent to the compositor to integrate various visual objects. A higher-level view of basic visual decoding is shown in Figure 5.42. Specialized decoding such as scalable, sprite, and error-resilient

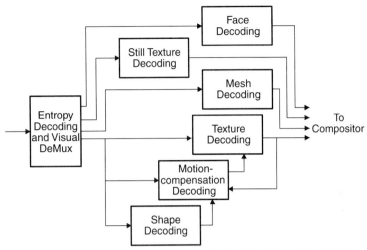

FIGURE 5.42   A high-level view of basic visual decoding [273].
©1998 ISO/IEC.

decoding are not shown [270]. With the exception of the IDCT, the decoding process is defined such that all decoders will produce numerically identical results. The IDCT specification is defined statistically such that different implementations for this function are allowed.

Figure 5.43 illustrates the video decoding process without any scalability. The diagram is simplified for clarity. The same decoding scheme is applied when decoding all the VOPs of a given session.

The decoder is mainly composed of three parts: the shape decoder, motion decoder, and texture decoder. The reconstructed VOP is obtained by combining the decoded shape, texture, and motion information.

The texture decoding process is used to decode the texture information of a VOP (see Figure 5.44).

By DC coefficients we mean $n=0$ in an INTRA coded block. n is the index of the coefficient in the appropriate zigzag scan order. The AC coefficients are obtained by decoding the variable length codes to produce EVENTs. An EVENT is a combination of a last nonzero coefficient indication, the number of successive zeros preceding the coded coefficient (RUN), and the nonzero value of the coded coefficient (LEVEL). The color component cc is related to the block number as specified in Table 5.5. Thus, cc is zero for the Y component, one and two for the first and second chrominance components, respectively.

One-dimensional data QFS[n] at the output of the variable-length decoder is converted into a two-dimensional array of coefficients denoted by

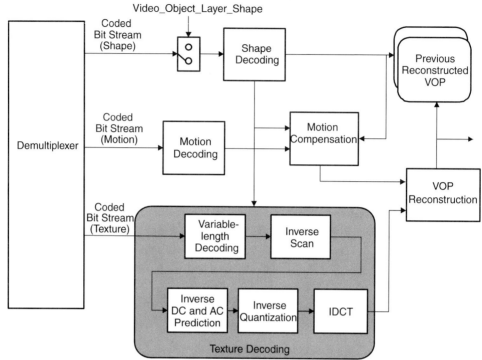

FIGURE 5.43 Simplified video decoding process [275].
©1998 ISO/IEC.

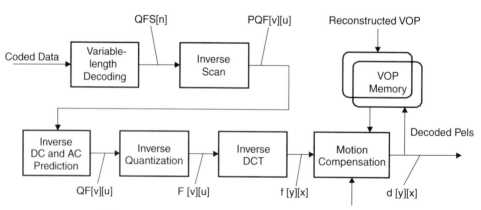

FIGURE 5.44 Video texture decoding process [275].
©1998 ISO/IEC.

PQF[v][u], where u and v both lie in the range of 0 to 7. n is in the range of 0 to 63. Three scan patterns are defined as shown in Figure 5.45: (a) alternate-horizontal scan, (b) alternate-vertical scan, and (c) zigzag scan. The scan that shall

TABLE 5.5   Color Component
Identification [275]

Block Number	cc 4:2:0
0	0
1	0
2	0
3	0
4	1
5	2

©1998 ISO/IEC.

be used is determined by the following method. For INTRA blocks, if acpred_flag=0, zigzag scan is selected for all blocks in a macroblock. Otherwise, DC prediction direction is used to select a scan on a block basis. If the DC prediction refers to the horizontally adjacent block, alternate vertical scan is selected for the current block. Otherwise (for DC prediction referring to vertically adjacent block), alternate-horizontal scan is used for the current block. For all other blocks, the 8×8 blocks of transform coefficients are scanned in the zigzag scanning direction.

The two-dimensional array of coefficients, QF[v][u], is inverse quantized to produce the reconstructed DCT coefficients. This process is essentially a multiplication by the quantizer step size. The quantizer step size is modified by two mechanisms; a weighting matrix is used to modify the step size within a block, and scale factor is used in order that the step size can be modified at the cost of only a few bits (as compared to encoding an entire new weighting matrix).

0	1	2	3	10	11	12	13
4	5	8	9	17	16	15	14
6	7	19	18	26	27	28	29
20	21	24	25	30	31	32	33
22	23	34	35	42	43	44	45
36	37	40	41	46	47	48	49
38	39	50	51	56	57	58	59
52	53	54	55	60	61	62	63

(a)

0	4	6	20	22	36	38	52
1	5	7	21	23	37	39	53
2	8	19	24	34	40	50	54
3	9	18	25	35	41	51	55
10	17	26	30	42	46	56	60
11	16	27	31	43	47	57	61
12	15	28	32	44	48	58	62
13	14	29	33	45	49	59	63

(b)

0	1	5	6	14	15	27	28
2	4	7	13	13	26	29	42
3	8	12	17	25	30	41	43
9	11	18	24	31	40	44	53
10	19	23	32	39	45	52	54
20	22	33	38	46	51	55	60
21	34	37	47	50	56	59	61
35	36	48	49	57	58	62	63

(c)

FIGURE 5.45   Three scan patterns: (a) alternate-horizontal, (b) alternate-vertical, (c) zigzag [275].
©1998 ISO/IEC.

Figure 5.46 illustrates the overall inverse quantization process. After the appropriate inverse quantization, the resulting coefficients, F"[v][u], are saturated to yield F'[v][u] and then a mismatch control operation is performed to give the final reconstructed DCT coefficients, F[v][u].

Once the DCT coefficients, F[u][v] are reconstructed, the inverse DCT is applied to obtain the inverse transformed values, f[y][x]. These values will be saturated so that: $-2^{N\_bit} \le f[y][x] \le 2^{N\_bit} - 1$, for all x, y.

Generalized Scalable Decoding. Generalized scalable decoding is the additional decoding process required for decoding scalable coded video. The scalability framework is referred to as *generalized scalability*, which includes the spatial and the temporal scalabilities. Figure 5.47 shows a high-level decoder structure for generalized scalability.

The base layer and enhancement layer bit streams are input for decoding by the corresponding base-layer decoder and enhancement-layer decoder. When spatial scalability is to be performed, midprocessor 1 performs spatial up or downsampling of input. The scalability postprocessor performs any necessary operations such as spatial up- or downsampling of the decoded base layer for display resulting at up outp_0, while the enhancement layer without resolution conversion may be output as outp_1.

When temporal scalability is performed, the decoding of base- and enhancement-layer bit streams occurs in the corresponding base- and enhancement-layer decoders as shown. In this case, midprocessor 1 does not perform any spatial resolution conversion. The postprocessor simply outputs the base-layer VOPs without any conversion, but temporally multiplexes the base- and enhancement-layer VOPs to produce a higher temporal resolution enhancement layer.

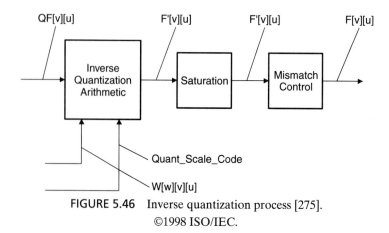

FIGURE 5.46 Inverse quantization process [275].
©1998 ISO/IEC.

FIGURE 5.47   High-level decoder structure for generalized scalability [275]. ©1998 ISO/IEC.

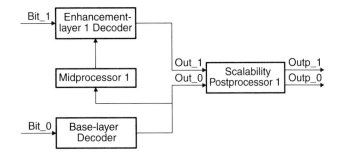

The reference VOPs for prediction are selected by reference select code as specified in Tables 5.6 and 5.7.

In coding of P-VOPs belonging to an enhancement layer, the forward reference is one of the following four: the most recently decoded VOP of the enhancement layer, the most recent VOP of the reference layer in display order, the next VOP of the lower layer in display order, or the temporally coincident VOP in the reference layer.

TABLE 5.6   Prediction Reference Choice in Enhancement-Layer P-VOPs for Scalability [275]

ref_select_code	Forward Prediction Reference
00	Most recently decoded enhancement VOP belonging to the same layer
01	Most recent VOP in display order belonging to the reference layer
10	Next VOP in display order belonging to the reference layer
11	Temporally coincident VOP in the reference layer (no motion vectors)

©1998 ISO/IEC.

TABLE 5.7   Prediction Reference Choices in Enhancement-Layer B-VOPs for Scalability [275]

ref_select_code	Forward Temporal Reference	Backward Temporal Reference
00	Most recently decoded enhancement VOP of the same layer	Temporally coincident VOP in the reference layer (no motion vectors)
01	Most recently decoded enhancement VOP of the same layer	Most recent VOP in display order belonging to the reference layer
10	Most recently decoded enhancement VOP of the same layer	Next VOP in display order belonging to the reference layer
11	Most recent VOP in display order belonging to the reference layer	Next VOP in display order belonging to the reference layer

©1998 ISO/IEC.

In B-VOPs, the forward reference is on of the following two: the most recently decoded enhancement VOP, or the most recent lower-layer VOP in display order. The backward reference is one of the following three: the temporally coincident VOP in the lower layer, the most recent lower-layer VOP in display order, or the next lower-layer VOP in display order.

Temporal scalability involves two layers, a lower layer and an enhancement layer. Both the lower and the enhancement layers process the same spatial resolution. The enhancement layer enhances the temporal resolution of the lower layers and, if temporally remultiplexed with the lower layer, provides full temporal rate. In the case of temporal scalability, the decoded VOPs of the enhancement layer are used to increase the frame rate of the base layer. Figure 5.48 shows a simplified diagram of the motion-compensation process for the enhancement layer using temporal scalability. Predicted samples p[y][x] are formed either from frame stores of the base layer or frame stores of the enhancement layer. The difference data samples f[y][x] are added to p[y][x] to form the decoded samples d[y][x].

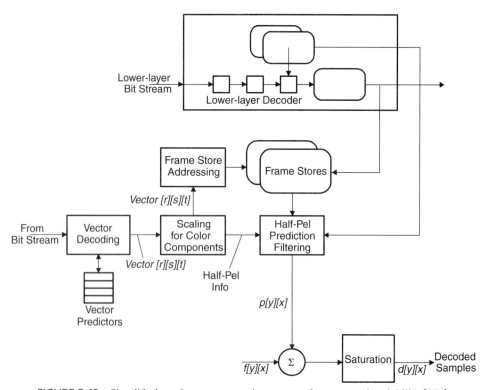

FIGURE 5.48 Simplified motion-compensation process for temporal scalability [275].
©1998 ISO/IEC.

There are two types of enhancement structures indicated by the "enhancement_type" flag. When the value of enhancement_type is 1, the enhancement layer increases the temporal resolution of a partial region of the base layer. When the value of enhancement_type is 0, the enhancement layer increases the temporal resolution of an entire region of the base layer.

The decoding process of the base layer is the same as the nonscalable decoding process. The VOP of the enhancement layer is decoded as I-VOP, P-VOP, or B-VOP. The shape of the VOP is either rectangular or arbitrary.

In the case of spatial scalability, the enhancement bit stream is used to increase the resolution of the image. When the output with lower resolution is required, only the base layer is decoded. When the output with higher resolution is required, both the base layer and the enhancement layer are decoded.

Figure 5.49 is a diagram of the video decoding process with spatial scalability. The decoding process of the base layer is the same as the nonscalable decoding process. A motion-compensated temporal prediction is made from reference VOPs in the enhancement layer. In addition, a spatial prediction is formed from the lower-layer decoded frame ($d_{lower}[y][x]$). These predictions are selected individually or combined to form the actual prediction.

In the enhancement layer, the forward prediction in P-VOP and the backward prediction in B-VOP are used as the spatial prediction. The reference VOP is set to the temporally coincident VOP in the base layer. The forward prediction in B-VOP is used as the temporal prediction from the enhancement-layer VOP. The reference VOP is set to the most recently decoded VOP of the enhancement layer. The interpolate prediction in B-VOP is the combination of these predictions.

In the case that a macroblock is not coded, either because the entire macroblock is skipped or the specific macroblock is not coded, there is no coefficient data. In this case f[y][x] is zero, and the decoded samples are simply the prediction, p[y][x].

Forming the spatial prediction requires definition of the spatial resampling process. The information is performed at the midprocessor. The resampling process is defined for a whole VOP; however, for decoding macroblocks, only the 16×16 region in the upsampled VOP that corresponds to the position of this macroblocks is needed.

The spatial prediction is made by resampling the lower-layer reconstructed VOP to the same sampling grid as the enhancement layer. In the first step, the lower-layer VOP is subject to vertical resampling. Then, the vertically resampled image is subject to horizontal resampling.

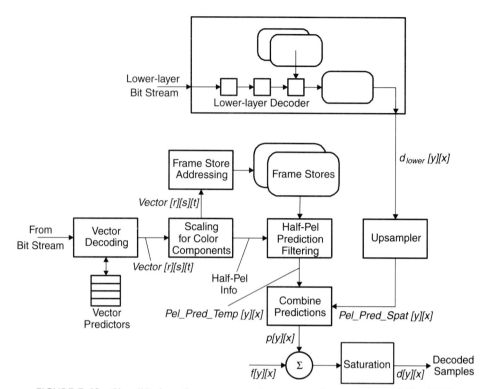

FIGURE 5.49   Simplified motion-compensation process for spatial scalability [275].
©1998 ISO/IEC.

5.6.9   Still Texture Object Decoding

The block diagram of the still texture object decoder is shown in Figure 5.50. The basic modules of a zero-tree wavelet-based decoding scheme are as follows:

- Decoding of the lowest subband using a predictive scheme
- Arithmetic decoding of the bit stream into quantized wavelet coefficients and the significance map for the other subbands
- Zero-tree decoding of the higher subband wavelet coefficients
- Inverse quantization of the wavelet coefficients
- Composition of the texture using Inverse Discrete Wavelet Transform (IDWT)

The wavelet coefficients of the DC band are decoded independently from the other bands. First the magnitude of the minimum value of the coefficients "band_offset" and the maximum value of the coefficients "band_max_value" are decoded from the bit stream. The parameter "band_offset" is negative or

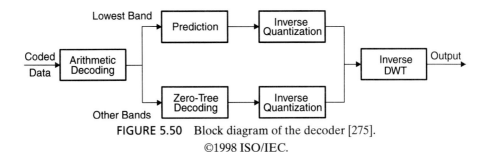

FIGURE 5.50   Block diagram of the decoder [275].
©1998 ISO/IEC.

zero integer, and the parameter "band_max" is a positive integer, so only the magnitude of these parameters are read from the bit stream.

The arithmetic coder model is initialized with a uniform distribution of "band_max_value-band_offset+1" number of symbols. Then, the quantized wavelet coefficients are decoded using the arithmetic decoder in a raster scan order, starting from the upper-left coefficient and ending at the lowest-right one. The model is updated with decoding of each predicted wavelet coefficient to adopt the probability model to the statistics of DC band.

The "band_offset" is added to all the decoded values, and an inverse predictive scheme is applied. Each of the current coefficients w_x is predicted from the three other quantized coefficients in its neighborhood (that is, w_a, w_b, and w_c) (see Figure 5.39), and the predicted value is added to the current decoded coefficient. If any of nodes A, B, or C are not in the image, its value is set to zero for the purpose of the inverse prediction. Finally, the inverse quantization scheme is applied to all decoded values to obtain the wavelet coefficients of DC bands.

In order to achieve a wide range of scalability levels efficiently as needed by different applications, three different zero-tree scanning and associated inverse quantization methods are employed. The encoding mode is specified in bit stream with quantization_type field as one of 1) single_quant, 2) multi_quant, or 3) bilevel_quant. The quantization types are shown in Table 5.8.

TABLE 5.8   The Quantization Types [275]

Code	Symbol
01	single_quant
10	multi_quant
11	bilevel_quant

©1998 ISO/IEC.

In single_quant mode, the bit stream contains only one zero-tree map for the wavelet coefficients. After arithmetic decoding, the inverse quantization is applied to obtain the reconstructed wavelet coefficients, and at the end, the inverse wavelet transform is applied to those coefficients. In multi_quant mode, a multiscale zero-tree decoding scheme is employed. Figure 5.51 illustrates the concept of this technique.

The wavelet coefficients of the first spatial (and/or SNR) layer are read from the bit stream and decoded using the arithmetic decoder. Zero-tree scanning is used for decoding the significant maps and quantized coefficients and locating them in their corresponding positions in trees. These values are saved in the buffer to be used for quantization refinement at the next scalability layer. Then, an inverse quantization is applied to these indices to obtain the quantized wavelet coefficients. An inverse wavelet transform can also be applied to these coefficients to obtain the first decoded image. The above procedure is applied for the next spatial/SNR layers.

The bilevel_quant mode enables fine granular SNR scalability by encoding the wavelet coefficients in a bit plane-by-bit plane fashion. This mode uses the same zero-tree symbols as the multi_quant mode. In this mode, a zero-tree map is decoded for each bit plane, indicating which wavelet coefficients are nonzero relative to that bit plane. The inverse quantization is also performed bit plane-by-bit plane. After the zero-tree map, additional bits are decoded to refine the accuracy of the previously decoded coefficients.

In single_quant mode, the wavelet coefficients are scanned in the tree-depth fashion, meaning that all coefficients of each tree are decoded before starting decoding of the next tree. In single_mode, the wavelet coefficients are scanned in the tree-depth fashion, meaning that all coefficients of each tree are decoded before starting decoding of the next tree.

In multi_quant mode, the wavelet coefficients are decoded in multiscalability layers. In this mode, the wavelet coefficients are scanned in the subband-by-subband fashion, from the lowest- to the highest-frequency subbands.

In bilevel_quant mode, the band-by-band scanning is also employed, similar to the multi_quant mode. When bilevel quantization is applied, the coefficients that are already found significant are replaced with zero symbols for zero-tree forming in later scans.

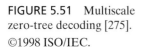

FIGURE 5.51   Multiscale zero-tree decoding [275]. ©1998 ISO/IEC.

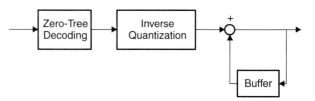

EXAMPLE 5.1

Figure 5.52 is an example of the scanning order for a 16×16 image, with three levels of decomposition. In this figure, the indices 0,1,2,3 represent the DC band coefficients, which are coded separately. The remaining coefficients are decoded in the order shown. As an example, indices 4,5, . . . ,24 represent one tree. At first, coefficients in this tree are decoded starting from index 4 and ending at index 24. Then, the coefficients in the second tree are decoded starting from index 25 and ending at 45. The third tree is decoded starting from index 46 and ending at index 66, and so on.

0	1	4	67	5	10	68	73	6	7	11	12	69	70	74	75
2	3	130	193	15	20	78	83	8	9	13	14	71	72	76	77
25	88	46	109	131	136	194	199	16	17	21	22	79	80	84	85
151	214	172	235	141	146	204	209	18	19	23	24	81	82	86	87
26	31	89	94	47	52	110	115	132	133	137	138	195	196	200	201
36	41	99	104	57	62	120	125	134	135	139	140	197	198	202	203
152	157	215	220	173	178	236	241	142	143	147	148	205	206	210	211
162	167	225	230	183	188	246	251	144	145	149	150	207	208	212	213
27	28	32	33	90	91	95	96	48	49	53	54	111	112	116	117
29	30	34	35	92	93	97	98	50	51	55	56	113	114	118	119
37	38	42	43	100	101	105	106	58	59	63	64	121	122	126	127
39	40	44	45	102	103	107	108	60	61	65	66	123	124	128	129
153	154	158	159	216	217	221	222	174	175	179	180	237	238	242	243
155	156	160	161	218	219	223	224	176	177	181	182	239	240	244	245
163	164	168	169	226	227	231	232	184	185	189	190	247	248	252	253
165	166	170	171	228	229	233	234	186	187	191	192	249	250	254	255

FIGURE 5.52   Scanning order of a wavelet block for a 16×16 image in the single_quant mode [275].
©1998 ISO/IEC.

The zero-tree symbols and quantized coefficient values are all decoded using an adaptive arithmetic decoder and a given symbol alphabet. The arithmetic decoder adaptively tracks the statistics of the zero-tree symbols and decoded values. The arithmetic decoder and all models are initialized in the beginning of each color loop. In order to avoid start-code emulation, the arithmetic encoder always starts with stuffing one bit 1 at the beginning of the entropy encoding. It also stuffs on bit 1 immediately after it encodes every 22 successive 0s. It stuffs one bit 1 to

EXAMPLE 5.2

Figure 5.53 is an example of decoding order for a 16×16 image with three levels of decomposition. The DC band is located at the upper-left corner (with indices 0,1,2,3) and is decoded separately as described in DC band decoding. The remaining coefficients are decoded in the order shown, starting at index 4 and ending at index 255. At the first scalability layer, the zero-tree symbols and the corresponding values are decoded for the wavelet coefficients of that scalability layer. For the next scalability layers, the zero-tree map is updated along with the corresponding value refinements.

0	1	4	5	16	17	18	19	64	65	66	67	68	69	70	71
2	3	6	7	20	21	22	23	72	73	74	75	76	77	78	79
8	9	12	13	24	25	26	27	80	81	82	83	84	85	86	87
10	11	14	15	28	29	30	31	88	89	90	91	92	93	94	95
32	33	34	35	48	49	50	51	96	97	98	99	100	101	102	103
36	37	38	39	52	53	54	55	104	105	106	107	108	109	110	111
40	41	42	43	56	57	58	59	112	113	114	115	116	117	118	119
44	45	46	47	60	61	62	63	120	121	122	123	124	125	126	127
128	129	130	131	132	133	134	135	192	193	194	195	196	197	198	199
136	137	138	139	140	141	142	143	200	201	202	203	204	205	206	207
144	145	146	147	148	149	150	151	208	209	210	211	212	213	214	215
152	153	154	155	156	157	158	159	216	217	218	219	220	221	222	223
160	161	162	163	164	165	166	167	224	225	226	227	228	229	230	231
168	169	170	171	172	173	174	175	232	233	234	235	236	237	238	239
176	177	178	179	180	181	182	183	240	241	242	243	244	245	246	247
184	185	186	187	188	189	190	191	248	249	250	251	252	253	254	255

FIGURE 5.53   Scanning order for multi_quant and bilevel_quant modes [275].
©1998 ISO/IEC.

the end of bit stream in the case in which the last output bit of arithmetic encoder is 0. Thus, the arithmetic decoder reads and discards one bit before it starts entropy decoding. During the decoding, it also reads and discards one bit after receiving every 22 successive 0s. The arithmetic decoder reads one bit and discards it if the last input bit to the arithmetic decoder is 0.

Decoding shape-adaptive wavelet coefficients is the same as decoding regular wavelet coefficients except for keeping track of the locations of where to put the decoded wavelet coefficients according to the shape information. Similar to decoding of regular wavelet coefficients, the decoded zero-tree symbols at a lower subband are used to determine whether decoding is needed at higher subbands. The difference is now that some zero-tree nodes correspond to the pixel locations outside the shape boundary and no bits are to be decoded for these out_nodes. Root layer is defined as the lowest three AC subbands, and leaf layer is defined as the highest three AC subbands. For a decomposition level of one, the overlapped root layer and leaf layer shall be treated as a leaf layer. The following description for shape-adaptive zero-tree decoding is the decoding process in the single quantization mode.

The shape information for both shape-adaptive zero-tree decoding and the inverse shape-adaptive wavelet transform is obtained by decomposing the reconstructed shape from the shape decoder. Assuming a binary shape with 0 or 1 indicating a pixel being outside or inside the arbitrarily shaped object, the shape decomposition procedure can be described as follows:

- For each horizontal line, collect all even-indexed shape pixels together as the shape information for the horizontal low-pass band, and collect all odd-indexed shape pixels together as the shape information for the horizontal high-pass band, except for the special case where the number of consecutive 1s is one.

- For an isolated 1 in a horizontal line, whether at an even-indexed location or at an odd-indexed location, it is always put together with the shape pixels for the low-pass band, and a 0 is put at the corresponding position together with the shape pixels for the high-pass band.

- Perform the preceding operations for each vertical line after the operations on all horizontal lines.

- Use the preceding operations to decompose the shape pixels for the horizontal and vertical low-pass bands further until the number of decomposition levels is reached.

5.6.10   Mesh Object Decoding

An overview of the simplified two-dimensional (2D) mesh object decoding process is shown in Figure 5.54.

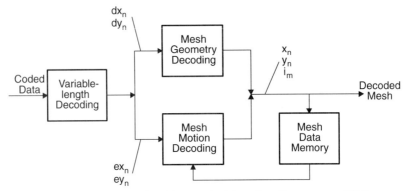

FIGURE 5.54   Simplified 2D mesh object decoding process [275].
©1998 ISO/IEC.

Variable-length decoding takes the coded data and decodes either node-point location data or node-point motion data. Node-point location data is denoted by dx_n, dy_n, and node-point motion data is denoted by ex_n, ey_n, where n is the node point index (n=0, . . . ,N-1). Next, either mesh-geometry decoding or mesh-motion decoding is applied. Mesh-geometry decoding computes the node-point locations from the location data and reconstructs a triangular mesh from the node-point locations. Mesh-motion decoding computes the node-point motion vectors from the motion data and applies these motion vectors to the node points of the previous mesh to reconstruct the current mesh.

The reconstructed mesh is stored in the mesh data memory so that the motion decoding process for the next mesh may use it. Mesh data consists of node-point locations $(x_n \ y_n)$ and triangles t_m, where m is the triangle index (m=0,...,M-1) and each triangle t_m contains a triplet <i,j,k>, which stores the indices of the node points that form the three vertices of that triangle.

After the mesh-object start code has been decoded, a sequence of mesh-object planes is decoded, until a mesh-object end code is detected. The new mesh flag of the mesh-object plane class determines whether the data that follows specifies the initial geometry of a new dynamic mesh, or whether it specifies the motion of the previous mesh relative to the current mesh, in a sequence of meshes. First, the decoding of mesh geometry is described; then, the decoding of mesh motion is described. In this specification, a pixel-based coordinate system is assumed, with the x-axis points to the right from the origin, and the y-axis points down from the origin.

5.6.11   Face Object Decoding

The coded data is decoded by an arithmetic decoding process. Following the arithmetic decoding, the data is determined by an inverse quantization process.

The Face Adaptation Processes (FAPs) are obtained by a predictive decoding scheme (see Figure 5.55).

For a given frame FAPs in the decoder, assume one of the following states:

- Set by a value transmitted by the encoder
- Retains a value previously sent by the encoder
- Interpolated by the decoder

FAP values, which have been initialized in an INTRA coded FAP set, are assumed to retain those values if subsequently masked out unless a special mask mode is used to indicate interpolation by the decoder. The decoder must estimate FAP values, which have never been initialized. For example, if only FAP group 2 (inner lip) is used and FAP group 8 (outer lip) is never used, the outer lip points must be estimated by the decoder. In a second example, the FAP decoder is also expected to enforce symmetry when only the left or right portion of a symmetric FAP set is received (for example, if the left eye is moved and the right eye is subject to interpolation, it is to be moved in the same way as the left eye).

In the case of DCT-based face-object decoding, the bit stream is decoded into segments of FAPs, where each segment is composed of a temporal sequence of 16 FAP object planes. The DCT-based decoding process (see Figure 5.56) consists of the following three basic steps:

1. Differential decoding the DC coefficient of a segment.
2. Decoding the AC coefficients of the segment.
3. Determining the 16 FAP values of the segment using IDCT.

5.6.12   Visual-Systems Composition Issues

Background composition is used in forming the background region for objects at the enhancement layer of temporal scalability when the value of both the enhancement type and background composition is 1. This process is useful when the enhancement VOP corresponds to the partial region of the VOP

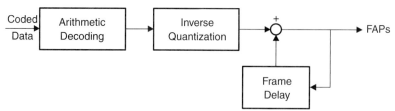

FIGURE 5.55   Face adaptation process decoding [275].
©1998 ISO/IEC.

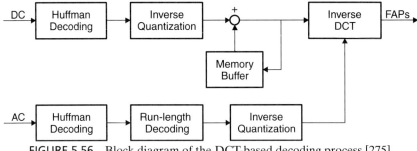

FIGURE 5.56   Block diagram of the DCT-based decoding process [275].
©1998 ISO/IEC.

belonging to the reference layer. In this process, the background of a current enhancement VOP is composed using the previous and the next VOP in display order belonging to the reference layer.

Figure 5.57 shows the background composition for the current frame at the enhancement layer. The dotted line represents the shape of the selected object at a previous VOP in the reference layer (called *forward shape*). As the object moves, a broken line (called *backward shape*) represents its shape at the next VOP in the reference layer. For the region outside these shapes, the pixel value from the nearest VOP at the reference layer is used for the composed background. For the region occupied only by the forward shape, the pixel value from the next VOP at the reference layer is used for the composed frame. This area is shown as lightly shaded in Figure 5.57. On the other hand,

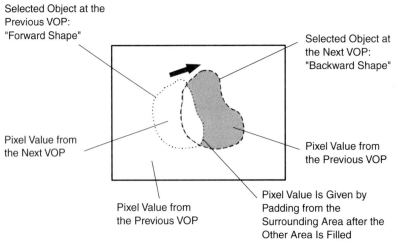

FIGURE 5.57   Background composition for the current frame at the enhancement layer [275].
©1998 ISO/IEC.

for the region occupied only by the backward shape, pixel values from the previous VOP in the reference layer are used (shaded dark area in Figure 5.57). For the region where the areas enclosed by these shapes overlap, the pixel value is given by padding from the surrounding area. The pixel value that is outside of the overlapped area should be filled before padding operation.

A mathematical description of the background composition method is as follows:

$$
\begin{aligned}
&\text{if } s(x,y,ta) = 0 \quad \text{and} \quad s(x,y,td) = 0 \\
&\qquad fc(x,y,t) = f(x,y,td) \quad (|t\text{-}ta| > |t\text{-}td|) \\
&\qquad fc(x,y,t) = f(x,y,ta) \quad (\text{otherwise}) \\
&\text{if } s(x,y,ta) = 1 \quad \text{and} \quad s(x,y,td) = 0 \\
&\qquad fc(x,y,t) = f(x,y,td) \\
&\text{if } s(x,y,ta) = 0 \quad \text{and} \quad s(x,y,td) = 1 \\
&\qquad fc(x,y,t) = f(x,y,ta) \\
&\text{if } s(x,y,ta) = 1 \quad \text{and} \quad s(x,y,td) = 1
\end{aligned}
$$

The pixel value of $fc(x,y,t)$ is given by repetitive padding from the surrounding area, where

fc	Composed background
f	Decoded VOP at the reference layer
s	Shape information (alpha plane), 0: transparent, 1:opaque
(x,y)	The spatial coordinate
t	Time of the current VOP
ta	Time of the previous VOP
td	Time of the next VOP

Two types of shape information $s(x,y,ta)$ and $s(x,y,td)$ are necessary for the background composition. $s(x,y,ta)$ is a forward shape, and $s(x,y,td)$ is a backward shape. If $f(x,y,td)$ is the last VOP in the bit stream of the reference layer, it should be made by copying $f(x,y,ta)$. In this case, two shapes $s(x,y,ta)$ should be identical to the previous backward shape.

The static sprite technology enables you to encode very efficiently video objects whose content is expected not to vary in time along a video sequence. For example, it is particularly well suited to represent backgrounds of scenes (decor, landscapes) or logos.

A static sprite (sometimes referred to as *mosaic* in the literature) is a frame containing spatial information for a single object, obtained by gathering information for this object through the sequence in which it appears. A static sprite can be a very large frame: it can correspond, for instance, to a wide-angle view of a panorama.

The MPEG-4 syntax defines a dedicated coding mode to obtain VOPs from static sprites: the so-called *Sprite VOPs*. Sprite VOPs are extracted from a static sprite using warping operations consisting of a global spatial transformation driven by a few motion parameters (0,2,4, or 8).

5.6.13   Error Resilience

MPEG-4 provides error robustness and resilience to allow accessing image or video information over a wide range of storage and transmission media. The error resilience tools developed for MPEG-4 can be divided into three major categories: resynchronization, data recovery, and error concealment [268].

Resynchronization.   Resynchronization tools attempt to enable resynchronization between the decoder and the bit stream after a residual error or errors have been detected. The resynchronization approach adopted by MPEG-4, referred to as a *packet approach*, is similar to the Group of Blocks (GOBs) structure used by the ITU-T standards such as H.261 and H.263 [237, 240]. In these standards, a GOB is defined as one or more rows of Macroblocks (MB). At the start of a new GOB, a GOB header is placed within the bit stream. The header information contains a GOB start code, which is different from a picture start code, and allows the decoder to locate this GOB. Furthermore, the GOB header contains information that allows the decoding process to be restarted. The GOB approach to resynchronization is based on spatial resynchronization. That is, once a particular macroblock location is reached in the encoding process, a resynchronization marker is inserted into the bit stream. A potential problem with this approach is that since the encoding process is variable rate, these resynchronization markers will most likely be unevenly spaced throughout the bit stream. Therefore, certain portions of the scene, such as high motion areas, will be more susceptible to errors, which will be more difficult to conceal.

The video packet approach adopted by MPEG-4 is based on providing periodic resynchronization markers throughout the bit stream. In other words, the length of the video packets is not based on the number of macroblocks, but instead on the number of bits contained in that packet. If the number of bits contained in the current video packet exceeds a predetermined threshold, then a new video packet is created at the start of the next macroblock.

A resynchronization marker is used to distinguish the start of a new video packet. This marker is distinguishable from all possible VLC code words as well as the VOP start code. Header information is also provided at the start of a video packet. Contained in this header is the information necessary to restart the decoding process and includes the macroblock number of the first macroblock contained in this packet and the quantization parameter necessary to decode that first macroblock. The macroblock number provides the necessary spatial resynchronization, while the quantization parameter allows the differential decoding process to be resynchronized. It should be noted that when using the error resilience tools within MPEG-4, some of the compression efficiency tools are modified. For example, all predictively encoded information must be confined within a video packet, to prevent the propagation of errors.

Data Recovery.   After synchronization has been reestablished, data recovery tools attempt to recover data that in general would be lost. These tools are not simply error-correcting codes, but also encode the data in an error-resilient manner. For example, one particular tool that has been endorsed by the Video Group is Reversible Variable Length Codes (RVLC). In this approach, the variable-length code words are designed such that they can be read both in the forward as well as reverse directions. Examples of such code words are 111, 101, 010. Code words such as 1000 would not be used. Obviously, this approach reduces the compression efficiency achievable by the entropy encoder. However, the improvement in error resiliency is substantial.

Error Concealment.   Error concealment is an extremely important component of any error robust video codec. Similar to the error resilience tools discussed earlier, the effectiveness of an error concealment strategy is highly dependent on the performance of the resynchronization scheme. If the resynchronization method can effectively localize the error, then the error concealment problem becomes much more tractable. For low bit rate, low delay applications, the current resynchronization scheme provides very acceptable results with a simple concealment strategy, such as copying blocks from the previous frame. In recognizing the need to provide enhanced concealment capabilities, the Video Group has developed an additional error resilient mode that further improves the ability of the decoders to localize an error. Specifically, this approach uses data partitioning by separating the motion and the texture. This approach requires that a second resynchronization marker be inserted between motion and texture information.

5.6.14 Profiles and Levels

Profiles and levels provide a means of defining subsets of the syntax and semantics and, therefore, the decoder capabilities required to decode a particular bit stream. Visual object profiles are presented in Table 5.10. A profile is a defined subset of the entire bit stream syntax. A level is a defined set of constraints imposed on parameters in the bit stream.

The purpose of defining conformance points in the form of profiles and levels is to facilitate bit stream interchange among different applications. The discretely defined profiles and levels are the means of the bit stream interchange among applications. Bit streams that represent a particular object corresponding to an object profile shall not use any of the tools for which the take does not have an "X." Visual combination profiles are shown in Table 5.9. The combination profiles can be grouped in three categories: natural visual (combination profile numbers 1–5), synthetic visual (combination profile numbers 6 and 7), and synthetic/natural hybrid visual (combination profile numbers 8 and 9). Table 5.10 lists the tools included in each of the object profiles.

5.7 MPEG-7 STANDARDIZATION OF MULTIMEDIA CONTENT DESCRIPTION INTERFACE

In October 1996, ISO/IEC JTC/SC29/WG11 started the MPEG-7 (multimedia content description interface) standardization process to increase the limited capabilities of current specific solutions. At present, more and more information is available in digital form, and we want to use it in different applications. However, before we start to use it, it is necessary to locate the information, which happens to be a very difficult problem, with the increasing availability of potentially interesting material [259]. The existing solutions enable text browsing: online database indexing and searching (machines like AltaVista, Yahoo!, Infoseek, HotBot for World Wide Web browsing); and client-based search implemented through *agents* (programs that look for the documents similar to the set of input documents) [276]. However, there does not exist a generally adopted scheme of audio/video material description, which would enable browsing such as "20 minutes of video material according to your preferences for today." Only in specific applications there exists the solution: *multimedia databases* enable browsing of images using characteristics such as color, texture, and information about objects in an image. It appears, however, that completely new applications that require browsing of content (the choice of possibly interesting TV/radio programs, in a growing number of available [digital] channels, and so on), are emerging.

The objective of the MPEG-7 standardization process is to provide an interoperable solution to extend the capabilities of today's proprietary solutions in identifying multimedia content. It is expected that MPEG-7 will be a successful standard that will transform demands from all fields converging to

TABLE 5.9 Visual Combination Profiles [275]

Object Profiles / Combination Profiles	Simple	Core	Main	Simple Scalable	12-bit	Basic Anim. Texture	Anim. 2D Mesh	Simple Face	Simple Scalable Texture	Core Scalable Texture
1. Simple	X									
2. Simple B-VOP Scalable	X			X						
3. Core	X	X								
4. Main	X	X	X						X	X
5. 12-bit	X	X			X				X	
6. Simple Scalable Texture									X	
7. Simple FA								X		
8. Hybrid	X	X				X	X	X	X	X
9. Basic Animated 2D Texture						X		X	X	X

©1998 ISO/IEC.

TABLE 5.10 Visual Object Profiles [275]

Visual Tools	Simple	Core	Main	Simple Scalable	12-bit	Basic Anim. Texture	Anim. 2D Mesh	Simple Face	Simple Scalable Texture	Core Scalable Texture
Intra Coding Mode (I-VOP)	X	X	X	X	X	X	X			
Inter Prediction Mode (P-VOP)	X	X	X	X	X	X	X			
AC/DC Prediction	X	X	X	X	X	X	X			
Slice Resynchronization	X	X	X	X	X	X	X			
Data Partitioning	X	X	X	X	X	X	X			
Reversible VLC	X	X	X	X	X	X	X			
4MV, Unrestricted MV	X	X	X		X	X	X			
Binary Shape Coding		X			X	X	X		X	

TABLE 5.10 Visual Object Profiles [275] *(Continued)*

Visual Object Profiles

Visual Tools	Simple	Core	Main	Simple Scalable	12-bit	Basic Anim. Texture	2D Anim. 2D Mesh	Simple Face	Simple Scalable Texture	Core Scalable Texture
H.263/MPEG-2 Quantization Tables		X	X	X	X		X			
P-VOP based temporal scalability Rectangular Shape		X	X	X	X		X			
P-VOP based temporal scalability Arbitrary Shape		X	X		X		X			
Bi-directional Pred. Mode (B-VOP)		X	X	X			X			
OBMC			X	X						
Temporal Scalability Rectangular Shape				X						
Temporal Scalability Arbitrary Shape										
Spatial Scalability Rectangular Shape				X						
Static Sprites (include low latency mode)			X							
Interlaced tools			X							
Grayscale Alpha Shape Coding			X							
4- to 12-bit pixel depth					X					
2D Dynamic Mesh with Uniform topology						X	X			
2D Dynamic Mesh with Delaunay topology							X			
Facial Animation Parameters								X		
Scalable Wavelet Texture (rectangular, Spatial & SNR Scalable)						X	X			X
Scalable Wavelet Texture (spatial scalable)							X		X	
Scalable Wavelet Texture (all tools, including Shape Adaptive)						X	X			X

©1998 ISO/IEC.

multimedia industry in technical specifications and at the right time. At the same time, the standard has to leave enough free space for further improvement of technical solutions through competition in the market. A standard defines only a description of multimedia content but not the feature extraction and searching techniques. Therefore, extensive research effort in the fields of digital image processing, compressing video/audio signals, artificial intelligence, and computer graphics will be necessary in order to generate promising solutions and to iteratively develop the standard.

5.7.1 Objectives, Scope, and Requirements

The working method on the MPEG-7 standard is similar to those on previous ones [259]. After defining the requirements, a call for proposals of technical solutions is opened and after evaluation of arrived suggestions (competitive stage), promising solutions are selected, and are then jointly developed (collaborative stage) (see Table 5.11).

MPEG-7 will specify a standard set of descriptors D (Descriptors) that can be used to describe various types of multimedia information. MPEG-7 will also standardize DDL (Description Definition Language) for definition of other descriptors as well as structures DS (Description Schemes) for the descriptors and their relationships. A combination of descriptors and schemes shall be associated with the multimedia content itself, to enable fast and efficient search for material of user's interest. Multimedia material may include still images, graphics, 3D models, audio, speech, video (both natural and synthetic), and information about how these elements are combined in a multimedia environment. The special types of this general data may include facial expressions or personal characteristics.

MPEG-7 builds on the other standard representations PCM, MPEG 1/2/4. For example, a shape descriptor used in the MPEG-4 standard is useful in the context of MPEG-7. At the same time, it can be applied in motion prediction in

TABLE 5.11   MPEG-7 Work Plan [277]

Requirements	October 1996
Call for proposals	October 1998
WD (Working Draft)	December 1999
CD (Committee Draft)	October 2000
FCD (Final Committee Draft)	February 2001
DIS (Draft International Standard)	July 2001
IS (International Standard)	September 2001

©1998 ISO/IEC.

MPEG-1, 2. MPEG-7 is being developed for standardized description of audio/video contents. However, existing solutions for text documents description will be also taken into consideration (HTML, SGML, and so on) if they are suitable for description of audio/video content. They will be standardized as a link between audio/video content description and textual data. The following standards are also important for the development of MPEG-7:

- ISO 8879 SGML Standardized General Markup Language
- ISO 9541 Font Interchange Standard
- ISO 10179 DSSSL Document Style Semantics Specification Language
- ISO 10180 SPDL Standard Page Description Language
- ISO 10744 HyTime Hypermedia time based structuring
- ISO HTML Hypertext Markup Language
- SMDL Standardized Music Description Language
- SMSC Standardized Multimedia Scripting Language
- XML Extensible Markup Language
- ISO DIS 14772 VRML Virtual Reality Modeling Language

It is important to emphasize that MPEG descriptors *will not depend* on the way the content is coded or archived. Moreover, it is possible to add an MPEG-7 descriptor to analog video signal and an image printed on a paper. However, MPEG-7 is largely built around the MPEG-4 standard, which codes audio/video material as objects that have certain relation in time (synchronization) and space (location on the scene).

MPEG-7 will have different *granularities* of description that offer different levels of content discrimination. It will be also possible to describe the same material using different characteristics that are appropriate for applications. On a low level of abstraction (it is possible to extract characteristics automatically), video material can be described with descriptors such as shape, size, texture, color, moving trajectory, and location in the scene. The upper level of abstraction contains semantic description of a scene (it requires interaction with experts). All these descriptors should be efficiently coded in the sense that enables their efficient browsing! Physically, they can be archived together with the material to which they are added, or can be located anywhere else on the distributed computer system (when a two-way link is needed).

MPEG-7 will support the application of database searching ("pull" applications: online/offline video databases retrieval, and search/location of multimedia information) and data distribution ("push" models on the Internet, filtering according to user behavior, and agents [broadcasting and Web casting]).

In Figure 5.58, the most general block diagram of an MPEG-7 application is shown: extraction of characteristics (analyze), standardized description, and search engine (application). Analyze and search are not standardized because they are not necessary for interoperability and they leave room for industry for continuous development and solution improvement.

Figure 5.59 illustrates a block diagram of an application that uses the MPEG-7 standard for description of multimedia content. Final performances of an application crucially depends on a database structure: the indexing information will have to be *structured* (for example, in a hierarchical or associative way). The way the MPEG-7 data will be used to answer user queries is outside the scope of the standard. This means, for example, that video material may be queried using video, music, speech, and so forth. It is up to the search engine to match the query data and the MPEG-7 AV description. A few query examples are

> **Music.** Play a few notes on a keyboard and get in return a list of musical pieces containing (or close to) the required tune, or images somehow matching the notes (for example, in terms of emotions).
>
> **Graphics.** Draw a few lines on a screen and get in return a set of images containing similar graphics, logos, and ideograms.
>
> **Image.** Define objects, including color patches or textures, and get in return examples from which you select the interesting objects to compose your image.
>
> **Movement.** On a given set of objects, describe movements and relations between objects and get in return a list of animations fulfilling the described temporal and spatial relations.
>
> **Scenario.** On a given content, describe actions and get a list of scenarios where similar actions happen.
>
> **Voice.** Using an excerpt of Pavarotti's voice, get a list of Pavarotti's records, video clips where Pavarotti is singing, or video clips where Pavarotti is present.

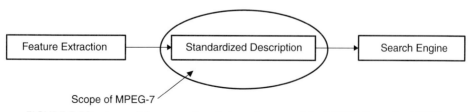

FIGURE 5.58   A possible processing chain and scope of the MPEG-7 standard [277].
©1998 ISO/IEC.

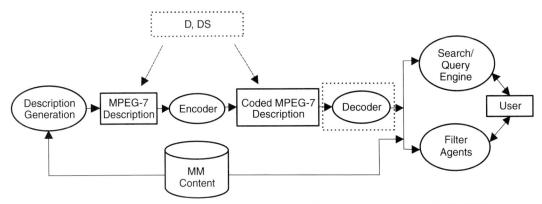

FIGURE 5.59 An abstract representation of possible applications using MPEG-7 [277]. ©1998 ISO/IEC.

There are numerous possible applications: digital libraries (image catalog, music dictionaries), multimedia catalog of services, program selection (radio/TV channels), and multimedia editing (personalized services of electronic news). Potential applications cover wide domains: education, journalism, tourist information, entertainment, geographical informational system, multimedia application, commercial, architecture, film/video/radio archive, and more.

A MPEG-7 search/query engine could freely access any complete or partial description associated with any AV object in any set of data, perform a ranking and retrieve the data for display by using the link information. An example architecture is illustrated in Figure 5.60.

Figure 5.61 is a functional block diagram of the Experimentation Model (XM) [280]. The XM is the portion of the MPEG-7 standard that serves as the basis for core experiments. The XM is also the reference model for the MPEG-7 standard. The relationships among XM components are essentially a detailed version of Context and Objectives [277]. The XM is divided into major functional components: an extraction component, an encoder, a systems layer, a decoder, a search/filtering component, and an evaluation application with user and media interfaces.

These components are further described next.

1. **Extraction**

   Descriptors. A Descriptor (D) defines the syntax and semantics of a representation entity for a feature. The representation entity is composed of an identifier of the feature and a data type. An example might be *Color: string*. The data type can be composite, meaning that it may be formed by a combination of data types. An example might be: *RGB-Color: [int,int,int].*

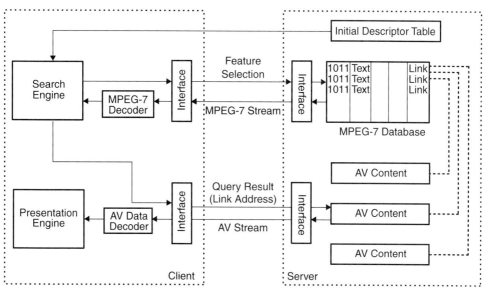

FIGURE 5.60   Example of a client/server architecture in an MPEG-7-based data search [277].
©1998 ISO/IEC.

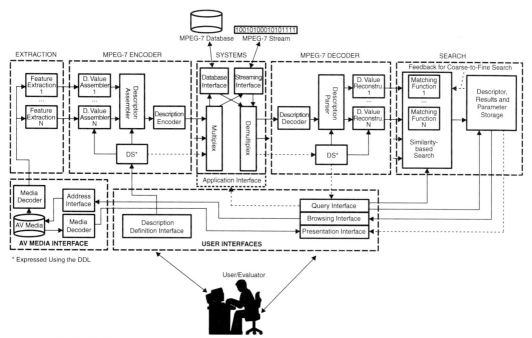

FIGURE 5.61   System components of the XM Ver 0.5 [280].
©1998 ISO/IEC.

It is possible to have several descriptors representing a single feature; that is, to address different relevant requirements. Examples for descriptors are a time-code for representing duration, color moments and histograms for representing color, and a character string for representing a title.

Description Scheme. A Description Scheme (DS) consists of one or more descriptors and description schemes. The DS specifies the structure and semantics of the relationships between them.

A simple description scheme for describing technical aspects of a shot might look like this, where those elements written in bold represent other DSs.

2. MPEG-7 Encoder

The MPEG-7 encoder takes descriptors from the extraction module, application-supplied descriptor schemes, and forms coded descriptions.

DDL. Description Definition Language. This is the language in which description schemes are specified. The DDL allows the creation of new description schemes and descriptors, and the extension of existing description schemes.

Description Coding Schemes. Description Coding Schemes provide coded representations of descriptions to satisfy requirements of compactness, and so on.

3. Systems Layer

Systems tools deal with integration of MPEG descriptions in other media standards, databases, and I/O considerations for encoded MPEG-7 descriptions.

4. MPEG-7 Decoder

The MPEG-7 decoder decodes encoded MPEG-7 descriptions and delivers these descriptions to the application. The decoder performs syntax parsing and decoding.

5. Search and Filtering Tools

Search tools permit the identification of data represented by MPEG-7 descriptions desired by the application. This may involve descriptor matching, similarity-based search, and so on.

6. Server Applications

Server applications (user interface in Figure 5.61) provide input to the extraction and encoding modules. These inputs consist of specification of features to be extracted, description schemes to be used, specific encoding schemes, and so on.

7. Client Applications

Client applications (user interface in Figure 5.61) provide the search engine with the features of the data item they are interested in locating.

8. Evaluation Tools

Evaluation tools (not shown in Figure 5.61) permit measurement and evaluation of normative components during the core experiments. Similar tools may be used for future conformance and validation exercises. These tools frequently provide graphical interfaces for examination of similarity based retrieval comparisons, and so on.

As shown in Table 5.12, MPEG-7 will standardize [278]:

- A set of descriptors D and description schemes DS
- The language for description schemes specification (DDL)
- Algorithms for coding the description of contents (coded description)

Description (D), by definition, attaches one (or more) representative value to the characteristic of multimedia material. Description Scheme (DS) defines structure and semantics with two or more D or DS and their relation in order to model multimedia content. The language for description definition (DDL) specifies description schemes DS. This language will enable generation of new DS and expansion of existing DS. Algorithms for coding of descriptors and description schemes have to enable efficient representation of multimedia content description. They have to be robust against errors and loss of information. They also have to support information about copyrights, authentication, and integrity of multimedia material.

TABLE 5.12   Typical Feature Types, Features, and Descriptors [278]

Characteristic Type	Features	Descriptors
N-dimensional spatial-temporal structure	Musical segment duration	Time code
	Object trajectory	Chain code
Statistical information	Color	Histogram, ...
	Frequency content of a video signal	Frequency component averaging
Object features	Object color	Histogram
	Object contour	Polygons, moments
	Object texture	Set of wavelet coefficients
Subjective features	Emotions	Text ...
	Style	Text ...
Production features	Author	Text, ...
	Producer	Text, ...
Composition information	Scene composition	Tree graph
Concepts	Events	Text, ...
	Activities	Text ...

©1998 ISO/IEC.

Examples of multimedia data are JPEG coded images and MPEG-2 compressed video. Color feature of an image is a description scheme and an image color histogram is a descriptor.

5.7.2 Applications

Classification of MPEG-7 applications can be implemented in different ways according to the way of distribution of multimedia material, media, the type of contents, user groups, and so forth [279, 281, 282, 283].

1. **Pull Applications**

   Storage and retrieval of video databases. TV and film archives contain huge quantities of multimedia material in different formats and with precise information about content, which may or may not be time-coded. It is necessary that MPEG-7 enable retrieval of existing databases: indexing and compression of a new material by digitization to use different descriptive information in different phases of video production. Some search/retrieval systems are [281]

   - QBIC (Query by Image Content) is the first commercial retrieval system.
   - Virage content-based image search engine.
   - RetrievalWare content-based image retrieval engine.
   - NeTra-V is a video analysis and retrieval system (search and retrieval of video objects).
   - MARS is a multimedia analysis and retrieval system.
   - ART MUSEUM content-based retrieval system.
   - VisualSeek is a fully automated content-based image query system.
   - VideoQ online search engine supporting automatic object-based indexing and spatio-temporal queries.
   - WebClip system for browsing and editing compressed video over WWW. VideoQ can now be used to retrieve video clips and then send them to WebClip to perform useful video compositing functions and special visual effects.

   Delivery of pictures and video for professional media production. The task of broadcast studio is to transmit to TV channels the video material, either complete or partially. With the support of a single query on the user side, MPEG-7 has to enable searching of distributed databases. Feedback information has to contain video-abstract, copyright information, material price, and a measure of technical quality of source video.

Commercial musical application. The main problem of today's music industry is how to reach the consumers with a growing diversity of musical tastes. An ideal way of presentation of accessible music to the customers is to enable easy (with no effort) search of musical material [282].

Sound effects libraries. As the method of retrieval of existing bases is not standardized, it is unsuitable for everyday work. It is necessary to enable designers to efficiently search the space of similar sound effects using prototypes, or even onomatopoeia [283].

Movie scene retrieval by memorable auditory events. It is not hard to imagine a new market growing up around micro-viewing (and micro-payment) short film clips that are searched through short, easily memorable auditory events. One should be able to look up a movie (and rent a viewing of a particular scene, for example) by quoting catch phrases [284].

2. **Push Applications**

User agent driven media selection. It is assumed that media broadcasting will be replaced with personalized multimedia programs on the Web. The application of agents and Internet technology will enable selection of contents by user, in a much more efficient way than existing video-on-demand applications [285].

Intelligent multimedia presentation. Increased amount of available information has caused a necessity for automatic presentation of this data. Intelligent systems that perform this automation, combine a knowledge about content, users, and applications [286].

Information access facilities for people with special needs. Active information representation can help people with motor, cognitive, or eyesight disability to overcome these problems. The main solution is to achieve multimodal communication, optimized for each user [287].

3. **Specialized Applications**

Teleshopping. It is typical for a customer to choose a product and not be sure if it is the correct choice. Hence, the MPEG-7 application has to enable fine-tuning of the search process [288].

Biomedical applications. Medical diagnosis requires permanent visual recognition of pathological changes in diagnostic 2D/3D data of different modalities and their comparison with the atlas. The MPEG-7 application has to enable separation of regions of interest and browsing the atlas with the data that contain similar regions of interest at different scales [289].

Also, efficient searching of 3D biomolecule structures is very important when developing a new drug, because biomolecular reactions depend essentially on the 3D shape of components, since it is very hard to predict biomolecular structure on the basis of primary structures.

Remote sensing applications. At present, a database of images taken from satellites contains a huge amount of data collected with different acquisition modalities (panchromatic, multispectral, hyperspectral, and thermal). Potential users are very heterogeneous, and telecommunication capacities have very much increased, so that there appears to be a need for standardized description of the content. Until now, information search in an image library is based on textual information such as scene name, geographic, and spectral and temporal information. MPEG-7 has to enable searching according to textual query, image query, content-based retrieval, confidentiality, and data protection [290].

Educational applications. The aim of using multimedia in educational software is to provide efficient support to different pedagogical approaches. MPEG-7 has to offer direct access to short video clips in large databases (history, performing arts, music on films, and so on) [289].

Surveillance applications. There are many applications in which a camera monitors sensitive areas and the system must trigger an action if some events occur. The system may build its database from no information or limited information, and accumulate a video database and metadata as time elapses. As time elapses and the database is sufficiently large, the system should have the ability to support operations on the database, such as search for a specific event, find similar events in the past, and make a decision [290].

Visually based control. Instead of programming commands based on text, it is possible to use figures, video objects, or sequence of images for specification of control behavior. Accumulation of control and video information allows visually based functions such as redo, undo, or search-by-task [291].

5.7.3 Research Areas

Access to multimedia material according to its content includes the following scientific/technical fields and research areas [292]:

- Digital image processing (scene, face, and gesture detection)
- Processing of audio signals (phrase detection, word spotting, and so on)

- The problems of semantic and artificial intelligence (natural languages, understanding in general sense)
- Interface problems (query entering, results representation)
- Computer networks (databases and distributed processing)
- Servicing problems (delivery, copyrights, payment)

Theory and tools for browsing and image/video manipulation are at present in the initial state of their development and many of the problems are still unsolved. For decades, image processing researchers have focused on problems related to medical and military images. Access to multimedia material according to its content includes a number of different scientific fields: digital image/audio processing, solving problems semantically with artificial intelligence, interface problems, communication networks, and others [293–297].

1. **Digital Image Processing**

   Image content recognition is a general problem, intensively investigated in military applications. The aim of the detection algorithm is to maximize the possibility of detection for a given value of false alarm. However, for applications of searching a multimedia content, it is necessary to develop new criteria because the false alarm might correspond to pictures the user did not request but may be worth seeing.

   Find interest regions. Image segmentation is traditionally defined as partitioning images into homogenous regions. A dual problem is edge detection. Nevertheless, optimal image segmentation is unnecessary when searching by content! Segmentation is defined as finding the regions of an image that are of interest to a user. A possible solution is a dynamical hierarchy of set of models that are optimized for different targets.

   Video parsing. Instead of processing a whole video, it is useful to divide video based on shots (an unbroken sequence of frames from one camera), scenes (a sequence of shots that focus on the same point of interest), and segments (a sequence of scenes that forms a story unit). However, until now, research is limited on shot detection and based on "edge" detection in time, while detection of scenes and sequences are much more complicated problems that are not systematically investigated.

   Space-time segmentation. A combination of information about space and motion is necessary when finding regions of interest for operations such as "separate the persons who are walking." Until now, only a small number of researchers have dealt with this problem.

Motion analysis. Motion analysis can be divided into scene motion (actions) and camera motion. Recognition of this motion is a completely new field of research (stroboscopic, mosaic images, and summary frames) that includes affine models with correction of parallax.

2. **Digital Image Compression**

Existing image/video compression techniques are optimized to achieve a maximal compression ratio with minimal perceptual image distortion and limited complexity of algorithms. "The fourth criterion" (possibility of access to content) is very poorly researched! It is supposed that there exists a significant (an important) *synergy* between image compression, feature extraction, and searching. First, the complexity of processing is significantly reduced due to a smaller amount of data in the compressed domain. Second, an important quantity of multimedia material is already compressed in such a way that the processing overhead due to decoding is reduced as reencoding of existing material. Third, efficient compressing techniques actually already perform some form of information filtering (motion estimation) and content decomposition (spatial-frequency decomposition) and present a good foundation for subsequent image content analysis. In the ideal case, analyzing techniques are applied directly on compressed data. In the suboptimal case, minimal decoding of compressed data is still necessary for extraction of useful data [295]. The key problem is to define a set of models that enable image compression and data access at the same time, and to define a measure of similarity of images suitable for a human visual system.

Compressed-domain image/video indexing and searching. Texture represents low-level characteristics of real-world images that allow feature-based query. Psychophysical studies have shown that humans perceive textures by decomposing a signal into components with different frequencies and orientations. Compression techniques that are based on transforms (DCT, wavelet) actually perform spatial-frequency decomposition of an image before quantization. Investigation of robust texture segmentation is still in progress [292].

Compressed-domain image manipulation. Manipulation of images includes a set of linear and nonlinear operations (filtering, convolution, geometrical transformation). By using a property of separable orthogonal transforms (DCT, DWT), it is possible to perform linear filtering directly in the transform domain. Nevertheless, manipulation of a video is not possible directly in compressed domain because of estimation and compensation of motion. There exist partial solutions based on inverse compensation of motion, which produces additional overhead [293].

3. Compression of 3D Graphical Models

Three-dimensional graphical models became very accessible to general end users due to rapid development of 3D scenes and Virtual Reality Modeling Language (VRML). However, complex objects, modeled with the polygonal mesh method, represent a big challenge even for high-end computers (manipulation and visualization of 3D objects require huge memory resources and a rendering speed) and for telecommunication data transmission systems.

A three-dimensional graphic model includes two types of information: structural data (specify connectivity information among vertices and characterize the topology of the model) and attribute data (describe information of each individual vertex—position, color, surface normal). Three-dimensional graphical files specify structural data as a list of vertex indices, and it is necessary to compress them without damaging data, which is hard to achieve at a high compression ratio. Possible solutions are algorithms for model specification and progressive coding [296]. Attribute data are characterized by a significant local correlation, so that they can be efficiently compressed preserving a coding error below some tolerable level.

4. Evaluation Criteria

A general agreeable set of evaluation criteria and benchmarking procedures are essential for facilitating advances in emerging technical fields. Objective and subjective metrics focusing on the signal quality have been used in image/video compression [88]. Proposal package description and test set in the MPEG-7 standardization process are described in [297–299]. Properties for good evaluation criteria [300, 301] of MPEG-7 technical solutions are

- Accommodation of existing DSs
- Expression efficiency
- Effectiveness
- Distinctiveness
- Processing efficiency (amenability for fast processing)
- Storage-space efficiency
- Scalability
- Flexibility

Due to its actual, sometimes aggressive working schedule, the MPEG-7 group should be able to contribute to and achieve an effective working solution that is acceptable in practical applications.

5.8 CONCLUDING REMARKS

The standards developed over five years by the MPEG explore every possibility of the digital environment. Recorded images and sounds coexist with their computer-generated counterparts, a new language for sound promises compact-disk quality at extremely low data rates, while the multimedia content could even adjust itself to suit the transmission rate and quality [302]. The worldwide acceptance of MPEG-2 in consumer electronics has led to large production scales, making MPEG-2 decoder equipment inexpensive and therefore also attractive for other related areas such as video communications and storage and multimedia applications in general. Because MPEG-2 was designed as a transmission standard, it supports a variety of packet formats (including long and variable-length packets of sizes from 1 to 64 Kbits) and provides error correction capability that is suitable for transmission over cable TV and satellite links. Since MPEG-2 video does not standardize the encoding method, but only the video bit stream syntax and decoding semantics, there have evolved two generalized video codecs: one for nonscalable video coding and one for scalable video coding [302, 303].

The H.263 video standard [304–306] is based on techniques common to many current video coding standards. The corresponding video codec is based on the DCT and motion compensation techniques. The key technical features of H.263 are block-size motion compensation, OBMC, pixel extrapolating motion vectors, 3D run-level-variable-length coding, median vector prediction, and more efficient header information signaling. H.263 supports five standardized picture formats: sub-QCIF, QCIF, CIF, 4CIF, and 16CIF. H.263+ is a revision of the original version of H.263. It contains approximately 12 new features that do not exist in H.263: new coding modes that improve compression efficiency, support for scalable bit stream, several new features to support packet networks and error-prone environments, and added functionality and support for a wider variety of video formats. H.263+ offers many improvements over H.263. It allows the use of a wide range of custom source formats as opposed to H.263, wherein only five video source formats defining picture size, picture shape, and clock frequency can be used. This added flexibility opens H.263+ to a broader range of video scenes and applications, such as wide format pictures, resizable computer windows, and higher refresh rates. Another major improvement of H.263+ over H.263 is scalability, which can improve the delivery of video information in error-prone, packet-lossy, or heterogeneous environments by allowing multiple display rates, bit rates, and resolutions to be available at the decoder. Furthermore, picture segment dependencies may be limited, likely reducing error propagation.

H.26L is designed to have low complexity, thereby permitting software implementation, enhanced error robustness, and adaptable rate control mechanisms. To learn more about ITU-T recommendations, H.263, H.263+, H.263++, and H.26L, references [304–308] are suggested.

Possibly, the greatest of the advances made by MPEG-4 is that viewers and listeners need no longer be passive. The height of interactivity in audiovisual systems today is the user's ability merely to stop or to start video in progress. MPEG-4 allows the user to interact with the objects within the scene, whether they derive from the so-called real sources (such as moving video), or from synthetic sources (such as computer-aided design output or computer-generated cartoons). Authors of content can give users the power to modify scenes by deleting, adding, or repositioning objects, or to alter the behavior of the objects. The MPEG-4 video coding standard is enabling content-based functionalities by introducing the concept of Video Object Planes (VOPs). MPEG-4 integrates most of the capabilities and features of multimedia into one standard, including live audio/video, synthetic objects, and text. Multi-point conversations can be facilitated by displays tailored to each viewer of a group of viewers. Multimedia presentations can be sent to auditoriums, offices, homes, and mobile locations, with delivery scaled to the capabilities of the various receivers. One of the outstanding features of MPEG-4 is the possibility of object-based image access to coded video data. Multiple video objects can be coded independently and multiplexed into a single data stream. At the receiver's end, placing decoded audiovisual objects at any arbitrary position in a two- or three-dimensional virtual space can recompose the audiovisual scene. Thus, the user has the possibility to interact with the audiovisual scene by selecting single objects, move the object within the virtual scene, and change object attributes such as size or orientation. The problems associated with rate control for coding multiple video objects were addressed as well. This type of algorithm is useful in supporting the object-based functionalities that are central to the MPEG-4 standard. A number of rate control tools have been proposed to provide a framework for efficient coding of multiple video objects at a wide range of bit rates and various spatial and temporal resolutions. The additional references [309–314] allow the enthusiasts to pursue the subject matter in depth and specific details for implementations.

MPEG-7 aims to standardize a set of multimedia description schemes. MPEG-7 will also address the coding of these descriptors and description schemes. It aims to support a number of audio and visual descriptions, including free text, N-dimensional spatio-temporal structure, statistical information, objective attributes, subjective attributes, production attributes, and composition information. For visual information, descriptions will include color, visual objects, texture, sketch, shape, volume, spatial relations, motion, and deformation. MPEG-7 also aims to support a means to describe multimedia material hierarchically, according to abstraction levels of information in order to efficiently represent a user's information need at different levels. Further discussion of different aspects concerning MPEG-7 is given in [302, 309, 315].

Some Issues Involved in Asynchronous Transfer of Video

SUMMARY

Video transfers across ATM networks have received much attention during the last 10 years by the relevant researchers. Various video services are expected in the future enabled by the rapid development in broadband network technology. While the wired network has been moving toward BISDN with ATM concepts for high data rates, wireless personal communication networks are also experiencing fast development. This chapter presents the issues involved in asynchronous video transfer. Overviews of rate control, multiplexing delay, and error and loss control are given. Other issues relating to video delivery over ATM, such as bandwidth management and video over wireless ATM networks, are discussed. Most of these areas are still the focus of debate. With the potential that ATM networks have for the delivery of video services, it is clear that these topics will continue to be of great interest in the near future. The success of Wireless ATM (WATM) relies on the success of ATM/BISDN in wired networks. When ATM networks become a standard in the wired area, the success of WATM will be realized.

6.1   RATE CONTROL

The purpose of the rate control is to enforce the specification of the bit stream. Source coding of video produces a variable bit rate because not all video frames have the same entropy [316–318]. The network has to be informed about the particular behavior that may be anticipated from a source in order to offer delay and loss guarantees. A suitable stochastic model characterizes the time varying rate from the coder, or its envelope is given some specified bound. The bound could be stochastic or deterministic. The block scheme of the general system for bit rate control is shown in Figure 6.1. The bit stream from the coder is fed into a buffer at a rate $R'(t)$ and it is served at some rate $\mu(t)$ so that the output bit rate $R(t)$ meets the specified behavior. The buffer smoothes the bit stream whenever the service rate is above or below the input rate. The size of the buffer is determined by delay and implementation constraints. Therefore, it is common to add a back pressure signal from the buffer to the encoder, so that the compression rate is increased when buffer overflow is at risk.

The flow control changes the quantization or other parameters, which may in turn reduce the quality. The recipient of the video may notice disturbing variations in the quality if there are frequent changes in quantization levels. One of the arguments used to promote asynchronous transfer of video is that the rate control would no longer be needed. The benefits would be a less complex encoder, less buffering delay, and a quality that would be constant since the transfer would use whatever capacity is needed for the unrestrained bit stream. However, in [319] it is shown that a fixed quantizer does not result in constant quality because sections of the video signal that are easy to encode should be more coarsely quantized than the average to maintain a uniform quality level. Second, it would be difficult to find an accurate and concise description of the uncorrelated bit rate in order to provide quality guarantees. This means that the bit stream from the coder should be regulated even for asynchronous transfers. The resource sharing in the network is improved when the flows are smooth.

The issue is thus to *reduce* the variability of the rate function $R(t)$ while minimizing the effects on the consistency of the perceptual quality [320]. The joint problem of traffic characterization and rate control is thus to find a suitable description of the bit stream to be useful to the network that can be enforced without throttling the compression rate.

FIGURE 6.1 General system for bit rate control [353].

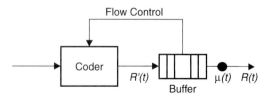

Modeling is a means to describe a bit rate function to the network. There are several attempts to model the variable-rate coded video bit stream R'(t) [321–332]. Most of these studies combine the modeling with some queuing analysis to determine multiplexing performance. There is good evidence that this bit rate process exhibits long-range behavior [333, 334]. This means that accurate characterization seems intractable by most conventional stochastic processes such as various Markov processes. The apparent long-range behavior could also be explained by lack of stationarity [335].

Provided that a model has been chosen, the user should then estimate the parameters for it and find a way to regulate the service rate $\mu(t)$ so that R(t) strictly obeys the specification. The network would then have the possibility to verify that the traffic is in accordance with its specification.

A model-based characterization that can be enforced without noticeably affecting the video quality is described in [336]. The method forces the bit stream to obey a Markov chain model. The admissible rate will be restricted to a few levels with geometrically distributed holding times.

Most of the models cannot be easily enforced and verified and are thus of limited value to the network for call acceptance control.

6.1.1 Rate Function Bounding

A more easily enforceable and verifiable specification of a bit rate function is to bound its envelope. The simplest is a single value that limits the rate function. The limit may be anywhere in the range of values that $R'(t)$ may assume. It is usually above the average. The limit, $\hat{R}$, does not have to be fixed for the duration of the session and could be renegotiated when permitted by the network control [337, 338]. Several bit rate control schemes suitable for enforcing a constant rate are presented in [339–343]. The decisions that the algorithms must take are when to apply back pressure and to what degree.

The leaky bucket (Section 3.6) is the most commonly suggested form of deterministic bounding with more than a single limit [344]. It is characterized by three parameters: the sustainable rate $\bar{R}$, the peak rate $\hat{R}$, and the maximum burst duration $\hat{b}$. The output rate R(t) from the buffer, measured over some interval at time t, is restricted by $R(t) \leq \hat{R}$, $\forall t$ and

$$\sum_{i=t}^{t+k} R(i) \leq (\hat{R} - \bar{R})\hat{b} + \bar{R}k, \forall t, k \tag{6.1}$$

The accumulated bit rate within a window of k time intervals is bounded by two areas, one fixed and one proportional to k, as shown in Figure 6.2. The worst behavior of a constrained source is a sustained rate of $\bar{R}$ with a single

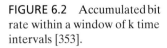

FIGURE 6.2 Accumulated bit rate within a window of k time intervals [353].

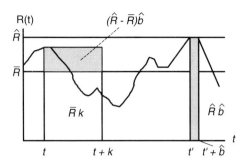

burst of $\hat{R}\,\hat{b}$ bits at some instance. An on-off behavior with periodic bursts at peak rate is also possible. The leaky bucket (Section 3.6) has been studied for realistic but unregulated video sequences [345]. However, there is evidence that it is the limiting function best suited to the characteristics of video sources. The leaky bucket is promoted in order to specify traffic of all types uniformly. That may indeed be more important than having several bounding functions, each with a claimed optimality for a specific type of traffic.

In the case for playback of stored video, the coder cannot be regulated. Then, some smoothing is possible and the server rate is adjusted according to the slow drift of the buffer occupancy level. Here, the goal is to minimize the probability of buffer overflow and the frequency of rate changes while meeting some prescribed characterization that the network uses for call acceptance. How this class of control works is described in [346, 347]. The network or receiver may send congestion or flow control notifications to the sender [348, 349]. These messages could be used in order to regulate the service rate, $\mu(t)$. If a restriction on the bit rate persists, then it will eventually lead to buffer feedback and increased compression. However, it is preferable that the flow and congestion control can be handled within the existing framework of the bit rate control.

6.2 MULTIPLEXING IN AN ATM NETWORK ENVIRONMENT

In order to transfer the information to the destination, the network performs the generic functions of multiplexing and routing. The routing functions, in order to provide connectivity, are not dependent on the information type in the transfers. On the other hand, multiplexing is highly dependent on the requirements by the information type and application context since multiplexing determines much of the transfer quality in the network. The optimization criteria for the transfer are to minimize the queuing and to maximize the utilization. A joint optimization is possible if the multiplexed streams are shaped to minimize the temporal variability.

Asynchronous time division multiplexing enables statistical multiplexing but does not mandate it. Statistical multiplexing has been successfully used for data communication for three decades and, more recently, in radio networks by means of spread spectrum techniques. The network provides fair access to the transmission capacity and routing. The end equipment is responsible for the quality of the transmission by means of retransmission and forward error correction. Quality guarantees have traditionally been accomplished by deterministic multiplexing—synchronous TDM (see Chapter 7).

For the network provider, the interesting issue is the video session's need for quality guarantees and the best way for providing it in the network [350]. Capacity allocation could be deterministic or statistic. The choice of multiplexing mode for asynchronous transfers depends on several issues, as illustrated in Figure 6.3 [351–353]. Here, the link has capacity C_{link}, while the source has peak rate $\hat{R}$, mean rate $\bar{R}$, and maximum burst length $\hat{b}$. Q denotes the required quality.

Deterministic multiplexing is the natural choice when the peak rate is close to the link rate, when the mean is close to the peak rate, when traffic bursts are long compared to the buffers in the network, or when the quality requirements are stringent.

As for general service classes, we may define three classes:

- Deterministic multiplexing with fixed quality guarantees
- Statistical multiplexing with probabilistic quality guarantees
- Statistical multiplexing without quality guarantees

FIGURE 6.3   Choice of multiplexing mode [353].

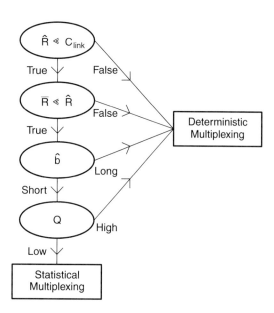

For ATM, in the terminology of the ITU-T Draft Recommendation I.371 [353], these classes are referred to as *ATM-layer bearer capabilities*. The classes are called Deterministic Bit Rate (DBR), Statistical Bit Rate (SBR) [referred to as constant and variable bit rate by the ATM Forum], and unspecified bit rate (UBR). In the Internet world, they correspond to guaranteed, predictive, and best-effort service [354]. The latter is offered by Internet protocol (IP). Video may be transferred in all of the listed service classes.

6.2.1 Deterministic Multiplexing

Deterministic multiplexing means that all flows are deterministically bounded and that enough capacity and buffers are reserved in the network to assure complete absence of overflow. The quality that can be guaranteed is therefore an absence of packet or cell loss and bounded maximum delay [355]. The delay variations may also be limited. The case when all queues are first come, first served, and the flows are bounded at the network access is analyzed in [356]. Tighter bounds on delay and buffer space can be achieved if more general services are allowed that shape the resultant multiplexed flow [357], or that maintain the shape of the individual flows through the multiplexing [358, 359].

The common objection to deterministic multiplexing is that the reserved capacity is poorly used when only loose bounds such as a peak rate limit can be placed on the flows. The traffic control architecture can, however, be designed so that service classes with statistical multiplexing can be offered in addition to the deterministic service. Traffic in the statistical classes can thus expend any slack in the reserved capacity. The issue is therefore one of tariffs. Namely, can guaranteed service be offered at nearly equal cost to a statistical bit rate service, for a fixed level of perceived quality, given that slack in the reserved capacity can be resold to other traffic classes? This question will remain open until the tariff structures are determined.

6.2.2 Statistical Multiplexing without Quality Guarantees

The simplicity of deterministic multiplexing is equaled by that of statistical multiplexing without quality guarantees. Since the network does not offer any guarantees of the multiplexing performance, the amount and the characteristics of the traffic entering are ignored. The perceived quality may vary depending on the momentary load in the network [360]. Despite the total absence of guarantees, this service class may still be of use for video transfers. Many of the applications using video are unidirectional and do not pose stringent delay limits. This allows, at least in principle, retransmissions to be used in order to reach a specified perceived quality. The quality can also be increased by means of forward error correction, especially in conjunction with spatial dispersion of the traffic to randomize losses [361, 362].

For ATM, there is a variant defined on the unspecified bit rate service known as Available Bit Rate (ABR). It is basically an unregulated service, but the cell-loss ratio is minimized for sources that obey congestion notifications from the network. Such messages are used to regulate the service rate of the buffer at the encoder. ABR could be offered with a low amount of reserved capacity which, for instance, could be chosen according to the bit rate needed for the required quality.

6.2.3 Statistical Multiplexing with Quality Guarantees

In order to offer quality guarantees, although probabilistic, a network must know its current inflow of traffic. New flows are allowed entry if they can be guaranteed the quality they request and their characteristics do not violate the quality of already accepted flows. This means that the network has to estimate the multiplexing behavior with a precision that matches the connection with the highest quality.

For a predictive service, one possible procedure is to measure the load on all links in the network and estimate the amount of capacity that can safely be allocated [363]. A call to be added is specified by its peak rate. If the unused portion of the capacity on all links along a route is above the requested level, the call is accepted. It is subsequently a part of the measurements needed for future requests. The advantage is that all calls are specified uniformly by a single parameter and that the acceptance decision is straightforward. The open issues are how to best estimate the available capacity and determine what kind of quality guarantees can be offered.

The SBR bearer capability for ATM is equally simple to formulate. The call request specifies the traffic that will be sent and states its desired quality. The network control computes the multiplexing performance that is obtained if the call is added to a specific route. If the resultant quality is sufficient for both the requested call and for existing ones, the call will be accepted over the route. The network subsequently monitors the traffic to verify that indeed the traffic of the new call behaves according to its specification.

The multiplexing performance has to be computed for a heterogeneous set of traffic characterizations. It is not sure that a single model can characterize all types of video. In addition, video has to share resources with other traffic types within a given service class.

Bounding offers a method of specifying all sources—not only video but also audio, data, and mixed ones—by a common set of parameters. The most popular is the leaky bucket (Section 3.6). The parameters for it may, however, be difficult to estimate before the call has commenced. A method for determining traffic parameters by measurements and the associated call acceptance are presented in [364]. One remaining problem is that multiplexing can make a traffic stream more bursty than specified at the network access. This problem may be solved by shaping multiplexed flows or by accepting lower utilization at nodes inside the network.

6.2.4 Multiplexing of MPEG Video Sources

The multiplexer can be modeled as a finite capacity queuing system with buffer size B (in ATM cells) and one server with fixed output rate R_{out}. The input of the multiplexer consists of various video sources. The model of the multiplexer is illustrated in Figure 6.4. There are different interleaving schemes for putting data from various sources into the common buffer at two time scales: frame time and cell time [365–367].

In a frame interleaving scheme, the information of each video source is multiplexed in the unit of a frame. It is assumed that each video source has a buffer that can store one frame of information, while all sources are synchronized in the frame boundary. At each frame time, the multiplexer scans each source and puts the information into the common buffer.

In a cell interleaving scheme, the multiplexing process is performed in the unit of a cell. It is assumed that all sources are transmitted at their peak rates from the sources to the multiplexer, and the cells in each frame are uniformly spaced. Each video source is synchronized in a frame. An example of frame-based and cell-based interleaving schemes is given in Figure 6.5.

It is obvious that the difference in the cell rates of different picture types in MPEG video is quite large. If the multiplexer can keep track of the picture type at each video source, it is possible to design a scanning order that has smaller loss probability. For example, after scanning an I picture, the buffer

FIGURE 6.4 Multiplexer model [327]. ©1996 IEEE.

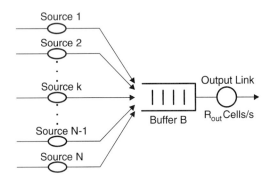

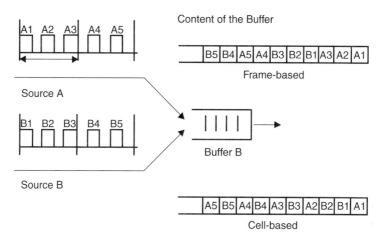

FIGURE 6.5   Example of multiplexing: frame-based and cell-based
interleaving scheme [327].
©1996 IEEE.

will have less chance of filling when the multiplexer scans a B picture rather
than an I or P picture, since the number of bits required to code a B picture is
much smaller than for an I or P picture. In order to arrange the scanning order
in each multiplexing cycle by considering the picture type of each MPEG
source, two rules are used:

- The source to be scanned followed by the I- or P-frame source is a B-
  frame source. If there is no B-frame source, the multiplexer will visit
  a P-frame source.
- The source to be visited followed by a B-frame source is an I-frame source. If
  there is no I-frame source, the multiplexer will visit a P-frame source.

One way to schedule the visiting order of the multiplexer to fulfill the
preceding rules is to arrange the starting frame of each MPEG source according to its polling order and the compression pattern in a GOP. Given the i-th
MPEG source, the starting frame should be the m-th frame in the compression
pattern of the GOP. Here, m=i mod P. With this arrangement, it will not have
two consecutive I pictures or P pictures in the scanning order, while the chance
for getting lost will become smaller.

6.2.5   ATM Multiplexer for Multiple Two-Layer Video Streams

The queuing model of the two-layer coder multiplexer is shown in Figure 6.6.
The multiplexing queue is managed by a push-out strategy that allows the
buffer to be fully shared by both traffic layers. Cells at the secondary layer are

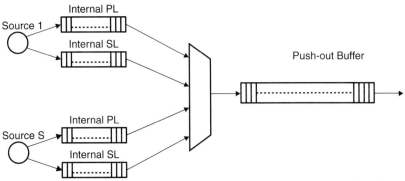

FIGURE 6.6   ATM video multiplexer for two-layer video streams [489].
©1996 IEEE.

lost if the number of cells from both the primary and secondary layers in the buffer are greater than the buffer size. The cells at the primary layer are lost when the total number of cells from the primary layer is greater than the buffer size. We can assume that the cell spacing is uniformly distributed over a frame interval by means of a smoothing scheme for a video source [368]. The multiplexer places the incoming cells in a common buffer with capacity B, and then transmits them over a 155.5 Mbps channel. When a large number of video sources are multiplexed, a Poisson arrival process can be assumed. We can also assume that the service process is Poisson. If we quantize the arrival rates into L levels as proposed in [369], and specify the overall arrival rate λ_i with probability p_i, then the Cell Loss Rate (CLR) can be evaluated as

$$CLR = \sum_i p_i \times \frac{\rho_i^N}{1 - \rho_i^{N+1}} \times (1 - \rho_i) \text{ where } \rho_i = \frac{\lambda_i}{C} \tag{6.2}$$

and C is the channel speed. Simulation results show that there is no cell loss rate at the primary layer due to network congestion. The CLR given by (6.2) corresponds to that at the secondary layer.

The traffic of an individual video source is bursty due to scene changes and motion. The overall multiplexed cell rate per frame can be further reduced by uniformly distributing the number of I frames transmitted in each frame interval.

6.3 VIDEO DELAY

Information is delayed in ATM networks and since we consider asynchronous transfers, these delays will not be constant, not even for deterministic multiplexing. This delay has to be considered end-to-end since delay limits are posed by the application. The video signal is delayed as protocol functions are executed and when the signal is transmitted across the network. The following instances may cause the end-to-end delays:

- Acquisition and display of the video
- Encoding, rate control, and decoding
- Segmentation and reassembly
- Protocol processing
- Wave propagation and transmission
- Queuing

The acquisition is the time it takes to capture a field or a frame depending on scanning, to digitize it and to perform color and scanning (interlaced to progressive) conversions. The reciprocal functions are performed before display. If there is no scanning conversion, then the delay can be on the order of a single-pixel instance.

The functions closer to the network are the segmentation of service data—units or streams into protocol data—units and their reassembly. The time to fill a packet or a cell might be excessive at low rates. For example, it takes 125 µs per octet at 64 Kbps. If the rate is temporarily or constantly low, it may be necessary to enforce a time limit, to send partially filled cells or packets of restricted length. Reassembly delay depends on message length and transfer rate. For instance, there is no delay for unstructured stream-oriented data. There may be restrictions on the Maximum Transfer Unit (MTU) to achieve acceptable delay.

The MTU is then dependent on the transfer rate, or the minimum acceptable rate is determined by the MTU size.

Protocol processing is a major cause of delay. It includes framing of information, calculation of checksums, and address look in hosts and switches-routers. In general, protocols should be implemented to reduce maximum delay and to maximize throughput.

Wave propagation is limited by speed of light. It takes roughly 100 ms to reach halfway around the globe (5 µs per kilometer in fiber). The transmission time is the length of packet or cell on the transmission line. The wave propagation determines when the first bit of a packet reaches the end of a transmission line, and the transmission time specifies how much later the last bit arrives. Increasing the line capacity and reducing the number of links per route reduces the transmission delay.

Since the multiplexing is asynchronous, there will be queuing in the network. Queuing delays in the network vary dynamically from cell to cell and packet to packet for a given route. The delay depends on the instantaneous load in each multiplexer, number of multiplexing hops on the route, amount of buffer space per node, and whether deterministic or statistical multiplexing is used. The scheduling discipline affects the distribution of the delays.

6.3.1   Cell Delay Variation

Cell Delay Variation (CDV), or jitter, can have a significant impact on the quality of a video stream (Chapter 8). MPEG-2 video systems use a 27-MHz system clock in the encoder and decoder. This clock is used to synchronize the operations at the decoder with those at the encoder. This enables video and audio streams to be correctly synchronized, and also regulates the retrieval of frames from the decoder buffer to prevent overflow and underflow. To keep the encoder and decoder in synchronization with each other, the encoder places Program Clock References (PCRs) periodically in the Transport Streams (TS). These are used to adjust the system clock at the decoder as necessary. If there is jitter in ATM cells, the PCRs will also experience jitter. Jitter in the PCRs will propagate to the system clock, which is used to synchronize the other timing functions of the decoder. This will result in picture quality degradation.

6.3.2   Delay Control

There are two control issues regarding delay: The variations must be equalized to maintain the isochronal sample rate, and the absolute value must be limited for interactive applications.

Most results that give the delay aspects of video aim at reducing the queuing delay. Basically, any of the listed functions can yield delay that exceeds the acceptable level for interactive applications. It is possible to limit the delay variations in the network, or to remove them from an arriving stream at the ATM adaptation layer or the transport layer. The delay can also be equalized at the application layer where the signal is reconstructed. The delay variations (jitter) control in the network comes at a cost of having either a high minimum delay or more complex scheduling. Since not all applications require jitter-free service, jitter removal should preferably be done outside the network when needed.

Equalization at the network interface of the receiver is not sufficient unless all subsegment protocol processing and data transfers within the end system are fully synchronous. This means that equalization will basically always be needed at the application layer. It is, in fact, the most appropriate location since the bit stream can be synchronized to the display system (the digital-to-analog converter). It should be noted that each stage of equalization introduces more delay.

In Figure 6.7, buffering data up to the acceptable limit D_L equalizes the delay. Segments that are delayed by more than the limit are treated as if they are lost. Equalization of delay variations is basically done by buffering data delivered by the network to a predetermined limit before delivery. Late data is discarded (there is no loss if $D_L \geq D_{max}$). The general problem with this approach concerns the choice of D_L to find a proper trade-off between delay and loss, and to determine that each pixel has been delayed by D_L when displayed.

A common simplification is to equalize queuing delay at the reassembly point. It is at the adaptation layer in ATM and at the transport layer in IP. Jitter introduced in the end system is then removed before or after the decoding to obtain signal synchronization.

The delay equalization requires the end system to have a clock that is synchronized in frequency to the sending clock. Usually the clocks at the sender and the receiver will have the same nominal frequency. The jitter is of much larger magnitude than the clock difference. Synchronization could be obtained by locking both clocks to a common reference clock, as carried by the global positioning system and by synchronous digital networks, or by using the network time protocol [370]. If a clock reference is not available, then the sender clock has to be estimated from the arriving packet stream. This technique uses a phase-locked loop presented in Figure 6.8. The input signal to the loop can be either time stamps carried in the cells or packets, or the buffer-full level [371]. Once the clocks are sufficiently synchronized and the data stream is sent completely isochronously, then the delay is equalized by simply reading the application frames from the buffer with the same time intervals as sent.

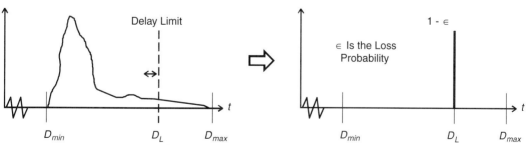

FIGURE 6.7   Equalization of delay variations [353].

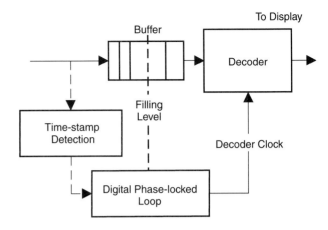

FIGURE 6.8 Phase-locked loop for the sender-clock frequency estimation [353].

Variable-rate video complicates the equalization since it is difficult to know how much of the time between arrivals is due to the generating process and how much is due to queuing in the network. Therefore, time stamps in every cell or packet are needed to mark their generating instances.

Signal synchronization is finally obtained after decoding. The frame buffer absorbs much of the delay variations in the decoding, and the residual could be eliminated by repeating or skipping frames to make adjustments to fit the display's clock. If the display allows an external clock, finer adjustments can be made by stretching and shortening the vertical and horizontal tracing times of the cathode ray tube's display. When several video streams emanating from different sources are displayed together, only one of the received signals can be used to synchronize the display system. The other signals must be stretched or contracted to fit that time base.

6.4 ERRORS AND LOSSES IN ASYNCHRONOUS TRANSFER MODE OF VIDEO

Video communication systems cause information errors and losses. For example, the camera has a limited bandwidth and the analog-to-digital conversion causes the quantization error. In addition, the encoding process introduces controlled amounts of distortion in order to compress the signal. The video signal will also be exposed to bit errors induced in the electronics and in the optics. The probability of bit error is low, below 10^{-8}, but not negligible. More troublesome is the information loss in the ATM network when full stretches of the signal are deleted. The causes of loss are transmission burst-errors, loss of cells and packets due to multiplexing overload, misrouting due to inaccurate addresses or entries in address tables, and delay above the acceptable threshold.

Undetected loss in a signal can place encoders and decoders out of phase. Burst errors caused by loss of synchronization and equipment failure have durations of 20–40 ms. Their probability of occurrence has been estimated to be below 10^{-7} [372]. Loss, especially due to multiplexing overloads, appears to be the most common signal corruption caused by the ATM network.

Error recovery is based on limited error propagation and correction or concealment of the missing portion of the signal. Proper framing of the bit stream restricts error propagation so that errors and loss can be detected.

6.4.1 Cell Losses in ATM Networks

Generally speaking, in the ATM network a cell can be lost due to two reasons: channel errors and limitations of network capacity and statistical multiplexing.

A communication channel is subject to different impairments. If an uncorrectable error occurs in the address field of an ATM cell, the cell will not be delivered to the right destination. This cell is considered lost. This is a rare cause of loss in ATM networks.

An ATM network takes advantage of statistical multiplexing, but also takes the risk of simultaneous traffic peaks of multiple users. Although a buffer can be used to absorb the instantaneous traffic peak to some extent, there is still a possibility of buffer overflow in case of congestion. In the case of network congestion/buffer overflow, the network congestion control protocol will drop cells. The malfunction or inefficient network management will also cause the cell loss. For example, loss of synchronization and lack of recovery measures in the physical layer would result in a stream of cell loss in the resynchronization/acquisition phase.

In an ATM network, cell discarding can occur on the transmitting side if the number of cells generated are in excess of allocated capacity, or the receiving side if a cell has not been received within the delay time of the buffer memory. Cells can be discarded in the ATM network by the congestion control procedure.

If the incoming traffic exceeds allocated capacity and causes the buffer overflow, the sender could be informed by the network traffic control protocol to reduce the traffic flow or switch to a lower-grade service mode by subsampling and interlacing.

If the network becomes congested and the input buffer overflows, then it will drop some cells to reduce the traffic and assume the normal communication phase.

If the error occurs in the cell header, especially in the address field, the cell may be misdelivered or go astray in the network. In the receiver, if a cell is not received within the maximum time-out window, the cell is considered to be lost. The loss of a cell leads to the loss of 384 consecutive bits, which may cause

---

EXAMPLE 6.1

The mean cell loss rate and the mean burst of consecutive cells lost can be calculated from the probabilities of cell loss. These equations are then rearranged in order to express the cell loss probabilities in terms of the mean burst of consecutive cells lost. Let the probability that any cell is lost is given by P, the probability that a cell is lost given that the previous one was not lost is given by P_n, and the probability that a cell is lost given that the previous one was lost is given by P_i. A lost cell can occur in two ways: immediately after a cell has been lost, and after a cell has been received. The probability that a cell is lost is given by

$$P = PP_i + (1 - P) \cdot P_n \quad \text{or} \quad P = \frac{P_n}{1 - P_i + P_n} \tag{6.3}$$

A burst of lost cells is defined as consecutive cells, all of which are marked as lost. It is preceded by and followed by one or several cells that are marked as not lost. The length of the burst of lost cells is defined as the number of cells in a burst that are marked as lost. The mean burst of consecutive cells lost is defined as the mean burst length. This number must always be greater than or equal to 1. A burst starts when a cell is lost after one or more cells have not been lost. The mean burst length is given by
$B = (1 - P_i) + 2P_i(1 - P_i) + 3P_i^2(1 - P_i) + \dots$.
Summing this series leads to the result

$$B = \frac{1}{1 - P_i} \tag{6.4}$$

Some rearranging gives

$$P_i = 1 - \frac{1}{B} \tag{6.5}$$

while for (6.3), we obtain

$$P_n = \frac{P(1 - P_i)}{1 - P}$$

Using (6.4), (6.5) can be expressed as

$$P_n = \frac{P}{B(1 - P)} \tag{6.6}$$

Equations (6.5) and (6.6) allow the probabilities of cell loss to be calculated from the average cell loss rate and the mean length of bursts of lost cells.

---

a serious degradation in picture quality for VBR compressed video signals. If the cell loss is caused by network congestion, a few consecutive cells, which contain thousands of bits of information, may be lost. Furthermore, the cell loss may affect the subsequent frames if an interframe coding scheme is employed. Therefore, the cell loss is a major problem encountered in VBR coding in the ATM environment. A cell loss may cause the loss of code synchronization. Since a variable number of data are packed into a cell, there is no way of knowing how much information is lost when a cell loss occurs unless some side information is available. Cell loss can occur unpredictably in ATM networks. It is assumed to be random, with the probability of cell loss depending only on whether a previous cell of the same priority was lost.

6.4.2   Cell Loss Process—The Gilbert Model

Cell loss in an ATM network is caused mainly by random bit errors in the cell header or by cell congestion in ATM nodes due to buffer overflow. Random transmission bit errors in the cell header result in cell discard and cell misdelivery. An 8-bit cyclic redundancy check code is used as a Header Error Control (HEC) function to protect the cell header. This HEC function can correct single bit errors or detect multiple bit errors. However, there is no protection against the buffer overflow, and cells tend to be lost consecutively whenever congestion arises at cell multiplexers.

The cell discard process is approximated using the Gilbert model, which is a two-state Markov model [373]. Its state transition diagram is shown in Figure 6.9. Parameters P, Q, p, and q represent the transition probabilities where

$$P + Q = 1 \qquad (6.7)$$
$$p + q = 1 \qquad (6.8)$$

Hence, the consecutive cell discard distribution is expressed as

$$P_B(n) = (1 - q)q^{n-1} \qquad (6.9)$$

where n denotes the cell discard length, while q represents the transition probability from Bad state to Bad state. In this model, cell loss is controlled by the average cell loss ratio of the channel P_D and the q value.

$$P_D = \frac{P}{P + p} \qquad (6.10)$$

FIGURE 6.9 State transition diagram of the Gilbert model [373].
©1990 ITU-T.

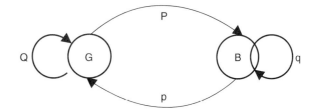

Thus, if the cell loss ratio P_D and the probability of consecutive cell loss q are given, other parameters such as P, Q, and p can be determined. The simulation results obtained in [374] show that even when the input signals are less bursty and the link utilization factor is not large, cells are still consecutively discarded, while the appropriate range for q is between 0.1 and 0.4. The larger the value of q, the longer the burst length [375].

6.4.3   Cell Loss Rate Characteristics as a Function of Time

Consider the busy ratio of the buffer. The buffer is modeled by two states: busy (buffer full), and idle (buffer is not full). A time length during the busy state is denoted by τ_i. Thus, the ratio of the busy state is given by $\tau_b/(\tau_i + \tau_b)$ where τ_b is the time until the state changes from busy to idle. It can be approximated by a cell transmission time (service time of the cell). Since cell loss occurs only when the buffer is busy, τ_i is approximated by the time interval of the cell loss. In an ATM network, since the cell length is fixed, the cell transmission time is a constant. Thus, τ_b is a constant, and only τ_i is a random variable.

Let now T_c be the cell transmission time, and suppose T_b to be the random variable of the interval time of cell loss occurrence. From the busy ratio, we define the time rate of cell loss as follows:

$$C_t = \frac{T_c}{T_c + T_b} \tag{6.11}$$

If the average of C_t is assumed to be C_{ave} and the average of T_b is assumed to be T_{bave} then C_{ave} is given by

$$C_{ave} = \frac{T_c}{T_c + T_{bave}} \tag{6.12}$$

C_{ave} reaches a value close to the cell loss rate [373]. While both of them generally do not have the same value, C_t is enough to display cell loss characteristics as a function of time.

Consider the relative frequency of C_t to observe the time rate of cell loss. We can obtain the relative frequency of C_t from the cell loss interval times T_{bn}, total lost cells N_{tb} in an observation period, and total lost cells N_t in all observation periods. A time rate of cell loss for an interval T_{bn} is given by $T_c/(T_c+T_{bn})$. If the cell loss with a cell loss interval of T_{bn} occurs N_{tb} times, then the time rate at this point, assumed to be C_{tn}, is given by

$$C_{tn} = \frac{T_c}{T_c + T_{bn}} \cdot \frac{N_{tb}}{N_t} \tag{6.13}$$

In order to develop a short-term congestion control method, it is important to clear dynamically changing cell loss rate characteristics. So, cell loss characteristics are analyzed as a function of time. A short-term congestion control method can be created from these cell loss rate characteristics.

6.4.4   Cell Jitter Reduction

The main objective here is to reduce the cell loss rate for I frames, which would enhance the quality of service. In order to decrease the cell loss for I frames, a cell jitter reduction is applied at the User Network Interface (UNI). This algorithm makes use of the information within the MPEG stream and produces an output in which the cell loss rate within a frame remains uniform. The cost is an increased jitter on a frame-to-frame basis, which implies that larger buffers would be required at both the sending and receiving ends. The increased buffer size requirements makes the algorithm unsuitable for real-time duplex communications, because of the increased delay and variance of the delay. However, it will work fine for distributive video services such as video on demand, multimedia mailing, and so forth.

In an MPEG stream, the number of bits required to code I frames is around seven times larger than the number of bits for B frames, and three times larger than for P frames. In a typical MPEG stream, on average, every twelfth frame is an I frame. The decoding time at the MPEG video decoder depends on the frame type. We will assume that the decoding time, t_{dec}, always is less than the display time, T_{disp}. This implies that each frame has to be received at the decoder at least T_{disp} before the time at which it needs to be displayed. Figure 6.10 shows how the transmission rate of an MPEG sequence varies as a function of time. In this case, only a simple smoothing algorithm has been implemented at the sending end to keep the transmission rate uniform within a frame. The transmission rate can vary significantly from frame to frame. It is

FIGURE 6.10   Transmission rate as a function of time where only interframe traffic smoothing has been applied [376].
©1996 IEEE.

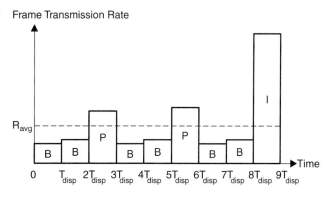

evident that I frames require the highest transmission rates and will place the heaviest load on the buffers.

The simplest method for traffic smoothing is to buffer the cells generated by a particular layer of the MPEG hierarchy, and flush them in the layer period T_{layer} with the cell rate

$$R_{cell} = \frac{N \; number \; of \; cells}{T_{layer}} \qquad (6.14)$$

Such smoothing algorithm can be applied at any layer of the MPEG hierarchy; for example, a slice, a frame, or a GOP. However, while smoothing at higher layers results in more uniform bit rates, there is a penalty involved, including larger buffer requirements and longer delays.

Transmission rate as a function of time with traffic shaping applied is shown in Figure 6.11 [376]. This cell reduction algorithm attempts to transmit all frames at a rate as close as possible to the average transmission rate without violating the timing requirements at the receiving end. Namely, every frame has to reach the decoder at least T_{disp} seconds before it needs to be displayed. When you compare Figures 6.10 and 6.11, it is easy to deduce that the standard deviation at the multiplexer buffering stage will decrease if the cell reduction algorithm is applied.

The first task to perform here is to extract information from the MPEG stream about frame sizes and types. This could be accomplished by scanning the MPEG stream at the input of the buffering stage at the user network interface. We will assume that the average bit rate, R_{avg} is known a priori. This is a fair assumption since the average bit rate is one of the traffic negotiations in the traffic contract between user and network. The algorithm operates on an I frame-to-I frame cycle. Then the total cycle transmission time T_c, can be expressed as (N is # of cells)

$$T_c = T_{disp} \times N \qquad (6.15)$$

This sets an upper limit on the buffer size required at the UNI. With this algorithm there is no need to buffer more than an I frame-to-I frame cycle.

FIGURE 6.11   Transmission rate as a function of time with traffic shaping is applied [376]. ©1996 IEEE.

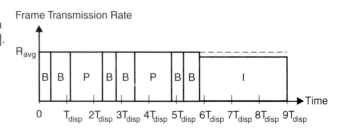

The next step is to use the extracted frame size information. By dividing the frame size by the display time, we obtain a calculated value for the unsmoothed transmission rate

$$R_{calc} = \frac{Frame\ size}{T_{disp}} \tag{6.16}$$

Two cases may arise when comparing R_{calc} with R_{avg}:

- In the case $R_{calc} > R_{avg}$, we will send the frame at a transmission rate of R_{avg}. The transmission time will therefore be less then T_{disp} and we will "gain" time. The gained time, t_g can be expressed as

$$t_g = T_{disp}\left(1 - \frac{R_{calc}}{R_{avg}}\right) \tag{6.17}$$

- A variable is used to keep track of the accumulated (gained) time, t_{acc}.
- In the case $R_{calc} \leq R_{avg}$, we will first consider B and P frames. The B or P frames will be transmitted at R_{avg} if there is enough accumulated time, t_{acc}. Naturally, t_{acc} has to be adjusted accordingly. All accumulated time is used when an I frame is transmitted. This will reset the value of t_{acc} at the end of each cycle. The time used to transmit an I frame can be expressed as $T_I = T_{disp} + t_{acc}$. This implies a transmission rate that can be either higher or lower than R_{avg}. The elapsed time in an I frame to I frame cycle will be restricted to $T_c = T_{disp} \times N$.

This algorithm is not suitable for real-time applications due to the delays involved in the buffering mechanism. It is, however suitable, for distribution video services and interactive multimedia applications with moderate buffer size requirements.

6.4.5 Network Framing

Asynchronously multiplexed networks such as those based on ATM have cells and packets as multiplexing units that are shorter than a full cell (session). The multiplexing unit in traditional TDM networks is a *call* (a session). Network framing means that appropriate control information is added to each multiplexing unit. An example of application framing is the MPEG slice layer, which packs bits for 16 consecutive lines together. The purpose of the network framing is to detect and possibly correct lost and corrupted multiplexing units. Errors and loss handling are shown in Figure 6.12. [377]. Errors may be detected by a Cyclic-Redundancy Check (CRC) of sufficient length [372]. Loss is detected by means of sequence members that turn it into erasures (known location, unknown values).

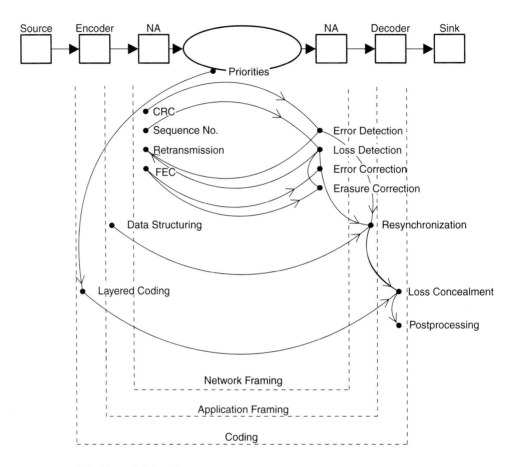

NA - Network Adaptation

FIGURE 6.12 Errors and loss handling [353].

It is important that the sequence number is based on the number of transferred data octets. Knowing that a cell or a packet has been lost does not tell how much data it contained [378].

Errors and loss can be identified by a CRC on the application frame after reassembly. It is important that frame length is known a priori since the length of a faulty frame cannot be ascertained. The failed CRC could be caused by a bit error, which would not affect its length or by a lost packet or cell.

In regular data communication, a lost or corrupted network frame would be retransmitted. There are complications with the use of retransmissions for video: First, the delay requirements might not allow it since it adds at least another round-trip delay that is likely to violate end-to-end delay requirements for conversational services. Second, the jitter introduced is much higher than that induced by queuing. Delay equalization is thus further complicated. Even if this is acceptable, the continuously arriving data stream must be buffered until the missing frame eventually is received.

There are several reasons to be cautious about Forward Error Correction (FEC) of cell and packet loss. First, it adds a fairly complex function to the system, which will be reflected in its cost. Second, the interleaving adds delay. Third, loss caused by multiplexing overload is likely to be correlated since the overload is caused by traffic bursts and more loss may thus occur than what the code can correct. If an interleaving matrix cannot be corrected, then the full matrix is useless, and the loss situation is in fact made worse. The interleaving matrix should of course be made to cope with burst losses, but, again, it increases the delay. Fourth, the coding adds overhead.

6.4.6   Error Concealment Strategies for ATM Networks

In general, the design of specific error concealment strategies depends on the system design. For example, if two-layered transmission is used, the receiver should be designed to conceal high-priority error and low-priority error with different strategies.

Moreover, if some redundancy (steering information) could be added to the encoder, the concealment could be more efficient. Figure 6.13 shows a block diagram of a generic one/two-tier video decoder with error concealment. As can be seen, there are two stages of decoder concealment: in the codeword domain and in the pel domain. Codeword domain concealment, in which locally generated decodable codewords (for example, B-picture motion vectors, end-of-block code, and so on) are inserted into the bit stream, is convenient for implementation of simple temporal replacement functions that can in principle also be performed in the pixel domain. The second stage of pel domain processing is for temporal and spatial operations not conveniently done in the codeword domain. Advanced spatial processing will generally have to be performed in the pel domain, although limited codeword domain options can also be identified.

6.4.7   Codeword Domain Error Concealment

The codeword domain concealment receives video data and error tokens from the transport processor/Variable Length Decoder (VLD). Under normal conditions, no action is taken and the data is passed along to the video decoder. When an error token is received, damaged data is repaired to the extent possible by insertion of locally generated codewords and resynchronization codes. An error region ID is also created to indicate the image region to be concealed

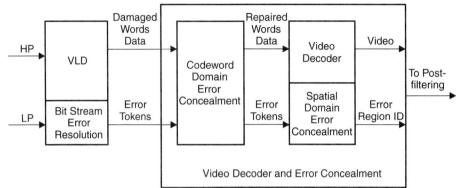

FIGURE 6.13   Video decoder with error concealment [23].
©1997 Signal Processing.

by subsequent pixel domain processing. Two mechanisms have been used in codeword error concealment: Neglect the effect of lost data by declaring an End Of Block (EOB), and replace the lost data with a pseudo code to handle the Macroblock (MB) types or other VLC codes.

If high-level data such as dc or a macroblock header is lost, the codeword domain concealment with pseudo codes can only provide signal resynchronization (decodability), and replaces the image scene with a fixed gray level in the error region. Further improvement is needed in the video decoder. This task is implemented with the error concealment in the video decoder. It is desirable to replace erased I- or P-picture regions with a reasonably accurate estimate to minimize the impact of frame-to-frame error propagation.

6.4.8   Spatio-Temporal Error Concealment

In general, two basic approaches are used for pel domain error concealment: temporal replacement and spatial interpolation. Error concealment using temporal replenishment with motion compensation is shown in Figure 6.14. In temporal replacement, the damaged blocks in the current frame are replaced by the spatially corresponding ones in the previously decoded data with motion compensation, if motion information is available. This method exploits temporal redundancy in the reconstructed video signals and provides satisfactory results in areas with small motion and for which motion vectors are provided. If motion information is lost, this method will fail in the moving areas.

Error concealment using spatial interpolation is shown in Figure 6.15. In the method of spatial interpolation, the lost blocks are interpolated by the data from the adjacent good blocks with maximally smooth reconstruction criteria or other techniques. The correlation among adjacent blocks in the received and reconstructed video signals is exploited.

FIGURE 6.14   Error concealment using temporal replenishment with motion compensation [379]. ©1992 ISO/IEC.

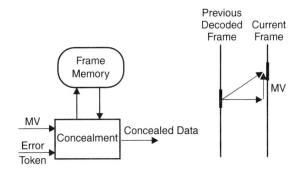

Severe blurring will result from this method if data in adjacent blocks are also lost.

In the MPEG decoder, groups of pixels (blocks, macroblocks, or slices) are separately decoded, so that pixel values and motion information corresponding to adjacent picture regions are generally available for spatial concealment. Estimation from horizontally adjacent blocks may not always be useful since cell loss tends to affect a number of adjacent blocks due to the MPEG and ATM data structures. Differential encoding between horizontally adjacent blocks tends to limit the utility of data obtained from such neighbors. Therefore, most of the usable spatial information will be located in blocks above or below the damaged region.

For I pictures, the damaged data can be reconstructed either by temporal replacement from the previously decoded anchor frame or by spatial interpolation from good neighbors. For P and B pictures, the main strategy to conceal the lost data is to replace the region with pixels from the corresponding and possibly motion-compensated region in the previously decoded anchor.

6.4.9   Adaptive Error Concealment for Intracoded Frames

A schematic block diagram for implementation of adaptive error concealment for intracoded frames is given in Figure 6.16. Corrupted macroblocks are first indicated by error tokens obtained via the transport interface. Then, a decision

FIGURE 6.15   Error concealment using spatial interpolation with the data from good neighbors [379]. ©1992 ISO/IEC.

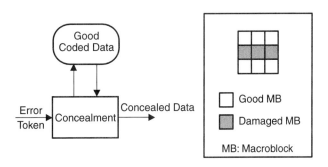

regarding which concealment method (temporal replacement or spatial inter-polation) should be used is based on easily obtained measures of image activity from the neighboring macroblocks (that is, top and bottom). The corrupted macroblocks are first classified into two classes according to the local activities. If local motion is smaller than spatial detail, the corrupted macroblocks are defined as the first class on which temporal replacement is applied. When local motion is greater than local spatial detail, the corrupted macroblocks are defined as the second class and they will be concealed by spatial interpolation. The overall concealment procedure consists of two stages. First, temporal replacement is applied to all corrupted macroblocks of the first class through-out the whole frame. After the temporal replacement stage, the remaining unconcealed damaged macroblocks of the second class are more likely to be surrounded by valid macroblocks. A stage of spatial interpolation is then per-formed on them. This will now result in less blurring, or the blurring will be limited to smaller areas. Therefore, a good compromise between shearing (dis-continue or shift of edge or line) and blurring can be obtained.

6.4.10 Spatial Scalable Error Concealment

This approach for error concealment of MPEG video is based on the scalability (or hierarchy) feature of MPEG-2 [379] (Section 4.6). Hierarchical transmission pro-vides more possibilities for error concealment, when a corresponding two-tier trans-mission media is available. A block diagram for the general principle of coding system with spatial scalability and error concealment is shown in Figure 6.17 [23].

In spatial scalable error concealment, the encoder produces two separate bit streams: one for basic low resolution and another for high-resolution enhancement. The high-resolution layer encoder uses an adaptive choice of temporal prediction from previous frames and compatible spatial prediction

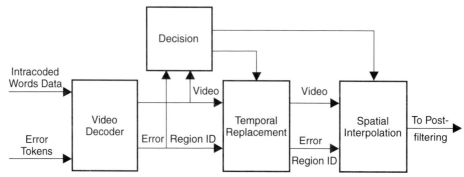

FIGURE 6.16 Two-stage error concealment strategy for intracoded frames [23].
©1997 Signal Processing.

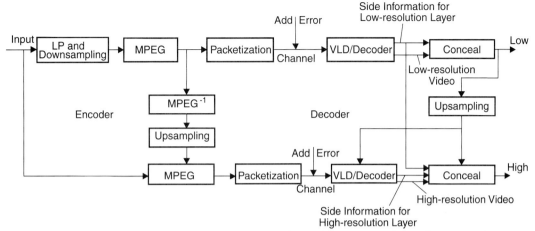

FIGURE 6.17   Block diagram of spatial scalability with error concealment (here MPEG and MPEG-1 imply encoder and decoder, respectively) [23].
©1997 Signal Processing.

corresponding to current temporal reference. In the decoder, redundancies that exist in the scaling data greatly benefit the error concealment processing. There are two kinds of information in the lower layer that can be used to conceal the data loss in the high-resolution layer: upsampled picture data and scaled motion information.

6.4.11   Encoding Parameter Adjustment

Error concealment is a method of reducing the magnitude of errors and cell loss in the video stream. This method includes temporal concealment, spatial concealment, and motion-compensated concealment. With temporal concealment, the errored data in the current frame is replaced by the unerrored data from the previous frame. In video sequences where there is little motion in the scene, this method will be quite effective. Another method of concealing errors is spatial concealment. Spatial concealment involves interpolating the data that surrounds an errored block in a frame. This method is most useful if the data does not contain a high level of detail.

Motion compensated concealment involves estimating the motion vectors from neighboring error-free blocks. This method could be used to enhance spatial or temporal concealment techniques. I frames cannot be used with this technique because they have no motion vectors.

The encoding parameters for a video stream can be adjusted to make a stream more resistant to bit errors and cell loss. Scalable coding (see Chapter 4) is supported by MPEG-2. It allows multiple qualities of service to be encoded in the same video stream. When congestion was not present in the network, all the cells would arrive at the decoder and the quality would be optimal. When congestion was present, the coding could be performed so that cells that provided a base layer of quality would reach the decoder, while the enhancement cells would be lost. Temporal localization is another method that can improve the quality of the video in the presence of cell loss. This involves adding additional I frames to the video stream. Additional I frames prevent long error propagation strings when a cell is lost since errors rarely are propagated beyond the next I frame encountered [380]. The additional I frames require more bits than the P or B frames they replace, and compression efficiency will be reduced. In addition, the greater bit rate required for these added I frames can contribute to network congestion. A third technique that can be performed at the encoder is to decrease the slice size. Since resynchronization after an error occurs at the start of the next slice, decreasing the slice size will allow this resynchronization to occur sooner.

6.4.12   MPEG Video Error Concealment

To effectively transmit video traffic over ATM networks, we need to study the issues involved in packetizing encoded video sequences. In particular it is important to study the effect of ATM cell loss and develop postprocessing techniques that can be used for error concealment. Error concealment approaches in [381] have assumed that both encoding and decoding occur simultaneously, with the decoder communicating to the encoder the location of damaged picture blocks. Many of these techniques are not realistic for real-time applications since they require retransmission of ATM cells. Prioritization approaches to ATM cell loss concealment have been proposed in [179, 382, 383]. Techniques involving interleaving data have also been proposed [384, 385], along with postprocessing techniques for error concealment [386–390]. In all of these techniques, there has been no mention of how the loss of macroblocks is detected. Figure 6.18 shows block diagram of the packing/error concealment scheme using ATM. The cell depacketization operation also provides information as to which macroblocks are missing [391].

This information is passed to the error concealment algorithm, which attempts to conceal the missing blocks. The goal of video error concealment is to estimate missing macroblocks in the MPEG data that were caused by dropped ATM cells. The use of spatial, temporal, and picture quality concepts are exploited.

Two error recovery approaches for MPEG encoded video over ATM networks are described in [391] The first approach aims at reconstructing each lost pixel by spatial interpolation from the nearest undamaged pixels. The sec-

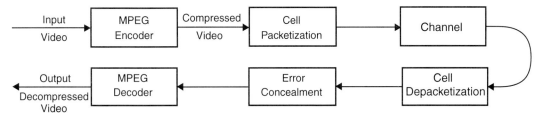

FIGURE 6.18   Block diagram of the packing/error concealment scheme [391].
©1995 IEEE.

ond approach recovers lost macroblocks by minimizing intersample variations within each block and across its boundaries.

One method to conceal the lost blocks in the damaged frame is to replace them from the corresponding regions of the previous frame (frame replenishment). Spatial, temporal, and frequency interpolations are used to conceal the lost blocks in [384]. Projection onto Convex Sets (POCS) is implemented in [390] in order to do the spatial interpolation, which has good performance in the presence of irregular motion or scene cuts. These methods merely exploit the redundancies on a small scale.

The objective here is to recover the lost blocks of the damaged image from the motion correlation between itself and the previous frame. The motion can be described by an affine model. The affine model includes translation, zoom, and rotation movements, and can be expressed as

$$u(x, y) = a_1 + a_2 x + a_3 y$$

$$v(x, y) = a_4 + a_5 x + a_6 y$$

(6.18)

The affine motion parameters $a_1, a_2, ... a_6$ are computed by minimizing the squared error between the damaged image frame and the previous frame

$$Error = \sum_{x, y \in R} [I(x, y, t) - I(x - u, y - v, t - 1)]^2 \tag{6.19}$$

where R is the region where the motion is estimated.

The preceding equation can be approximated by expanding $I(x - u, y - v, t - 1)$ with the Taylor series. Then we have the following equation

$$Error = \sum_{x, y \in R} (I_t + u I_x + v I_y)^2 \tag{6.20}$$

where I_t, I_x, and I_y are derivatives with respect to time, x and y, respectively.

Since this approximation is true only if the frame-to-frame displacement is a fraction of a pixel, a multiresolution approach is necessary [392]. In the multiresolution representation, a large displacement in high resolution can be reduced to a small displacement in low resolution, thereby satisfying the Taylor series approximation.

In many applications where there is significant camera motion (remote surveillance), the evolution from frame to frame can be well described by the affine motion. Registering images within a multiresolution pyramid carries out the motion estimation. The global motion is estimated in the lowest resolution level, and is then used to update and refine the local motion. The local motion is further refined iteratively at higher resolution levels. An affine transform is used to extract translation, scaling, and rotation parameters.

6.4.13   Loss Concealment

A loss is detected either by means of the network or application framing information. The corrupted application frame can be considered useless. The application framing should contain sufficient information to allow the next correctly received segment to be decoded. This means that the location within the picture of the information in the segment must be known, and that there cannot be any coding dependencies between the information in the segments. The latter condition implies that there cannot be any prediction dependencies across segment boundaries, and that variable-length codewords are not split by segment boundaries [393].

The decoded picture will contain an empty area that corresponds to the lost information. This area can be concealed by using surrounding pixels in time and space [15, 239, 382]. For example, the corresponding area in the previous frame can be used [393]. It might be best to repeat the full frame if the corruption is severe. When the coded motion vectors are correctly received, they can be used to find the most appropriate replacement in the previous frame. The prediction error is the only remaining error in the area.

Thoughtful packing of the information, such as separate transfers of motion vectors and prediction errors can improve loss concealment. A more general framework is often referred to as *layered* or *hierarchical coding*.

6.5   BANDWIDTH MANAGEMENT

The ABR service has been currently standardized as an ATM layer service and ATM layer transfer mechanism at the ATM Forum and ITU-T SG13 [394,

395]. ABR service traffic is sensitive to cell loss rather than transfer delay and is difficult to be predicted because the burstiness of traffic is very large. In addition, bandwidth utilization of source traffic is variable due to the flow control according to the network state. This is because the ABR service uses the remaining bandwidth unused by CBR and VBR services. The ABR service is used for the data transmission service, which has a large burst, such as LAN traffic, high-speed file transfer, and so forth.

As the flow control method for the ABR service, the closed-loop rate-based mechanism was adopted by the ATM Forum in October 1994 and supplemented continuously. Figure 6.19 shows the principle of the closed-loop rate based method for the flow control algorithm of ABR traffic [341]. Source End System (SES) transmits a forward Resource Management (RM) cell after sending N_{rm} data cells, and before receiving a backward RM cell, it transmits data cells continuously at the same transmission speed. If the source receives a backward RM cell with Congestion Indicator (CI) = 0 No Increase (NI) = 0, via Destination End System (DES), it increases the transmission rate. If the received backward RM cell contains congestion state information of CI = 1, the source decreases the transmission rate as the network indicates. It prevents the network from the congestion state by reducing input traffic to the network when the network is congested.

It is difficult to monitor the ABR input traffic exactly in the UPC mechanism, which monitors source input traffic in the network. This is because the transmission rate of the ABR traffic at the source changes depending on the network control, and the round-trip delay occurs between the source and UPC mechanism [396].

For traffic control of the ABR service, the bandwidth management and allocation mechanism is one of the important study items including the flow control and dynamic UPC. As the ABR service uses the remaining bandwidth, which the Constant Bit Rate (CBR) or VBR service does not use to improve its efficiency by the network control, the ATM network requires the bandwidth management and allocation mechanism that can guarantee the QoS of all services.

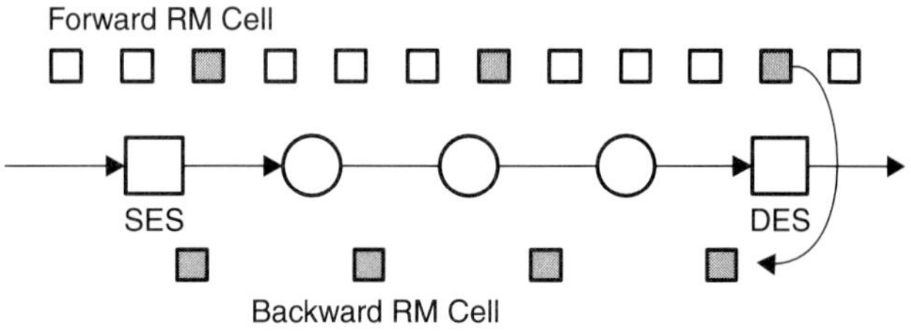

FIGURE 6.19   Closed-loop rate-based method for the flow control [341].
©1996 IEEE.

6.5.1   Bandwidth Management for the ABR Service

Connection Admission Control (CAC) accepts an ABR connection request when the network can guarantee the required QoS based on the Minimum Cell Rate (MCR). If the MCR is set to zero, a requested ABR connection is always accepted. The meaning of the MCR = 0 is that the source transmission rate may be zero according to the network control. When the ABR service is accommodated in the ATM network, it will increase the throughput of a transmission link using the remaining bandwidth, which the CBR or VBR service does not use and does not affect the QoS of the CBR or VBR service having high priority. The network guarantees MCR as a bandwidth for the ABR service and controls Allowed Cell Rate (ACR) of the terminal transmission rate by transmitting Explicit Rate (ER) to the terminal according to the network congestion.

The use of the remaining bandwidth for the ABR service in the ATM network means that the cells stored in the ABR buffer are filled up to empty slots in the transmission link as shown in Figure 6.20. The dedicated buffer is required for the ABR traffic at the ATM switch node to execute the ABR traffic flow control. The flow control of the ABR service can increase the transmission link utilization using the available bandwidth of the cell level generated by the burst characteristic of the VBR service.

When the connection holding time is short and the connection is frequently requested at the connection level, existing flow control mechanisms may cause the congestion since the closed-loop rate-based method controls the source transmission rate using ER calculated by the ABR buffer status when the congestion is expected or has occurred. The congestion can be protected by executing the Preventive Bandwidth Management (PBM) procedure shown in Figure 6.21 after the CAC process, and by transmitting the bandwidth modification information to the terminal in advance for the efficient bandwidth management.

6.6   VIDEO OVER WIRELESS ATM NETWORKS

Due to the success of ATM on wired networks, Wireless ATM (WATM) has become the direct result of the ATM "anywhere" movement. WATM can be

FIGURE 6.20 Transmission bandwidth use of ABR traffic [341].
©1996 IEEE.

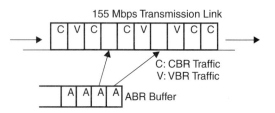

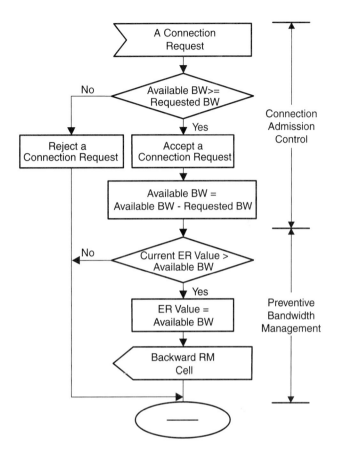

FIGURE 6.21   Bandwidth management procedure for ABR connection [341]. ©1996 IEEE.

viewed as a solution for next-generation personal communication networks, or as a wireless extension of the BISDN networks. The ATM Forum is currently involved in defining the baseline of a WATM system. The specification for both mobility control in ATM infrastructure networks and seamless radio extension of ATM to mobile devices are under development [397].

There has been a great deal of interest recently in the area of wireless networking. Issues such as bit error rates and cell loss rates are even more important when transmitting video over a wireless network. A high-performance wireless local area network that operates in the 60 GHz millimeter waveband can experience cell loss rates of 10^{-4} to 10^{-2} [397]. To provide adequate picture quality to the user, some form of error correction or concealment must be employed. One option is to use the MPEG-2 error resilience techniques and to modify the MPEG-2 standard slightly when it is used over wireless ATM networks. This technique is known as *macroblock resynchronization* [397]. In macroblock resynchronization, the first macroblock in every ATM cell is coded absolutely rather then differentially. This allows for resynchronization of the video stream much more often than would be possible if resynchronization could only take place at the slice level. It would be relatively simple to incorporate this method with the existing MPEG-2 coding standard by adding an interworking adapter at the boundary between the fixed and wireless network [361]. A second proposal for improving error resilience in wireless network is to use Forward Error Correction (FEC) methods. In addition, improved performance can be achieved by using a two-layer scalable MPEG-2 coding scheme rather than one layer [398].

6.6.1   Wireless ATM Reference Models

A system reference model for WATM is shown in Figure 6.22. The overall system consists of a fixed ATM network infrastructure and a radio access segment. In the fixed ATM network, the switches, which communicate directly with wireless station or wireless end-user devices, are mobility enhanced ATM switches. These switches set up connections on behalf of the wireless devices. They serve as the "entrance" to the infrastructure wired ATM networks. The other ATM switching elements in the wired ATM networks remain unchanged. Based on the different types of wireless applications, the radio access segment falls into a number of areas which that may need different solutions.

6.6.2   Fixed Wireless Components

In fixed wireless LANs, or network interconnection via satellite or microwaves links, the end-user devices and switching devices are fixed. They establish connections with one another via wireless channels. In these applications, the data transmissions are wireless, yet without mobility.

6.6.3   Mobile End Users

In digital cellular, Personal Communications Service (PCS), and wireless LANs, the end-user devices, which are mobile, communicate directly with the fixed network switching devices via wired or wireless channels. To support the ATM connections, the end-user devices are required to be equipped with a wireless terminal adapter that communicates with the wireless access point in the fixed switching elements.

6.6.4   Mobile Switches with Fixed End Users

End-user devices are connected to switches via wired or wireless channels. The end-user device and the switch, as a unit, are mobile. There can be more than one end-user device attached to one switch. An end-user device is fixed to one switch instead of roaming around different switches. The switch is responsible for establishing connections with the fixed infrastructure network component, through either wired channel or wireless channel. In this case, the fixed mobility enhanced ATM switches and the mobile switches need wireless access points and wireless terminal adapters.

6.6.5 Mobile Switches with Mobile End Users

In this case, end-user devices are mobile. There are also some mobile switching elements. When the end user wants to establish a connection, it first sets up a connection with the fixed network switch, which then sets up a connection with the fixed

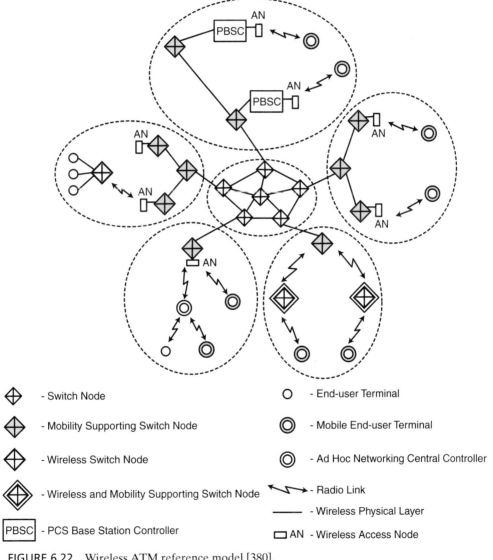

FIGURE 6.22   Wireless ATM reference model [380].
(Figure based on G. A. Coffey, "Video over ATM Networks," 1997, The ATM Forum.)

network switches, either directly or via other mobile switches. Wireless access points and wireless terminal adapters are needed to support the mobility.

6.6.6 Interworking with the Personal Communication Service

In PCS networks, the users are PCS terminals. PCS terminals send data to proper PCS base stations via wireless links, which then establish connections to the fixed network switching elements through a base station controller. The base station controller is a logical element that functions as the ATM-> PCS translator.

6.6.7 Wireless Ad Hoc Networks

An ad hoc network is the cooperative engagement of a collection of mobile terminals without the required intervention of any centralized access point. An auto-configuration of a wireless ATM network will be required for this kind of application. In wireless ad hoc networks, an end user can communicate with the mobility enhanced ATM switches, either directly or via a central controller.

6.6.8 Wireless ATM Design Issues

WATM adopts ATM to provide the data communication services so the overall architecture is based on the ATM protocol stack. To support mobility, appropriate extensions need to be added to the ATM protocol stack. The wireless segment of the network will require new mobility functions.

The protocol architecture currently proposed by ATM Forum is shown in Figure 6.23 [399]. The WATM items are divided into two distinct parts: mobile ATM (control plane) and radio access layer (wireless control). Mobile ATM deals with the higher-level control/signaling functions needed to support mobility. These include handover, location management, routing, addressing, and traffic management. The radio access layer is responsible for the radio link protocols for wireless ATM access. The radio access layer consists of the Physical layer (PHY), Media Access Layer (MAL), Data Link Control (DLC), and Radio Resource Control (RRC). At present, only PHY and MAL are under consideration. The protocols and approaches for DLC and RRC have not been proposed yet.

6.6.9 Mobile ATM

Mobile ATM defines the design functions of control/signaling. In WATM networks, a mobile end user establishes a Virtual Circuit (VC) to communicate with another end user, either mobile or ATM end user. When the mobile end user moves from one Access Point (AP) to another AP, proper handover is required. To minimize the interruption to cell transport, an efficient switching

FIGURE 6.23   WATM proto-
col architecture [399].

(Figure based on J. Deane,
WATM PHY Requirements,
1996, The ATM Forum.)

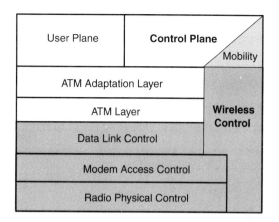

of the active VCs from the old data path to new data path is needed. In addition, the switching should be fast enough to make the new VCs available to the
mobile users. During the handover, an old path is released and a new path is
reestablished. In this case, no cell is lost and cell sequence is preserved. Cell
buffering consists of uplink buffering and downlink buffering. If the VC is broken when the mobile user is sending cells to AAPs, uplinking buffering is
required. The mobile user will buffer all the outgoing cells. When the connection is up, it sends out all the buffered cells so that no cells are lost unless the
buffer overflows. Downlink buffering is performed by APs to preserve the
downlink cells for sudden link interruption congestion, or retransmissions. It
may also occur when the handover is executed [400]. When the handover occurs,
the new data path may not support the current QoS. In this case, a negotiation is
required to set up new QoS. Since the mobile user may be in the access range of
several APs, it will select the one that can provide the best QoS.

When a connection is established between a mobile ATM endpoint and
another ATM endpoint, the mobile ATM endpoint needs to be located. There
are two basic location management schemes: the mobile scheme and the location register scheme. In the mobile scheme, when a mobile ATM moves, the
reachability update information only propagates to the nodes in a limited
region. The switches within the region have the correct reachable information
for the mobiles. When a call is originated by switching in this region, it can use
the location information to directly establish the connection. If a switch outside this region originates a call, a connection is established between this
switch and the mobile's Home Agent, which then forwards the cells to the
mobile. This scheme decreases the number of signaling messages during a local
handover [401]. In a location register scheme, an explicit search is required
prior to the establishment of connections. A hierarchy of location registers,
which is limited to a certain level, is used.

Due to the mobility feature of mobile ATM, routing signaling is a little bit different from that for the wired ATM network. First, mapping of mobile terminal routing in the network is necessary. In addition, rerouting is needed to reestablish connection when the mobile ATMs move around. The addressing issue of WATM focuses on the addressing of the mobile terminal or mobile end user device. The current solution is that each mobile terminal has a name and a local address. The name of the mobile terminal is a regular ATM end system address. It is constant and does not change while the terminal moves. When a terminal is up, its name is advertised by the switch it attaches to the other switches. A local or temporary address is assigned when the mobile terminal attaches to a different switch during roaming. This switch assigns a local significant address to the terminal. A mapping takes place in order to map the terminal's name to its temporary address [402].

The mobility feature parts additional impact on traffic control and QoS control. A reference model for resource allocation in WATM is still unavailable. Support for dynamic QoS renegotiations and extensions to ABR control policy to deal with handover and other related design issues has not yet been proposed. In wireless networks, the topology is changing with time. This, as well as other mobility features, present a unique set of network management challenges. Specific methods must be designed to maintain the dynamic nature of network topology. Some other issues, such as network and user administration, fault identification and isolation, and performance management, also need to be considered.

6.6.10   Radio Access Layer

To support wireless communications, new wireless channel-specific physical, medium access, and data link layers need to be added below the ATM network layer. These layers are called *radio access layers* in the WATM network. The design issues of the radio access layer are presented next.

A several-GHz spectrum would be required to provide high-speed wireless transmission. Currently, 5-GHz band is considered to be adequate to provide a 51 Mbits/s channel with advanced modulation and special coding techniques. Although 155 Mbits/s is unreachable due to the limitation of today's techniques, people believe that it will soon be available in the 60-GHz band, and 622 Mbits/s would be reached in the not-too-distant future. Based on this, two separate Physical layer (PHY) specifications are recommended, one for a 5-GHz band and one for a 60-GHz band, since they will require different operations [399].

WATM Media Access Control (MAC) is responsible for providing functional point-to-point links for using the higher protocol layer. To identify each station, both 48-bit address and lack significant address (which is assigned dynamically within a cell) are allowed. Each station registers its address to its hub during a hub-initiated slotted-content period for new registration so that it makes itself known by others. In a shared environment, there must be some control over the use of the medium to guarantee QoS. An extended network, which satisfies Peak Cell Rate (PCR), Sustainable Cell Rate (SCR), and Maximum Burst Size (MBS) requests, is suggested. Each station may use the media only when it is informed by the control elements (hub). Each can send out several packets at a time. To minimize overhead, the MAC should support multiple ATM cells in a packet. Another design issue of MAC layer is to support multiple PHY layers. Currently, people are interested in different wireless bands, which include infrared medium, 5-GHz radio band, and 60-GHz band. Different PHYs will be needed for different media. WATM MAC should support all of them. Some other design issues such as error recovery and support for sleep, are also under consideration [403].

Data Link Control (DLC) is responsible for providing service to the ATM layer. Multigating the effect of radio channel errors should be done in this layer before cells are sent to the ATM layer. In order to fulfill this requirement, error detection/retransmission protocols and forward error correction methods are recommended. Currently, the DLC protocol and syntax, interface to MAC layer, and interface to ATM layer have not been proposed.

Radio Resource Control (RRC) is needed for support of control plane functions related to the radio access layer. It should support radio resource control and management functions for PHY, MAC, and DLC layers, signaling support for mobile ATM and interface to the ATM control plane.

6.7   CONCLUDING REMARKS

The ATM technology that was chosen for the BISDN promises to be flexible and fast enough to support all the requirements demanded by new services. ATM is expected to be used in the central transmission system between the service providers and the access networks, which together connect the consumer. However, even with ATM, the amount of data generated by uncompressed video services is still hard to handle. Approximately 270 million bits are required to represent only one second of raw uncompressed video data (using broadcast quality). The bandwidth and hardware resources that would be needed to transmit this amount of data would make the service much too expensive. A widely accepted solution was found by compressing the video. The fact that one network can convey all of these different types of information, with different demands on bandwidth, burstiness, and so forth, is primarily due to ATM technology. The information coming from the different services, such as file transfers or video transmission, are segmented to fit into the ATM cell by the ATM adaptation layer and multiplexed into one stream of the ATM cells. The fact that the ATM cell is of fixed size instead of variable size enables simpler and much faster processing in all network components such as interface cards and switches. In contrast to Synchronous Transfer Mode (STM) or Time Division Multiplexing (TDM), ATM uses the bandwidth of a connection in a fairly efficient way. TDM guarantees the required bandwidth with an acceptable, constant delay. However, it is inefficient in its use of the transmission capacity. In ATM, the access to the network is in principle unlimited, dependent only on the capacity available. This is also referred to as *statistical multiplexing*. ATM uses statistical multiplexing in order to use network resources in an efficient manner. Typically, a combination of many variable bit rate and constant bit rate connections are multiplexed together via the ATM layer. A discussion of different aspects of the multiplexing in ATM network environment is given in [404–410].

Statistical multiplexing does have the drawback, however, that situations can occur where ATM cells must be dropped due to network congestion. Furthermore, huge buffers and long transmission lines can cause delay. Varying buffer size/use of the network, along with varying congestion conditions, can cause cell delay variation. Cell loss can be a more serious problem as more information is lost, especially if no Forward Error Correction (FEC) implementations are used. Long constant cell delay may be a problem if the applications are interactive, as relatively long waiting times may be experienced. High Cell Delay Variation (CDV) is under all circumstances a problem in video applications as it may violate the timing model used by the systems layer. CDV can cause program clock reference jitter, which again can cause degraded picture quality, seen as color distortion or blockiness. To get more information about video delay, errors, losses, and bandwidth management, some references such as [411–420] are recommended.

CHAPTER 7

Asynchronous Transfer of Video in the Internet

7.1   INTRODUCTION
7.2   THE GLOBAL INTERNET
7.3   INTERNET NETWORK ARCHITECTURE
7.4   INTERNET AND ATM
7.5   INTERNET INTEGRATED SERVICES
7.6   MPEG-4 VIDEO TRANSPORT OVER THE INTERNET
7.7   CONCLUDING REMARKS

SUMMARY

The concept of asynchronous transfer of video in the Internet is introduced. The global Internet is described first. The emphasis is on the Internet network architecture and ATM. This is followed by integrating Internet protocols and ATM. Finally, this is extended to Internet integrated services. We include Internet Engineering Task Force (IETF) integrated services, controlled-load service, and guaranteed service. Architectural considerations of MPEG-4 video transmission over the Internet are also included.

7.1   INTRODUCTION

The speed of available data links has grown from 56 kbits/s in the 1960s, to 1.544 Mbits/s in the 1970s, to Internet backbone speeds of 45 Mbits/s by 1990, and is projected to grow to well over 1 Gbits/s in the near future. During the 1990s, telecommunications engineers have exercised great efforts to develop a Broadband Integrated Services Digital Network (BISDN) architecture based on a transmission technology called Asynchronous Transfer Mode (ATM). ATM provides integrated data and real-time communications high-speed links using virtual circuits.

The history of the Internet is a story of the cooperation of engineers and computer professionals. Three groups conducted independent research on packet switching in the early 1960s. Baran wrote a RAND report on a potential packet switching network [421], while Kleinrock performed the first performance analysis of packet switched networks [407, 421]. Davis and Scantlebury worked on packet switching at the National Physical Laboratory in the U.K. [422]—the word "packet" comes from that project. Concurrently, the Massachusetts Institute of Technology Defense Advanced Research Project Agency (DARPA) group developed the concept of a global interconnected network of computers. This resulted in Robert's proposal for the Advanced Research Project Agency Network (ARPANET) in 1967 [422]. Tomlinson wrote the first email program in 1972 [422]. The same year, Kahan introduced the idea of open-architecture networking [421]. Because the network control protocol of ARPANET did not provide end-to-end error control, a new protocol, which became known as Transmission Control Protocol/Internet Protocol (TCP/IP), was developed [423].

While it is not possible to determine the exact size of the Internet, it is clear that the number of connected computers is growing rapidly and usage is probably growing even more rapidly. Figure 7.1 illustrates the growth in the number of host computers registered in the Internet domain. The exponential graduations on the vertical axis can be noted.

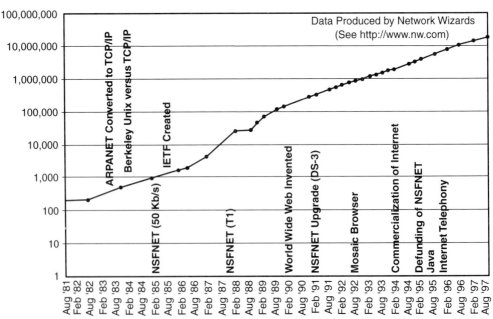

FIGURE 7.1   The growth of Internet hosts from August 1981 through August 1997 [423].
©1997 IEEE.

In 1990, Berners-Lee proposed a hypermedia software interface to the Internet, which in 1991 he named the "World Wide Web" (WWW) [422]. The demand for video as an additional information type in the WWW is certainly present. This demand resulted in a couple of activities to make the current Internet protocol environment suitable to carry real-time traffic such as video and audio [424]. The great popularity in the WWW has stimulated the continued rapid growth of Internet traffic. In 1997, various Internet Service Providers (ISPs) have been reporting traffic growth in the range of 10%–20% per month.

Telecommunication networks and computer networks have been developed from different perspectives. Telecommunication networks have relied on circuit switching. The circuits have provided either a constant bandwidth or a constant data rate. When telephone circuit switches became so complicated that new services required three or four years of switch software modification, the telecommunications industry developed a new architecture called the "Intelligent Network" (IN) to facilitate the introduction of new services. IN defines interface-to-switch call-processing software so that central computers at a service control point can instruct the switch on how to handle a call.

Computer networks have adopted packet switching, which facilitates statistical multiplexing of burst data transmissions from different sources. Furthermore, computer networks have relied on the processing power of customer premises equipment to control the network. For example, IP wide area networks have used connectionless packet-forwarding routers in the network nodes, as they have relied on the endstations to establish and maintain reliable TCP connections.

Whereas the global telephone network was originally designed to support one service (voice), the Internet was architected to support a broad range of data communications services. In addition, IP was designed to operate over a wide range of network technologies. Like other network architectures, the Internet has a layered set of protocols. IP is simple, and it defines an addressing plan and a packet delivery service. An effort is made to deliver each packet, but there are no guarantees concerning the transmit time or even the reliability. Many protocols can run on top of IP. The most common one is TCP, which provides a guaranteed delivery service. Many creative services have been developed to run on a TCP/IP network. However, TCP/IP is not appropriate for real-time delivery of data such as audio and video.

IP does not guarantee the delivery of packets, and TCP/IP is subject to unpredictable delays. As the Internet expands, however, new protocols such as the Real-Time Transport Protocol (RTP) and Resource Reservation Protocol (RSVP) are being developed. Indeed, RSVP software is already available from some router vendors, but the Internet Engineering Task Force (IETF) is still developing specifications for policy software. Another group of IP-based protocols supports multicasting, which increases the efficiency of network utilization for applications such as Internet radio and videoconferencing. Multimedia applications are being transferred from server to client, and people are experimenting with voice and video real-time connections over the Internet [423].

7.2   THE GLOBAL INTERNET

Many researchers in the computer science and electrical engineering fields already receive a larger number of Internet email messages than telephone calls, fax messages, or ordinary mail. This has now extended to all fields. For private use, the online services compete to provide comprehensive Internet access.

One feature that makes the Internet unique from the perspective of a telecommunications researcher is the ability to use the Internet itself as a research testbed and research forum, even without being directly affiliated with a network operator. Its usability as a research tool has been facilitated by several factors. First, the protocols are relatively simple to implement. Another factor is the integration of the measurement and facilities into architecture; for example, to check delay and packet loss, or to trace routes through the network. Moreover, tools and applications are often made available at no charge through the Internet itself. The flat-fee tariff structure in large parts of the Internet sped up the important experimentation with new services, long before there were paying customers to justify them. This flat-fee service has also greatly facilitated the free sharing of programs and information, as the information provider does not have to worry about having to pay for the bits leaving his site [425].

It is generally accepted that in the near future, large computer networks will be connection oriented, with at least data link layer connectivity being provided by ATM. These networks need to communicate with existing networks. For the huge existing investment in IP networks to remain useful, we must devise mechanisms to carry IP traffic over ATM networks. A fundamental issue is how to carry datagrams over virtual circuits. It is clear that the arrival of an IP datagram should cause a virtual circuit to be opened, if one is not opened already [389]. However, it is not clear how to handle the open circuit thereafter. It would be desirable to keep it open for some time, and to amortize the cost of opening the circuit over many packets. On the other hand, if no more packets are to arrive soon, it is better to close the connection. The ATM adaptation layer must decide heuristically how long to hold the circuit open, since the IP datagrams do not contain information about the length and rate of any higher layer conversations.

7.3   INTERNET NETWORK ARCHITECTURE

The Internet started about 25 years ago. The architecture and technology conceived at that time are, with some minor refinements, still at the foundation of the current worldwide network connecting millions of subnetworks and hosts. Central to the Internet approach is the ability to conceal heterogeneous networks and systems [426]. Until 1995, the Internet worldwide network was based on the model adopted in the United States, whereby a high-speed backbone was funded by the government while regional and access networks were either funded by the government or commercialized by private companies. At the beginning of 1997, the number of Internet access subscribers worldwide was around 30 million, while the population of Internet users was estimated at more than twice that number [427]. According to the current business model, a user signs a contract with an ISP and pays any applicable charge to connect to that ISP. ISPs connect those end users to Internet backbone networks. Backbone providers route traffic between ISPs and interconnect with other backbone providers.

One of the key points of the Internet paradigm is the definition of an abstract network service capable of decoupling the underlying networking technologies from the applications. These applications can be developed independently of the network technology. The Internet reference network architecture is composed of end nodes (hosts) linked by subnetworks as shown in Figure 7.2. All the hosts belonging to the same subnetwork exchange data directly. The crossing of subnetwork boundaries is enabled by means of intermediate nodes. Hosts and routers exchange data by means of the IP—the universal protocol used by the heterogeneous networks components to offer a unified abstraction of the network service.

The IP is capable of offering a network service in which the information is packaged in data units, named *packets* or *datagrams*. The network offers no assurance on the delivery of the packets to the intended recipient (best-effort service). Intermediate nodes decide where to route a packet addressed to a given destination on the basis of routing tables built by exchanging information with other intermediate nodes by means of custom protocols such as Routing Information Protocol (RIP), Open Shortest Path First (OSPF), and Border Gateway Protocol (BGP). The Internet Control Message Protocol (ICMP) supports IP by offering some basic control capabilities, such as sending

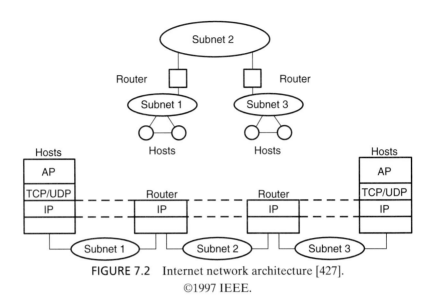

FIGURE 7.2   Internet network architecture [427].
©1997 IEEE.

reachable packets and asking an upstream packet source to slow down the packet transmission rate in the event of congestion [428].

The end-to-end protocols add the capability to multiplex/demultiplex multiple flows of packets at the end nodes and they may add reliability. In particular, the user datagram protocol (UDP) offers an unreliable service and adds a differentiation of packet flows within a host by means of port numbers [429]. The Transmission Control Protocol (TCP) offers a reliable sequenced delivery of byte streams on top of the datagram service offered by the IP [430]. TCP is a connection-oriented protocol and enables connections with significance only at the end nodes. A windowing scheme is applied to enforce flow control; that is, to avoid the overrunning of slow receivers, as well as to allow the traffic source to adapt to network overload. In particular, the number of outstanding packets—that is, the number of packets a source is entitled to transmit while waiting for an acknowledgment—is timed according to a probing of available bandwidth.

Figure 7.3 illustrates the classical Internet protocol stack, which includes end-user applications such as the Simple Mail Transfer Protocol (SMTP) for the exchange of electronic mail messages [431], and network-specific applications such as the Domain Name System (DNS) for the node naming service [432]. In Figure 7.3, other user application-specific protocols are the remote terminal (Telnet), the File Transfer Protocol (FTP), and the Network News Transfer Protocol (NNTP) for exchange of newsgroup information.

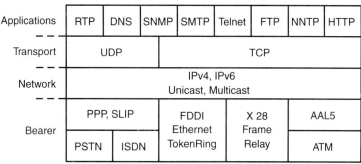

Applications	RTP	DNS	SNMP	SMTP	Telnet	FTP	NNTP	HTTP
Transport	UDP			TCP				
Network	IPv4, IPv6 Unicast, Multicast							
Bearer	PPP, SLIP		FDDI Ethernet TokenRing	X 28 Frame Relay	AAL5			
	PSTN	ISDN			ATM			

FIGURE 7.3   Internet protocols [427].
©1997 IEEE.

The popular WWW client/server applications [433, 434] based on the HyperText Transfer Protocol (HTTP) have been introduced in recent years. Among the key features of these applications is the capability to access a huge amount of multimedia information distributed worldwide in a transparent and user-friendly manner. The browsing of information is enabled by use of the hypertext structure, where a document formatted using HyperText Markup Language (HTML) contains links to other documents [435].

The management of network resources in the Internet is carried out in the frame of the Simple Network Management Protocol (SNMP) [436]; that is, an application layer protocol running over UDP for resilience designed to exchange management information among network nodes. An upgrade of the basic SNMP (SNMP Version 2) has been proposed to improve the security capabilities and resolve the issue of distribution of network management functions [437]. SNMP is a relatively simple protocol widely used by the network management stations to execute management applications [438]. The nonrealtime user and network applications tolerate packet delays and loss.

7.4   INTERNET AND ATM

A comparison of the IP and ATM approaches, in terms of network architecture and protocols, offers a view on the convergence of the computer and telecommunications industries. The original IP paradigm has evolved by taking into account the paradigm shift from a data-only network to multimedia internetworking, while the ATM approach, originally conceived in the telecommunications field, has been largely influenced by the computer networking style in the ATM Forum [427]. The main features of IP and ATM are compared in Table 7.1.

TABLE 7.1   IP/RSVP versus ATM/SVC [427]

Feature	IP	ATM
Addressing	32/128 bit (v4/v6)	160 bit NSAP
Transfer mode	Datagram/Flow	PVC/SVC/Fast Resource management
Size adaptation	MTU discovery	Segmentation and reassembly
Signaling	RSVP	UNI/NNI
Quality of service Reservation	ISA service classes	ATM service classes
Orientation	Receiver-oriented	Sender-oriented
Mix	Heterogeneous	Homogeneous VCs
QoS	Dynamic QoS	Dynamic QoS
Network state	Soft state	Hard state

©1997 IEEE.

The IPv6 128-bit address identifies a network node interface with an assumption of network hierarchy that greatly reduces the work needed to route packets over the Internet. This is achieved by allocating all addresses within a domain—that is, a set of network nodes administered by a single organization—so that they have a common prefix. When two domains want to exchange routing information, they only need to pass the domain prefixes to each other. It is recommended that domains that are close in the physical topology of the Internet are given domain prefixes that themselves have a common prefix. How large the different parts of the prefix need to be is dictated by the topology and size of the domains and may vary on different parts of the Internet. ATM uses the E.164 addresses that are defined by ITU-T to identify an interface uniquely to a public network [439]. The 20-byte Network Service Access Point (NSAP) format is designed for ATM addresses within private ATM networks. NSAP-format ATM addresses consist of three components: Authority and Format Identifier (AFI), which identifies the type and format of the Initial Domain Identifier (IDI); the IDI, which identifies the address allocation and administration authority; and the domain-specific part, which contains actual addressing information.

IP adopts a connectionless approach, while ATM is connection oriented. IPv6 has enriched IPv4 best-effort forwarding of IP datagrams with the capability to link data packets belonging to an end-to-end communication with uniform requirements. That is the concept of a *flow*. Network nodes can handle IP packets with the same flow identifier in the same manner. RSVP provides a means to exchange resource control information at the host router and at the router-router interfaces in order to negotiate and establish soft resource allocation. IP routers operate according to RSVP, upon receiving periodic refresh messages calling for resource reservation, and cache a link resource allocation state [440]. Resource allocation is implemented by sharing the output links of the routers according to a proper IP packet-scheduling algorithm.

7.4.1 Integrating IP and ATM

ATM offers Virtual Circuits (VCs) providing QoS guarantee in terms of data loss, bounded delay, and jitter. On the other hand, network resource control mechanisms are being introduced at the network layer of the Internet protocol with the objective of giving real-time traffic a priority with respect to nondelay-sensitive traffic. The effectiveness of the action of resource-control mechanisms applied at the network layer is limited by the capability of lower-layer protocols operated by subnetworks to enforce resource-control mechanisms. The sharing of the capacity of a point-to-point link among several traffic flows can be effectively operated by applying resource-control mechanisms at the network layer [441].

Although the Internet community is sponsoring ATM as the promising high-speed bearer technology of subnetworks, the vision of the Internet is still focusing on the protocol suite to be executed exclusively among hosts at network edges and routers in subnetwork boundaries. The perspective is to consider ATM as a high-speed data pipe technology and to guarantee QoS by means of RSVP [422, 424, 427].

Cooperation between RSVP and ATM signaling protocols to guarantee QoS is an attractive perspective for building novel broadband networks to carry Internet traffic over public infrastructures and over enterprise internets. The underlying subnetwork layer protocols are cooperating with the Internet network layers' protocols to provide QoS. Application support for QoS is shown in Figure 7.4.

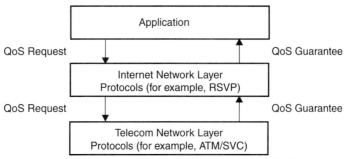

FIGURE 7.4   Application support for QoS [427].
©1997 IEEE.

A number of proposals have been introduced recently to integrate IP and ATM protocols. Examples are the IP switching [442] and tag switching [443] schemes. The former addresses a radical substitution of conventional routers and switching technologies to build high-speed IP backbones. The latter suggests a smoother overlay approach to be implemented over conventional routers and switching technology.

IP switching nodes dynamically shift between store-and-forward and cut-through switching [441, 442]. IP switches base their operation on the traffic flow concept. The IP flow feature introduced by IPv6 and RSVP is based on explicit flow identifiers. In this case, a traffic flow is a sequence of IP packets sent from a particular source to a particular destination, sharing the same protocol type, the same type of service, and other characteristics as determined by examining information in the packet header. Prior to cut-through, an IP switch acts like a router with store-and-forward routing of IP datagrams.

Tag switching enables the forwarding of IP packets directly across a network of tag switching compliant routers [443]. A tag switching network is made of two types of nodes: tag edge routers and tag switches. The former are routers at the edge of the tag switching network that apply tags and perform Internet network layer functions. The information can be carried in data units in two ways:

- As a part of the ATM layer header
- As a part of the Internet network layer header

Tag switching is independent of the routing protocols employed.

7.5   INTERNET INTEGRATED SERVICES

Until 1995, the Internet has been a "single-service" network, with all packets being treated more or less equally. Cooperative congestion control, operating at the endpoints through TCP, assured high overall utilization between customers and applications. If the Internet is also to carry real-time services and thus become an "integrated-services network," there have to be incentives for the network providers to provide the appropriate low-delay, highly reliable infrastructure. This will only occur when a significant number of people start using the Internet for "production" real-time use, or when mechanisms for incremental charging for such real-time-capable capacity have been implemented. Incremental charging is made more difficult by the large number of service providers—both ends of an audio conversation, for example, may rarely be served by the same provider.

The original design goal of the Internet was to serve a highly fault-tolerant network for the defense community. To this end, the amount of state shared between the network and end systems is minimized, being merely sufficient information to calculate a set of routers and, for each packet sent by an end system, to determine the best current route. In its original implementation, a great deal of attention was paid to this distributed, dynamic route calculation and not much to the performance aspects of packet forwarding.

Over time, it became apparent that traffic management for different applications, for different users, and for overloaded networks would be essential. A number of stages in the evolution of the protocols and implementations of the Internet have followed.

The first service differentiation was by application and the idea of Type of Service (ToS) forwarding was proposed [445]. Conceptually, routers distinguish traffic either by examining special bits in the IP packet header or by application protocol.

Telnet, File Transfer Protocol (FTP), and the WWW's application protocol, HyperText Transfer Protocol, all operate over TCP to provide ordered reliable delivery.

Group communication is very useful for applications that involve multiple simultaneous senders and receivers. The multicast backbone is a virtual overlay on the current Internet that provides multicast, which results in a massive reduction of load on the network for such applications [446].

Typical applications based on User Datagram Protocol (UDP) offer an approximately fixed rate of packets to the network. Fundamentally, to support arbitrary numbers of users of these applications and not suffer overload, the Internet has to be enhanced in some way. A number of possibilities exist: overengineering, resource reservation, and usage-based charging. The overengineering approach may work for a large class of applications, but many researchers and practitioners believe that there will always be some applications that can dominate the network capacity. In that case, resource reservation and perhaps usage-based charging are needed as well.

7.5.1 Internet Engineering Task Force Integrated Services

In response to the growing demand for an Integrated Services (IS) Internet, the Internet Engineering Task Force set up an Integrated Service Working Group. This group has defined several service classes that, if supported by the routers traversed by a data flow, can provide the data flow with certain QoS commitments [447]. A data flow identifies the set of packets to receive the special QoS. It is defined by a "session" comprising the IP address, transport layer protocol type and port number of the destination, along with a list of specific senders to that session that are entitled to receive the special QoS. Source address and port number identify each sender, while its protocol type must be the same as for the session.

The original Internet integrated service model supports three types of service classes: best effort, guaranteed, and predicted [444]. The network makes no service commitment to carry best-effort traffic except the promise not to delay and drop data unnecessarily. The network works properly and if the traffic generated by the source is conforming with the declared traffic profile, the network commits itself to give to guaranteed traffic hard delay bounds and lossless delivery to conforming traffic. The predicted service class provides low packet loss and a maximum delay bound, although occasional delayed or lost packets are tolerated. The traffic exceeding the declared profile is carried as best effort with no explicit identification, while in ATM networks, nonconformant traffic is explicitly tagged as lower priority and is carried with no guarantee.

The IETF has considered various QoS classes. Two of these, controlled load service and guaranteed service, have been formally specified for use in resource reservation protocol (RSVP) [448, 449].

7.5.2 Controlled-Load Service

Controlled-load service provides approximately the same QoS under heavy loads as under light loads. A description of the traffic characteristics for the flow desiring the controlled-load service must be submitted to the routers as for the case of guaranteed service, although it is not necessary to include the peak rate parameter. If the flow is accepted for controlled-load service, then the router makes a commitment to offer the flow a service equivalent to that seen by the best-effort flow on a highly loaded network. The important difference from the traditional Internet best-effort service is that the controlled-load flow does not noticeably deteriorate as the network load increases. This will be true regardless of the level of load increase. The controlled-load service is intended for those classes of applications that can tolerate a certain amount of loss or delay, provided it is kept to a reasonable load. Example applications in this category include adaptive real-time applications [450].

Controlled-load has some rather simple implementations in terms of the queuing systems in routers. It also functions adequately for the existing multicast backbone applications, which can adapt to the modest (small) scale end-to-end delay, variations, and jitter that it may introduce through the use of adaptive play and buffering.

7.5.3 Guaranteed Service

Guaranteed service provides an assured level of bandwidth, a form end-to-end delay bound, and no queuing loss for conforming packets of a data flow [451]. It is intended for applications with stringent real-time delivery requirements such as certain audio and video applications that have fixed "play-out" buffers and are intolerant of any datagram arriving after their playback time. Guaranteed service really addresses the support of "legacy" applications that expect a delivery model similar to traditional telecommunications circuits.

Each router characterizes the guaranteed service for a specific flow by allocating a bandwidth R and buffer space B that the flow may consume. This is done by approximating the "fluid model" of service so that the flow effectively sees a dedicated wire of bandwidth R between the source and receiver [452]. In a perfect fluid model, a flow conforming to a token bucket of rate r and depth b will have its delay bounded by b/r, provided $R \geq r$. To allow for deviations from this perfect fluid model in the router's approximation, two error terms, C and D, are introduced. These errors arise from the finite packet sizes that are being dealt with. For example, any packet may experience an excess delay as it is forwarded due to the size of the packets in the same queue and due to inaccuracies in scheduling from packets (of a possibly different size) in other queues bound for the output link. The delay bound becomes $b/r + C/R+D$.

With guaranteed service, however, a limit is imposed on the peak rate p of the flow, which results in a reduction of the delay. In addition, the packetization effect of the flow needs to be taken into account by considering the maximum packet size M. While the IP in principle permits a wide range of packet sizes, in practice the range supported makes this upper limit practical and realistic. These additional factors result in a more precise bound on the end-to-end queuing delay as follows:

$$Q_{delay\ end\text{-}to\text{-}end} = \frac{(b-M)(p-R)}{R(p-r)} + \frac{(M+C_{tot})}{R} + D_{tot}, \quad (case\ \ p > R \geq r) \qquad (7.1)$$

$$Q_{delay\ end\text{-}to\text{-}end} = \frac{(M+C_{tot})}{R} + D_{tot}, \quad (case\ \ R \geq p \geq r) \qquad (7.2)$$

The terms C_{tot} and D_{tot} represent the summation of the C and D error terms, respectively, for each router along the end-to-end data path. In (7.1), there are three delay terms, made from the contributions of the bursts of packets b (the bucket depth) sent at the peak rate p and serviced at the output link rate R, plus the sum over all hops of errors introduced at each hop due to a packet-size worth of fluid flow approximation, plus a third term made up of cross-traffic scheduling approximation contributions. In (7.2), the first term is absent. Because the link rate is greater than the peak, there are no packets queued from this flow itself.

For a router to invoke guaranteed service for a specific data flow, it needs to be informed of the traffic characteristics of the flow along with the reservation characteristics. Furthermore, to enable the router to calculate sufficient local resources to guarantee a lossless service requires the terms C_{sum} and D_{sum}, which represent the summation of the C and D error terms, respectively, for each router along the path.

7.6 MPEG-4 VIDEO TRANSPORT OVER THE INTERNET

MPEG-4 [273] is an emerging ISO/IEC standard that intends to establish a flexible content-based audiovisual environment that can be customized for specific applications (see Chapter 5). Efficient coding, access, and transmission of natural/synthetic audio/video for low bit rate (mobile) communications terminals and the Internet are supported. It is very important that MPEG-4 content may be transported over any transport mechanism, such as ATM or the Internet protocol.

Preparing MPEG-4 encoded content for transport starts with placing objects in Elementary Streams (ESs). Video and audio objects will have a single stream. Other objects may have two or more. Higher-level data describing the scene (Binary Format for Scene description (BIFS), updating, and positioning the media objects) is conveyed in its own ES. To inform the system which ES belongs to a certain object, MPEG-4 uses Object Descriptors (ODs). Object descriptors in turn contain Elementary Stream Descriptors (ESDs) to tell the system what decoders are needed to decode a stream. With another field, optional textual information about the object can be supplied. Object descriptors are sent in their own ES, which allow them to be added or deleted dynamically as the scene changes.

The play-out of the multiple MPEG-4 objects is coordinated at a layer devoted solely to synchronization. Here, elementary streams are split into packets, and timing information is added to the payload of these packets. These packets are then ready to be passed on to the transport layer. Timing information for the decoder consists of the speed of the encoder clock and the time stamps of the incoming streams, which are relative to the clock. Two kinds of time stamps exist: one indicates when a piece of information must be decoded, and the other indicates when the information must be ready for presentation. The distinction between the types of stamps is important. In many video coding schemes, some frames are calculated as an interpolation between previous and following frames. Thus, before such a frame can be decoded and presented, the one after it must be decoded (held in a buffer).

In terms of the ISO seven-layer communications model, no specific transport mechanism is defined in MPEG-4. Existing transport formats and their multiplex formats suffice, including the MPEG-2 transport stream, Asynchronous Transfer Mode (ATM), and Real-Time Transport Protocol (RTP) on the Internet. A separate transport channel could be set up for each data stream, but there can be many of these for a single MPEG-4 scene. A small toll in MPEG-4, FlexMux, was designed to act as an intermediate step to any suitable form of transport. In addition, another interface defined in MPEG-4 lets the application ask for connections with a certain quality of service, in terms of parameters like bandwidth, error rate, or delay. Application designers can write their own code without having to worry about the underlying delivery mechanisms. The next release of the standard MPEG-4 version 2 will allow differing channels to be used at either end of a transmission/receive network.

MPEG-4 video transmission over the Internet is in initial stages of the standardization process. In [453] architectural considerations of MPEG-4, video transmission over the Internet is presented. It captures the issues that have been raised and tries to highlight the commonalities and differences in MPEG and IETF concepts for MPEG-4 transport over the Internet.

- MPEG-4 over IP or MPEG-4 over the Internet?
- Architecture of session configuration and control.
- Architecture of stream description and mapping to transport channels.
- Fundamentals of the timing model.
- Two IP/MPEG-4 payload format integration approaches [454–456].
- Multiplexing and buffering.
- How much delivery awareness does the compression layer need?
- Data partitioning versus "real" scalability.

7.7 CONCLUDING REMARKS

It is apparent that IP will become the dominant networking protocol for the next decade. The Internet has evolved from a classical, closed-community data network into a true multiservice network that can support the emerging multimedia applications and their protocols with appropriate performance. Real-time services over the Internet, which include video and voice transmission, do not tolerate packet delay, jitter, and loss. The requirement to deliver information within a given play-out deadline prevents real-time applications from using TCP to enforce reliable information delivery. For that reason, video and voice applications developed for the Internet are based on UDP. UDP-based applications do not back off in case of network congestion, and interfere heavily with data traffic.

The RTP is designed to carry real-time continuous media data (video) over the Internet. RTP runs over UDP and sets a protocol framework tailored to each application via profile specification by assessing a set payload type code and its mapping to payload formats [454, 456]. Application control information specific to RTP is sent by using the RTCP. RTCP periodically sends receiver and sender reports to enable the calculation of packet loss, packet delay, jitter, and round-trip time, and to offer support for synchronization. The feedback information delivered in the receiver reports is used to estimate the network state (unloaded, loaded, or congested) and to perform software source code control and bandwidth variations.

WWW servers and browsers play back streaming video by a helper or plug-in application as the data are received. The Real-Time Streaming Protocol (RTSP) enables servers to connect to any standard-compliant client program [427]. RTSP operates on top of RTP and allows streaming servers to negotiate with client programs to find the most convenient data format and delivery rate that can be supported on a link and to control the streaming session while in progress. Optionally, RTSP allows the setting of parameters for permission, copyright control, and encryption.

Therefore, asynchronous transfer of video over the Internet faces many technical challenges, such as real-time data over nonreal-time network, high data rate over limited network bandwidth, and unpredictable availability of network bandwidth. For more detailed information on these topics, papers [427, 447, 503] are recommended.

C H A P T E R   8

Quality of Service for Packet Video over ATM Networks

SUMMARY

In this chapter, we outline the issues concerning Quality of Service (QoS) for packet video over ATM networks. An overview of video service classes defined by the ATM Forum is provided. Whether ATM is successful or not depends on whether good utilization of networking resources can be achieved. In this case, ATM would make full use of available capacity while maintaining QoS guarantees to all services. After presenting QoS parameters, we discuss QoS requirements.

Video communications are quite sensitive to network performance such as cell loss, cell transfer delays, and delay variations. The optimal association of ATM networking and video coding techniques will have to assure a flexible and reasonable QoS for video communications. In this chapter, we also treat traffic management functions and QoS requirements, and discuss the QoS protocol reference model and perceptual quality of the received video.

8.1   INTRODUCTION

Video is expected to be one of the major services offered in BISDN based on ATM [471], and will probably be the dominant traffic through such networks. Transmitting video over digital networks requires sophisticated compression techniques in order to limit bit rate requirements and to provide high-quality, reliable service to customers. To transmit video, multiple encodings and decodings, without any serious degradation are required. For example, the transmission of video in an ATM network requires QoS with $10^{-9} \leq$ Bit Error Rate (BER) $\leq 10^{-6}$, and a Cell Loss Ratio (CLR) $\leq 10^{-8}$. In the case of cell-structured transmission of video in an ATM network, packet losses may occur due to heavy traffic causing the buffers in the network nodes to overflow. Loss may also occur if packet transmission delay increases to the point that the packet arrives too late for playback on the terminal or storage overflow in the exchanges or impairment of the Virtual Channel Identifier (VCI) caused by bit errors. In either case, the result is loss of data in units of packets, and occasionally a burst of packet losses will occur. This results in a serious degradation of the quality of service, which is not acceptable for video either at variable and/or constant bit rates. Some common techniques such as error correction coding and protection by packet priority can be used for minimizing the degradation due to transmission errors [457].

A natural approach to protect the packets is to ensure an appropriate level of quality for each service class by assigning some sort of priority to packets. The definition of the priority can be done explicitly by assigning the Cell Loss Priority (CLP) field into the packet header in an ATM network [458].

In BISDN with ATM, various kinds of traffic—such as video, data, and voice—share the common transmission resources; in other words, they are multiplexed into one bit stream. This is a useful technique to use the link capacity efficiently. In the aspect of transfer delay, each type of traffic requires its own QoS. For example, real-time traffic, such as video, is sensitive to delay and delay jitter. In contrast to the real-time traffic, the nonreal-time data traffic is insensitive to delay, but sensitive to transmission error. Traffic control mechanisms are, therefore, required to meet the different QoS requirements of individual traffic. There are many kinds of traffic control mechanisms such as connection admission, usage parameter, and priority. Among these traffic control mechanisms, time priority control is generally used to meet different requirements of QoS regarding the delay constraint for high-priority traffic such as video and for low-priority traffic such as data [458].

With the finalization of MPEG video coding standards, digital video is being used in various applications such as CD-ROM recording, digital TV,

Digital Video Disc (DVD) recording and playback, Video on Demand (VoD), and High Definition Television (HDTV) [96]. Variable Bit Rate (VBR) video, packetized and transmitted over packet switched networks such as ATM, has a number of advantages over constant bit rate video. VBR bit stream is allowed, and therefore consistent quality video can be obtained, in an open loop operation with a constant Quantization Parameter (QP) for all pictures in a video sequence. Significant quality gain is expected. On the communication network side, packet-based transmission can achieve Statistical Multiplexing Gain (SMG) by multiplexing multiple video sources.

For constant quality, a video encoder is operated in an open loop, which is sometimes called "free VBR." The bit stream is packetized and sent to the network without buffering. The highly variable MPEG bit stream reduces the network throughput. On the other hand, it is always to the benefit of broadcasters and network operators to multiplex more channels without reducing video quality too much. The higher multiplexing requirement results in tighter traffic constraints on video sources. An encoder buffer is used to smooth variable bit streams to meet the traffic constraints. The extreme case is the CBR video, where a large buffer is required to smooth a VBR bit stream to a CBR bit stream. A high multiplexing gain can be achieved with CBR video, but the video quality is not, in general, consistent. Several studies showed that higher SMG could be achieved if an encoder buffer is used to smooth the highly variable MPEG bit stream [459, 460]. However, the finite buffer requires a closed loop operation, which will vary video quality and introduce additional delays. Thus, there exists a trade-off between consistent video quality and higher SMG.

For video over ATM networks, since video sources are located remotely on the network, open loop flow control uses a model to describe the traffic of each source. The model is called the Traffic Descriptor (TD), which has to be agreed upon by both the source and the network [461].

The leaky bucket (Section 3.6) has been used as a traffic policing mechanism for various studies [462, 463]. In order to guarantee that the video source is compliant with its leaky bucket parameters, some excess packets have to be dropped or marked as low-priority packets. Packet loss is inevitable due to unexpected bit stream changes in a video sequence. Because sizes of encoder and decoder buffers are finite, buffer overflow can also cause packet loss. Packet loss should be avoided for video services [462]. Thus, a source-based joint control of both encoder bit rate and channel transmission rate is necessary and can reduce or eliminate packet loss.

In the scenario where information from a group of video sessions is to be delivered as a bundle, compression and multiplexing of video streams should occur together before packetization. We call this *video aggregation*. Application areas of video aggregation include video broadcast, VoD, transport of long distance videophone data, and others. Video streams from various subscribers targeted for a common remote area may be aggregated at a local central office before being delivered as a bundle to the remote control office serving the area [464].

8.2 INTEGRATED VIDEO SERVICES OVER ATM

The ATM, a connection-oriented fast packet switching technique, is particularly adequate for the integration of a wide spectrum of services such as data, voice, image, video, or multimedia with different bit rate and QoS requirements. Its roots go back to the early 1980s when it became obvious that fast hardware switching and buffering circuits were able to cope with these challenges. For example, in 1986, the new sets of standards for the BISDN on ATM were set up [31]. Future broadband integrated services based on the ATM technology are expected to carry information from a large variety of different services and applications. However, video traffic is likely to dominate because of the large-bandwidth nature of images.

The format ATM is universal for any network: local or wide area, public, or private. This has the potential not only to provide a uniform scheme for integrating various types of services, but also to integrate local and wide area networking. Some large corporations are already installing ATM in Local Area Networks (LANs), thereby redrawing the boundary between their own networks and public networks, capturing more and more of the functionality and added value to their side. New applications, such as LAN interconnection, multimedia videoconferencing, or VoD, observe quite different traffic profiles and characteristics. A satisfactory service quality can be achieved only by proper traffic control schemes, such As Usage Parameter Control (UPC), cell loss control, resource dimensioning, and management [465].

One of the major advantages of the BISDN/ATM is the integration of different services. Multiple traffic management policies can be integrated and high network utilization can be achieved. The network can use sophisticated cell scheduling and queue management methods in order to support complex traffic management policies [466, 467].

A network switch element can employ cell queuing in order to prevent cell loss when congestion occurs in the switch element. Congestion takes place when the traffic load on an output port exceeds the output port's link rate. Figure 8.1 illustrates a switch element with queuing units. The queuing units can be located at the input, the output, or internal to the switch unit ports.

FIGURE 8.1   A switch element with queuing units [468].
©1998 IEEE.

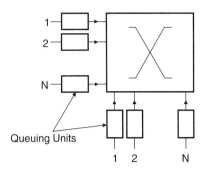

Three different queuing unit architectures are shown in Figure 8.2. The
cell scheduling and queue management methods most often found in ATM
networks today is First-In First-Out (FIFO) scheduling with a single queue
shared by all connections (see Figure 8.2a). In order to support integration of
traffic with different service requirements, the shared queue can be segmented
into multiple shared queues that are scheduled according to defined priorities
(see Figure 8.2b). A cell scheduling and buffer management method that
offers several advantages compared to shared queue methods is weighted fair
queuing (see Figure 8.2c). The queuing is per connection with FIFO queues,
while scheduling is performed according to a weighted allocation policy. The
weighted fair queuing method can provide [468]:

- **Weighted bandwidth allocation policies with enforcement of that policy.** Bandwidth is allocated on a per-connection basis, according to relative weights.
- **Isolation of users.** Well-behaved users can be protected from misbehav-
  ing users exceeding their allowed transmission rates, thereby improving
  network robustness.
- **Allocation of queue length can be allocated** along a network connection
  path on a per-connection basis.
- **Scalability.** Queue capacity can be scaled to match a connection's distance, speed, and number of traversed nodes.
- **Smooth flow of cells.**

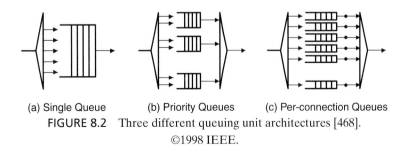

(a) Single Queue   (b) Priority Queues   (c) Per-connection Queues
FIGURE 8.2   Three different queuing unit architectures [468].
©1998 IEEE.

From these features, it can be understood that weighted fair queuing has strong theoretical support. Fairness and robustness are some of the major advantages that weighted fair queuing can provide.

8.3 SERVICE CLASSES DEFINED BY THE ATM FORUM

ATM has to manage a combination of constant and variable bit rate services with a wide range of bandwidth characteristics and varying sensitivities to data loss. The ATM Forum has attempted to find the same classification for the services expected in BISDN. In this way, they could identify the necessary transfer requirements for a few broad traffic classes and pack user data in an efficient manner for each class. They decided on four major service classes, which are listed in Table 8.1 [469]. In order to facilitate the efficient transfer of all these services, several methods are used to pack data into the 48 user bytes of an ATM cell. These methods are referred to as the ATM Adaptation Layers (AALs). Each AAL has a different segmentation and reassembly scheme that performs the packing and unpacking in a manner optimized for a specific class.

As for the asynchronous transfer of video, traffic on a particular link will consist of randomly interleaved cells belonging to different circuits. The network guarantees that all cells of a circuit follow the same route, and hence are delivered in the same order in which they were sent. The intention is that ATM networks should be able to guarantee the quality of service in terms of cell loss, as well as maximum delay and delay variations (Chapter 6).

Impairments play a central role in service definition and network design. The possible impairments are delay, cell delay variation, cell loss, and cell misinsertion. Delay includes packetization delay, queuing delay, and depacketization delay.

TABLE 8.1   General BISDN Service Classes Defined by the ATM Forum [469]

Service Class	Description
Constant Bit Rate (CBR)	Used for circuit emulation. The source must send blank cells if necessary to maintain a constant bandwidth.
Variable Bit Rate (VBR)	There are two types of VBR services: real-time, which are delay sensitive, and nonreal-time.
Available Bit Rate (ABR)	This class was developed for computer data. It uses as much bandwidth as is left on the network. As congestion increases, ABR bandwidth is reduced.
Unspecified Bit Rate (UBR)	Similar to the ABR class, UBR is expected to transfer the same types of services, but with no bounds on cell loss or delay.

Additionally, there may be switching delays as well as propagation delay. Cell delay variation means that different cells belonging to a particular virtual connection will generally suffer different delays in passing through the network because of queuing. Cell loss may be caused by transmission errors that corrupt cell headers, or by congestion due to traffic peaks or equipment failure. Cell misinsertion appears because corruption of the cell header may cause a cell to be routed to a wrong recipient. Such cells would be lost to the intended recipient and inserted into the wrong connection. Control of these impairments in order to provide an appropriate quality of service over a potentially very wide range of services is one of the dominating topics of ATM.

8.4 ATM SERVICE CATEGORY ALTERNATIVES

Five standardized ATM service categories specify which traffic and QoS parameters are associated with the connection. The numerical values of the parameters are used to establish a connection through the ATM network. In the case of a residential broadband access network operated by a telephone or cable company, the connection would be established from its own video server if it is supplying the content, or from the server of another company in the case of access to third-party content. When the network operator's server is used, proprietary service categories can be used in addition to the standardized ones. However, its features would need to be implemented on all ATM equipment in the network.

The first determination of service category is the bit rate. Since the number of bits varies from one frame to another, MPEG is naturally a variable bit rate coding scheme. However, many commercial MPEG codecs generate a constant bit rate, so their traffic can be transported over circuit-based networks such as Asymmetric Digital Subscriber Line (ADSL) or T1 systems. The conversion to CBR is achieved by means of a buffer on the output of the VBR codec as shown in Figure 8.3 [470]. To prevent overflow of the buffer, a feedback mechanism controls the quantization parameter of the codec in response to buffer fill level. CBR transport can therefore be used at the expense of varying video quality. A CBR codec is more costly to manufacture than a VBR codec, and is used prior to the widespread deployment of broadband VBR transport technologies such as ATM. Consequently, there is currently a significant installed base of CBR MPEG codecs, so that even when ATM transport is available, there is a requirement to transport CBR MPEG traffic over ATM.

FIGURE 8.3   Constant Bit
Rate (CBR) and Variable Bit
Rate (VBR) MPEG [470].
©1997 IEEE.

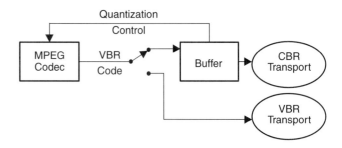

For nonreal-time traffic, there are three types of VBR service at the ATM level:

- **Nonreal-Time** (nrt), suited to packet traffic that is sensitive to error.
- **Unspecified Bit Rate** (UBR), similar to LAN service (for example, Ethernet) and suited to packet traffic that requires no performance guarantees from the network.
- **Available Bit Rate** (ABR), suited to packet applications that can reduce the rate of offered traffic in response to congestion control requests from the network.

The characteristics of these three service categories are listed in Table 8.2. Further details can be found in [394, 467].

nrt-VBR service can be used for MPEG traffic with the Maximum Burst Size (MBS) related to the number of MPEG transport packets obtained from a single MPEG frame, and to the number of MPEG transport packets that are batched together for segmentation into ATM cells.

The congestion control capability of ABR service is desirable if the traffic is VBR at the MPEG level. As the number of bits required for I frames are significantly larger than those for P and B frames, congestion can occur during the transport of multiple VBR MPEG streams. The tariff for ABR can be

TABLE 8.2   Characteristics of Nonreal-Time ATM Service Categories [470]

	nrt-VBR	ABR	UBR
Traffic parameters	PCR, SCR, MBS	PCR, MCR	PCR
QoS parameters	CLR	CLR	None
Congestion control	No	Yes	No

Note: PCR: Peak Cell Rate; SCR: Sustained (average) Cell Rate; MBS: Maximum Burst Size; MCR: Minimum Cell Rate; QoS: Quality of Service; CLR: Cell Loss Ratio.

©1997 IEEE.

expected to be less than the tariff for VBR because the source is assisting the network operator to control congestion. The congestion control method in ABR that is standardized by the ATM Forum is known as *Explicit Rate* (ER) [394, 467]. It allows the network to specify to the source the cell rate that should be offered within the range from MCR to PCR. When the source is constrained to retain cells because of network congestion, the buffer at the source may fill beyond an acceptable threshold. At this point, a feedback mechanism, such as the one illustrated in Figure 8.3, can be brought into operation to adjust the quantization of the codec to produce a more compressed code. Thus, a codec suited to ABR service is similar to a CBR codec in design and cost, whereas for VBR and UBR services the codec does not require any quantization feedback.

UBR is suited to applications in which video quality can be sacrificed in order to achieve low-cost transport [470]. It allows spare bandwidth from other applications to be used with no QoS guarantees. Although bandwidth can be requested, it cannot be guaranteed due to traffic through routers that do not implement the Internet bandwidth reservation protocol. Research and distance education content is suited to UBR residential broadband service since low tariffs are required, despite the fact that many applications incur a high transport cost. A summary of service category selection is shown in Figure 8.4.

8.5   VIDEO AGGREGATION

Compression methods of a video stream can be divided into two classes: VBR compression and CBR compression. In VBR compression, the output bit rate of the encoder varies according to the bandwidth requirement of the underlying video sequence. The image quality is more or less constant. In CBR compression, the output bit rate of the encoder is forced to be constant. The image

FIGURE 8.4   ATM service category selection [470]. ©1997 IEEE.

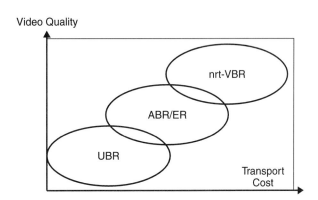

quality varies over time since scenes that demand high bandwidth may have their bandwidths cut down to maintain the constant output bit rate [471]. Bit rate and quality characteristics of VBR and CBR video compression schemes are shown in Figure 8.5. Compression schemes that lie somewhere between the two extremes are also possible.

The question that often arises is how to achieve both the advantage of VBR compression, which offers relatively constant image quality, and those of CBR transport, which facilitates simple network operation. The answer is that this is possible when several video streams are to be transported as a bundle. A common CBR channel can be used to transport the VBR compressed streams as a whole. It means that, as a group, the video bundle is CBR, but individually, the video streams are VBR.

In video aggregation, video sequences are compressed collaboratively so that (a) the sum of the bit rates of the video sequences is almost equal to, but not greater than, the reserved bit rate of the constant bit rate channel; (b) within each video stream, data discarded are less important than those retained; and (c) different video streams have roughly the same image quality according to some Signal-to-Noise Ratio (SNR) or distortion metric.

In video compression schemes, the output data can be divided into segments. Each segment has a certain number of bits. If needed, some of the bits can be dropped at the expense of image quality. Within each segment, bits can be ordered according to their significance, so that those of lower significance will be dropped first if necessary. The segments could be "blocks," while the bits are from codewords representing the nonzero frequency components in the blocks. The bits in a block can be ordered according to frequency. The codewords of low frequencies are generally more significant to image quality [472].

Let n be the number of video streams, and k the number of segments taken from each stream for aggregation. In this case, the total number of

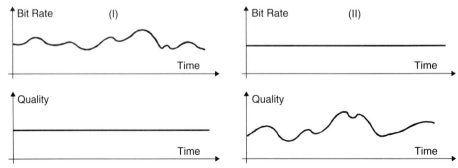

FIGURE 8.5   Bit rate and quality characteristics of VBR and CBR video compression scheme: (I) VBR video compression, (II) CBR video compression.

segments collected from all sources is $m = nk$. Let B_i be the number of bits reserved for sharing among the m segments. When B_i is insufficient to accommodate all bits of the segments, we can compute the number of bits $B_i(D)$ that must be retained for each segment i in order to maintain a distortion level of D. In order to select a specific but common operating distortion level for all segments, we find a distortion level D' so that

$$B_1(D') + B_2(D') + ...B_m(D') = B_i \qquad (8.1)$$

For each of segment i, the least-significant bits are then dropped so that the number of bits remaining is $B_i(D')$. In practice, our goal is to transport no more than $B_i(D)$ bits and to minimize the difference between distortion levels of any two segments.

MPEG traffic shows high fluctuation in bit rates because each frame type has a different mean bit rate. In [473], it is shown that the mean bit rate of I frame traffic in the MPEG stream, is nine times larger than that of B frame traffic. Thus, burstiness of aggregated MPEG traffic is significantly affected by starting positions of I frames. Figure 8.6 shows a block diagram for analysis of asynchronously aggregated MPEG traffic [473].

An input MPEG video signal is split into I, B, and P frames according to frame types and aggregate respective I-, B-, and P-frame traffic. Statistical characteristics of the aggregated MPEG traffic are computed from those of aggregated I, B, and P traffic. Figure 8.7 shows the diagram of asynchronously aggregated I-frame traffic. Aggregation of I-frame traffic reduces burstiness compared to a single MPEG traffic case. Traffic generated by different traffic sources is independent of one another.

The method for computation of the effective bandwidth of aggregated MPEG traffic was proposed in [473].

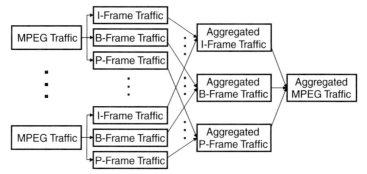

FIGURE 8.6   Block diagram for analysis of asynchronously aggregated
MPEG traffic [473].
©1996 IEEE.

FIGURE 8.7   Diagram of
asynchronously aggregated
I-frame traffic [473].
©1996 IEEE.

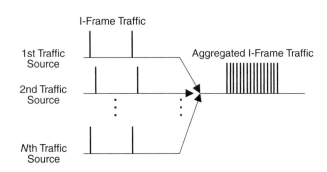

Figure 8.8 shows the block diagram of the proposed method. The effective bandwidth of the aggregated I-frame traffic is computed by the Gaussian bound because the aggregated I-frame traffic has very low correlation across frames. The aggregated B-frame traffic and the aggregated P-frame traffic are combined because they show similar exponentially decaying correlation characteristics across frames. The effective bandwidth of the aggregated MPEG traffic is computed by adding the Gaussian bound of the aggregated I-frame traffic and the modified equivalent capacity of the combined B- and P-frame traffic.

8.5.1   Modeling the Aggregated Traffic

Several video traffic models are proposed to model a single source at frame level [13, 32, 328, 474, 475, 476] and for subdivisions of the frame [477, 478]. However, the models for aggregate traffic should reproduce the distribution of cells in time, caused by the aggregation of the traffic of several sources with a determined packetization process. In previous work, the aggregate video traffic was modeled with the sum of bits generated by frame [328]. These models do not consider the possibility of sources with the random offset in time.

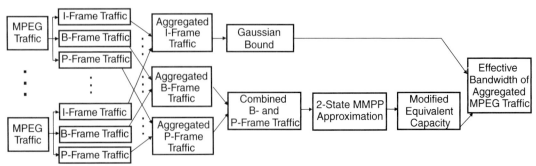

FIGURE 8.8   Proposed method for computation of the total effective bandwidth of aggregated MPEG traffic [473].
©1996 IEEE.

To model the aggregated traffic more accurately, assume the proposed scale: cells generated in a scale interval. A model should capture the essential properties of the source in order to generate an equivalent traffic artificially. In this way, the model can be used in simulations at the place of real traffic, with the computational load saving that this implies. The autocorrelation function is the most important statistical function related to the time [479]. The marginal distribution also has an important impact in the behavior of the model. The series number of cells generated in a slice interval could be seen as a time series that could be described with an Autoregressive Moving Average (ARMA) model. The ARMA model, unlike Markovian [13, 475, 479] and autoregressive [13, 32, 326, 328, 474, 475, 476] models, allows you to generate sequences with a more accurate autocorrelation function. An ARMA model is simply a digital filter with zeroes and poles excited with white noise. The filter permits that the output sequence has the autocorrelation function desired. The obtained sequence has a Gaussian distribution [21]. A transformation of the sequence is required if another type of distribution is desired [474].

8.6   QUALITY OF SERVICE

The existing definition of QoS lacks the clarity required to express separately the service provider's and customer's viewpoints, as illustrated in Figure 8.9. QoS required by the customer is a statement of the level of quality of a particular service required or preferred by the customer. The level of quality may be expressed by the customer in technical or nontechnical language. A typical customer is not concerned with how a particular service is provided or with any of the aspects of the network's internal design, but only with the resulting end-to-end service quality. It must be recognized that the customer's QoS requirements can be sometimes subjective. These requirements are useful, although subjective. It is up to the service provider to translate them into something of objective use [470].

QoS offered by the service provider is a statement of the level of quality that is offered to the customer. This is the level of service that the service provider can achieve with the design of the network. The level of quality is expressed by values assigned to network performance parameters, which cover the network and network support [471].

QoS achieved by the service provider is a statement of the level of quality achieved by the service provider. It is a record of the levels of quality that have been achieved. These are expressed by values assigned to the parameters specified for the offered QoS. These performance values are summarized for specified periods; for example, for the previous three months and/or on an annual basis.

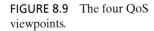

FIGURE 8.9   The four QoS
viewpoints.

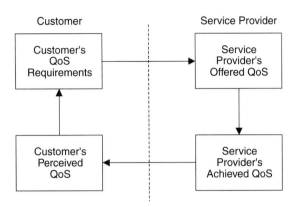

QoS perceived by the customer is a statement expressing the level of quality experienced by the customer. The perceived QoS is expressed usually in degree of satisfaction and not in technical terms. The perceived QoS is accessed by various methods, including customer's surveys, customer's comments, and customer's complaints. Figure 8.10 shows how the various QoS viewpoints interrelate with one another. The service provider and the network provider have been separated in the diagram to illustrate the fact that the service provider need not always be the network provider.

The services provider must always take full responsibility for the QoS offered to the customer. From the intrarelationships between the QoS viewpoints, it can be concluded that both the customer's and service provider's quality interest must be in a state of equilibrium in order to have successful business relationships. Therefore, it is necessary to manage the activities and

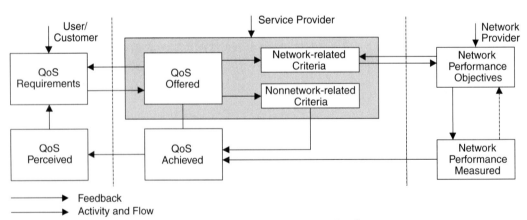

FIGURE 8.10   Various QoS viewpoints: intrarelationships [470].
©1997 IEEE.

relationships associated with QoS viewpoints to obtain the optimum quality levels in accordance with the price the customer is willing to pay.

The effect on end-to-end image quality of packet loss is not yet well defined. In early MPEG reference models, cell loss rates lower than 10^{-9} were proposed, but rates of 10^{-4} are currently being considered as acceptable. The effect of cell loss is not dependent only on the average cell loss rate, but also on the distribution of cell loss over time. Periods of high cell loss due to network congestion can have a serious detrimental impact on image quality [480].

Delay requirements vary depending on the application. For interactive video applications, a maximum end-to-end delay of some 100 ms is appropriate, while a much longer delay would be tolerable for a user simply watching a recorded clip or movie in a video playback application. Delay requirements have a strong impact on the type of the network service to be provided [481, 482]. For example, in the case of video playback, a large buffer in a settop box can absorb considerable variation in network delays of successive cells. On the other hand, the tight delay constraints for real-time communication limit the possibility of dealing with the congestion on network lines by cell buffering. Coding delays must be included in the overall delay budget, thus limiting the scope for rate smoothing in a closed-loop coder producing CBR output.

8.7   QUALITY OF SERVICE PARAMETERS

QoS is defined by specific parameters for cells that are conforming to the traffic contract. It is defined on an end-to-end basis. This perspective is actually meaningful to an "end user," which can be the end workstation, a customer premises network, a private ATM UNI, or a public ATM UNI. QoS is defined in terms of the one of the following measurement outcomes. The measurement is done with respect to cells sent from an originating user to a destination user.

- A transmitted cell from the originating user.
- A successfully transferred cell to the destination user.
- A lost cell that does not reach the destination user.
- An error cell that arrives at the destination but has errors in the payload.
- A misinserted cell that arrives at the destination but was not sent by the originator. This can occur due to an undetected cell header error or a configuration error.

The QoS parameters are defined in terms of the preceding outcomes by the following definitions [482]:

$$\text{Cell Loss Ratio} = \frac{\text{Lost Cells}}{\text{Transmitted Cells}} \tag{8.2}$$

$$\text{Cell Error Ratio} = \frac{\text{Errored Cells}}{\text{Successfully Transferred Cells + Errored Cells}} \tag{8.3}$$

$$\text{Severely Errored Cell Block Ratio} = \frac{\text{Severely Errored Cell Blocks}}{\text{Total Transmitted Cell Blocks}} \tag{8.4}$$

A severely errored cell block is defined as the case in which more than M out of N cells are in error, lost, or misinserted.

$$\text{Cell Misinsertion Rate} = \frac{\text{Misinserted Cells}}{\text{Time Interval}} \tag{8.5}$$

The Cell Transfer Delay is comprised of the following components illustrated in Figure 8.11. Let

- T1 = Coding and decoding delay
    T11 = Coding delay
    T12 = Decoding delay
- T2 = Segmentation and reassembly delay
    T21 = Sending-side AAL segmentation delay
    T22 = Receiving-side AAL reassembly/smoothing delay
- T3 = Cell transfer delay (end-to-end)
    T31 = Inter-ATM node transmission delay
    T32 = Total ATM node processing delay (due to queuing, switching, routing, and so on)

Delay can occur on the sending and receiving sides of the end terminal, in intermediate ATM nodes, and in the transmission links connecting ATM nodes.

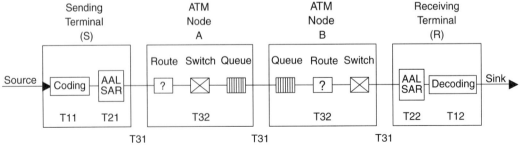

FIGURE 8.11   Sources of delay [482].

(Reprinted with the permission of The McGraw-Hill Companies from D.E. McDysand and D.L. Spohn, *ATM Theory and Applications*, McGraw-Hill, 1995.)

Cell Delay Variation (CDV) is currently defined as a measure of cell clamping, which is heuristically how much more closely the cells are spaced than the nominal interval. CDV can be computed at a single point against the nominal intercell spacing, or from an entry-to-exit point. Cell clamping is of concern because if too many cells arrive too closely together, then cell buffers may overflow.

The error rate is principally determined by fiber-optic error transmission characteristics, and is common to all QoS classes. Average delay is largely impacted to the propagation delay in the WAN, and average queuing behavior. A lower bound on loss is determined by fiber-optic error characteristics, with higher values of loss dominated by the effects of queuing strategy and buffer sizes. Delay, delay variations, and loss are impacted by buffer size and buffering strategy [483].

For those connections that do not (or cannot) specify traffic parameters and QoS class, there is a capability defined by the ATM Forum as "best effort" where no QoS guarantees are made and no specific traffic parameters need be stated. This traffic can also be viewed as "at risk" since there are no performance guarantees. In this case, the network admits this traffic and allows it to utilize capacity unused by connections that have specified traffic parameters and have requested a QoS class. It is assumed that connections utilizing the best-effort capability can determine the available capacity on the route allocated by the network.

The main problem of QoS parameters estimation is essentially that ATM traffic has almost no statistical structure. The underlying processes we are interested in are the occurrences of losses, the cell delay, and the cell delay variation processes in an ATM connection. If we assume Wide Sense Stationarity (WSS) in these processes, even fulfilled for self-similar traffic, the estimation of the delay's distribution is biased since at least the variance and all ordinary moments of degree two and higher are biased. The bias of the variance estimator of any random variable X is given by

$$E[VarX] = VarX\left(1 - 2\sum_{j=1}^{N-1} \frac{\left(1 - \frac{j}{N}\right)\rho_j}{N-1}\right) \tag{8.6}$$

where N is the number of samples and ρ_j is the normalized Autocovariance Function (ACF) of the process X at log j [483]. As the number of samples N (the measurement window) are increased, this bias tends toward zero, even if the ACF does not decrease quickly, as is the case in self-similar processes. The online measurement of the losses shows, due to correlation effects, similar behaviors as the delays process. In other words, the measured QoS parameters only converge toward a constant value as long as the traffic is at least ergodic and WSS. These conditions are generally fulfilled in simulations but not in reality. Thus, since nonstationarity means that the distributions are time dependent, all moments of the measured process are also time dependent.

The main consequence is that any window-based measurement will give wrong results. The longer the measurement is (that is, the wider the window is), the more the effects of nonstationarity will be taken into account.

EXAMPLE 8.1

Let us define the occurrences of losses of stochastic process $X_k = n$ $(n \geq 0)$, the number of losses in one connection at slot time k. Since from the beginning until the end of the connection, the random variable X has an assigned value for each time slot, the number of samples N is the number of ATM slots in the connection. The mean of this process is an estimator of the CLR. This estimator converges with increasing N since the bias of the variance becomes negligible as seen in (8.6).

EXAMPLE 8.2

Consider the time needed to measure a CLR of 10^{-5} in a 1.5 Mbps connection. For about 100 cells lost, this time is about 45 minutes. For the same connection, the 10^{-6} delay quantile is in the range of 10 seconds. The losses and delays in such a connection are correlated. The same estimator used in different time periods over a connection will provide different estimations in the same QoS parameter.

8.7.1 QoS Classes

In order to make things simpler on users, a small numbers of predefined QoS classes are defined, with particular values of parameters prespecified by a network in each of a few QoS classes [500]. The ATM Forum *UNI specification version 3.0* defines the five numbered QoS classes and example applications summarized in Table 8.3.

TABLE 8.3   ATM Forum QoS Classes [482]

QoS Class	QoS Parameters	Application
0	Unspecified	"Best effort" "At risk"
1	Specified	Circuit emulation, CBR
2	Specified	VBR video/audio
3	Specified	Connection-oriented data
4	Specified	Connectionless data

(Reprinted with the permission of The McGraw-Hill Companies from D.E. McDysand and D.L. Spohn, *ATM Theory and Applications*, McGraw-Hill, 1995.)

In the unspecified QoS class, the network operator for the performance parameters specifies no objective. Services using the unspecified QoS class may have explicitly specified traffic parameters. An example application of the unspecified QoS class is the support of best-effort service, where effectively no traffic parameters are specified. For this type of "best effort" service, the user does not effectively specify any traffic parameters and does not expect a performance commitment from the network. One component of the best-effort service is that the user application is expected to adapt to the time-variable, available network resources. The interpretation and clearer definition of the best-effort service is an ongoing activity in the ATM Forum. The current name for this type of service is the Unspecified Bit Rate (UBR).

For each specified QoS class, there is one specified objective value for each performance parameter, where a particular parameter may be essentially unspecified (for example, a loss probability of 1). Initially, each network provider should define the ATM performance parameters for at least the following service classes from ITU-T *Recommendation I.362* in a reference configuration:

- Service Class A: Circuit emulation, constant bit rate video
- Service Class B: Variable bit rate audio and video
- Service Class C: Connection-oriented data transfer
- Service Class D: Connectionless data transfer

In the future, more QoS classes may be defined for a given service class [482]. The following specified QoS classes are defined by the ATM Forum:

Specified QoS Class 1 supports a QoS that meets service class A performance requirements. This class should yield performance comparable to current digital private-line.

Specified QoS Class 2 supports a QoS that meets service class B performance requirements. This class is intended for packetized video and audio in teleconferencing and multimedia applications.

Specified QoS Class 3 supports a QoS that meets service class C performance requirements. This class is intended for interoperation of connection-oriented protocols, such as frame relay.

Specified QoS Class 4 supports a QoS that meets service class D performance requirements. This class is intended for interoperation of connectionless protocols.

Figure 8.12 shows a concrete example of how the QoS parameters for cell loss ratio for the CLP=0 flow and cell delay variation might be assigned for the four specified QoS classes. A network operator may provide the same performance for

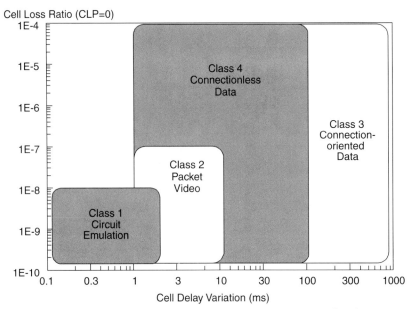

FIGURE 8.12   Example of QoS class value assignments [482].
(Reprinted with the permission of The McGraw-Hill Companies from D.E. McDysand and D.L. Spohn, *ATM Theory and Applications*, McGraw-Hill, 1995.)

all or a subset of specified QoS classes, subject to the constraint that the requirements of the most stringent service class are met.

8.8   QUALITY OF SERVICE REQUIREMENTS

Various applications have different QoS requirements. For example, some well-known requirements exist for voice after 30 years of experience in telephony. If voice has greater than about 15 ms of delay, then echo cancellation is usually required. Packetized voice can accept almost a 1 percent cell loss rate without being objectionable to most listeners. Newer applications do not have such a basis, or well-defined requirements; however, there are some general requirements.

Video application requirements depend upon several factors, including the video coding algorithm, the degree of motion required in the image sequence, and the resolution required in the image. Loss generally causes some image degradation, ranging from distorted portions of an image to loss of an entire frame, depending upon the extent of the loss and the sensitivity of the video-coding algorithm. Also, variations in delay of greater than 20 to 40 ms can cause perceivable jerkiness in video playback.

Users of interactive applications are also sensitive to loss and variations in delay due to retransmissions and inconsistent response time, which can decrease productivity. Consistent response time (or lack thereof) can affect how users perceive data service quality.

Distributed computing and database applications can be very sensitive to absolute delay, loss and variations in delay. The ideal is infinite bandwidth with latency close to the speed of light in fiber. A practical model is that of performance comparable to a locally attached disk drive or CD ROM, which ranges from 10 to 100 ms.

In ATM networks, QoS will be selectable and controllable from both terminal capability and network performance. Thanks to VBR communication realized by ATM, the terminal can generate its coded data at any bit rate regardless of the constants or variables during communication. This means that terminals will be able to demand any QoS they wish.

However, it is not possible to use the maximum QoS for all communications without any limitations. The important constraint may be the cost or charging of ATM network services. The better QoS will require higher costs when the amount of data transmitted during communication is the same. Users will have to consider a trade-off between QoS and cost of communications. This implies that, in principle, QoS of communication will be left to the user [497].

Since ATM networking and video coding techniques are closely related in the context of end-to-end QoS, interactions and relationships of terminal capability and the network performance need to be examined to assure a flexible and reasonable QoS for video communications. One of the goals of ATM networks is to support different traffic superpositions with different bandwidth and QoS requirements. At the same time, network resources have to be optimized.

The BISDN should be able to meet different requirements of the ATM layer [426, 444]. These QoS requirements are specified in terms of objective values of some of the network performance parameters specified in [485]. This parameters are Cell Loss Ratio (CLR), Cell Transfer Delay (CTD), and Cell Delay Variation (CDV). The negotiation of the QoS class takes place at connection establishment and is part of the traffic contract. From the legal point of view, it is a commitment for the network to respect this contract and offer the required QoS to the user [486]. This means that the Connection Acceptance Control (CAC) function must know whether the network can respect a contract under negotiation [487]. This function must access some measured parameters that will allow to decide whether required resources may be allocated or not, while respecting all other contracts of the already established connections (see Section 8.10).

ATM connection duration is not limited and may last from few seconds to several hours. Since each connection will negotiate a contract with the network and the users will pay for the negotiated QoS, it is not so obvious what exactly this long-term commitment is.

8.9 QUALITY OF SERVICE AND BASIC CODING TECHNIQUES

ATM, which has been recommended by the ITU, has the transfer mode in broadband ISDN networks, supports transmission of VBR traffic via statistical multiplexing, and assigns priorities to the signals being transmitted. ATM was proposed to achieve both high-speed transmission and flexibility. Video applications ranging from video telephony to High Definition TV (HDTV) require a variety of network bandwidths, and need to satisfy real-time constraints; for example, delay and Cell Loss Rate (CLR). The performance of ATM networks in handling video applications depends on the way in which the video signals are coded and packetized. Compressed video data are packetized into cells with a fixed size. Each cell is switched and transmitted independently, and is subject to a delay due to coding, packetization, switching, transmission, and queuing. If the delay exceeds the human vision tolerance limit, excessively delayed cells will have to be discarded and regarded as lost cells. Coding and packetization of video data must be designed to minimize the effects of cell loss on the QoS.

Hierarchical video coding has proven to be a powerful technique in alleviating the problem of cell loss in ATM networks. The benefits of coding VBR video signals into hierarchical layers in ATM networks include:

- Hierarchical coding to select presentation quality according to the type of service.
- When video signals are packetized into ATM cells, video signals from the same hierarchical level must be packed into the same cells. In addition, during network congestion, only the least important cells from the higher layers are dropped This ensures that the cells from the lowest layer are successfully transmitted, which, in turn, guarantees satisfactory QoS.
- Hierarchical coding allows error protection since the important video signals from the lower layers in the hierarchy constitute a small fraction of the total video signals, and error occurrence in important video signals is reduced.
- Hierarchical coding permits video signals to pass through a large number of different bandwidths during multicasting.

In recent years, more and more attention has been paid to two-layer video coders, since ATM networks support two levels of priority traffic. A simple partition scheme, using a cut-off frequency, was proposed to partition the

DCT coefficients into two layers [179]. Since both layers are coded by the MPEG-2 standard [96], the traffic at both layers is variable and bursty. Furthermore, since the same quantizer scale applies to the video signals at both layers, it is impossible to adapt the traffic at one layer without affecting the other. Another two-layer coder is discussed in [488] where the video signals at the primary layer are coded at a low bit rate with moderate picture quality.

The residual coding distortion, which is the difference between the input video and the decoded output of the primary layer, is coded in a secondary stage to provide an enhancement layer of data. However, this scheme requires a number of successive passes over each frame of data to refine the picture. In [489], a novel two-layer coding technique and its characteristics are investigated wherein the video signals of a video stream, after block DCT and quantization, are divided into two layers (primary and secondary layers). A hybrid coding scheme of a Vector Quantization (VQ) technique and an entropy coder is exploited to code the DCT coefficients at the primary layer. The error (DCT) components between the original quantized DCT and the decoded output of the primary layer are coded at the secondary layer by an entropy coder.

8.10   TRAFFIC MANAGEMENT FUNCTIONS AND QOS REQUIREMENTS

The QoS of video communication depends first on the capabilities of sending terminals, which will perform coding to source pictures and organize picture data into transmission signals. The QoS perceived at the receiving end will be affected by the network's transmission impairments referred to as *network performance*. Thus, the end-to-end QoS from the viewer's point of view can be represented as a function of two factors: terminal capability and network performance: for example,

$$QoS = f \text{ (terminal capability, network performance)} \qquad (8.7)$$

A typical parameter of terminal capability is the number of coded frames per second that will correspond to the fidelity of reproduced motion at the receiving end. On the other hand, network performance will be expressed by ATM-based parameters such as cell losses, cell-transfer delays and delay variations, and bit errors in the cell payload.

In order to ensure that the QoS in terms of cell loss and cell delay of the ATM connections meets the requirements of the supported services and applications, traffic management functions must be implemented in the ATM network. A key traffic management function is Connection Admission Control

(CAC), which accepts or rejects a new call. CAC, as a part of the resource management of the BISDN, will accept or reject the user's request, depending on available network resources. For performing this CAC, the terminal will be requested to inform the network of the necessary bandwidth and QoS class. The bandwidth and QoS can be negotiated between the terminal and the network. If the terminal follows the negotiated bandwidth and does not exceed traffic above the negotiated value, the network will have to assure the QoS. CAC estimates the resource requirements of an ATM connection based on the connection's traffic descriptors and QoS requirements [490].

The ITU defines a mandatory traffic descriptor, the Peak Cell Rate (PCR), based on the minimal time interval between two consecutive cells of the connection [395]. It also defines the Cell Delay Variation Tolerance (CDVT) parameter that allows some variation of the PCR. In the ATM Forum, an additional pair of traffic descriptors, the Sustainable Cell Rate (SCR) and the burst tolerance, are defined based on a Generic Cell Rate Algorithm (GCRA), which is equivalent to the so-called "leaky bucket" algorithm (Section 3.6). In general, the CAC will admit a new call if the sum of all equivalent rates, including that of the new call, does not exceed the link capacity.

Two types of control mechanisms have been proposed for ATM networks: preventive and reactive. The first corresponds to traffic control, the second to congestion control. The purpose of the traffic control is to minimize congestion. When a new call arrives, the network must perform admission control by determining whether to accept this call or not, based on the current network utilization, this call's traffic descriptor, the required QoS of the calls, and the network efficiency [490].

Given the types of services and the QoS requirements, the network must first determine the acceptance region within which all QoS requirements can be satisfied. In the case where the acceptance region is not known, the network has to make admission decisions on a real-time basis. *Network efficiency* can be defined by high throughput or high economic efficiency.

In spite of preventive control measures, congestion may occur. Reactive actions are necessary to minimize the intensity, spread, and the duration of the congestion. However, congestion control requires considerable exchange of information among the nodes of the network. At the switching nodes, buffers are required to solve switching conflicts that arise when several cells are switched simultaneously to the same destination link. When too many cells arrive at the same time, the buffer can be saturated. Unpredictable fluctuations of traffic flows and a wrong modeling at the source behavior may also be at the root of this saturation. The exchange of information among the nodes occurs through the headers of data cells and through some control cells.

Two types of congestion notifications are used: forward and backward [491]. In a forward congestion-based scheme, when a switch is congested, forward notifications are sent to the destination to inform it that the congestion was encountered at the same point along the Virtual Circuit/Virtual Path (VC/VP) [467]. The current ATM network architecture for resource management contains two levels: VC and VP. A *virtual path* is a group of connections sharing a common path from source to destination. Virtual circuits are the individual connections within a virtual path. When a call arrives, the network first checks whether a virtual path for the source and destination pair exists. If the virtual path exists, then the network verifies whether there is enough capacity within the VP for a new VC to accommodate this call. Once the call is admitted, no call processing is required at transit nodes, and cells will be delivered in order. If the virtual path does not exist, or if there is no capacity for the VC within the existing VP, the network can reject the call, request more resources if the virtual path exists, or create a new virtual path. Upon receiving the marked cells, the destination returns the control cells to inform the source about the congestion status. The source works with this feedback information to increase or decrease the bit rate.

In the backward congestion notification, a rate-based scheme similar to the forward case can be used, except that no notifications are sent directly from the congested point to the source.

Another important element is routing based on QoS requirements. A typical resource reservation process has two essential steps: finding resources and making reservations. Resource reservation can only be made when routing has found paths with sufficient resources to meet user requirements. Therefore, to support the resource reservation, routing has to take into consideration the wide range of QoS requirements [484]. In order to support the wide range of QoS requirements, routing protocols need to have a more complex model where the network is characterized with multiple metrics such as bandwidth, delay, and loss probability. The basic problem of QoS routing is to find a path that satisfies multiple constraints. As current routing protocols are already reaching the limit of feasible complexity, it is important that the complexity introduced by the QoS support not impair the scalability of routing protocols.

8.11 QOS PROTOCOL REFERENCE MODEL

The QoS protocol reference model provides a generic framework to integrate, coordinate, and manage system components to provide end-to-end guaranteed QoS for a wide range of applications. Figure 8.13 illustrates the proposed QoS protocol reference model [28]. It consists of a number of layers and planes.

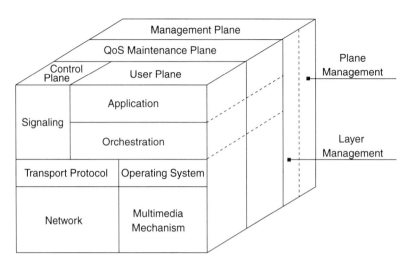

FIGURE 8.13   QoS protocol reference model [28].
©1997 IEEE.

The layer architecture consists of the application, orchestration, and communication layer.

- The application layer corresponds to the generic application platform.
- The orchestration layer is responsible for maintaining playback continuity in single streams and coordination across multiple related multimedia streams.
- The communication layer provides real-time scheduling at the host system, and real-time delivery via the network.

The communication layer is further divided into two different parts: network and multimedia host system.

The layered architecture hides the complexity of multimedia communications and the diversity of multimedia requirements from the upper layers. The lower layers provide services to the upper layers, and the upper layers specify service requirements. Figure 8.14 depicts the relationship between the layered architecture and the ISO OSI protocol reference stack [492].

There are also four planes in the reference model: user, control, QoS maintenance, and management.

The **user plane** is for the transport of multimedia data from the source to the destination.

The **control plane** is for the signaling of multimedia call establishment, maintenance, and disconnection. Such signaling can be transmitted out of band (that is, in a different channel from the data) to decouple the different service requirements between the data and the control messages.

Application				Application
Orchestration				Presentation
				Session
Generation	Transport	Presentation		Transport
				Network
				Data Link
				Physical

The **QoS maintenance plane** guarantees contracted QoS levels to multi-media applications on an end-to-end basis. The main functions performed on this plane include QoS management, connection management, and admission control. The QoS managers span all system layers, and each is responsible for QoS negotiation, QoS translation between the adjacent layers, and interaction with the corresponding layer (for example, to gather the status of messages about QoS from that layer). The connection manager is responsible for the connection establishment, maintenance, and disconnection. The connection manager also has to adapt dynamically to QoS degradation (connection management is discussed in Sections 8.12 and 8.13). Admission control is responsible for performing the admissibility test. Such tests include the schedulability test, bandwidth allocation test, and buffer allocation test. The connection manager is required to interact closely with the QoS manager and with admission control to achieve guaranteed performance.

The **management plane**, including layer management and plane management is responsible for operation, administration, maintenance and provision services. Layer and plane management provides intraplane and interplane management for communication.

8.12   QoS: Maintenance, Monitoring, Adaptation

A systemwide resource manager is required to manage the various system components and to perform admission control to guarantee the QoS of the existing connections. The packet loss model accounts for packet losses of both the server and the network and can be used as the basis for systemwide admission control [28]. QoS maintenance for each component may include congestion control and flow control in the network, as well as real-time scheduling at the host systems and media servers.

QoS monitoring performs traffic policing to prevent the user from violating the negotiated traffic characteristics. For example, traffic-shaping mechanisms such as the leaky bucket scheme may be applied [493]. If the user violates the service contract, penalties may be imposed, such as lowering the service priority or charging more.

Since the traffic is dynamic, sometimes the system may be overloaded. If the negotiated QoS cannot be guaranteed, or the user would like to change the negotiated parameter values during the connection, renegotiation between the user and the system will be required.

8.13   PERCEPTUAL QUALITY OF THE RECEIVED VIDEO

The communication system for packet video with ATM has to limit the loss and delay so that the perceptual quality of the received video is adequate for its intended use [494]. Most of the information loss objectively measured would be incurred at the source encoding when used. The coding is done in accordance with the signal properties, and possibly also based on the application context. The introduced error can therefore be made as imperceptible as possible. Information loss during transfer may interfere with the signal at any point and, although the probability of loss may be low, it could cause annoying effects in the reconstructed video. Acceptable levels for transfer loss and error are difficult to determine. They depend on the criteria such as the use and cost of the video transfer, the duration of the session, the quality of the source material, and the appearance of the loss and errors in the reconstructed signal [495–497]. It is possible to reduce visibility of loss by signal processing means. The probability of occurrence may also be reduced by forward error correction when the loss events are independent.

The factors that have the greatest impact on quality are the number of lost cells and packets, the number of pixels in an impaired region and its shape, and the "burstiness" of the loss. For the latter, random cell or packet losses are found to yield greater quality degradation than clustered losses at equal loss ratios. Thus, for a given loss probability, one may safely assume that uncorrelated loss will give an upper bound on the quality degradation [494].

The delays will vary from packet to packet since the transfer is asynchronous. The most common approach to handling the variations is to impose a delay limit and to delay all data up to that limit. The delay variations are of little concern when the maximum delay in the network is below the tolerable end-to-end limit. When this is not the case, arrivals with delay above the limit are discarded upon reception, and excessive delay is therefore turned into loss.

For a given delay distribution, there is consequently a balance between the amount of delay and the probability of loss [495].

There are limits under which further improvements in delay and loss are unnoticeable to the eye. Passing these limits does not lead to improvements for the user, and it may increase the complexity of the control functions and the wasted capacity in the network.

8.14   CONCLUDING REMARKS

In the business climate, it will be disadvantageous for a service provider to ignore the demands on quality specified by customers. A methodology, which could simplify the identification and management of tasks associated with QoS, is favorable. The service provider who offers credible quality at a lower price wins. However, service providers still need to learn how to achieve a viable balance between cost and quality.

Topics for future work are to incorporate a more detailed network with dynamic usage parameter control, admission control, and the ATM access switch, and to estimate the actual statistical multiplexing gain. Through the implementation of VBR coding, we expect to better understand the trade-offs among video quality, network components on the service quality, and other possible service types. On the system structure, communication with media server, dispatching packets, and storage management can be included. To significantly improve system performance, new disk technology has to be used in the future. The future evolution phase involves the integration of advanced intelligent networks into ATM.

Video in Multimedia Communications

SUMMARY

Multimedia communications have been used by various distributed applications. Videoconferencing/retrieval systems and video on demand will address all network types. The development of interactive television on a large scale presents numerous technical challenges in a variety of areas. As progress continues to be made in all these areas, trial deployments of all interactive services are necessary to ascertain consumer interest in this new form of communication.

Many issues relating to video delivery over ATM are discussed in this chapter. These include distributed multimedia systems and applications: interactive television, video on demand, scalability with respect to multimedia, routing, and pricing. Most of these areas are still the focus of debate. With the potential that ATM networks have for the delivery of video services, it is clear that this topic will continue to be of great interest in the near future.

9.1 INTRODUCTION

Multimedia itself denotes the integrated manipulation of at least some information represented as continuous media data, as well as some information encoded as discrete media data (text and graphics). Here, we have the act of capturing, processing, communicating, presenting, and/or storing.

We understand continuous media data as time-dependent data in multimedia systems (audio and video data), which is manipulated in well-defined parts per time intervals according to a contract. Multimedia communication deals with the transfer, protocols, services, and mechanisms of discrete media data (text, graphics) and continuous media data (audio, video) in/over digital networks. Such communication requires that all involved components be capable of handling a well-defined Quality of Service (QoS). The most important QoS parameters are required capacities of the involved resources, compliance to end-to-end delay and jitter as timing restrictions, and restriction of the loss characteristics. A protocol designed to reserve capacity for continuous media data, transmitted in conjunction with the discrete media data over, for example, an Asynchronous Transfer Mode-Local Area Network (ATM-LAN) is certainly a multimedia communication issue [262].

A Distributed Multimedia System (DMS) is an integrated communication, computing, and information system that enables the processing, management, delivery, and presentation of synchronized multimedia information, which the quality of service guarantees [28]. Multimedia information may include discrete media data, such as text, data, and images, and continuous media data, such as video and audio. Such a system enhances human communications by exploiting both visual and aural senses, and provides the ultimate flexibility in work and entertainment, allowing one to collaborate with remote participants, view movies on demand, and access online digital libraries from the desktop.

In networked multimedia applications, various entities typically cooperate in order to provide the mentioned real-time guarantees to allow data to be presented at the user interface. The requirements are most often defined in terms of QoS. We distinguish four layers of QoS: user QoS, application QoS, system QoS, and network QoS [481]. The user QoS parameters describe requirements for the perception of multimedia data at the user interface. The application QoS parameters describe requirements for the application services possibly specified in terms of media quality (for example, end-to-end delay) and media relations (for example, inter/intrastream synchronization). The system QoS parameters describe requirements of the communications services resulting from the application QoS. These may be specified in terms of both quantitative (for example, bits per second or task processing time) and qualitative (for example, multicast, interstream synchronization, error recovery, or ordered delivery of data) criteria. The network QoS parameters describe requirements on network services (for example, network load or network performance).

Multimedia applications negotiate a desired QoS during the connection setup phase either with the system layer or possibly directly with the network layer, if the system is not able to provide QoS for applications. If both are not capable of providing the desired QoS, many current multimedia applications try to set up end-to-end connection and take care of QoS themselves.

Interactive Television (ITV) is a new form of digital consumer multimedia service that can give viewers much greater control over the content of the programs than is possible with conventional analog television. Advances in audio/video compression, multimedia database systems, ongoing deployment of broadband networks, inexpensive home terminals, and user-friendly interfaces provide the infrastructure for offering a wide variety of interactive video services to consumers at home via standard television [201]. Such services include Video on Demand (VoD), video telephony, multimedia information retrieval, distance education, home shopping, and multiplayer/multilocation video games. The most important aspect of ITV is the ability of the viewer to exercise both coarse and fine-grain control over the contents of the programming being viewed. The selected multimedia material could contain still images, video, and audio. Creating a customized entertaining experience with audio/video whose quality is comparable to state-of-the-art conventional TV programming is the challenge of ITV. Each viewer of an ITV application is totally independent. This requires that a separate instance of an application be executed by the ITV system for each viewer, although the stored or synthesized media elements are shared. Economically providing the appropriate computing, storage, and communication facilities required for each viewer of an ITV system is key for such services. An ITV system deals with data types (audio, video) that are typically large, even after compression, and must be processed within real-time constraints. The data throughput or bandwidth required for each viewer can be 25 to 100 times that required for standard voice telephony.

9.2   DISTRIBUTED MULTIMEDIA SYSTEMS

Distributed Multimedia Systems (DMS) will create an electronic world in which people are able to shop, work, or learn at home, watch video programs on demand, access online digital libraries from the desktop, and so forth [28]. Technological advances in computers, high-speed networks, data compression, and consumer electronics—coupled with the availability of multimedia resources, mechanisms, and manipulation functions, the development of the relevant standards, and the convergence of the computers, telecommunications, and cable television industries—are accelerating the realization of such systems. The ability to accommodate continuous as well as discrete media in an integrated system is the distinguishing feature of multimedia systems. An example of a DMS is a number of multimedia PCs and/or workstations interconnected with continuous media servers via the Internet that allow users to retrieve, browse, and manipulate video or audio. Such networked multimedia systems dramatically enhance the existing CD-ROM-based multimedia applications and encourage newly emerging broadband applications—at the expense of higher complexity due to the requirements of guaranteed QoS. These include constraints on bit error rates, packet loss probabilities, and delivery delays required in a traditional point-to-point information delivery system. Additional constraints are introduced due to the orchestration of distributed media in a DMS, such as the synchronization among multiple media streams from distributed sources to achieve a meaningful presentation. Formally, we can define a DMS as an integrated communication, computing, and information system that enables the processing, management, delivery, and presentation of synchronized multimedia information with QoS guarantees. Figure 9.1 summarizes a DMS.

The inputs of the system consist of the important factors that drive a DMS from concept to reality, and the outputs consist of a wide range of distributed multimedia applications. The system inputs (see Figure 9.1) can be divided into three orthogonal dimensions: The inputs shown on the left are the major contribution industries, including the computers, telecommunications, cable TV, entertainment, and consumer electronics industries. The inputs shown on the right are the important issues in the development of a DMS, including the technical, standardization, regulation, copyright, market, and

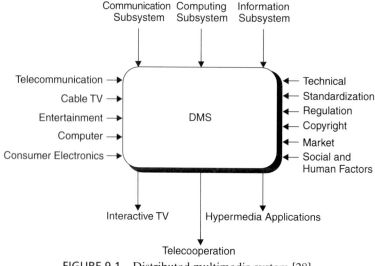

FIGURE 9.1   Distributed multimedia system [28].
©1997 IEEE.

social and human factors. The inputs shown at the top are a collection of the enabling technologies of the information subsystem (for storage), the communication subsystem (for transmission), and the computing subsystem (for processing). The information subsystem consists of the multimedia servers, information archives, and multimedia database systems. It stores and retrieves multimedia information, serves a large number of simultaneous user requests with QoS guarantees, and manages the data for consistency, security, and reliability. The communication subsystem consists of transmission medium and transport protocols. It connects the users with distributed multimedia resources and delivers multimedia materials with QoS guarantees, such as real-time delivery for video or audio data and error-free delivery for text data. The computing subsystem consists of a multimedia platform (ranging from a high-end graphics workstation to a multimedia PC equipped with a CD-ROM drive, speaker, sound card, and video card), Operating System (OS), presentation and authoring tools, and multimedia manipulation software. It allows users to manipulate the multimedia data. An authoring tool is specialized software that allows a producer or designer to design and assemble multimedia elements for a multimedia presentation. The outputs of the system can be broadly classified into three different types of distributed multimedia applications: ITV, telecooperation, and hypermedia. ITV allows subscribers to access video programs and interact with them. Services include home shopping, interactive video games (which can be classified as hypermedia applications), financial transactions, VoD, news on demand, and so forth. Telecooperation overcomes time and location restrictions and allows remote participants to join a group activity. Services include remote learning, telecommuting, teleservicing, teleoperation, multimedia email, videophone, desktop conferencing, electronic meeting rooms, joint editing, and group drawing. A hypermedia document is a multimedia document with "links" to other multimedia documents that allows users to browse multimedia information in a nonsequential manner. Services include digital libraries, electronic encyclopedias, multimedia magazines, multimedia documents, information kiosks, computer-aided learning tools, and the World Wide Web.

9.2.1   Main Features of DMS

The main features of a DMS can be summarized as follows [498]:

> **Technology integration:** Integrates information, communication, and computing systems to form a unified digital processing environment.
>
> **Multimedia integration:** Accommodates discrete data as well as continuous data in an integrated environment.

Real-time performance: Requires the storage systems, processing systems, and transmission systems to have real-time performance. Hence, huge storage volume, high network transmission rate, and high CPU processing rate are required.

Systemwide QoS support: Supports diverse QoS requirements on an end-to-end basis along the data path from the sender, through the transport network, and to the receiver.

Interactivity: Requires duplex communication between the user and the system, and allows each user to control the information.

Multimedia synchronization support: Presents the playback continuity of media frames within a single continuous media stream, and temporal relationships among multiple related data objects.

Standardization support: Allows interoperability despite heterogeneity in the information content, presentation format, user interfaces, network protocols, and consumer electronics.

9.3   REQUIREMENTS OF DISTRIBUTED MULTIMEDIA APPLICATIONS

Distributed multimedia applications have several requirements with respect to the service offered to them by the communication system [28]. These requirements depend on the type of the application and on its usage scenario. For example, a nonconversational application for the retrieval of audiovisual data has different needs than a conversational application for live audiovisual communication.

The requirements of the applications regarding the communications services can be divided into traffic and functional requirements. The functional requirements are multicast transmission and the ability to define coordinated sets of unidirectional streams. The traffic requirements include transmission bandwidth, delay, and reliability. They depend on the type, number, and quality of the data streams.

The traffic requirements can be satisfied by the use of resource management mechanisms. They establish a relationship between transmitted data and resources, and ensure that the audiovisual data are transmitted in a timely manner. For this, during the transmission of data, the information about the resource needs must be available at all nodes participating in distributed applications (that is, end systems and routers). Hence, resources must be reserved and state must be created in these nodes, which means that a connection is established. This connection should then be used for transmission of data.

EXAMPLE 9.1

A bandwidth of 1.15 Mb/s is typically required for the playback of Motion Picture Experts Group (MPEG-1) coded video. The end-to-end delay is more stringent for conferencing than for playback applications. In the former case, the delay should not be more than 150 ms. The play-out of related streams must be done in tight synchronization (< 80 ms skew). Hence, appropriate measures must be obeyed during the data transfer. On the other hand, the reliability requirements are sometimes lower than for traditional communication applications (that is, if a fault-tolerant data encoding scheme is used). Furthermore, retransmissions (which are used traditionally for the provision of reliability) increase end-to-end delay and are often worse than lost data for multimedia applications.

For various multimedia applications, especially in the conferencing realm, multiple receivers are interested in receiving the same data. For example, in a talk distributed via the network, all listeners must receive the same data. Sending each person a single copy wastes resources because the same nodes are traversed for parts of the path from the sender to the receivers. Thus, multicast should be used, which provides for the transmission of a single copy of data to multiple receivers. In addition to reduced network load, multicast also lowers the processing load of the sender. Multicast must not be limited to a single sender. In conferencing scenarios, it is usual to have several senders who normally do not use the resources at the same time (only one person is speaking).

The delivery of audiovisual data to large receiver groups (for example, the distribution of Internet Engineering Task Force meetings over the multicast backbone) must take into account that the resource capabilities of the participants can vary widely. These capabilities can range from high-speed network links and fast workstations to low-end personal computers connected via narrowband links. Therefore, support for heterogeneous systems must be provided with respect to networks as well as end systems. One way to handle this heterogeneity is the filtering of data streams; dropping data in the network that either cannot be transmitted due to a lack of bandwidth or cannot be presented by the end system due to a lack of computing power.

9.4 DISTRIBUTED MULTIMEDIA APPLICATIONS

Multimedia integration and real-time networking create a wide range of opportunities for multimedia applications. According to the different requirements imposed upon the information, communication, and computing subsystems, distributed multimedia applications may be broadly classified into three types: ITV, telecooperation, and hypermedia [28, 201].

ITV requires a very high transmission rate and stringent QoS guarantees. It is therefore difficult to provide such broadband services over a low-speed network, such as the current Internet, due to its low bandwidth and best-effort-only services. ITV typically demands point-to-point switched connections, good customer services, and excellent management for information sharing, billing, and security. Bandwidth requirement is asymmetric in that the bandwidth of a downstream channel that carries video programs from the server to the user is much higher than that of the upstream channel from the user to the server.

Telecooperation requires multicast, multipoint, and multiservice network support for group distribution. In contrast to the strict requirement on the video quality of ITV, telecooperation (such as videophone and desktop conferencing) allows lower picture quality and therefore has a lower bandwidth requirement. It is possible to provide such services with the development of the real-time transport protocols over the Internet. Telecooperation requires powerful multimedia database systems rather than just continuous media servers, with the support of visual query and content-based indexing and retrieval.

Hypermedia applications are retrieval services and require point-to-point or multipoint-to-point and switched services. They also require user interfaces, powerful authoring, and presentation tools.

9.5 INTERACTIVE TELEVISION

The four main components of interactive television systems are: a home terminal, commonly known as the Set-Top Box (STB) or Customer Premises Equipment (CPE); an access network; a network-based server; and a powerful user-friendly interface. Typical configuration of an ITV system is shown in Figure 9.2 [201]. It shows a variety of services such as video telephony, games, and ITV. The system consists of servers and a distributed network, as well as the STB.

9.5.1 Customer Premises Equipment

The cost of the CPE is a dominant factor in the overall cost of the ITV system. The less expensive the CPE is, the more likely it is that people will try the service and become repeat users. The CPE (or STB) typically takes the form of a box sitting on top of the TV set. This CPE connects to both the television and an external communication network via a subscriber "drop" or "loop" [201].

When interactive services are offered, the complexity and cost of the STB increases. Since the digital services are new "add-ons," the new STB must

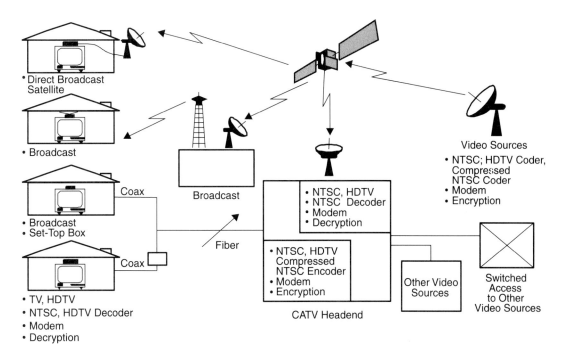

FIGURE 9.2   ITV system configuration [201].

© 1997 Chapman and Hall.

provide both the analog functions outlined previously and the digital functions of audio and video decompression, demodulation to recover the digital feeds, decryption, an upstream modem for communicating consumer control requests back to the program source, and a user-friendly interface [201].

The basic interactive STB just described is capable of supporting a variety of interactive video services. Among them are the popular ones such as movies-on-demand and home shopping. To support these services, a source of interactive service programming (a *server*) sends an individual, digitally compressed bit stream to the STB of the consumer currently using a particular service provided from a server [201].

The bit stream representing the audio/video program sent to the basic interactive STB needs to be decompressed and fed to the TV set. All of the processing required to create the real-time interactive program is usually performed at the program server. This might include the composition of multiple audio and video elements to create the final presentation [201].

This partitioning of functionality assures that the cost of STB is minimized. Sharing a network-based functionality to reduce CPE, and thereby the total system cost, is common in the network-based services industry, including telephony. However, this strategy of reducing CPE costs by sharing functionality in the network can restrict the types of interactive applications that can be effectively supported [201].

A consumer's remote control input is transmitted from the STB back to the server in the network. This input can change the flow of the program being executed by the server on behalf of that consumer. The audio and video bit stream produced by the server is compressed, often in real time, and modulated for transmission to the consumer's STB. In many instances, the server may store bit streams compressed previously in nonreal time. In some other instances, an uncompressed bit stream may be sent to the STB. The STB then simply demodulates the received signal to recover the transmitted bit stream and decompresses it to create the presentation on the TV set [201].

9.5.2 Interactive Television Servers

ITV servers are a collection of computing, storage, and communications equipment that implements interactive video services. A service may require that more than one server be implemented, or a server may implement more than one service. The overall architecture of a server is shown in Figure 9.3. The architecture of an ITV server includes several subsystems optimized for specific functions and a high-speed network connecting them. OAM and P refer to operations, administered, maintenance, and provisioning [201].

All subsystems of the server communicate with one another via a local high-bandwidth interconnect and a switch. This architecture can be used to scale capabilities of the server incrementally, and it provides isolation between the various subsystems.

A storage subsystem stores the media (audio/video/data) samples. It may use different combinations of types, disks, and semiconductor storage technologies to meet the capacity and latency requirements of the various applications.

FIGURE 9.3 Architecture of an ITV server [201].
©1997 Chapman and Hall.

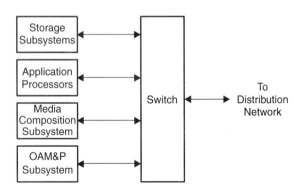

These storage technologies are typically combined into a hierarchy to optimize the performance for a given cost.

Application processors interact with the storage subsystem to deliver the output of various media to the subscriber's CPE, or to compose for eventual presentation.

Media composition subsystems use media samples from the storage subsystem and control commands from the application processors to create a single composite compressed audio and video bit stream as required by each STB.

A special class of servers known as *gateway servers* provide the navigation and other functions required to support the consumer's interface for the selection of services. These servers present "menus" of available services (for example, movies-on-demand, home shopping, and broadcast television), accept the consumer's selection, and then pass control to the server providing the selected service. The visual interface and navigation scheme of a gateway server is completely programmable. A high-end interactive media server can present a full-motion audio/video interface, whereas a low-end system can provide simple, text-based menus [201].

Two key components of the server technology are logical organization of the multimedia samples in a file system or database, and techniques by which media components can be continuously (real time) recorded or played back from the server.

Digital audio/video is a sequence of quanta (audio samples or video frames). Retrieval and presentation of such quanta require continuity in time. That is, a multimedia database server must ensure that the recording and presentation follows a real-time data rate. During presentation, for example, the server must retrieve data from a disc at a rate that prevents the output device from overflowing or running out of samples [201].

To reduce the initiation latency and buffering requirement, continuous presentation requires either a sequence of periodic tasks with deadlines, or retrieval of data from disks into buffers in rounds. In the first approach, tasks include retrieval of data from disks, and deadlines correspond to the latest time when data must be retrieved from disks into buffers to guarantee continuous presentation (see Figure 9.4). Since the data flow is bursty owing to varying compression ratio and jitter in the storage systems, buffers are required in the CPE and the server to ensure smooth data flow to the presentation hardware. In every round, sufficient data for each media stream is retrieved to ensure continuous presentation.

The server has to supply the buffers with enough data to ensure continuity of the playback processes. Efficient operation is then equivalent to preventing buffer

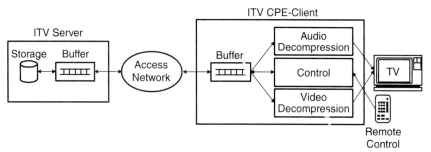

FIGURE 9.4   ITV server, access network, and ITV customer premises
equipment-client [201].
©1997 Chapman and Hall.

overflow/underflow while minimizing buffer size and the initiation latency. Since disk data transfer rates are significantly higher than a single stream's data rate, a small buffer should suffice for conventional file and operating system support for several media streams [201].

9.5.3   User Interface

User interface designs for ITV are more involved than those for standard TV, owing to the richness of the types of possible interactions with the consumer. They will most likely vary among different applications. There will be a small number of ITV generic program types, such as movies-on-demand, shopping, and so forth. Certain "look and feel" guidelines will emerge from user interfaces and for ITV programming in general [499]. Multimedia interfaces are typically designed using a mixture of four kinds of modules:

- Media editors
- Multimedia object locators and browser navigation
- Authoring tools for creating program logic
- Hypermedia object creation

9.5.4   Media Editors

A number of media editors already exist to create primitive media objects such as text, still images, and video and audio clips. A media editor is used for editing primitive multimedia objects to construct a composite object that is suitable as a multimedia presentation. The basic functions provided by the editor are delete, cut, copy, paste, move, and merge. The challenge is to present these basic functions in the most natural manner that is intuitive to the user.

EXAMPLE 9.2

The move operation is usually presented by highlighting text and dragging and dropping it to the new location. However, the same metaphor does not work for all multimedia objects. The exact implementation of the metaphor and the efficient implementation for that metaphor will distinguish such editors from each other.

9.5.5 Navigation

Navigation refers to the sequence in which the objects are browsed, searched, and used. Navigation can be either direct or predefined. If direct, then the user determines the next sequence of actions. If predefined, searching for the next program start, the user needs to know what to expect with successive navigation actions. The navigation can also be in a browse mode, in which the user wants to get general information about a particular topic. Browsing is common in systems with graphical data. ITV systems normally provide direct navigation as well as browsing options. The browse mode is typically used to search for a specific attribute or a subobject.

EXAMPLE 9.3

In an application using dialog boxes, the user may have traversed several dialog boxes to reach a point where the user is ready to play a sound object. A browse mode may be provided to search the database for all sound objects appropriate for that dialog box. An important aspect of any multimedia system is to maintain a clear perspective on the objects being displayed, and the relationship between these objects. The relationships may be associative if they are a part of a set or hierarchical.

Navigation is the first generic application for ITV. Various flavors have been created. Some examples are mapping of ITV programs to channel numbers, and interfaces that show "picture-in-picture." Navigation is rightly the first application focus, acknowledging the challenge ahead in helping viewers find their way in the proliferation of programming in the interactive world.

9.5.6 Content Creation for ITV

A good authoring system must access predefined media and program elements, sequence these elements in time, specify their placement spatially, initiate actions in parallel, and indicate specific events and the actions that may result from them. Both the CPE and the server may perform some of these algorithmic actions when the application is executed. Existing commercial tools for creating interactive multimedia applications run the gamut, from low-level programming languages to packages that support the relatively causal creation of interactive presentations. Two very broad categories are visual tools for use by nonprogrammers, and programming languages. The design of an authoring system requires careful analysis of the following issues:

- Hypermedia design details
- User interfaces
- Embedded/linking multimedia objects to the main presentation
- Multimedia object storage and retrieval
- Synchronization of components of a composite multimedia stream

A variety of authoring systems exist depending on their role and flexibility required. Some of these are described next.

Dedicated authoring systems are designed for single users and single streams. The authoring is typically performed using desktop computer systems on multimedia objects captured by a video camera or on an object stored in a multimedia library. They need to be engineered to provide user interfaces that are extremely intuitive and follow real-world metaphors. Flexibility and functionality have to be carefully limited to prevent overly complex authoring.

In a timeline-based authoring system, objects to be merged are placed along a timeline. The author specifies objects and their positions in the timeline. For presentation in a proper time sequence, each object is played at a prespecified point in the time scale. In early timeline systems, once the multimedia object was captured in the timeline, it was fixed in location and could not be manipulated easily. Editing a particular component caused all objects in the timeline to be reassigned because the position of objects is not fixed in time, only in sequence. Newer systems define timing relations directly between objects. This makes inserting and deleting objects much easier because the start and end of each object are more clearly defined.

Structured multimedia authoring is based on structured object-level construction of presentations. Explicit representation of the structure allows modular authoring of the individual component objects. The timing constraints are also derived form the constituent data items. A well-structured system also allows the user to define an object hierarchy and to specify the relative location of each object within it. Some objects may have to undergo temporal adjustment, which allows them to be expended to better fit the available time slot. The navigation design of the authoring system should allow the author to view the overall structure, while at the same time being able to examine specific object segments more closely. The benefit of an object hierarchy is that removing the main object also removes all subobjects that are meaningful only as overlays on the main object. The design of the view must show all relevant information for a specific view. For example, views may be needed to show the object hierarchy plus individual component members of that hierarchy, and to depict the timing relation between the members of the hierarchy.

Early structured systems did not allow authors to express automatic functions for handling certain routine tasks in the authoring process. Programmable authoring systems provide such additional capability in two areas:

- Functions based on audio and image processing and analysis
- Embedded program interpreters that use audio and image processing functions

Thus, the main improvement in building user programmability into the authoring tool is not only to perform the analysis, but also to manipulate the stream based on the analysis results. This programmability allows the performing of a variety of tasks through the program interpreter rather than manually. Advances in authoring systems will continue as users acquire a better understanding of stored audio and video and the functionality needed by users.

9.5.7 Hypermedia Applications

Hypermedia applications present a unique set of design issues not commonly encountered in other applications. A good user interface design is crucial to the success of a hypermedia application. The user interface presents a window to the user for controlling storage and retrieval, connecting objects to the presentation, and defining index marks for combining different multimedia streams. While the objects may be captured independently, they have to be played back together for authoring. The authoring system must allow coordination of many streams to produce a final presentation.

9.6 VIDEO ON DEMAND

The Audiovisual Multimedia Services Technical Committee of the ATM Forum released the *Video on Demand Specification 1.1* in March 1997 [500]. This document represents the first phase of a study of multimedia issues relating to ATM. Specification 1.1 only addresses issues relating to the transport of constant packet rate of MPEG-2 Single Program Transport Streams (SPTS) over ATM networks. While the scope of the document is very limited, many believe it will serve as a guide for carrying of a wide range of video over ATM networks.

Video on Demand (VoD) Specification 1.1 provides a reference configuration (see Figure 9.5) for the network supplying VoD services. The reference

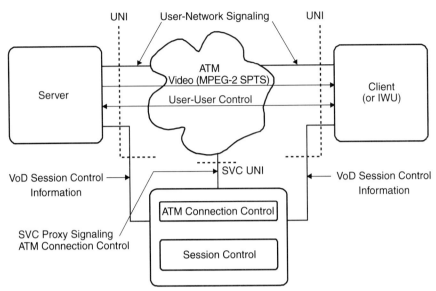

FIGURE 9.5   Video on demand reference configuration from ATM Forum VoD
Specification 1.1 [500].

model consists of a server, client, and a separate session/connection control
unit. The client could be either a Set-Top Terminal (STT) or Interworking Unit
(IWU). The reference depicts five communication links, which would be
served by five separate Virtual Connections (VC).

   If the server and client both supported signaling (*ATM Forum Signaling
Specification 4.0*), then the user-to-network signaling VCs would be as shown.
In the event that either the server or the client or both did not support signal-
ing, proxy signaling would be employed. The MPEG-2 Single Program Transport Stream (SPTS) traffic would be accommodated on a separate VC [501].
This VC would be the last VC connection established. The user-to-user control
VC would be used for implementation-specific information flows. *Video on
Demand Specification 1.1* indicates that one of the main purposes for this VC
would be to exchange program selection information between the client and
the server. This would allow the end user to select a specific item for viewing
and inform the server of that selection. The VoD session control VC would be
used for session control information [502]. This link would be used to facilitate
connection setup between the server and the client in the event that proxy signaling is required. Proxy signaling is supported when either the server or the
client or both do not support signaling. The basic procedure outlined for proxy
signaling is that the client contacts the session controller. The session controller
provides the client with a list of servers from which to choose. When the client

selects a server, the session controller informs the ATM connection controller to establish a VC for the user to control information. The client will then make a specific program selection. The VC would then be established for the transfer of MPEG-2 SPTS video from the server to the client.

9.7   SOME OPEN ISSUES

Many topics related to overall infrastructure for distributed multimedia applications have been developed over the last few years. So far, only some parts have found their way into systems for daily use. Others will be developed in the future, while some have been put aside for varying reasons (complexity, questionable usefulness, "political incorrectness," and so on). Various parts for the multimedia communication infrastructure are still missing, and they must be developed in the future to offer a complete solution. Examples of missing or incomplete parts, especially with respect to the QoS provisioning part of multimedia communications, are QoS routing and pricing mechanisms. Perhaps most important will be the verification of the suitability of the proposed mechanisms for large-scale use, for multicast sessions with many receivers as well as for many small concurrent sessions.

9.7.1   Scalability with Respect to Multimedia Applications

The multimedia communications methods designed for shared and distributed components must be scalable. With respect to multimedia applications (for example, multicast video conferences), scalability has at least two aspects [503]:

- Scalability with respect to the number of participants in one application
- Scalability with respect to the number of concurrent applications

The first requirement states that it must be possible to transmit a flow (distributed via multicast) to a potentially large number of participants. To fulfill these requirements, mechanisms for resource sharing among the participants and for the aggregations of reservations must be provided. Furthermore, there should be no central component that has to process requests from new participants joining old participants leaving such a conference.

The second requirement demands that it should be possible to support many independent applications, and hence, flows; for example, thousands of videoconferences (probably with very few participants) and video-retrieval sessions. Therefore, the processing and storage effort per flow must be very small.

Which type of scalability is more important depends on the predominant usage scenario. Currently, it seems that more attention has been given to the first issue: the scalability of one application. In the future, small-sized applications will probably be more important; hence, more consideration should be given to the second issue, the scalability of concurrent applications.

9.7.2 Routing

QoS-driven routing algorithms are needed for the efficient establishment of reservations. These algorithms suggest one or multiple suitable parts toward a given target considering a given set of QoS requirements. Then one attempts to make a reservation on such a path. Without appropriate routing mechanisms that take QoS requirements into account, the setup reservation becomes a trial-and-error approach [503].

A QoS-driven routing algorithm has to consider the currently available capacity of a resource to avoid an immediate rejection of the reservation attempt and the QoS requirements of the reservation to find a route best suited for this QoS. It should also consider the resource load after the routing decision to avoid using up the majority of resources on this route.

Some of the problems to be solved with QoS routing are

- How much state information should be exchanged among routers?
- How often should this system information be updated?
- Must there be a distinction between exterior and interior systems and, if yes, how can it be made?
- Is it possible to hide internal details of an autonomous system?
- Can the complexity of path computation be managed?

QoS routing is still in its infancy. At least in the Internet, its necessity, and the ability in principle to perform QoS routing and the proposed approaches are currently under controversial discussions.

9.7.3 Pricing

An important issue for the future success of distributed multimedia applications is the cost for any data transmission with or without QoS. The question, "Why should a user ask for less than the best quality?" has always been answered with "costs" [503, 504]. QoS methods have to take this into account as an additional, possibly negotiable, parameter. However, most research has focused on cost issues; architecture issues have most often been neglected [505–507]. Among many others, the issues to be addressed are

- Who pays for a service, and how is this indicated, especially if the receiver benefits from the transmitted data?

- Can the user specify a limit on his or her expenditures?
- How can fairness be provided such that each receiver within a multicast session pays his or her share?
- How can payment cross a firewall?
- How can a department or a group be charged instead of the overall company?

In addition to these issues, which apply to transmissions without QoS, further questions have to be answered in QoS provisioned systems [508, 509, 510, 394]. Some of these are: how can resource consumption be "weighted" (delay versus loss), what QoS do users accept for a specific price, which pricing schemes do they understand, and how can fairness be provided such that all users, benefiting from a reservation made for multicast transmission, share a cost in a fair manner?

9.8 CONCLUDING REMARKS

The success of ATM for multimedia communications depends on the successful standardization of its signaling mechanisms, its ability to attract the development of the native ATM applications, and the integration of the ATM with other communications systems. ATM will have its role in the backbone, so integration with the Internet is needed. The integration of ATM into the Internet world is under investigation. If there will be ATM applications such as video on demand, then there is also the need for a "side-by-side" integration of ATM and Internet protocols [262].

The multimedia communication systems developed so far have addressed several of the necessary aspects. Yet, not all issues have been tackled. Solutions for these issues have to be developed and have to find their way through the standardization activities to provide for a complete multimedia communications infrastructure, which is needed to support distributed multimedia applications [260, 503].

Distributed multimedia applications emerge from advances in a variety of technologies, spanning new applications that in turn push such technologies to their limits and demand fundamental changes to satisfy a diversity of new requirements. With the rapid development of the Internet, distributed multimedia applications are accelerating the realization of the information superhighway, thereby creating gigantic potential new markets and ushering in a new era of human communications. Up-to-the-minute information, computer-simulated experiences such as virtual reality, on-demand services, and telecommuting, for example, will be the way of life in the future.

Many research issues still need to be resolved before distributed multimedia applications can be widely deployed. Such applications consume considerable system resources, require systemwide QoS guarantees to ensure their correct delivery and presentation, and must be provided with user-friendly interfaces [28].

More user control and interactivity are desired. Faster processors and hardware, higher network bandwidths, and data compression ratios and improvements in a variety of related technologies are necessary. Standardization is also important to accommodate the heterogeneity of techniques and to provide portability of applications. Last, but not least, for these applications to be commercially viable, costs will be an important consideration.

APPENDIX A

Information on the Internet

A.1 DOCUMENTS
A.2 SOFTWARE/HARDWARE
A.3 PRODUCTS, MANUFACTURERS, AND VENDORS

This appendix lists Web sites maintained by standards bodies (international, regional, and national), research institutes, private organizations, universities, industry, professional/technical societies, and others. The list is quite extensive and the information was up-to-date at the time of writing. In view of the rapid changes, some sites may no longer exist and new ones may have been developed. The main objective is to provide the reader with the wealth of information available on the Internet.

A.1 DOCUMENTS

A.1.1 ISO/IEC International Organization for Standardization

http://www.jtc1.org

> (ISO/IEC JTC1/SWG-GII, Joint Technical Committee on Information Technology, Special working group on Global Information Infrastructure GII for Global Information Society, March 1994, Recomm. Y.100, 110, 120)

> (ETSI European Telecommunications Standards Institute, EII European information infrastructure SRC6 Sept. 1994)

> (Japan TTC Telecommunication Technology Committee, IITG Information Infrastructure Task Group, TTC WGS-GII)

ISO/IEC JTC1/SC29 Coding of Audio, Picture, Multimedia, and Hypermedia Information

http://www.chips.ibm.com/.sc29

> (ISO/IEC JTC1 TC Technical directions: Multimedia and representation, Subcommittees SC29 Working groups:

WG1 Joint Photographic Experts Group

WG11 Moving Picture Experts Group

WG12 Multimedia and Hypermedia Experts Group)

ISO/IEC JTC1/SC29/WG11 MPEG (Moving Picture Experts Group)

(MPEG SubGroup on Requirements, Systems, Video, Audio, SNHC, Test, Implementations studies, DSM, Liaisons)

http://www.chips.ibm.com/.mpeg

    (MPEG Homepage: Plenary meetings and subgroup meetings)

http://www.cselt.it/mpeg

    (MPEG-1 IS11172(1-5), MPEG-2 IS13818(1-10), MPEG-4 DIS14496(1-6), MPEG-7)

http://garuda.imag.fr/MPEG4

    (MPEG-4 Systems)

http://www.hhi.de/mpeg-video

    (MPEG-4 Natural video coding)

http://www.es.com/mpeg-4snhc

    (MPEG-4 SNHC Synthetic and natural hybrid coding)

http://www.tnt.uni-hannover.de/project/mpeg/audio

    (MPEG-4 Audio coding)

http://sound.media.mit.edu/~eds/mpeg4

    (MPEG-4 Structured audio)

http://www.darmstadt.gmd.de/mobile/MPEG7

    (MPEG-7 Homepage)

http://www.meta-labs.com/mpeg-7-aud

    (MPEG-7 Audio)

ISO/IEC JTC1/SC29/WG1 (ITU-T SG8) JPEG/JBIG

http://www.jpeg.org

    (ISO/IEC IS 10918 (1-4) T.81, JPEG Joint Photographic Experts Group Homepage)

http://pr.jpeg.org

    ISO/IEC JTC1/SC29/WG1 WD15444 JPEG2000)

    (Verification Model 2.0 WG1N1047, WG1N1096, WG1N875, WG1N989)

    (Architecture: MCAP&CREW+, algorithm: Marcellin's W/TCQ wavelet and trellis-based coder)

http://eurostill.epfl.ch

    (European initiative toward JPEG2000: New image coding system) *http://www.hpl.hp.com/loco*

> (ISO/IEC DIS14495-1 ITU/T.81 JPEG-LS Lossless and near-lossless compression of continuous-tone still images: based on HP LOCO-I codec; software)

http://disc.org.uk

> (ISO/IEC ITU-T.82 IS11544 JBIG)

http://spmg.ece.ubc.ca/research/jbig/main.html

> (ISO/IEC JTC1/SC29/WG1 WD14492 JBIG-2)

http://www.jpeg.org/public/jbigpt2.htm

> (JBIG2 WD14492 can be downloaded in gzipped PS or PDF)

ISO/IEC JTC1/SC29/WG12 MHEG (Multimedia & Hypermedia Experts Group)

http://www.mheg.org

> (ISO/IEC JTC1/SC29/WG12 IS13522(1-7), MHEG Multimedia & Hypermedia Experts Group)

http://www.fokus.gmd.de/ovma/mug

> (MHEG-5 Users group)

http://www.mheg5.com/links.html

> (MHEG-5 Resource center)

A.1.2   ITU-T International Telecommunications Union

http://www.itu.int/publications

> (ITU-T Standardization sector)

http://www.itu.ch/itudoc/itu-t/rec/q.html

http://www.itu.int/itudoc/itu-t/com7.html

> (Mapping between ISO/IEC and ITU-T Recommendation, Jan. 1998)

ITU-T JCG on AVMMS (Joint Coordination Group on Audio-Visual Multimedia Services)

ITU-T SG1	BISDN services principle
ITU-T SG2	Network and service operation
ITU-T SG3	Tariff and accounting principles, economic and policy issues
ITU-T SG4	Telecommunication management network and network maintenance
ITU-T SG7	Data networks and open system communications
ITU-T SG8	Characteristics of telematic systems
ITU-T SG9	
ITU-T SG11	Signaling requirements and protocols

ITU-T SG12   End-to-end transmission performance of networks and terminals (Q10 Subjective audiovisual quality, Q11 Objective audiovisual quality, Q22 Speech quality experts group)

ITU-T SG13   General network aspects (BISDN UNI specification (physical layer, ATM layer, AAL), NNI specification, interworking with NISDN, FR)

ITU-T SG14

ITU-T SG15   Transport networks, systems and equipment (BISDN NNI specification)

ITU-T SG16   Multimedia systems and services (Q.3 Data protocols for multimedia conferencing, Q9 Accessibility to multimedia for people with disabilities, Q11 Videoconferencing for circuit switched networks ISDN and POTS; Q12-14 Videoconferencing for packet switched networks LAN and Internet: Q.12 BISDN multimedia systems and terminals, Q.13 Packet switched multimedia systems and terminals, Q.14 Common protocols, MCUs and protocols for interworking with H.300-series terminals; Q15 Video coding, Q20 Audio coding)

ITU-T SG12 Performance
ftp://its.bldrdoc.gov/dist/ituvidq

(ITU-T SG12 Q10 Performance: Subjective audiovisual quality)
ftp://its.bldrdoc.gov/dist/ituvidq

(ITU-T SG12 Q11 Performance: Objective audiovisual quality)
ftp://its.bldrdoc.gov/dist/sg12q22

(ITU-T SG12 Q22 Performance: Speech quality)

ITU-T SG16 Multimedia Systems and Services
http://www.itu.ch/itudoc/itu-t/com16.html

(ITU-T SG16 Study Group Multimedia systems and services)
ftp://ftp.imtc-files.org/imtc-site

(ITU-T SG16 Q.3 Data protocols for multimedia conferencing)
ftp://standard.pictel.com/h324-site

(ITU-T SG16 Q11 Circuit-Switched Network Systems Experts Group: Videoconferencing ISDN H.320, POTS H.324 and T.122 transport, Mobile H.324/C and H.223/M multiplex) *ftp://standard.pictel.com/video-site*

(ITU-T SG16 Q15 AVC Advanced Video Coding Experts Group: Recommendation H.120, H.261, H.263, H.263+, H.263++, H.26L)

ftp://standard.pictel.com/sg16_q20

(ITU-T SG16 Q20 Audio coding: G.711, G.722, G.723.1, G.728, G.729)

ftp://standard.pictel.com/avc-site

(ITU-T SG16 Q12-14 Videoconferencing for packet switched networks ATM H.310 & H.321, ISO-Ethernet H.322, LAN Ethernet H.323: Q.12 BISDN multimedia systems and terminals, Q.13 Packet switched multimedia systems and terminals, Q.14 Common protocols, MCUs and protocols for interworking with H.300-series terminals)

A.1.3   ATM Forum

http://www.ATMforum.com

(ATM Forum TC worldwide technical committee of 13 Working groups; Market awareness and education committee, User committee, Cookbook solutions committee; 6 Interest groups; ATM Forum Wireless ATM)

ftp://ftp.ATMforum.com/pub/approved-specs

(ATM Forum Approved specifications)

ftp://ftp.ATMforum.com/ATM/documents/letter-ballot

(ATM Forum Specifications in letter ballot)

ftp://ftp.ATMforum.com/ATM/documents/straw-ballot

(ATM Forum Specifications in straw ballot)

ftp://ftp.ATMforum.com/ATM/documents/btd

(ATM Forum Specifications in preparation)

ftp://ftp.ATMforum.com/pub/contributions

(ATM Forum Contributions)

http://www.ATMforum.com/specs/specs.html

(ATM Forum: Technical specifications)

ATM Forum Audiovisual Multimedia Services (AMS)

(ATM Forum, Audio/visual multimedia services (AMS), v.1.0, Jan. 1996.)

(ATM Forum, Traffic management, v.4.0, Apr. 1996. with TM available bit rate addendum, Jan. 1997.)

(ATM Forum Implementation Agreement, Video on demand specification 1.0, af-saa-0049.000, Dec. 1995)

(ATM Forum Implementation agreements UNI 3.1, 1994.)

(ATM Forum, LAN emulation over ATM specification 1.0, Jan. 1995.)

ftp://netlab.ohio-state.edu/pub/jain/ATMf/af-prf22.ps

(Performance testing effort at the ATM Forum)

http://www.itu.ch/itudoc/itu-t

(ITU-T Rec. I.150, I.361, I.362, I.363, I.356 QoS, I.371, I.327, I.311, I.211, I.413, I.413, I.321, I.432, I.610)

(ITU-T Rec. Q.2110, Q.2130, Q.293, Q.2931, Q.2130, Q.2110)

(ITU-T Rec. Q.2610 Q.2650 Q.2931 Q.293x Q.2961 Q.2963 Q.2964 Q.297x Q.298x)

(ITU-T Rec. J.82 Mapping of MPEG-2 in AAL-1/AAL-5, ITU-T G.804)

(ITU-T Rec. I.363.5, BISDN ATM adaptation layer (AAL) specification: Type 5 AAL, 08/1996)

(ITU-T Rec. I.361, BISDN ATM layer specification, 11/1995)

(ITU-T Rec. I.363.5, BISDN ATM adaptation layer (AAL), specification: Type 5 AAL, 08/1996)

(ITU-T Rec. I.413 Rev. 1, BISDN user-network interface, version WTSC 1993, published December 1993)

(ITU-T Rec. I.430 Rev. 1, Basic user-network interface—Layer 1 specification, WTSC 1993, March 1994)

(ITU-T Rec. I.432 Rev. 1, BISDN user-network interface—Physical layer specification, WTSC 1993, January 1994)

ftp://standard.pictel.com/AVC-site

(Videoconferencing for packet switched networks ATM H.310, H.321)

http://web.ansi.org/…

(ATM: ANSI standards: T1.624, T1.627)

ftp://thumper.bellcore.com/pub/smq/

(Bellcore's standard archive)

http://info.bellcore.com

ftp://ftp.tele.fi/ATM

(Archive: Standards drafts)

http://wuarchive.wustl.edu

http://cell-relay.indiana.edu/cell-relay

(Cell-relay or broadband technologies: Archives, Getting started, ATM documents, Network bibliography, Trade press sources, ATM sites, ATM software)

ftp://cell-relay.indiana.edu/pub/cell-relay

(/archive, /FAQ, /docs, /bib, /publications, /conferences, /vendors) *http://cell-relay.indiana.edu/cell-relay/archives*

    (Archives)

http://cell-relay.indiana.edu/cell-relay/FAQ/ATM-FAQ

    (ATM FAQ: References, Industry forums and vendor information, Technology questions, ATM vs. XYZ technology, Reference implementations)

http://cell-relay.indiana.edu/cell-relay/ReferenceSources.html

    (ATM: Dictionary, Glossary, Acronyms)

http://cell-relay.indiana.edu/cell-relay/docs/docs.html

    (ATM related documents: Standards, Tech reports)

http://cell-relay.indiana.edu/cell-relay/publications/software

    (ATM software)

http://www.frforum.com/4000/frATM/frATM.toc.html

    (ATM vs. Frame Relay)

http://cif.cornell.edu

    (CIF Cells in Frames: ATM over LAN)

http://sulu.lerc.nasa.gov/ctdreps.html

    (ATM over satellite)

http://info.gte.com/ieee-tcgn/conference/gbn95/schulzrinne.abstract.txt

    (ATM drawbacks/deficiencies)

http://www.cis.ohio-state.edu/~jain

    (R. Jain's Recent advances in networking: Class Lectures, Seminars, Student Reports, References, Tutorials, Courses)

ftp://ftp.netlab.ohio-state.edu/pub/jain

    (OSU archive)

http://www.cis.ohio-state.edu/~jain/refs/all_refs.htm

    (Hot topics in networking references)

http://www.cis.ohio-state.edu/~jain/refs/ATM_refs.htm

    (ATM networking references)

http://www.cis.ohio-state.edu/~jain/refs/ATM_book.htm

    (ATM books)

http://www.cis.ohio-state.edu/~jain/...

    (Tutorials on ATM networks)

http://www.cis.ohio-state.edu/~jain/cis788.htm

    (Reports on recent advances in networking)

http://www.cis.ohio-state.edu/~jain/cis788-97/video_over_ATM/index.htm

    (Video over ATM)

http://www.cis.ohio-state.edu/~jain/cis788-97/tcp_over_ATM/index.htm

    (IP over ATM)

http://www.cis.ohio-state.edu/~jain/cis788-97/tcp_over_ATM/index.htm

    (TCP over ATM)

http://www.cis.ohio-state.edu/~jain/cis788/frame_relay/index.html

    (Frame Relay overview)

http://www.cis.ohio-state.edu/~jain/cis788/gigabit_ethernet/index.html

    (Gigabit Ethernet)

http://www.cis.ohio-state.edu/~jain/cis788/isdn/index.html

    (ISDN overview)

http://www.infotech.tu-chemnitz.de/~paetz/ATM

    (ATM Homepage)

http://www-atp.llnl.gov/atp/ATM.html

    (ATM Information resources)

ftp://ftp.magic.net

    (IP over ATM tutorial)

A.1.4   IETF (Internet Engineering Task Force)

http://www.ietf.org

    (IETF Internet Engineering Task Force: Internet standard specification)

http://info.isoc.org/internet-history

    (ISOC Internet Society: evolution and stability of Internet)

http://www.iab.org/iab

    (IAB Internet Architecture Board)

http://www.ietf.org/iesg.html

    (IESG Internet Engineering Steering Group: management of tech. activities)

http://www.iana.org

    (IANA Internet Assigned Number Authority: tables of assigned numbers)

http://www.ietf.org/html.charters

    (IETF Working groups areas: Applications, General, Internet Operations and management, routing, security, transport and user services)

    (IETF Working group and GII: IP over cable data network, IP over vertical blanking interval, IP over ADSL, IP over Satellite)

http://www.rfc-editor.org

    (RFC Editor)

    (RFCs are series of formal documents with status: informational, experimental, standards track, best current practice, historic)

(IETF Standardization process: Internet drafts, Draft standard, Internet standard STD1)

http://www.ietf.org/lid-abstracts.html

(Internet Drafts)

(RFC 2026, The Internet standards process—Revision 3, Oct. 1996)

(RFC 2028, The organizations involved in the IETF standards process, Oct. 1996)

(RFC 2200, Internet official protocol standards, June 1997)

(RFC 1796, Not all RFCs are standards, Apr. 1995)

(RFC 1150, FYI on FYI: Introduction to the FYI notes, Mar. 1990)

(RFC 1958, Architectural principle of the Internet, June 1996)

(RFC 791, Internet Protocol (IP), Internet Society)

(RFC 792, Internet Control Message Protocol, September 1981.)

(RFC 793, Transmission Control Protocol (TCP), J. Postel, 09/01/1981 STD-7)

(RFC 768, User Datagram Protocol (UDP), J. Postel, 08/28/1980 STD-6)

(RFC 959, File Transfer Protocol (FTP), Internet Society)

(RFC 791, Internet Protocol (IP Addressing), J. Postel, 09/01/1981 STD-5)

(RFC 821, Simple Mail Transfer Protocol (SMTP), August 1982)

(RFC 1034, Domain names—Concept and facilities, November 1987)

(RFC 1332, The PPP Internet Protocol Control Protocol (IPCP), G. McGregor, 05/26/1992)

(RFC 1825, Security Architecture for the Internet Protocol, R. Atkinson, August 1995)

(RFC 1866, Hypertext markup language (HTMLv2.0), November 1995)

(RFC 1945, Hypertext transfer protocol (HTTPv1.0), May 1996)

(RFC 1112 IP Multicasting)

(RFC 2002 IP Mobility support)

(RFC 2022 MARS Multicast Address Resolution Server and Multicast over ATM)

(RFC1883 1884, 1970, 1971 IPv6)

(RTP Transport protocol for real-time applications RFC1889, RFC1890, RFC2038)

(RTP payload format for H.263/ H.263+/ MPEG4 elementary streams)

(RTSP Real-time streaming protocol)

IETF Audio/Video Transport Group (AVT)

http://www.ietf.org/html.charters/avt-charter.html

>   (AVT Audio/video transport group)

>   (MPEG2 Elementary stream, MPEG in RTP RFC2038, RTP RFC1889, Routers RSVP+IPv6+Multicast)

>   (RFC2035,   RFC2032,   RFC2029,   RFC2190,   RFC2198,   RFC2250, RFC2343, RFC2354)

http://www.ietf.org/html.charters/rsvp-charter.html

>   (RSVP Resource reservation setup protocol)

>   (RSVPv1, Internet draft, Functional specification, R. Braden, 1996)

http://www.ietf.org/proceedings/directory.html

>   (Proceedings of IETF meetings)

http://www.ietf.org/html.charters/ion-charter.html

>   (NBMA working group)

http://www.ietf.org/html.charters/atommib-charter.html

>   (ATM MIB working group)

>   (RFC1633, Integrated services in the Internet architecture: An overview, P. Braden, D. Clark, and S. Shenker, June 1994)

>   (RFC1821, Integrated services)

http://ds.internic.net/internet-drafts/draft-ietf-intserv-guaranteed-svc-06.txt

>   (Internet draft, Specification of guaranteed quality of service)

http://www.com21.com/pages/ietf.html

>   (IETF IP over ATM)

>   (RFC1483,   RFC1754,   RFC1755,   RFC1932,   RFC2022,   RFC1483, RFC1577, RFC1626, RFC1695, RFC2098)

>   (RFC 1577, M. Laubach, Classical IP and ARP over ATM, 1994)

>   (RFC 1483, Multiprotocol Encapsulation over ATM Adaptation Layer 5, J. Heinanen, 07/20/1993)

>   ip-ATM-request@hpl.hp.com

>   (IP over ATM, mailing list)

http://ipmulticast.com

>   (IPMI IP Multicast Initiative Forum)

http://www.best.com

>   (The Multicast Backbone, MBone)

>   (IP/VBI protocol: IP over Vertical Blanking Interval of TV, extension of IP Multicast)

http://www.bell-labs.com/mailing-lists/iptel

    (IP Telephony)

http://www.von.com

    (IP Telephony)

http://www.etsi.fr/tiphon

    (Telecommunications and Internet protocols)

http://www.dc.net/ilazar

    (Internet resources)

http://nic.nordu.net

    (Internet-Drafts directories)

ftp://ftp.nis.garr.it

http://ds.internic.net/ds/dspg0intdoc.html

    (Internet Drafts)

ftp://ftp.isi.edu/in-notes

    (Request for Comments)

ftp://ds.internic.net/rfc

    (Request for Comments)

ftp://nic.funet.fi/pub/doc/rfc

    (Request for Comments)

http://www.etsi.fr/tiphone

    (ETSI Telecommunication and Internet protocols)

http://playground.sun.com/pub/ipng/html/ipng-main.html

    (IP Next generation Homepage)

http://www.merit.edu

    (Internet architecture)

http://www.irtf.org/irtf

    (IRTF Research of evolution of the future Internet)

http://www.iana.org

    (IANA Central coordinating functions of the Internet)

http://www.w3.org/TR

    (W3C—World Wide Web Consortium)

A.1.5   DAVIC (Digital Audio-Visual Council)

http://www.davic.org/speci.htm

    (DAVIC Digital Audio-Visual Council: Public available specification for end-to-end interoperability of broadcast and interactive audiovisual information)

(DAVIC Technical committee: Applications and requirements, Content representation and API and security, System design and integration)

(Standardization process: strategy, public call for proposals, public draft 1/2, finalize, publish)

(DAVIC technical specification/report 1.4 (1-14): requirements and framework, architectural guides, technology toolsets, system integration-implementation-conformance)

http://www.iso.ch/davic/s16501e.pdf

(ISO/IEC JTC1/SC29 DIS16500(1-9), DIS16501(DAVIC Part 1))

http://davic.eureca.ru/orga.htm

(DAVIC specification and digital TV standards show a scenario for digital TV evolution to interactive multimedia services: VOD video-on-demand, storage based VOD, switched video broadcast, enhanced data broadcast, interactive data broadcast, Internet access, institutional multimedia retrieval)

http://www.opentv.com

(OpenTV technology standard)

http://www.cabot.co.uk

(Cabot Software: MHEG5 Engine, MHEG5 Authoring tool, Web browser for digital TV)

http://www.webtv.com

(Microsoft WebTV)

A.1.6   Digital Television

http://www.atsc.org/stan&rps.html

(ATSC Advanced Television Systems Committee)

(Doc. A53 ATSC Digital television standard, Doc. A54 Guide to the use of the ATSC digital television standard) (Doc. A.56 System information for digital television ATSC standard)

(Doc. A52 Digital audio compression standard AC-3)

(Doc. A65 Program and system Information for protocol for terrestrial broadcast and cable)

http://www.ebu.ch

(EBU European Broadcasting Union)

http://www.dvb.org

(EBU DVB Direct Video Broadcasting)

DVB provides a unified framework for delivering digital audio/video and data using, cable and terrestrial transmission infrastructures. The DVB project is a group of 200 companies from over 25 countries which was formed in 1993 to standardize systems for digital broadcasting of video and data over cable and terrestrial networks.

http://www.digitag.org

(EBU Digital Terrestrial Television Action Group)

http://www.itc.org.uk

(DTTV UK Terrestrial digital TV)

http://www.dtg.org.uk

(UK Digital TV Group)

(NADIB Narrow Band Digital Broadcasting consortium)

(BDB British (Terrestrial) Digital Broadcasting)

(BSkyB satellite analog broadcasting)

http://www.etsi.fr

(ETSI European Telecommunications Standards Institute)

(European Commission's Directive 95/47/EC: the transmission standard is ISO/IEC13818, and the common scrambling algorithm SCA is defined by ETR 298)

(ETS 300 421, DVB Digital broadcasting systems for television, sound and data services; Framing structure, channel coding and modulation for 11/12 GHz satellite services, December 1994)

(ETS 300 429, DVB Digital broadcasting systems for television, sound and data services; Framing structure, channel coding and modulation for cable systems, August 1994)

(ETS 300 743, Digital Video Broadcasting, DVB subtitling)

(ETS300 744, DVB-Terrestrial, modification DVB-T Mobile test in trams and racing cars driving up to 300Km/h)

(ETS 300 468, Specification for Service Information (SI) in DVB Systems, January 1997)

(ETS 300 800, DVB-Cable modem)

(ETS 300 472, Digital broadcasting systems for television, sound, and data services, October 1996)

Specification for conveying ITU-R System B Teletext in Digital Video Broadcasting (DVB) bitstreams

(ETSI ETR, Asymmetrical Digital Subscriber Line ADSL, ETSI Technical report 328, December 1996)

(ETSI Technical Report 328 on ADSL, edition 1, December 1996)

(CENELEC EN 50083-9, Cable distribution systems for television, sound and interactive multimedia signals. Part 9: Interfaces for CATV/SMATV headends and similar professional equipment for DVB/MPEG-2 transport streams. March 1997)

(ETS 300 608 Digital cellular telecommunication system (Phase 2); Specification of the Subscriber Identity Module—Mobile Equipment (SIM-ME) Interface GSM11.11, August 1997)

http://www.ee.surrey.ac.uk/Contrib/WorldTV

(Worldwide TV standards)

http://www.bbc.co.uk/rd/whatsnew/index.htm

(BBC Research and Development)

http://www.smpte.org/index.html

(Society of Motion Picture and Television Engineers)

http://www.cablelabs.com/about_cl.html

(Cable television system operators)

(SCTE Society of Cable Telecommunications Engineers DVS/026-Digital Video: Subtitling methods for Broadcast Cable)

ITU-R (International Telecommunications Union—Radiocommunication Sector)
http://www.itu.int/itu-r/...

(ITU-R SG10 Broadcasting service—Sound)
http://www.itu.int/itu-r/...

(ITU-R SG11 Broadcasting service—Television, ITU Task Group 3)

(ITU-R BT.601-4, Encoding parameters of digital television for studios)

(ITU-R BT.1208, Video coding for digital terrestrial television broadcasting)

(ITU-R BT.709-1, Basic parameter values for the HDTV standard for the studio and for international program exchange)

A.1.7 Liaisons

http://www.iso.ch/VL/Standards.html

(Standards and Standardization Bodies)

http://www.iso.ch/infoe/catinfo.html

(ISO International Organization for Standardization: 75 Member Nations, 150+ Technical Committees, 600+ Subcommittees, 1500+ Working Groups)

http://www.bsi.org.uk/sc24

(ISO JTC1/SC24 Computer graphics and Image processing)

http://www.iec.ch/down-e.htm

   (IEC International Electrotechnical Commission: 41 Member Nations, 80+ Technical Committees, 100+ Subcommittees, 700+ Working Groups)

http://www.itu.int/ITU-Databases/TSBPatent

   (ITU-T patent disclosure policy)

http://web.ansi.org/default_js.htm

   (American National Standards Institute OnLine)

http://snad.ncsl.nist.gov/madvtg/IGOSS/igoss.html

   (NIST National Institute of Standards and Technology)

http://www.itu.int/itudoc/itu-t/com10.html

   (ITU-Radio Communication Sector SG10: Languages and general software aspects for telecommunication systems)

http://www.itu.int/itudoc/itu-t/com11.html

   (ITU-Radio Communication Sector SG11: Signaling requirements and protocols)

http://www.itu.ch/itudoc/itu-t/com16.html

   (Study Group 16 Multimedia services and systems)

http://www.tinac.com

   (TINA Telecom. Information Networking Architecture Consortium)

http://www.t1.org

   (Committee T1, Telecommunication subcommittee: T1A1, T1E1, T1M1, T1P1, T1S1, T1X1)

http://www.tiug.org

   (ISDN Users group)

http://www.xdsl.com

   (xDSL Homepage)

http://www.adsl.com/adsl_ATM.html

   (ADSL Forum TR-002, ATM over ADSL Recommendations, March 1997) (ANSI T1.413, Network and customer installation interfaces—ADSL Metallic Interface, version March 95)

http://www.frforum.com/4000/frATM/frATM.toc.html

   (Frame Relay/ATM PVC Service Interworking Implementation Agreement (FRF.8), Frame Relay Forum)

http://wwwhost.ots.utexas.edu/ethernet

   (Ethernet Homepage)

http://www.iol.unh.edu/consortiums/fe/index.html

   (Fast Ethernet Consortium)

http://www.gigabit-ethernet.org

   (Gigabit Ethernet Alliance)

http://www.fddi.be

   (FDDI Institute)

http://www.atis.org

   (SONET Interoperability Forum)

   (Bellcore document GR-253 Issue 02, Set: Synchronous Optical Network (SONET) Transport; Systems: Common Generic Criteria. December 1995)

   (ITU-T Recomm. G.707 Rev.2, Synchronous digital hierarchy bit rates,version WTSC 1993, August 1993)

   (ITU-T Recomm. G.804, ATM cell mapping into plesiochronous digital hierarchy (PDH), November 1993)

http://www.wapforum.org

   (WAP Wireless Application Protocol Forum, OSI Layers 4,5,6 and security)

   (ETSI standard for the networks based on Wideband CDMA and TD/CDMA)

http://www.itu.int/imt

   (IMT2000 International Mobile Telecommunications Q.1701, Q.1711, Q.1721:

   2 Mbps in fixed locations, 384 Kbps at pedestrian speeds, 144 Kbps at faster speeds)

   (GSM Global System for Mobile communications)

   (UMTS Universal Mobile Telecommunications System Forum)

   (UPT Universal personal telecommunications service, ITU-T SG1 Recomm. F.851, 852)

   (FPLMTS Future public land mobile telecom. system service, ITU-T SG1,2,4,11,13,15)

   (TMN Telecommunications Management Network, ITU-T SG 2,4,7,10,11,13,14)

http://www.imtc.org

   (International Multimedia Teleconferencing Consortium, Inc.)

http://www.stdvlab.com

   (U.S. Consumer Business Unit Digital Video Applications Group)

http://www.cemacity.org

   (Consumer electronics manufacturing association)

http://www.omg.org/omg/background.html
    (OMG Object Management Group)
http://vag.vrml.org
    (ISO DIS14772 VRML Virtual Reality Modeling Language, AG)
http://www.web3d.org
    (Web3D Consortium, formerly VRML Consortium)
http://www.rational.com/uml
    (Universal Modeling Language)

A.1.8 Links

http://www.cmpcmm.com/cc
    (Computer and Communications Standards)
http://www.gsc.etsif.fr
    (Global standard collaboration GSC4)
http://standard.pictel.com/webftp.html
    (PictureTel Co. Standards Page)
ftp://src.doc.ic.ac.uk
    (ITU-T Documents)
http://drogo.cselt.stet.it/ufv/leonardo
    (dr. L. Chiariglione Homepage)
http://www.vol.it/MPEG
    (MPEG Information page)
http://lenkkari.cs.tut.fi/~jleino/TCP_primer/tcp.html
    (Introduction to the Internet Protocols)
http://sunsite.informatik.rwth-aachen.de/dblp/db
    (Computer sciences bibliography)
http://www.ph.tn.tudelft.nl/PRInfo
    (TU Delft)
http://www.ieee.org
    (IEEE Homepage)
http://standards.ieee.org
    (IEEE Standards)
http://www.opera.ieee.org
    (IEEE Transactions on Multimedia, Proc. of the IEEE)
http://www.comsoc.org
    (IEEE Communications Magazine)

http://www.spie.org

    (SPIE Society of Photo-Optical and Instrumentation Engineers)

http://www.aes.org/standards.htm

    (AES Audio Engineering Society)

http://www.icspat.com/links.htm

    (ICSPAT Online)

http://iowegian.com/splat.htm

    (SPLAT SP links arranged taxonomically)

http://www.ee.princeton.edu/~icip95/iplink/index.html

    (Image processing Web sites)

http://www.internz.com/compression-pointers.html

    (Compression pointers)

http://spib.rice.edu/spib.html

    (SPIB Signal Processing Information Base)

http://www-isl.stanford.edu/~gray/iii.html

    (Signal Proc. MM Information Infrastructure)

http://www-isl.stanford.edu/~gray

    (Quality evaluation of lossy compressed images)

http://ipt.lpl.arizona.edu

    (Image Processing for Teaching)

http://farnsworth.mit.edu

    (The Digital Information Infrastructure Guide)

http://viswiz.gmd.de/MultimediaInfo/

    (Index to Multimedia information sources)

http://cuiwww.unige.ch/OSG/info/MultimediaInfo/mmsurvey

    (Multimedia Research, Standards and Products)

http://www.cablelabs.com/PR/950327mpeg_ipr.html

    (MPEG Intellectual Property Rights Licensing Group)

http://www.powerweb.de/mpeg/mpegfaq

    (MPEG FAQ)

http://www.netwideo.com/technology

    (MPEG-2)

http://www.cablelabs.com/PR

    (MPEG-2)

http://www.cs.brandeis.edu/~dcc

    (IEEE Data Compression Conference)

http://icmit.mit.edu

(The International Consortium for Medical Imaging Technology)

http://www.xray.hmc.psu.edu/dicom/dicom_home.html

(DICOM Digital Imaging and Communications in Medicine)

http://www.faqs.org/faqs/compression-faq

(FAQ Frequently Asked Questions)

http://www.cis.ohio-state.edu/hypertext/faq/usenet/compression-faq/part1/faq-doc-15.html

(Compression FAQ)

A.2   SOFTWARE/HARDWARE

The test model TMN and verification model VM are documents that describe examples of encoders compliant with H.263 and MPEG-4 syntax, respectively, and are usually updated at each of the respective standards meetings.

ftp://standard.pictelcom/video-site/h263plus

(Doc.Q15D65 TMN10 Video codec test model, near-term)

(Doc.Q15C15 TMN9 Video codec test model, near-term)

http://spmg.ece.ubc.ca/h263plus

(Telenor/UBC TMN test model implementation in H.263+ codec v3.2)

ftp://dspftp.ee.ubc.ca/pub/tmn/ver-3.2

(/tmn-3.2.0.tgz, tmndec-3.2.0.tgz, tmnpatch-3.2.0.tgz)

ftp://bonde.nta.no/pub/tmn/software

(Telenor/UBC H.263+ codec v2.0)

http://www.nta.no/~brukere/DVC/h263_software

(H.263 documents, Telenor)

ftp://ftp.berkom.de/h263plus

(Deutsche Telekom test model implementation in H.263+ codec)

http://www-video.eecs.berkeley.edu/download

(TMN Matching pursuit H.263 codec v2.0)

http://www.gctech.co.jp

(H.261/H.263 Encoder/Decoder software)

http://www.icsl.ucla.edu/~wireless

(UCLA H.223 Multiplex Simulator)

http://www.chips.ibm.com/.mpeg

(Doc.N2552 MPEG-4 Verification Model VM12)

(Doc.N2205 MPEG-4 Simulation software)

http://www.gti.ssr.upm.es/projs/momusys.html

(MoMuSys project (EU-ACTS) MPEG4 systems and Video)

ftp://ftp.fzi.de

(MPEG-4 system software)

http://www.q-team.de/mpeg4/mpeg4pc.htm

(MPEG-4 Q-Team)

http://www.fhtw-berlin.de/Projekte/Wavelet

(Wavelet codec as contribution for MPEG-4)

ftp://ftp.netcom.com/pub/cfogg/mpeg2/mpeg2codecv1.1.tar.gz

(MPEG2 Codec Software Simulation Group)

ftp://mm-ftp.cs.berkeley.edu/pub/mpeg2/software

(MPEG2 Encoder/Decoder)

http://www.bok.net

(MPEG Pointers and Resources)

http://bmrc.berkeley.edu

(Berkeley MPEG Page)

http://www.ligos.com/downloads

(MPEG Video encoder software)

http://www.xingtech.com/downloads/sw

(XING Streamworks)

ftp://skynet.ecn.purdue.edu/pub/dist/delp/samcow

(MPEG-1, H.263 test sequences)

http://www.sarnoff.com/mpeg/test/bitstreams

(MPEG elementary streams or ATSC transport stream audio)

ftp://links.uwaterloo.ca/pub/Bragzone/...

(Test image files)

ftp://ipl.rpi.edu/pub/image/still/usc

(Test image files)

http://www.precisionimages.com/image_index.html

(Imaging Resources)

http://www.wavelet.org/wavelet/links.html

(Wavelet digest)

http://www.mat.sbg.ac.at/~uhl/wav.html

(Wavelet Internet sources)

http://www.aware.com

(WaveTool software toolbox)

http://www.mathworks.com/wavelet.html

    (MATLAB wavelet toolbox)

http://www.wolfram.com/wis

    (Wavelet Explorer)

http://www.mpeg.org/~tristan/MPEG/links.html#indexes

    (VideoAudio Compression Indexes)

http://www.mpeg.org/~tristan/MPEG/links.html#links

    (VideoAudio Compression WWW)

http://www.cis.ohio-state.edu/hypertext/faq/usenet/compression-faq/top.html

    (Comp.compression group FAQ)

http://www.bitscout.com/faqtoc.htm

    (Videoconferencing FAQ)

http://www.icsl.ucla.edu/~ipl/psnr_results.html

    (UCLA IPL Benchmarking)

http://links.uwaterloo.ca/bragzone.base.html

    (Benchmarking of compression programs)

http://www-mobile.ecs.soton.ac.uk/jurgen

    (Mobile Video Research at University of Southampton)

http://www-mobile.ecs.soton.ac.uk

    (Mobile Multimedia Research at University of Southampton)

http://www.tnt.uni-hannover.de/soft/info/ftp

    (TNT FTP Server)

ftp://ftp.tnt.uni-hannover.de/pub/MPEG/audio

    (TNT FTP Server)

ftp://ftp.uu.net/graphics/jpeg

    (Independent JPEG Group)

ftp://ftp.uu.net:/graphics/jpeg/jpegsrc.v5.tar.Z

    (Independent JPEG Group: C source code)

http://www.hpl.hp.com

    (JPEG-LS Information and software)

ftp://ftp.csd.uwo.ca

    (CALIC state-of-the-art arithmetic codec)

ftp://ipl.rpi.edu/lsp.tar.gz

    (LSP lossless version of SPIHT codec)

http://www.cs.pdx.edu

    (Papers and source code on lossless compression)

http://www.geocities.com

(Extensive archive comparisons of lossless coding)

http://www.cis.ohio-state.edu/hypertext/faq/usenet/compression-faq/part1/faq-doc-12.html

(Lossless Arithmetic Coder)

ftp://ftp.cpsc.ucalgary.ca/pub/projects/ar.cod

(Order-0 model arithmetic coder by Bell, Cleary, and Witten)

ftp://prep.ai.mit.edu/pub/gnu/gzip-1.2.4.tar.gz

(Documentation of GZIP program)

ftp://plg.uwaterloo.ca/pub/dmc/.c*

(Arithmetic coder using dynamic Markov modeling)

ftp://ftp.cis.upenn.edu/pub/eero/epic.tar.Z

(EPIC E. Simoncelli and E. Adelson, critically sampled dyadic subband decomposition and a combined run-length/Huffman entropy coder)

ftp://ftp.cis.upenn.edu/pub/eero/EPWIC-1.tar.gz

(EPWIC-1 Embedded Predictive Wavelet Image Coder, wavelet pyramid decomposition whose coefficients are encoded /one bitplane at a time/ using a static arithmetic encoder; C source software for X windows platforms)

ftp://ipl.rpi.edu/SPIHT.zip

(SPIHT Set Partitioning in Hierarchical Trees, S. Pearlman wavelet codec)

http://primacomp.com

(SPIHT)

http://www.focusweb.com/…

(SPIHT FocusWave Co. commercial program)

http://www.crc.ricoh.com/CREW

(CREW Compression with Reversible Embedded Wavelets)

http://www.code.ucsd.edu/RobustImage

(PZW Packetized Wavelet Zerotree Compression scheme for robust image compression and transmission over noisy channels)

http://www.harc.edu

(HARC-C Houston Advanced Research Center wavelet-based image codec)

http://www.cengines.com/products/products.htm)

(HARC-C commercial version Compression Engine L.L.C)

http://www.fhtw-berlin.de/Projekte/Wavelet/wavelet.html

(PACC Partitioning Aggregating Conditional wavelet coding)

http://www.engr.umbc.edu/~itl/project/medimg/compress/WT/wt.html

(Wavelet transform with Predictive Vector Quantization image compression) *http://www.ctr.columbia.edu/advent/waveform.html*

>   (WT, WP, WPS, SWP, DAG Space and frequency adaptive wavelet packet image compression demo programs)

ftp://ftp.cs.dartmouth.edu/pub/gdavis/wavelet.0.3.tar.gz

>   (Wavelet Image Tool Kit)

ftp://eceserv0.ece.wisc.edu/pub/nguyen/SOFTWARE/UICODER

>   (Transform codecs LOT and DWT, MATLAB)

ftp://eceserv0.ece.wisc.edu/pub/nguyen/SOFTWARE/UIFBD

>   (EQ and Context based; MATLAB programs)

http://math.dartmouth.edu/~strela

>   (Transform codec based on MultiWavelets, MATLAB programs)

ftp://links.uwaterloo.ca/pub/Fractals/Programs/Fisher

>   (Fractals based image codec, Y. Fisher, C source code)

http://www.iterated.com

>   (Fractal Imager, Iterated Systems)

http://inls.ucsd.edu/y/Fractals/#software

>   (Fractal image coding software)

http://spanky.triumf.ca

>   (Fractal image coding)

http://hpux.dsi.unimi.it

>   (Fractal image coding)

ftp://ftp.informatik.uni-freiburg.de

>   (Freiburg Fractal Image Compression FTP site)

http://www-syntim.inria.fr

>   (Fractal coding demonstrations from INRIA)

http://www-mddsp.enel.ucalgary.ca

>   (Model-Based Video Compression)

http://www-nt.e-technic.uni-erlangen.de

>   (Facial animation)

http://neuron.eng.wayne.edu

>   (Image Compression Using Neural Nets)

http://wwwqbic.almaden.ibm.com

>   (QBIC Query by image content, first commercial retrieval system)

http://www.virage.com/cgi-bin/query-e

>   (Virage content-based image search engine)

http://vrw.excalib.com/cgi-bin/sdk/cst/cst.bat

>   (RetrievalWare content-based image retrieval engine)

http://vivaldi.ece.ucsb.edu/Netra

   (Netra image retrieval system)

http://jadzia.ifp.uiuc.edu

   (MARS multimedia analysis and retrieval system)

http://www.videolib.princeton.edu/test/retrieve

   (ART MUSEUM content-based retrieval system)

http://www.ctr.columbia.edu/VisualSeek

   (VisualSeek: Content-based image query system, Demo)

http://www.ctr.columbia.edu/VideoQ

   (VideoQ: online search engine)

http://www.ctr.columbia.edu/webclip

   (WebClip: browsing & editing compressed video over WWW->VideoQ)

A.3   PRODUCTS, MANUFACTURERS, AND VENDORS

http://www.vol.it/MPEG

   (MPEG Companies listing)

   (MPEG LA Co: 35 key U.S. patents + 100 international)

http://www.mpeg.org/~tristan/MPEG/companies.html

   (MPEG Pointers and Resources: Companies)

http://www.empeg.org

   (MPEG Audio in the car radio)

http://www.mpeg2.de

   (MPEG2 and DVD)

http://www.videodiscovery.com/vdyweb/dvd/dvdfaq.html

   (DVD technology)

http://www.ima.org

   (Institute for Musical Arts)

http://www.videodiscovery.com

   (Publishers of innovative educational multimedia)

http://www.dval.com

   (Wake Board—capture and compression board)

http://www.videoconferencing.com/standards.htm

   (IVC Wavelet-based coder)

http://qi.com/products/oem/videowave/index.html

   (Qi Video Wave Wavelet video card)

http://www.vivo.com

    (Vivo Software Inc. H.320/H.324 software)

http://www.ATMforum.com

    (International Product and Service Guide)

http://www.cis.ohio-state.edu/~jain/cis788/ATM_prod/index.html

    (ATM Products)

http://www.fokus.gmd.de/atc

    (ATM Test and conformance center)

http://www.nwfusion.com

    (Buyer's Guide)

http://cell-relay.indiana.edu/cell-relay/publications/InternetResources/vendors/index.html

    (Vendors list)

http://www.cis.ohio-state.edu/~jain/cis788-97/ATM_products/index.htm

    (ATM Products Directory)

http://www.fore.com/products/video/index.html

    (Fore Systems Corporation)

http://www.fore.com/ATM-edu

http://www.k-net.co.uk/products/video.htm

    (K-net Corporation)

http://www.fvc.com/products/Dvgate.html

    (First Virtual Corporation)

http://www.icon-stl.net/~ststech/descrip.html

    (STS Technologies Corporation)

http://www.aherncorp.com/vcon/cruiser100.html

    (Ahern Communications Corporation)

http://siemens.com

    (Siemens)

http://alcatel.fr

    (Alcatel)

http://www.trillium.com

    (Trillium Software)

http://www.infotech.tu-chemnitz.de/~paetz/ATM

    (Vendors of ATM ICs and equipment)

http://www.chips.ibm.com/products/mpeg

    (IBM Co.)

http://www.c-cube.com
http://divicom.com
http://www.mp3.com
http://www.liquidaudio.com
http://www.dolby.com
http://www.ti.com

    (Texas Instruments DSP Solutions Homepage)

http://www.precisionimages.com/c80forum/c80forum.htm

    (TMSC80 Developers Forum)

http://www.bdti.com

    (A DSP technology analysis and software development firm)

http://www.netvideo.com

    (Internet Video Services, Inc.)

http://www.ftmedia.com/newmedia/index.html

    (Management reports)

ATSC Digital TV Standard Transport Packet Stream

B.1   ATSC TV LAYERED SYSTEM ARCHITECTURE WITH HEADERS/DESCRIPTORS
B.2   TRANSPORT PACKET STREAMS
B.3   COMPATIBILITY WITH OTHER TRANSPORT SYSTEMS

The U.S. Advanced Television Systems Committee (ATSC) was formed by the member organizations of the Joint Committee on Inter-Society Coordination, predicting that the prompt, efficient, and effective development of a coordinated set of national standards is essential to the current and future development of domestic TV services. On May 24, 1993, the three groups that developed the four final digital systems agreed to develop a single, state-of-the art system and propose it as a standard. The three groups (AT&T and Zenith Electronics; General Instruments and Massachusetts Institute of Technology; Philips Consumer Electronics, Thomson Consumer Electronics, and David Sarnoff Research Center, now called Sarnoff Corp.) have been working together as the "Digital HDTV Grand Alliance" [511]. The final ATSC system is based on their proposal to the Advisory Committee on Advanced Television Service (ACATS). On December 24, 1996, the FCC voted unanimously to adopt the ATSC digital television standard. Video and audio compression, the packetized data transport structure, and the modulation and transmission system specified in the ATSC standard are mandated by the FCC for use by terrestrial broadcasters. The specific video formats to be used for broadcast television are the subject of voluntary industry standards. This means that in order to be FCC compliant, a broadcaster need not transmit in one of the ATSC video formats, and a receiver need not display all of the ATSC video formats. The FCC initially mandated that all TV stations broadcast digital TV by 2006—it has since backed away from that deadline. Also, the ATSC standard has been adopted by Argentina, Canada, South Korea, and Taiwan.

    The ATSC Digital Television (DTV) standard [512] describes a system designed to transmit high-quality video, audio, and ancillary data over a single

6 MHz channel. The system can deliver reliably about 19 Mbits/s of throughput in a 6 MHz terrestrial broadcasting channel, and about 38 Mbits/s in a 6 MHz cable television channel.

The ATSC DTV system consists of three subsystems:

- **Source coding and compression** refer to the bit rate reduction schemes appropriate for application to the video, audio, and ancillary digital data stream. The digital TV system employs the MPEG-2 video bit stream syntax (main profile/high level) for the coding of video, and the digital audio compression (AC-3) standard for the coding of audio [514].

- **Service multiplex and transport** refer to the means of dividing the digital data stream into smaller packets of information, and the appropriate methods of multiplexing video data stream packets, audio stream packets, and ancillary data stream packets into a single data stream. In developing the transport mechanism, interoperability among digital media— such as terrestrial broadcasting, cable distribution, satellite distribution, recording media, and computer interfaces—was a prime consideration. The digital television system employs the MPEG-2 transport bit stream syntax for the packetization and multiplexing of video, audio, and data signals for digital broadcasting systems. The MPEG-2 transport stream syntax was developed for applications in which channel bandwidth or recording media capacity is limited and the requirement for an efficient transport mechanism is important. The transport protocol consists of 188-byte packets protected by an additional 20 bytes of redundant Forward Error Correction (FEC) data. This approach should give a robust and inherent error correction capability in noisy communication channels. The MPEG-2 transport stream was also designed to facilitate interoperability with the ATM transport mechanism [513].

- **RF/Transmission** refers to channel coding and modulation. The channel coder takes the data bit stream and adds additional information that can be used by the receiver to reconstruct the data from the received signal which, due to transmission impairments, may not accurately represent the transmitted signal. The modulation subsystem (or physical layer) uses the digital data stream information to modulate the transmitted signal. The modulation subsystem offers two modes: a terrestrial broadcast mode (8VSB) and a high data-rate mode (16VSB).

European manufacturers and broadcasters formed the voluntary Digital Video Broadcasting (DVB) group in September 1993. Their objective was to set standards for a digital TV system driven by commercial market needs. The

DVB group agrees on standards, which are then passed to the European Tele-communications Standards Institute (ETSI) for publication. The main technical differences between DVB and ATSC digital television standards may be summarized as follows:

- DVB DTV is based on standard-resolution TV (625-line, 50 MHz interlaced fields) and relies on the MPEG-2 audio/video compression. The wide screen variant has an aspect ratio of 16:9. In the optional high-definition mode, the number of lines is doubled (1250 interlaced) and the number of pixels per line is also doubled. High-definition TV is to be simulcast along with standard resolution TV. DVB sets a common standard for encryption, but broadcasters are free to use a conditional access system of their own choice.

- ATSC DTV is based on computer display standards that call for pictures to be transmitted at a rate of 24, 30, or 60 Hz to match cinema projection standards (24 frames per second) and the 60-field/30 frame NTSC analog TV system. ATSC resolution ranges from 1280 to 1920 pixels per scanning line, and scanning lines number from 720 to 1080. Like DVB, the ATSC standard hinges on MPEG-2 video coding. However, it uses Dolby Digital AC-3 stereo and multichannel surround sound, rather than MPEG-2 audio.

The DVB digital television standard [515] describes a system designed to transmit high-quality video, audio, and ancillary data over a single 8 MHz channel. The system can deliver reliably about 24 Mbits/s of throughput in an 8 MHz terrestrial broadcasting channel, and about 38 Mbits/s in an 8 MHz cable television channel. A modification of the terrestrial system (T-Mobile) makes heavier use of error correction, so the user data rate is reduced to 15 Mbits/s. The prime difference among the standards is the way the compressed signal is packed for transmission. The DVB standard for satellite transmission is based on quadrature phase-shift keying modulation, whereas cable uses quadrature amplitude modulation. For terrestrial TV, the modulation is coded orthogonal frequency-division multiplex. The TV signal is spread over several thousand narrow channels (8000/2000 subchannels).

B.1   ATSC TV LAYERED SYSTEM ARCHITECTURE WITH HEADERS/ DESCRIPTORS

1. **Picture layer:** Multiple picture formats and frame rates.
2. **Compression layer:** MPEG-2 video compression.
3. **Transport layer:** Packet format based on MPEG-2 transport, flexibility to deliver a wide variety of picture, sound, and data services. Flexibility in

the mix of video, audio, and data. Each type of data into separate packets (see Figure B.1). Capability to create new services: many stereo channels of audio, broadcast distribution of computer software, transmission of high-resolution still images to computers.

4. Transmission layer: The system can deliver reliably about 19 Mbits/s of throughput in a 6 MHz terrestrial broadcasting channel, and about 38 Mbits/s in a 6 MHz cable television channel.

The overall multiplexing approach can be described as a combination of multiplexing at two different layers. In the first layer, program transport streams are formed by multiplexing one or more elementary bit streams at the transport layer. In the second layer, the program transport streams are combined (using asynchronous packet multiplexing) to form the overall system.

B.2   TRANSPORT PACKET STREAMS

The ATSC DTV system separately packages video, audio, and auxiliary data in fixed-length packets. The data stream consists of a flow of packets (see Figure B.1):

- Transport streams are comprised of relatively short, fixed-length packets.
- Each packet contains a single type of data.
- There is no predetermined mix of video, audio, or auxiliary data.
- The service type mix can change dynamically.
- Transport streams are designed for error-prone channels.
- Provides excellent interoperability with ATM networks, satellite distribution, terrestrial broadcasting, recording media, and computer interfaces.
- The MPEG-2 transport layer is an emerging standard for a variety of applications.

This allows flexibility in the services that can be provided:

- "Second video program" in a user-selectable window
- Download program-related software to "smart receivers"
- Rapid enabling of pay-per-view decoders on cable
- Future enhancements

B.3   COMPATIBILITY WITH OTHER TRANSPORT SYSTEMS

The ATSC transport system interoperates with two of the most important alternate transport systems. It is syntactically identical to the MPEG-2 transport

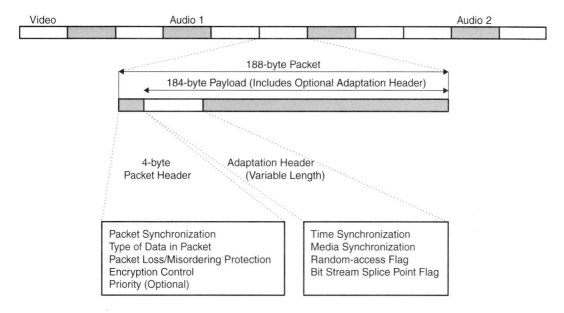

FIGURE B.1   ATSC DTV / MPEG-2 transport [513].

stream definition, with the Digital Television Standard being a subset of the MPEG-2 specification. The transport system also has a high degree of interoperability with the ATM. Furthermore, as several of the cable television and Direct Broadcast Satellite (DBS) systems currently in use or being designed employ MPEG-2 transport layer syntax, the degree of interoperability with such deployed systems should be quite high.

The first aspect of interoperability is syntactic and refers only to the coded representation of the digital television information. The second relates to the delivery of the bit stream in real time.

B.3.1   Interoperability with MPEG-2

The ATSC system is interoperable with MPEG-2 decoders, as the transport is a constrained subset of the MPEG-2 transport syntax. The constraints are imposed for reasons of increased performance with respect to channel acquisition, bandwidth efficiency, and decoder complexity.

The system also supports bit streams and services beyond the compressed video and audio services; for example, text-based services, emergency messages, broadcast distribution of computer software, many stereo channels of audio, transmission of very high-resolution still images to computers, and other future ancillary services. A means of identifying such bit streams is necessary, but is not part of the MPEG-2 definition.

B.3.2 Interoperability with ATM

The MPEG-2 transport packet size is such that it can be easily partitioned for transfer in a link layer that supports ATM transmission. The MPEG-2 transport layer and the ATM layer serve different functions in a video delivery application. The MPEG-2 transport layer solves MPEG-2 presentation problems and performs the multimedia multiplexing function. The ATM layer solves switching and network adaptation problems. Figure B.2 illustrates the differences between the format of an ATM cell and the format of the MPEG-2 transport packet.

There are several possible methods for mapping the MPEG-2 transport packet into the ATM format, and international standards organizations are standardizing the method to be used in different application domains.

Formation of the ATM cell with no AAL bytes, formation of the ATM cell with a single AAL byte, as well as formation of an ATM cell with dual AAL bytes are shown in Figures B.3, B.4, and B.5, respectively [516].

A popular method for Constant Bit Rate (CBR) sources in the Video-on-Demand (VoD) application, under standardization by the ITU-T and the ATM Forum, is to perform cell-aligned packet mapping with an AAL-5 Packet Data Unit (PDU). A preferred solution to cell/packet alignment is to encapsulate one or two transport packets into an AAL-5 PDU structure. This is illustrated in Figure B.6. Two MPEG-2 transport packets, consisting of 376 bytes, are concatenated, and the AAL-5 PDU trailer is computed and appended. The PDU is then segmented and the segments are inserted as the payload of

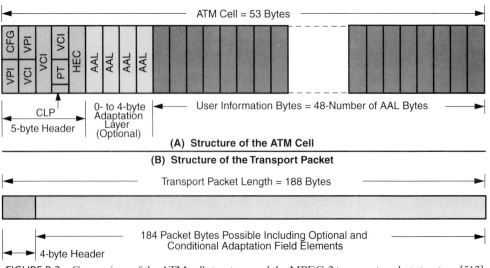

FIGURE B.2 Comparison of the ATM cell structure and the MPEG-2 transport packet structure [513].

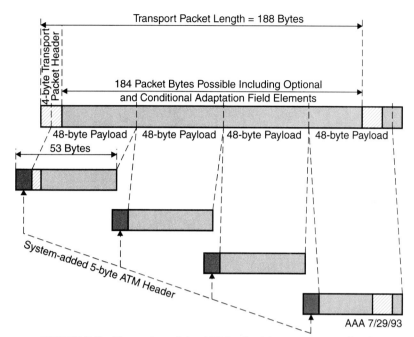

FIGURE B.3   Formation of the ATM cell with no AAL byte [516].

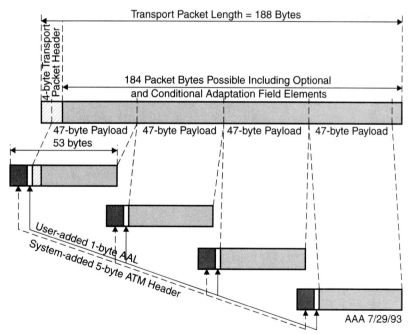

FIGURE B.4   Formation of the ATM cell with a single AAL byte [516].

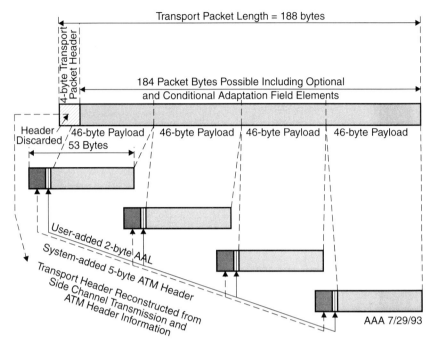

FIGURE B.5 Formation of an ATM cell with dual AAL bytes [516].

eight successive ATM cells. The ATM cell that contains the PDU header is identified by a special value in the PT field of the ATM cell header. Two processes can
contribute to the time jitter of each MPEG-2 packet as it traverses the ATM network. The first is that ATM cells may be delayed at network nodes as part of the
ATM cell scheduling and routing algorithms. This component is not controllable
by the encoder-side equipment. The second component is the packetization delay
in forming the two-packet (eight-cell) PDU.

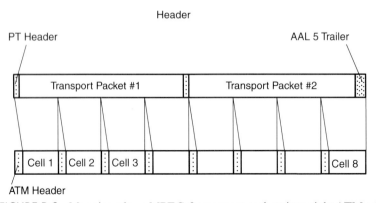

FIGURE B.6 Mapping of two MPEG-2 transport packets into eight ATM cells using
the AAL-5 PDU [513].

The AAL-5 PDU trailer performs error detection and Segmentation and Reassembly (SAR) functions. The PDU trailer is an 8-byte structure, with the elements summarized in Table B.1. The User-to-User (UU) field may be defined by the ITU-T and/or the ATM Forum with specific information for the VoD application. The field length is important to locate any padding that may be required to pad the PDU to be an incremental number of ATM cells. Padding will be required when it is necessary to issue a short PDU because a PCR packet has arrived at the PDU assembly processor. The CRC-32 provides an end-to-end error detection function.

TABLE B.1   Elements of the AAL-5 PDU Trailer [513]

PDU Field	Size (bytes)	Function
UU	1	User-to-User information to allow the encoder application to signal the decoder application with application-dependent information.
CPI	1	Reserved for future use.
Length	2	16-bit binary number that represents the length of the PDU payload. It allows padding to follow the PDU payload in applications that require it.
CRC-32	4	Cyclic Redundancy Check calculated over the payload of the PDU.

APPENDIX C

Multimedia and Standardization

Communications require standards that define the meaning and the syntax given to information at the source when it reaches the destination. The telecommunications industry bases its standards on the original consideration that there are impedance mismatches in passing from the wires of one telephone company to another. It is not the right way to promote communications; in other words, the telephone companies' business [260]. The digital speech is just a means to optimize transmission in the network, not something to be offered as an end-to-end service to customers.

The movie industry has settled on a small number of film formats, each characterized by a different audiovisual performance level. The hardware and software motion picture industry agreed that the ability to project a movie anywhere in the world was good for everybody's business.

The radio industry took the commendable approach of defining standards of worldwide reach. The television industry has defined its standards in such a way that users can only watch programs coming from a certain source. Nevertheless, a good 405 lines at 50 Hz television system was deployed in the U.K. in the late 1930s. In the early 1940s, the U.S. established its 525/30 system that improved on the U.K. system by some 20%. A few years later, Europe established its own 625/25 television system that did not improve bandwidth over the National Television System Committee's (NTSC) system (625×25 versus 525×30). With the addition of color to the monochrome signal, the number of "national paths" to television increased dramatically with NTSC, Phase Alternate Line (PAL), Sequential Couleur Avec Memoire (SECAM), and their almost countless variants.

The CATV industry, sitting in between television and telecommunications and by definition a local business, has an outlook toward standards depending on the country in which it operates.

The consumer electronics industry (mostly recording) has taken the most straightforward application of the definition of standards. It is considered a freely entered agreement between a manufacturer and a user to sell/buy a certain piece of equipment. Users can play back audio or video from media that are specific to the type of equipment purchased ("format") from a third party that agrees to produce the content in that format.

The computer industry takes a similar attitude, but it is considerably more articulated. The purchase of a computer is a freely entered agreement between a manufacturer and a user to provide hardware and some layers of software so that high-level applications can be developed or purchased from the manufacturer or from third parties.

In the electronic games industry, the purchase of an electronic game is a freely entered agreement between a manufacturer and a user to sell/buy hardware and software that runs exclusively on the hardware.

So far, the different industries have been diverging, but multimedia communications necessarily need some convergence zone that can only be achieved by standardization in key areas [516, 517]. Putting every stakeholder together and producing communication standards accepted by all is a big task. MPEG succeeded in doing that for its first-generation standards, MPEG-1 and MPEG-2, and the second-generation standard, MPEG-4 [518].

The working method on the emerging MPEG-7 standard is similar to those on previous ones [259]. After defining the requirements, a call for proposals of technical solutions is opened, and after evaluation of arrived suggestions (competitive stage), promising solutions are selected and then jointly developed (collaborative stage).

Table C.1 presents a summary of present and emerging standards for coding and representation of visual information.

TABLE C.1 Summary of Present and Emerging Standards for Coding and Representation of Visual Information

Standard	Standardization Body / Information on Internet	Main Target Bit Rate	Main Compression Technologies	Main Target Applications
JPEG IS 10918 (1, 2) Rec. T.81 1992.	ISO/IEC JTC1/SC29/WG1 ITU-T SG8 http://www.jpeg.org http://www.ijg.org	Compression ratio 2–30	DCT Perceptual Q Zigzag reordering Huffman coding Arithmetic coding Independent lossless coding	Internet imaging Digital photography Image and video editing Medical imaging
JPEG Extensions IS 10918 (3) 1996. Rec. T.84	http://jura.jpeg.org http://www.ijg.org		DCT Variable Q A selective refinement Provision for tiling SPIFF extension	Medical imaging Image processing and editing, Archival and hidden compression functions Image interchange Satellite imagery
JPEG2000 WD 15444 2000.	ISO/IEC JTC1/SC29/WG1 ITU-T SG8 http://pr.jpeg.org	Compression ratio 2–50	Flexible compression architectures process and/or format Arbitrary shape coding	Internet imaging Digital photography Image and video editing Printing Medical imaging Mobile applications Color fax Satellite imaging Photo and art digital libraries
JPEG-LS Part 1 DIS 14495 (1) 1998. Rec. T.87	ISO/IEC JTC1/SC29/WG1 ITU-T SG8 http://www.hpl.hp.com/loco		Context modeling Prediction Golomb codes	Lossless and near lossless coding of continuous tone still images
JPEG-LS Part 2 DIS 14495 (2) 1999.			Arithmetic coding More effective prediction Modified Golomb code	

TABLE C.1 Summary of Present and Emerging Standards for Coding and Representation of Visual Information (*Continued*)

Standard	Standardization Body / Information on Internet	Main Target Bit Rate	Main Compression Technologies	Main Target Applications
JBIG (JBIG1) IS 11544 Rec. T.82 1993. Rec. T.85 1995.	ISO/IEC JTC1/SC29/WG1 ITU-T IETF *http://disc.org.uk/.jpeg*	Compression ratio 20:1 (3–5 times higher than Fax Group 3,4/ MMR)	Context-based arithmetic coder (dynamically adaptive to the statistics of each pixel content)	Lossy Lossless Progressive (lossy to lossless) coding for fax apparatus Image browsing
MRC (Mixed Raster Content) 1998. Rec. T.44 IETF RFC 231		(Application profile of JBIG1 for facsimile)	Uses multilayered, multiresolution imaging model for compression Compression of compound images (Binary text and Continuous tone images) for both natural color and palletized images	Color fax over PSTN and Internet ITU-T Color fax IETF Internet Fax File format: (TIFF = Fx) TIFF for fax extended
JBIG 2 WD 14492 2000.	ISO/IEC JTC1/SG29/WG1 *http://www.jpeg.org/public* *http://spmg.ece.ubc.ca/ research/jbig/main.html*	Compression ratio 2–4 times higher than JBIG-1 High-performance decompression	Lossy, lossless, and lossy to lossless image compression High-quality progressive coding Content progressive coding Content-based (text, halftones, line art, large characters) decomposition and coding Model-based coding, soft pattern matching, pattern matching and substitution File formats to enclose the coded bilevel image data (both sequential and random access)	Document storage and archiving Coding images on WWW Wireless data transmission Print spooling Facsimile Teleconferencing Interactive multimedia

TABLE C.1 Summary of Present and Emerging Standards for Coding and Representation of Visual Information *(Continued)*

Standard	Standardization Body / Information on Internet	Main Target Bit Rate	Main Compression Technologies	Main Target Applications
MPEG-1 IS 11172 (1–5) 1992.	ISO/IEC JTC1/SC29/WG11 *http://www.cselt.it/mpeg* *http://www.mpeg.org*	Bit rates up to about 1.5 Mbits/s	DCT Perceptual Q Adaptive Q Zigzag scanning Predictive MC Bidirectional MC Half-sample accuracy ME Huffman coding Arithmetic coding	Storage on CD-ROM Consumer video Video-CD De facto standard on WWW
MPEG-2 IS 13812 (1–9) Rec. H.262 1995.	ISO/IEC JTC1/SC29/WG11 ITU-T *http://www.cselt.it/mpeg* *http://www.mpeg.org*	Bit rates 1.5 Mbits/s to about 50 Mbits/s	DCT Perceptual Q Adaptive Q Zigzag scanning Predictive MC Bidirectional MC Frame/field-based MC Half-sample accuracy ME Spatial scalability Temporal scalability Quality scalability Huffman coding Arithmetic coding Error-resilient coding	Digital TV Digital HDTV High-quality video Satellite TV Cable TV Terrestrial broadcast Video editing Video storage Stereoscopic video DVD Professional studio/postproduction processing DVB MPEG camera Set-top boxes

TABLE C.1 Summary of Present and Emerging Standards for Coding and Representation of Visual Information (*Continued*)

Standard	Standardization Body / Information on Internet	Main Target Bit Rate	Main Compression Technologies	Main Target Applications
MPEG-4 IS 14496 (1–6) Feb. 1999.	ISO/IEC JTC1/SC29/WG11 MPEG-4 Systems *http://garuda.imag.fr/ MPEG4* MPEG-4 Video *http://bs.hhi.de/ mpeg-video* MPEG-4 SNHC *http://www.es.com/ mpeg-snhc* MPEG-4 Audio *http://www.tnt.uni-hannover .de/project/mpeg/audio*	Bit rates 8 Kbits/s to about 35 Mbits/s	DCT Wavelet Perceptual Q Adaptive Q Zigzag scanning Horizontal/vertical scanning Zero-tree reordering Predictive MC Bidirectional MC Frame/field-based MC Half-sample accuracy ME Advanced ME Overlapping MC Spatial scalability Temporal scalability Quality scalability View dependent scalability Bitmap shape coding Sprite coding Face animation Body animation Dynamic mesh coding Huffman coding Arithmetic coding Error-resilient coding Shape adaptive DCT Shape adaptive Wavelet Object/content-based coding (shape, motion and texture) Synthetic and natural hybrid coding (SNHC) Feathering filter Deringing filter	Internet video Interactive video Visual editing Content manipulation Consumer video Professional video 2D/3D computer Graphics/animation Mobile multimedia communications Stereoscopic video Surveillance video

Standard	Standardization Body / Information on Internet	Main Target Bit Rate	Main Compression Technologies	Main Target Applications
MPEG-4 Version 2 2000.	ISO/IEC JTC1/SC29/WG11		Additional tools and functionalities Improved coding efficiency Improved error robustness Coding multiple views Body animation Coding of 3D meshes Media integration of text and graphics	
MPEG-7 2001.	ISO/IEC JTC1/SC29/WG11 *http://www.cselt.it/mpeg* *http://www.darmstadt .gmd.de/mobile/MPEG7*	Multimedia content description interface	Proposal package description Evaluation of proposals Test sets To standardize: -A set of description schemes and descriptions -A language to specify description schemes (Description Definition Language [DDL]) -A coding scheme for the description	Visual retrieval systems Auditory retrieval systems Beyond-search applications Education Surveillance Multimedia search and retrieval
MHEG IS13522 (1-7)	ISO/IEC JTC1/SC29/WG12 *http://www.mheg.org*	Multimedia and Hyper- media Experts Group	Methods for storage, exchange and display of multimedia presentations	CD-ROM-based encyclopedias Interactive books for learning Video- and news-on-demand systems Interactive television
Rec. H.261 Nov. 1990.	ITU-T ITU-T SG16 Q15 AVC *http://www.itu.ch/itudoc/ itu-t/com16.html*	Bit rates px 64 Kbits/s (p=1-30)	DCT Adaptive Q Zigzag scanning Predictive MC Integer-sample accuracy ME Huffman coding Error-resilient coding	ISDN videoconferencing

371

TABLE C.1 Summary of Present and Emerging Standards for Coding and Representation of Visual Information (*Continued*)

Standard	Standardization Body / Information on Internet	Main Target Bit Rate	Main Compression Technologies	Main Target Applications
Rec. H.263 Nov. 1995.	ITU-T ITU-T SG16 Q15 AVC *ftp://standard.pictel.com/video-site* *http://www.nta.no/~brukere/DVC/h263_software*	Bit rates 8 Kbits/s up to 1.5 Mbits/s	Bidirectional MC Half-sample accuracy ME Advanced ME Overlapping MC Huffman coding Arithmetic coding Error-resilient coding 3D VLC	POTS video-telephony Desktop video-telephony Mobile video-telephony
Rec. H.263 Version 2 (H.263+) Jan. 1998	ITU-T ITU-T SG16 Q15 AVC *ftp://standard.pictel.com/video-site* *ftp://standard.pictel.com/video-site/h263plus* *http://spmg.ece.ubc.ca/h263plus*		High degree of error resilience Negotiable coding options Advanced intracoding mode Deblocking filter Slice structure mode Supplemental enhancement Improved PB-frame mode Reference picture Selection mode Temporal, SNR, and spatial scalability modes Backward compatible with H.263 Horizontal/vertical scanning Reduced resolution mode New VLC for intra/frames Alternate VLC for interframes Modified quantization Wider variety of input video formats Independent segment decoding mode	Wireless or packet-based transport networks

TABLE C.1 Summary of Present and Emerging Standards for Coding and Representation of Visual Information (*Continued*)

Standard	Standardization Body / Information on Internet	Main Target Bit Rate	Main Compression Technologies	Main Target Applications
Rec. H.263 Version 3 (H.263++) Nov. 2000.	ITU-T ITU-T SG16 Q15 AVC *ftp://standard.pictel.com/ video-site*	Near-term standardization of enhancements to H.263 video codec	4×4 motion compensation and DCT Adaptive quantization Reference picture selection enhancement Scalability enhancement IDCT mismatch reduction Deblocking and deringing filters Error concealment Error resilience Packetization	Real-time telecommunication and related nonconversational services Compatibility between MPEG-4 and H.263
H.26L Middle 2002.	ITU-T ITU-T SG16 Q15 AVC *ftp://standard.pictel.com/ video-site*	Long-term standardization based on new (very low bit-rate) video coding technology	Enhanced visual quality Enhanced error robustness Low complexity Low end-to-end delays Adaptable rate control mechanisms Video scalability Streaming support	Real-time conversational services Internet video applications Sign language and lip-reading communication Video storage and retrieval service Video store and forward services (video mail) Multipoint communication over heterogeneous networks Future mobile communication environment (IMT-2000)

Bibliography

CHAPTER 2: PACKET VIDEO IN THE NETWORK ENVIRONMENT

[1] N. Jayant, "High quality networking of audio-visual information," *IEEE Comm. Magazine*, vol. 31, pp. 84–95, Sept. 1993.

[2] A. A. Lazar et al., "MAGNET: Columbia's integrated network testbed," *IEEE J. Selected Areas in Comm.*, vol. 11, pp. 859–871, Nov. 1993.

[3] A. A. Lazar and J. S. White, "Packetized video on MAGNET," *Optical Engineering*, vol. 26, pp. 596–602, Dec. 1986.

[4] P. Gonet, "Fast packet approach to integrated broadband networks," *Networks*, vol. 9, pp. 292–298, Dec. 1986.

[5] M. Devault et al., "The 'prelude' ATD experiment assessments and future prospects," *IEEE J. Selected Areas in Comm.*, vol. 4, pp. 1528–1532, Dec. 1986.

[6] J. Sidron and J. S. Gopal, "PARIS: An approach to integrated high-speed private networks," *Int. J. Digital Analog Cable Syst.*, vol. 1, pp. 77–85, 1988.

[7] L. Chiariglione and L. Corgnier, "System consideration for picture communication," *ICC'84*, pp. 245–249, Amsterdam, May 1984.

[8] Z. Bojkovic, "Some issues in packet video: modeling, coding, compression," *2nd Int. Workshop on Image and Signal Processing: Theory, Methodology, Systems and Applications*, pp. 2–23, Budapest, Hungary, Nov. 1995.

[9] Y. Q. Zhang et al., "Variable bit-rate video transmission in the broadband ISDN environment," *Proc. IEEE*, vol. 79, pp. 214–221, Feb. 1991.

[10]   T. Bially et al., "A technique for adaptive voice flow control in integrated packet networks," *IEEE Trans. Comm.*, vol. COM-28, pp. 325–333, March 1980.

[11]   Z. Bojkovic, "Speech signal coding in subband analysis," *MELECON'85*, pp. 163–166, Madrid, Spain, Oct. 1985.

[12]   M. Schwartz, *Telecommunications networks*, Reading, MA: Addison-Wesley, 1987.

[13]   B. Maglaris et al., "Performance models of statistical multiplexing in packet video communications," *IEEE Trans. Comm.*, vol. COM-36, pp. 834–844, July 1988.

[14]   W. Verbiest et al., "The impact of the ATM concept on video coding," *IEEE J. Selected Areas in Comm.*, vol. SAC-6, pp. 1623–1632, Dec. 1988.

[15]   G. Carlsson and M. Vetterli, "Packet video and its integration into the network architecture," *IEEE J. Selected Areas in Comm.*, vol. 7, pp. 739–751, June 1989.

[16]   P. Gonet, "Asynchronous time division switching: The way to flexible broadband communication networks," *Proc. International Zurich Seminar on Digital Communications*, Zurich, Switzerland, pp. 741–748, 1986.

[17]   M. Nomura, T. Fujii, and N. Ohta, "Layered packet loss protection for variable rate video coding using DCT," *II Intl. Workshop on Packet Video*, Torino, Italy, Sept. 1988.

[18]   A. J. Viterbi and J. V. Omura, *Principles of digital communication and coding*, New York, NY: McGraw-Hill, 1997.

[19]   A. K. Jain, *Fundamentals of digital image processing*, Englewood Cliffs, NJ: Prentice Hall, 1989.

[20]   A. S. Tom, *Channel equalization and interface reduction using scrambling and adaptive amplitude modulation*, Ph.D. Thesis, MIT, Dept. of Electrical Eng., June 1990.

[21]   J. G. Proakis, *Digital communications*, New York, NY: McGraw-Hill, 1983.

[22]   Z. Bojkovic, "Recent trends in packet video transmission on ATM networks," *Proc. Basis of Electronics Workshop '94*, pp. 17–105, Cluj Napoca, Romania, Oct. 1994.

[23]   H. Sun et al., "Error concealment algorithms for robust decoding of MPEG compressed video," *Signal Processing: Image Communications*, vol. 10, pp. 249–268, Sept. 1997.

[24]   N. Jayant, "Signal compression: Technology targets and research directions," *IEEE J. Selected Areas in Comm.*, vol. 10, pp. 796–818, May 1992.

[25]   J. L. Mitchell et al., *MPEG video compression standard*, New York, NY: Chapman and Hall, 1996.

[26]   A. N. Netravali and B. G. Haskell, *Digital pictures—representation, compression and standards*, New York, NY: Plenum Press, 1995.

[27]   K. R. Rao and P. Yip, *Discrete cosine transform: Algorithms, advantages, applications*, New York, NY: Academic Press, 1990.

[28]   V. O. K. Li and W. Liao, "Distributed multimedia systems," *Proc. IEEE*, vol. 85, pp. 1063–1108, July 1997.

CHAPTER 3: VIDEO COMMUNICATION USING ASYNCHRONOUS TRANSFER MODE TECHNIQUE

[29]   K. Sayood, *Introduction to data compression*, San Francisco, CA: Morgan Kaufmann, 1996.

[30]   T. M. Chen and T. Luckenbach, "Data communication in ATM networks," *IEEE Comm. Magazine*, vol. 32, Aug. 1994.

[31]   M. De Prucker, *Asynchronous transfer mode: Solution for broadband ISDN*, London, UK: Elias Harwood, 1993.

[32]   M. Nomura, T. Fuji, and N. Ohta, "Basic characteristics of variable rate video coding in ATM environment," *IEEE J. Selected Areas in Comm.*, vol. 7, pp. 752–760, June 1989.

[33]   W. Verbiest and L. Pinoo, "A variable bitrate codec for asynchronous transfer mode networks," *IEEE J. Selected Areas in Comm.*, vol. 7, pp. 761–770, June 1989.

[34]   R. Handel and M. N. Huber, *Integrated broadband networks: An introduction to ATM-based networks*, Reading, MA: Addison-Wesley, 1991.

[35]   L. Murphy, J. Murphy, and J. K. MacKie-Mason, "Feedback and efficiency in ATM networks," *IEEE ICC*, pp. 1045–1049, Dallas, TX, June 1996.

[36]   C. B. Lee, K. B. Ha, and R.-H. Park, "Computation of effective bandwidth of aggregated VBR MPEG video traffic in ATM networks using the modified equivalent capacity," *IEEE ICC*, pp. 627–631, Dallas, TX, June 1996.

[37]   D. Ruiu, "Testing ATM systems," *IEEE Spectrum*, vol. 31, pp. 25–27, June 1994.

[38]   D. Niehaus et al., "Performance benchmarking of signaling in ATM networks," *IEEE Comm. Magazine*, vol. 35, pp. 134–143, Aug. 1997.

[39]   ITU-T *Draft Rec. Q.2931, B-ISDN signaling ATM adaptation layer-service specific coordination function for support of signaling at the user-to-network interface (SSCF at UNI)*, Dec. 1993.

[40]   R. Kisimoto, Y. Ogata, and F. Lumaru, "General interval distribution characteristics of packetized variable rate video coding data streams in the ATM network," *IEEE J. Selected Areas in Comm.*, vol. 7, pp. 833–841, May 1989.

[41]   C. Scott, M. Bigger and D. Dorman, "Getting the picture-integrated video services in BISDN," *Telecom. J. Australia*, vol. 40, Feb. 1990.

[42]   K. Yamazaki and M. Wada, "Studies on video services and codings in BISDN," *IEICE Tech. Rep.* SSE 91–21, June 1991.

[43]   R. Handel, M. N. Huber, and S. Schroeder, *ATM networks—concepts, protocols, applications*, Reading, MA: Addison-Wesley, 1994.

[44]   A. F. Daginklas and M. Ghanbari, "Priority mechanisms in ATM switches carrying two layer video data," *Electronics Letters*, vol. 29, pp. 273–274, Feb. 1993.

[45]   Y. Sato and K. J. Sato, "Virtual path link capacity design for ATM networks," *IEEE J. Selected Areas in Comm.*, vol. 9, pp. 104–111, Jan. 1991.

[46]   J. Feng, K. T. Lo, and H. Mehrpour, "Statistical analysis and simulation study of two-layer MPEG video coding algorithm in ATM networks," *Intl. Symposium on Information Theory and Its Applications*, pp. 647–652, Sydney, Australia, Nov. 1994.

[47]   Q. F. Zhu, Y. Wang, and L. Shaw, "Coding and cell-loss recovery in DCT-based packet video," *IEEE Trans. CSVT*, vol. 3, pp. 248–258, June 1993.

[48]   A. Elavalid and D. Mitra, "Effective bandwidth of general Markovian traffic sources and admission control of high speed networks," *IEEE/ACM Trans. Networking*, vol. 1, pp. 329–343, June 1993.

[49]   A. R. Reibman and B. G. Haskell, "Constraints on variable bit rate video for ATM networks," *IEEE Trans. CSVT*, vol. 2, pp. 361–372, Dec. 1992.

[50]   R. J. Safranek, C. R. Kalmanek, and R. Garg, "Methods for matching compressed video to ATM networks," *IEEE ICIP*, vol. 1, pp. 13–16, Washington, DC, Oct. 1995.

[51]   W. Ding, "Joint encoder and channel rate control of VBR video over ATM networks," *IEEE Trans. CSVT*, vol. 7, pp. 266–278, April 1997.

[52] W. Lou and M. E. Zarki, "Adaptive data partitioning for MPEG-2 video transmission over ATM based networks," *IEEE ICIP*, vol. 1, pp. 17–20, Washington, DC, Oct. 1995.

[53] J. J. Chen and D. W. Liu, "Optimal coding of video sequence over ATM networks," *IEEE ICIP*, vol. 1, pp. 21–24, Washington, DC, Oct. 1995.

[54] P. Sen et al., "Models for packet switching in variable bit rate video sources," *IEEE J. Selected Areas in Comm.*, vol. 7, pp. 865–869, June 1989.

[55] S. Huang, "Modeling and analysis for packet video," *IEEE GLOBE-COM'89*, Dallas, TX, Nov. 1989.

[56] M. W. Garrett and M. Vetterli, "A joint source/channel model for real time services on ATM networks," *Third Intl. Workshop on Packet Video*, Morristown, NJ, March 1990.

[57] P. Panche and M. E. Zarki, "Modeling video sources for resource allocation in ATM-based B-ISDN," *Third Intl. Workshop on Packet Video*, Morristown, NJ, Mar. 1990.

[58] R. Grunenfeler et al., "Characterization of video codecs as autoregressive moving average processes and related queuing system performance," *IEEE J. Selected Areas in Comm.*, vol. 9, pp. 284–293, April 1991.

[59] C. Shim et al., "Modeling and call admission control algorithm of variable bit rate video in ATM networks," *IEEE J. Selected Areas in Comm.*, vol. 12, pp. 332–344, Feb. 1994.

[60] A. La Corte et al., "Modeling activity in VBR video sources," *Signal Process.: Image Comm.*, vol. 3, pp. 167–178, Aug. 1991.

[61] H. G. Mussmann, "A layered coding system for very low bit rate video coding," *Signal Process., Image Comm.*, vol. 7, pp. 267–278, Nov. 1995.

[62] D. E. Pearson, "Developments in model-based video coding," *Proc. IEEE*, vol. 83, pp. 892–906, June 1995.

[63] R. Shafer and T. Sikora, "Digital video coding standards and their role in video communications," *Proc. IEEE*, vol. 83, pp. 907–924, June 1995.

[64] P. Kauff et al., *Functional coding of video for MPEG-4 applications*, ISO/IEC MPEG, Doc. 395, Singapore, Nov. 1994.

[65] T. Sikora, *Video based multimedia retrieval-advanced coding techniques*, Internal Report-Project Description, Video Coding Group, Dept. ECSE, Monash University, Melbourne, Australia, Dec. 1993.

[66] T. Sikora and P. Kauff, "Functional coding of video using a shape adaptive DCT algorithm and object-based tools," *Picture Coding Symp.*, Melbourne, Australia, March 1996.

[67] P. Kauff et al., "Functional coding of video using a shape-adaptive DCT algorithm and an object-based motion-prediction toolbox," *IEEE Trans. CSVT*, vol. 7, pp. 181–195, Feb. 1997.

[68] G. Karlsson and M. Vetterli, "Sub-band coding of video for packet networks," *Optical Engineering*, vol. 27, pp. 574–586, July 1996.

[69] W. Werbiest, "Video coding in an ATM environment," *Third Intl. Conf. on New Systems and Services in Telecomm.*, Liege, Belgium, Nov. 1986.

[70] M. Duponcheel and W. Verbiest, *Simulation results for a hybrid transform video coding algorithm*, RACE project 2023, BTM-A 11-05-PR, 1986.

[71] M. L. Liou, "Overview of the px64 kbits video coding standard," *Comm. ACM*, vol. 34, pp. 59–63, April 1991.

[72] R. E. Crochiere, S. A. Webber, and J. L. Flanagan, "Digital coding of speech in subbands," *Bell Sys. Tech. J.*, vol. 55, pp. 1069–1085, Oct. 1976.

[73] M. Vetterli, "Multi-dimensional subband coding: Some theory and algorithms," *Signal Processing*, vol. 6, pp. 97–112, April 1984.

[74] J. W. Woods and S. D. O'Neil, "Subband coding of images," *IEEE Trans. ASSP*, vol. 34, pp. 1278–1288, May 1986.

[75] H. Gharavi and A. Tabatabai, "Subband coding of monochrome and color images," *IEEE Trans. Circuits and Syst.*, vol. 35, pp. 207–214, Feb. 1988.

[76] P. H. Westernik et al., "Subband coding of images using vector quantization," *IEEE Trans. Comm.*, vol. 36, pp. 713–719, June 1988.

[77] O. Johnsen, O. V. Shentov, and S. K. Mitra, "A technique for the efficient coding of the upper bands in subband coding of images," *ICASSP'90*, pp. 2097–2100, April 1990.

[78] C. J. Podilchuk, N. S. Jayant, and P. Noll, "Sparse codebook for the quantization of the non-dominant subband image coding," *IEEE ICASSP*, pp. 2101–2104, April 1990.

[79] C. J. Podilchuk, N. S. Jayant, and N. Farvardin, "Three-dimensional subband coding of video," *IEEE Trans. Image Processing*, vol. 4, pp. 125–139, Feb. 1995.

[80] N. Mohsenian and N. M. Nasrabadi, "Subband coding of video using an edge-based vector quantization technique for compression of the

upper bands," *IEEE ICASSP*, vol. III, pp. 233–236. San Francisco, CA, March 1992.

[81] N. Tanabe and N. Farvardin, "Subband image coding using entropy-coded quantization over noisy channels," *IEEE J. Selected Areas in Comm.*, vol. 10, pp. 926–943, June 1992.

[82] N. Farvardin and J. W. Modestino, "Optimum quantizer performance for a class of non-Gaussian memoryless sources," *IEEE Trans. Inform. Theory*, vol. 30, pp. 485–497, May 1984.

[83] Y. H. Kim and J. W. Modestino, "Adaptive entropy coded subband coding of images," *IEEE Trans. Image Process.*, vol. 1, pp. 31–48, Jan. 1992.

[84] P. A. Chou, T. Lookabaugh, and R. M. Gray, "Entropy-constrained vector quantization," *IEEE Trans. ASSP*, vol. 37, pp. 31–42, Jan. 1989.

[85] M. W. Marcellin, P. Sriram, and K. L. Tong, "Transform coding of monochrome and color images using trellis coded quantization," *IEEE Trans. CSVT*, vol. 3, pp. 270–276, Aug. 1993.

[86] P. Sriram and M. W. Marcellin, "Image coding using wavelet transforms and entropy-constrained trellis-coded quantization," *IEEE Trans. Image Processing,* vol. 4, pp. 725–733, June 1995.

[87] R. E. Van Dyck et al., "Wavelet video coding with ladder structures and entropy-constrained quantization," *IEEE Trans. CSVT*, vol. 6, pp. 483–495, Oct. 1996.

[88] N. S. Jayant and P. Noll, *Digital coding of waveforms*, Englewood Cliffs, NJ: Prentice Hall, 1984.

[89] D. J. Le Gall, "Subband coding of images with low computational complexity," *Picture Coding Symp.,* Stockholm, Sweden, June 1987.

[90] D. Esteban and C. Galand, "Application of QMF to split band voice coding schemes," *IEEE ICASSP*, pp. 191–195, May 1977.

[91] J. Princen and A. Bradley, "Analysis/synthesis filter bank design based on time domain aliasing cancellation," *IEEE Trans. ASSP*, vol. 34, pp. 1153–1161, Oct. 1986.

[92] J. W. Woods (Editor), *Subband image coding*, Norwell, MA: Kluwer Academic, 1991.

[93] Z. Bojkovic, A. Samcovic, and D. Milovanovic, "Upper bound on coding gain for video subband coding systems," in *Proc. Intelligent Terminals, source and channel coding, COST 229*, pp. 69–76, Budapest, Hungary, Sept. 1993.

[94] Z. Bojkovic, A. Samcovic, and D. Milovanovic, "One way for subband image coder choice using entropy measuring," in *Proc. Adaptive*

methods and emergent techniques for signal processing and communications, COST 229, pp. 257–260, Ljubljana, Slovenia, April 1994.

[95]   G. Karlsson and M. Vetterli, "Three dimensional subband coding of video," *ICASSP'88*, pp. 1110–1113, 1988.

[96]   K. R. Rao and J. J. Hwang, *Techniques and standards for image, video and audio coding*, Upper Saddle River, NJ: Prentice Hall PTR, 1996.

[97]   R. Kisimoto and K. Irie, "HDTV transmission system and coding method in an ATM network," *3rd Intl. Workshop on HDTV*, Tokyo, Japan, Aug. 1989.

[98]   H. S. Malvar, *Signal processing with lapped transforms*, Norwood, MA: Artech House, 1992.

[99]   H. Schiller, "Overlapping block transform for image coding preserving equal number of samples and coefficients," *Visual Communications and Image Processing'88*, edited by T. R. Hsing, SPIE vol. 1001, pp. 834–839, 1988.

[100]   P. M. Cassereau, D. H. Staelin, and G. DeJager, "Encoding of images based on a lapped orthogonal transform," *IEEE Trans. Comm.*, vol. COM-37, pp. 189–193, Feb. 1989.

[101]   H. S. Malvar and D. H. Staelin, "The LOT: Transform coding without blocking effects," *IEEE Trans. ASSP*, vol. ASSP-37, pp. 553–559, April 1989.

[102]   H. S. Malvar, "Lapped transforms for efficient transform/subband coding," *IEEE Trans. ASSP*, vol. ASSP-38, pp. 969–978, June 1990.

[103]   J. P. Princen, A. W. Johnson, and A. B. Bradley, "Subband/transform coding using filter bank designs based on time domain aliasing cancellation," *IEEE ICASSP*, Dallas, TX, pp. 2161–2164, April 1987.

[104]   H. S. Malvar, "Extended lapped transforms: properties, applications and fast algorithms," *IEEE Trans. Signal Proc.*, vol. 40, pp. 2703–2714, Nov. 1992.

[105]   R. L. de Queiroz and K. R. Rao, "Adaptive extended lapped transforms," *IEEE ICASSP*, vol. 3, pp. 217–220, Minneapolis, MN, April 1993.

[106]   R. Hoffman, *Data compression in digital systems*, New York, NY: Chapman and Hall, 1997.

[107]   H. M. Jung et al., "HD-VCR codec for studio application using quadtree structured binary symbols in wavelet transform domain," *IEEE Trans. CSVT*, vol. 6, pp. 506–513, Oct. 1996.

[108]   M. Antonini et al., "Image coding using wavelet transform," *IEEE Trans. Image Processing*, vol. 1, pp. 205–220, April 1992.

[109]   S. G. Mallat, "A theory for multiresolution signal decomposition: The wavelet representation," *IEEE Trans. Pattern Anal. Machine Intell.*, vol. 11, pp. 674–693, July 1989.

[110]   O. Rioul and M. Vetterli, "Wavelets and signal processing," *IEEE Signal Processing Magazine*, vol. 8, pp. 14–38, Oct. 1991.

[111]   J. M. Shapiro, "Embedded image coding using zerotrees of wavelet coefficients," *IEEE Trans. Signal Processing*, vol. 41, pp. 3445–3462, Dec. 1993.

[112]   P. Strobach, "Quadtree-structured recursive plane decomposition coding of images," *IEEE Trans. Signal Processing*, vol. 39, pp. 1380–1395, June 1991.

[113]   Y. K. Kim, H. G. Kim, and K. T. Park, "New tree structure with conditional height difference for wavelet transform image coding," *Electronics Letters*, vol. 31, pp. 90–92, Jan. 1995.

[114]   Y. Q. Zhang and S. Zafar, "Motion-compensated wavelet transform coding for color video compression," *IEEE Trans. CSVT*, vol. 2, pp. 285–296, Sept. 1992.

[115]   A. S. Lewis and G. Knowles, "Image compression using the 2-D wavelet transform," *IEEE Trans. Image Processing*, vol. 1, pp. 244–250, April 1992.

[116]   S. G. Mallat, "Multifrequency channel decomposition of images and wavelet models," *IEEE Trans. ASSP*, vol. 41, pp. 3445–3462, Dec. 1993.

[117]   E. A. B. daSilva and M. Ghanbari, "On the performance of linear phase wavelet transforms in low bit rate image coding," *IEEE Trans. Image Processing*, vol. 5, pp. 689–704, May 1996.

[118]   E. A. B. daSilva, D. G. Sampson, and M. Ghanbari, "Super high definition image coding using wavelet vector quantization," *IEEE Trans. CSVT*, vol. 6, pp. 399–406, Aug. 1996.

[119]   S. G. Mallat, *Multiresolution representation and wavelets*, Ph.D. Thesis, University of Pennsylvania, Philadelphia, PA, 1988.

[120]   M. Vetterli and C. Herley, "Wavelets and filter banks: Theory and design," *IEEE Trans. Signal Processing*, vol. 40, pp. 2207–2232, Feb. 1992.

[121]   P. Antal, "Wavelet decomposition of image signals," in *Proc. Intelligent terminals, source and channel coding COST229*, pp. 301–310, Budapest, Hungary, Sept. 1993.

[122]   E. A. Rosenfeld, *Multiresolution techniques in computer vision*, New York, NY: Springer-Verlag, 1984.

[123] I. Daubechies, "Orthonormal bases of compactly supported wavelets," *Comm. on Pure and Applied Math.*, vol. 41, pp. 909–996, Nov. 1998.

[124] M. J. T. Smith and T. B. Barnwell, "Exact reconstruction techniques for tree-structured subband coders," *IEEE Trans. ASSP*, vol. 34, pp. 434–441, June 1986.

[125] F. Mintzer, "Filters for distortion-free two-band multirate filter banks," *IEEE Trans. ASSP*, vol. 33, pp. 626–630, June 1985.

[126] P. P. Vaidyanathan, "Quadtree mirror filter banks, N-bands extensions and perfect-reconstruction techniques," *IEEE ASSP Magazine*, vol. 4, pp. 4–20, July 1987.

[127] P. P. Vaidyanathan, *Multirate systems and filter banks*, Englewood Cliffs, NJ: Prentice-Hall, 1993.

[128] M. Ohta, M. Yano, and T. Nishitani, "Wavelet picture coding with transform coding approach," *IEICE Trans. Fundamentals*, vol. E75-A, pp. 776–785, July 1992.

[129] Y. Huh et al., "Classified wavelet transform coding of images using vector quantization," Proc. of *SPIE on Video Comm. and Image Processing*, vol. 2308, pp. 207–217, Sept. 1994.

[130] W. Kou, *Digital image compression algorithms and standards*, Norwell, MA: Kluwer Academic, 1995.

[131] D. Milovanovic, Z. Bojkovic, and A. Samcovic, "On objective performance measures in image compression by subband coding," *IEEE Workshop on Nonlinear Signal and Image Processing*, pp. 202–205, Neos Marmaras, Greece, June 1995.

[132] Y. Huh, J. J. Hwang, and K. R. Rao, "Classified wavelet transform coding of images using two-channel conjugate vector quantization," IEEE ICIP, pp. 363–367, Austin, TX, Nov. 1994.

[133] Y. Huh, J. J. Hwang, and K. R. Rao, "Block wavelet transform coding of images using classified vector quantization," *IEEE Trans. CSVT*, vol. 5, pp. 63–67, Feb. 1995.

[134] I. Daubechies, *Ten lectures on wavelets*, Philadelphia, PA: SIAM, 1992.

[135] A. R. Lindsey, "Wavelet packet modulation for orthogonally multiplexed communication," *IEEE Trans. Signal Processing*, vol. 45, pp. 1336–1339, May 1997.

[136] P. P. Gandhi, S. S. Rao, and R. S. Pappu, "Wavelets for waveform coding of digital symbols," *IEEE Trans. Signal Processing*, vol. 45, pp. 2387–2390, Sept. 1997.

[137] K. C. Pohlmann, *Principles of digital audio*, New York, NY: McGraw-Hill, 1995.

[138] J. B. O'Neal Jr., "Differential pulse code modulation PCM with entropy coding," *IEEE Trans. Information Theory*, vol. IT-21, pp. 169–174, March 1976.

[139] M. Rabbani and P. W. Jones, *Digital image compression techniques*, Bellingham, WA: SPIE Optical Engineering Press, 1991.

[140] W. Verbiest, "Video coding in an ATM environment," in *Proc. 3rd Intl. Conf. on New Systems and Services in Telecomm.*, Liege, Belgium, Nov. 1986.

[141] M. Duponcheel and W. Verbiest, *Simulation results for a hybrid transform video coding algorithm*, RACE project 2023, BTM-A11-05-PR, 1986.

[142] S. S. Dixit, "Advances in compression techniques for transmission of video over packet switched networks," *1st World Electronic Media Symp. New Horizons in Electronic Media*, pp. 157–161, Geneva, Switzerland, Oct. 1989.

[143] W. A. Pearlman and P. Jakatdar, "The effectiveness and coding of hybrid transform/DPCM interframe image coding," *IEEE Trans. Comm.*, vol. COM-32, pp. 832–838, July 1984.

[144] Z. Bojkovic, "Analysis of output signal-to-noise ratio in hybrid DCT/DPCM image coding system," *EUSIPCO'88*, pp. 1649–1652, Grenoble, France, Sept. 1988.

[145] N. Nasrabadi and R. King, "Image coding using vector quantization: A review," *IEEE Trans. Comm.*, vol. 36, pp. 957–971, Aug. 1988.

[146] Y. Linde, A. Buzo, and R. M. Gray, "An algorithm for vector quantizer design," *IEEE Trans. Comm.*, vol. 28, pp. 84–95, Jan. 1980.

[147] C. Chan and C. Ma, "A fast method of designing better codebooks for image vector quantization," *IEEE Trans. Comm.*, vol. 42, pp. 237–242, Feb. 1994.

[148] T. Berger, *Rate-distortion theory*, Englewood Cliffs, NJ: Prentice Hall, 1971.

[149] M. Sabin and R.M.Gray, "Product code vector quantizers for waveform and voice coding," *IEEE Trans. ASSP*, vol. 32, pp. 474–488, June 1984.

[150] M. Antonini et al., "Image coding using lattice vector quantization of wavelet coefficients," *IEEE ICASSP*, pp. 2273–2276, Toronto, Canada, May 1991.

[151]   A. Gersho and R. M. Gray, *Vector quantization and signal compression*, Boston, MA: Kluwer Academic, 1992.

[152]   W. Li et al., "A video coding algorithm using vector transform-based techniques," *IEEE Trans. CSVT*, vol. 7, pp. 146–153, Feb. 1997.

[153]   J. Skavroski and I. Dologlou, "Image compression using permutative vector quantization," *Signal Processing: Image Communication*, vol. 11, pp. 39–47, Nov. 1997.

[154]   A. E. Jacquin, "Fractal image coding: A review," *Proc. IEEE*, vol. 81, pp. 1451–1456, Oct. 1993.

[155]   R. Boyd-Merrit, "Iterated claims advances in fractal compression," *Electronic Engineering Times*, p. 105, April 1995.

[156]   M. F. Barnsley, *Fractals everywhere*, New York, NY: Academic Press, 1988.

[157]   K. Sayood, *Introduction to data compression*, San Francisco, CA: Morgan Kaufmann, 1995.

[158]   M. F. Barnsley and J. Jackin, "Application of recurrent iterated function systems to images," in *Proc. SPIE*, vol. 1001, pp. 122–131, 1988.

[159]   A. E. Jacquin, "Image coding based on a fractal theory of iterated contractive image transformations," *IEEE Trans. Image Processing*, vol. 1, pp. 18–30, Jan. 1992.

[160]   D. J. Le Gall, "The MPEG video compression algorithm," *Signal Processing: Image Comm.*, vol. 4, pp. 129–140, April 1992.

[161]   G. H. Jozawa et al., "Two-stage motion compensation using adaptive global MC and local affine MC," *IEEE Trans. CSVT*, vol. 7, pp. 75–85, Feb. 1997.

[162]   M. Holter, "Differential estimation of the global motion parameters zoom and pan," *Signal Processing*, vol. 16, pp. 249–265, March 1989.

[163]   K. Kamkers and H. Watanabe, "Video coding for digital storage media using hierarchical interframe scheme," *SPIE/VCIP*, vol. 1360, pp. 1540–1550, Oct. 1990.

[164]   H. Sanson, "Motion affine models identification and application to television image coding," *SPIE/VCIP*, vol. 1605, pp. 570–581, 1991.

[165]   G. H. Jozawa, "Segment-based video coding using an affine motion model," *SPIE/VCIP*, vol. 2308, pp. 1605–1614, Sept. 1994.

[166]   M. Subbarao and A. M. Wakman, "Closed form selection to image flow equations for planar surface in motion," *Computer Vision, Graphics and Image Processing*, vol. 36, pp. 208–228, Nov. 1986.

[167]   Y. Nakaya and H. Harashima, "Motion compensation based on spatial transformations," *IEEE Trans. CSVT*, vol. 4, pp. 339–356, June 1994.

[168]   C. F. Chen and K. K. Pang, "On the characteristics of motion compensated frame difference signals in video coding," *Australian Video Comm. Workshop*, pp. 237–246, Melbourne, Australia, July 1990.

[169]   H. M. Hang, Y. M. Chan, and T. S. Chao, "Motion estimation using frequency components," *SPIE/VCIP*, vol. 1818, pp. 74–84, 1992.

[170]   M. I. Sezam and R. L. Lagendijk, *Motion analysis and image sequence processing*, Hingham, MA: Kluwer Academic, 1993.

[171]   G. Tziritas and C. Labit, *Motion analysis for image sequence coding*, Amsterdam, Netherlands: Elsevier Science, 1994.

[172]   M. J. Chen, L. G. Chen, and T. D. Chiueh, "One dimensional full-search motion estimation for video coding," *IEEE Trans. CSVT*, vol. 4, pp. 504–509, Oct. 1994.

[173]   H. G. Musmann, P. Pirsch, and H. J. Grallert, "Advances in picture coding," *Proc. IEEE*, vol. 73, pp. 523–548, April 1985.

[174]   K. A. Prabhu and A. N. Netravali, "Pel recursive motion compensated component color coding," *IEEE ICC.*, pp. 2G.8.1–8.5, Philadelphia, PA, June 1982.

[175]   D. R. Walker and K. R. Rao, "Improved pel recursive motion compensation," *IEEE Trans. Comm.*, vol. 33, pp. 1011–1015, Sept. 1985.

[176]   T. Koga et al., "Motion compensated interframe coding for video conferencing," *NTC, National Telecomm. Conf.*, pp. G.5.3.1–3.5, New Orleans, LA, Nov.–Dec. 1981.

[177]   J. R. Jain and A. K. Jain, "Displacement measurement and its application in interframe image coding," *IEEE Trans. Comm.*, vol. 29, pp. 1799–1808, Dec. 1981.

[178]   A. N. Netravali and J. D. Robbins, "Motion compensated television coding: some new results," *Bell Syst. Technical Journal*, vol. 59, pp. 1735–1745, Sept. 1980.

[179]   P. Pancha and M. E. Zarki, "MPEG coding for variable bit rate video transmission," *IEEE Comm. Magazine*, vol. 32, pp. 54–66, May 1994.

[180]   S. Dixit and P. Skelly, "MPEG-2 over ATM for video dial-tone networks: Issues and strategies," *IEEE Network, Special Issue on Digital Interactive Broadband Video Dial Tone Networks*, pp. 30–40, Sept./Oct. 1995.

[181]   L. Li and N. D. Georganas, "MPEG-2 coded and uncoded-stream synchronization control for real-time, multimedia transmission and presentation over B-ISDN," *Proc. of 2nd ACM Multimedia*, pp. 239–246, Oct. 1994.

[182]   L. Liu, "MPEG video for LAN-based video conferencing," *Multimedia Communications and Video Coding*, pp. 57–62, 1996.

[183]   M. Kawashima et al., "Adaptation of the MPEG video coding algo-rithm to network applications," *IEEE Trans. CSVT*, vol. 3, pp. 261–269, Aug. 1993.

[184]   W. Luo and M. E. Zarki, "MPEG2Tool: A toolkit for the study of MPEG2 video transport over ATM based networks," *SPIE*, vol. 2668, pp. 356–364, 1995.

[185]   F. Pereira, "MPEG4: A new challenge for the representation of audio-visual information," *Picture Coding Symposium*, Melbourne, Australia, March 1996.

CHAPTER 4: SCALABILITY TECHNIQUES

[186]   D. Taubman and A. Zakhor, "A common framework for rate and dis-tortion based scaling of highly scalable compressed video," *IEEE Trans. CSVT*, vol. 6, pp. 329–354, Aug. 1996.

[187]   ISO/IEC JTC1/SC29/WG11, Doc. N1643, *Coding of moving pictures and audio*, Bristol, UK, 1997.

[188]   F. Bosveld, R. Lagendijk, and J. Biemond, "A refinement system for hierarchical video coding," *SPIE/VCIP*, vol. 1360, pp. 576–586, Oct. 1990.

[189]   N. Chaddha, M. Vishwanath, and P. Chou, "Hierarchical vector quan-tization of perceptually weighted block transform," 5th *Data Com-pression Conf.*, Snowbird, UT, pp. 3–12, March 1995.

[190]   M. Civanlar and A. Puri, "Scalable video coding in frequency domain," *SPIE/VCIP*, vol. 1818, pt. 3, pp. 1124–1134, Boston, MA, Nov. 1992.

[191]   A. Erdem and M. Sezan, "Scalable extension of MPEG-2 for coding 10-bit video," *SPIE Symp. Image and Video Compression*, vol. 2186, pp. 245–256, San Jose, CA, Feb. 1994.

[192]   B. Girod, "Scalable video for multimedia workstations," *Comput. and Graphics*, vol. 7, pp. 269–276, May/June 1993.

[193]   C. Guillemot and R. Ansari, "Layered coding schemes for video transmission on ATM networks," *J. Visual Comm. and Image Repre-sentation*, vol. 5, pp. 62–74, March 1994.

[194]   J. Ohm, "Advanced packet-video coding based on layered VQ and SBC techniques," *IEEE Trans. CSVT*, vol. 3, pp. 208–221, June 1993.

[195]   J. Ohm, "Multi-rate 3-D subband coding of video," *IEEE Trans. Image Processing*, vol. 3, pp. 572–588, Sept. 1994.

[196]   Y. Ho, C. Baseile, and A. Miron, "MPEG-based video coding for dig-ital simulcasting," *Intl. Workshop on HDTV*, Kawasaki, Japan, 1992.

[197] A. Puri, "Video coding using the MPEG-2 compression standard," *SPIE/VCIP*, pp. 718–729, Nov. 1993.

[198] T. Chiang and D. Anastassiou, "Hierarchical coding of digital television," *IEEE Comm. Magazine*, vol. 32, pp. 38–45, May 1994.

[199] ISO/IEC 13818-2 Draft International Standard: *Generic coding of moving pictures and associated audio information—Video*, Nov. 1994.

[200] ISO/IEC JTC1/SC29/WG11 Doc. N400, Test model editing committee, *Test model 5*, April 1993.

[201] B. G. Haskell, A. Puri, and A. N. Netravali, *Digital video: an introduction to MPEG-2*, New York, NY: Chapman and Hall, 1997.

[202] R. Aravind, M. R. Civanlar, and A. R. Reibman, "Packet loss resilience of MPEG-2 scalable video coding algorithms," *IEEE Trans. CSVT*, vol. 6, pp. 426–435, Oct. 1996.

[203] M. R. Civanlar and A. Puri, "Issues in efficient frequency scalable coding," *Proc. PCS'93*, paper 12.2, Lausanne, Switzerland, 1993.

[204] ISO/IEC JTC1/SC29/WG11 CD13818, *Generic coding of moving pictures and associated audio*, Nov. 1993.

[205] S. H. Lee, S. H. Jang, and J. S. Koh, "Selective protection of coded bitstream and error concealment for ATM transmission of MPEG video," *IEEE Workshop on Visual Signal Processing and Comm.*, pp. 307–310, Melbourne, Australia, Sept. 1993.

[206] C. Herpel, *SNR scalability vs data partitioning for high error-rate channels*, ISO/IEC JTC1/SC29/WG11 Doc. N658, July 1993.

[207] C. Gonzales and E. Viscito, "Flexibly scalable digital video coding," *Signal Process.: Image Comm.*, vol. 5, pp. 5–20, Feb. 1993.

[208] T. Sikora, T. K. Tan, and K. N. Ngan, "A performance comparison of frequency domain pyramid scalable coding schemes within the MPEG framework," *Picture Coding Symp.*, pp. 16.1–16.2, March 1993.

[209] A. Puri and A. Wong, "Spatial domain resolution scalable video coding," *SPIE/VCIP*, pp. 1701–1713, Nov. 1993.

[210] D. Anastassiou, "Scalability for HDTV," *Intl. Workshop on HDTV, Signal Processing of HDTV IV*, pp. 9–15, 1993.

[211] D. Ginsburg, *ATM solutions for enterprise internetworking*, Reading, MA: Addison-Wesley, 1996.

[212] O. Poncin et al., *New results on spatial scalability*, ISO/IEC JTC1/SG29/WG11 Doc. N495, July 1993.

[213] ISO/IEC 13818-2 ITU-T *Rec. H.262, Generic coding of moving pictures and associated audio information—Video*, 1995.

[214]   A. Wang and C. T. Chen, "A comparison of ISO MPEG1 and MPEG2 video coding standards," *SPIE/VCIP*, pp. 1436–1448, Boston, MA, Nov. 1993.

[215]   M. Ghanbari, "An adapted H.261 two layer video codec for ATM networks," *IEEE Trans. Comm.*, vol. 40, pp. 1481–1490, Sept. 1992.

[216]   Y. Wang and A. Puri, *Spatial-temporal adaptive interlace extraction*, ISO/IEC JTC1/SC29/WG11, Doc. 509, Sept. 1992.

[217]   T. Naveen and S. C. Fhu, *Comparison of spatial and frequency keys*, ISO/IEC JTC1/SC29/WG11, Doc. 615, 1993.

[218]   A. Puri, L. Yan, and B. G. Haskell, *Syntax, semantics and description of temporal scalability*, ISO/IEC JTC1/SC29/WG11, Doc. 795, Sept. 1993.

[219]   A. Puri and B. G. Haskell, *Picture format scalable coding structures*, ISO/IEC JTC1/SC29/WG11 Doc. 673, 1993.

[220]   A. Puri, *Picture format scalable coding for HDTV*, ISO/IEC JTC1/SC29/WG11 Doc. 390, March 1993.

CHAPTER 5: MPEG AND ITU-T VIDEO STANDARDS

[221]   T. Sikora, "MPEG digital video-coding standards," *IEEE Signal Processing Magazine*, vol. 14, pp. 82–100, Sept. 1997.

[222]   V. Bhaskaran, and K. Konstantinides, *Image and video compression standards, algorithms and architectures*, Norwell, MA: Kluwer Academic, 1997.

[223]   D. J. Le Gall, "MPEG: A video compression standard for multimedia applications," *Comm. ACM*, vol. 34, pp. 47–58, April 1991.

[224]   ISO/IEC IS11172 (MPEG-1), *Information technology-coding of moving pictures and associated audio for digital storage media up to about 1.5 Mbit/s*, 1993.

[225]   S. F. Chang, "Content-based indexing and retrieval of visual information," *IEEE Signal Processing Magazine*, vol. 14, pp. 45–48, July 1997.

[226]   F. Pereira, *First proposal for MPEG-7 visual requirements*, ISO/IEC SC29/WG11 Doc. M1941, MPEG Bristol Meeting, April 1997.

[227]   MPEG Requirements Group, *MPEG-7: Context and objectives*, ISO/IEC SC29/WG11 Doc. N1678, MPEG Bristol Meeting, April 1997.

[228]   S. J. Wee, M. O. Polley, and W. F Schreiber, "A generalized framework for scalable video coding," *Multimedia Communications and Video Coding*, Plenum Press, edited by Y. Wang et al., pp. 483–490, 1996.

[229]   N. Ahmed, T. Natarajan, and K. R. Rao, "Discrete cosine transform," *IEEE Trans. Computers*, vol. C-23, pp. 90–93, Dec. 1974.

[230]   B. R. Halhed, "Videoconferencing Codecs: Navigating the MAZE," *Business Comm. Review*, vol. 21, pp. 35–40, 1991.

[231]   B. L. Tseng and D. Anastassiou, "Multiview point video coding with MPEG-2 compatibility," *IEEE Trans. CSVT*, vol. 6, pp. 414–419, Aug. 1996.

[232]   A. Puri, R. V. Kollaris, and B. G. Haskell, "Stereoscopic video compression using temporal scalability," *SPIE/VCIP*, vol. 2501, pp. 745–756, Taipei, Taiwan, May 1995.

[233]   T. Homma, *MPEG contribution: Report of the Ad Hoc Group on MPEG-2 applications for multi-view point pictures*," ISO/IEC SC29/WG11 Doc. 861, March 1995.

[234]   A. F. Inglis, *Video engineering*, New York, NY: McGraw-Hill, 1995.

[235]   A. Puri, "Video coding using the MPEG-2 compression standard," *SPIE/VCIP*, Boston, MA, Nov. 1993.

[236]   J. Ni, T. Yang, and D. H. K. Tsang, "CBR transportation on VBR MPEG-2 video traffic for video-on-demand in ATM networks," *ICC*, Dallas, TX, pp. 1391–1395, June 1996.

[237]   M. Ghanbari, "Two-layer coding of video signals for VBR networks," *IEEE J. Selected Areas in Comm.*, vol. 7, pp. 771–781, June 1989.

[238]   S. Tubaro, "A two-layer video coding scheme for ATM networks," *Signal Processing: Image Comm.*, vol. 3, pp. 129–141, June 1991.

[239]   L. H. Kien and K. N. Ngan, "Cell-loss concealment techniques for layered video codecs in an ATM network," *IEEE Trans. Image Processing*, vol. 3, pp. 666–677, Sept. 1994.

[240]   M. Khansari et al., "Approaches to layered coding for dual-rate wireless video transmission," *Intl. Conf. Image Processing*, vol. 1, pp. 258–262, Nov. 1994.

[241]   J. Mitchell, W. Pennebaker, A. Fogg, and D. LeGall, *MPEG Video: Compression standard*, Norwell, MA: Kluwer Academic, 1997.

[242]   ITU-T *Draft Recommendation H.263 Version 2, H.263+ Video coding for low bit rate communication*, Sept. 26, 1997.

[243]   ITU-T *Recommendation H.263, Video coding for low bit rate communication*, March 1996.

[244]   K. Rijkse, "H.263: Video coding for low-bit-rate communications," *IEEE Trans. Comm.*, vol. 34, pp. 42–45, Dec. 1996.

[245]   ITU-T *Recommendation H.261, Video codec for audiovisual services at px64 kbit/s*, March 1993.

[246]   M. Tekalp, *Digital video processing*, Upper Saddle River, NJ: Prentice-Hall, 1995.

[247]   ITU-LBC-97-094, *Draft 10 of H.263+, H.263+ Video group*, Nice, France, Feb. 1997.

[248]   M. Khansari and V. Bhaskaran, "A low complexity error-resilient H.263 coder," *IEEE ICASSP*, vol. 4, pp. 2737–2740, Munich, Germany, April 1997.

[249]   B. Erol, M. Gallant, and F. Kossentini, "The H.263+ video coding standard: Complexity and performance," *DCC'98*, Snowbird, UT, March, 1998.

[250]   ITU-T, Study Group 16, Video Coding Experts Group (Question 15), Doc. Q15F09, *Report of the ad hoc committee H.263++ development*, Seoul, Korea, Nov. 1998.

[251]   ITU-T, Study Group 16, Video Coding Experts Group (Question 15), Doc.Q15F10, *Report of the ad hoc committee H.26L development*, Seoul, Korea, Nov. 1998.

[252]   ITU-T, Study Group 16, Video Coding Experts Group (Question 15), Doc. Q15D62, *Recommended simulation conditions for H.263v3*, Tampere, Finland, April 1998.

[253]   ITU-T, Study Group 16, Video Coding Experts Group (Question 15), Doc. Q15D65d1, *Video codec test model, near-term, version 10 (TMN10), draft 1*, Tampere, Finland, April 1998.

[254]   ITU-T, Study Group 16, Video Coding Experts Group (Question 15), Doc. Q15D62, Call for proposals for H.26L video coding, Geneva, Switzerland, Jan. 1998.

[255]   *Liaison Statement from* ITU-T Q.11 and 15/WG 16 to SC 29/WG 11 on ITU-T *Rec. H.263 and MPEG-4 Video issues*, Q15-D-67, MPEG M3550, Q15D19, MPEG Doc. N2148.

[256]   J. Villasenor, *H.324 Overview*, ITU Mobile Group Meeting, Jan. 1997.

[257]   ITU-T SG16 Q.15, Doc. Q11F07, *Request to support MPEG-4 video in H.324 terminals*, Seoul, Korea, Nov. 1998.

[258]   ITU-T SG16 Q.15, Doc. Q11E27, *Liaison* to ITU-T SG16 on MPEG-4 video over H.324, ISO/IEC JTC1/SC29/WG11, Doc. N2384, July 1998.

[259]   L. Chiariglione, "Impact of MPEG standards on multimedia industry," *Proc. IEEE*, vol. 86, pp. 1222–1227, June 1998.

[260]   L. Chiariglione, "MPEG and multimedia communications," *IEEE Trans. CSVT*, vol. 7, pp. 5–18, Feb. 1997.

[261]   L. Chiariglione, *MPEG-4 project description*, Document ISO/IEC JTC1/SC29/WG11 Doc. N1177, Munich, Germany, MPEG Meeting, Jan. 1996.

[262]   M. Orzessek and P. Sommer, *ATM and MPEG-2: Integrating digital video into broadband networks*, Upper Saddle River, NJ: Prentice Hall PTR, 1998.

[263]   ISO/IEC JTC1/SC29/WG11, Doc. N1164, Jan. 1996.

[264]   ISO/IEC JTC1/SC29/WG11, Doc. N1022, July 1995.

[265]   ISO/IEC JTC1/SC29/WG11, Doc. N2172, March 1998.

[266]   R. Nell and A. Zakhor, "Very low bit rate video coding based on matching pursuits," *IEEE Trans. CSVT*, vol. 7, pp. 158–171, Feb. 1997.

[267]   ISO/IEC JTC1/SC29/WG11, Doc. N2196, March 1998.

[268]   L. Chiariglione, "The development of an integrated audio-visual coding standard: MPEG," *Proc. IEEE*, vol. 83, pp. 151–157, Feb. 1995.

[269]   [Online]Available WWW: http://cselt.it/mpeg

[270]   T. Sikora, "The MPEG-4 video standard verification model," *IEEE Trans. CSVT*, vol. 7, pp. 19–31, Feb. 1997.

[271]   VM Action Group, *MPEG-4 video verification model version 1.1*, Tech. Rep. ISO/IEC JTC1/SC29/WG11 Doc. N1172, Feb. 1996.

[272]   E. Reusens et al., "Dynamic approach to visual data compression," *IEEE Trans. CSVT*, vol. 7, pp. 197–211, Feb. 1997.

[273]   MPEG Video Group, *MPEG-4 video verification model version 12.0*, ISO/IEC JTC1/SC29/WG11 Doc. N2552, Rome, Italy, Dec. 1998.

[274]   J. Osterman, *Report on the ad hoc group on evaluation of tools and algorithms of video submissions for MPEG-4 in January 1996*, ISO/IEC JTC1/SC29/WG11 Doc. N1162, Munich, Germany, Jan. 1996.

[275]   ISO/IEC JTC1/SC29/WG11, Doc. N2202, Tokyo, Japan, March 1998.

[276]   V. Milutinovic et al., "A software package for experimenting in genetic search on Internet: Static versus mobile agents," *IEEE International Workshop on enabling technologies: Infrastructure for collective enterprises*, Stanford University, June 1998.

[277]   ISO/IEC JTC1/SC29/WG11, Doc. N2460, *MPEG-7: Context and objectives V.10*, Oct. 1998.

[278]   ISO/IEC JTC1/SC29/WG11, Doc. N2461, *MPEG-7: Requirements V.7*, Oct. 1998.

[279]   ISO/IEC JTC1/SC29/WG11, Doc. N2462, *MPEG-7: Applications V.7*, Oct. 1998.

[280]   ISO/IEC JTC1/SC29/WG11, Doc. N2571, *MPEG-7 Experimentation model (XM) Ver. 0.5*, Dec. 1998.

[281]   Y. Rui, T. S. Huang, and S.-F. Chang, "Image retrieval: past, present and future," *J. Visual Commun. and Image Representation*, vol. 10, pp. 39–62, March 1999.

[282]   A. Ghias et al., "Query by humming - musical information retrieval in an audio database," *ACM Multimedia'95*, San Francisco, CA, 1995.

[283]   R. L. Mott, *Sound effects: Radio, TV and film*, Focal Press, Boston, MA, 1990.

[284]   G. Davenport et al., "Cinematic primitives for multimedia," *IEEE Computer Graphics & Applications*, vol. 11, pp. 67–74, July 1991.

[285]   P. Maes, "Modeling adaptive autonomous agents," *Journal of Artificial Life*, vol. 1, no. 1&2, pp. 135–162, 1994.

[286]   E. Andre and T. Rist, "Generating coherent presentations employing textural and visual material," *Artificial Intelligence Review*, vol. 9, no. 2, pp. 147–165, 1995.

[287]   The Human Communication Research Centre [Online], Available http://www.hcrc.ed.ac.uk

[288]   A. Chavez, P. Maes, and A. Kasbah, "An agent marketplace for buying and selling goods," *IC on practical applications of intelligent agents and multi-agent technology*, London, UK, 1996.

[289]   R. C. Schak, "Active learning through multimedia," *IEEE Multi-Media*, vol. 1, no. 1, pp. 69–78, 1994.

[290]   J. Courtney, "Automatic video indexing via object motion analysis," *Pattern Recognition*, vol. 30, pp. 607–625, April 1997.

[291]   S. Palm, T. Mori, and T. Sato, "Bilateral behavior media: Visually based teleoperation control with accumulation and support," *Robotics and Automation Magazine*, 1998.

[292]   R. Picard, "Light-years from Lena: Video and image libraries of the future," *IEEE ICIP*, pp. 310–313, Washington, DC, Oct. 1995.

[293]   S. F. Chang, "Compressed-domain techniques for image/video indexing and manipulation," *IEEE ICIP*, pp. 314–317, Washington, DC, Oct. 1995.

[294]   M. Yeung et al., "Video browsing using clustering and scene transitions on compressed sequences," *SPIE*, vol. 2417, pp. 399–413, 1995.

[295]   M. Irani and P. Anandan, "Video indexing based on mosaic representation," *Proc. IEEE*, vol. 86, pp. 905–921, May 1998.

[296]   G. Taubin, W. Horn, and F. Lazarus, *The VRML compressed binary format*, IBM Research report, June 1997.

[297]   ISO/IEC JTC1/SC29/WG11, Doc. N2464, *MPEG-7 proposal package description (PPD)*, Oct. 1998.

[298]   ISO/IEC JTC1/SC29/WG11, Doc. N2469, *Call for proposals for MPEG-7 technology*, Oct. 1998.

[299]   ISO/IEC JTC1/SC29/WG11, Doc. N2467, *Description of MPEG-7 content set*, Oct. 1998.

[300]   ISO/IEC JTC1/SC29/WG11, Doc. M3921, *Testing methodologies for image indexing and content-based retrieval*, Oct. 1998.

[301]   ISO/IEC JTC1/SC29/WG11, Doc. N2463, *MPEG-7 evaluation process*, Oct. 1998.

[302]   R. Koenen, "MPEG-4: multimedia for our time," *IEEE Spectrum*, vol. 36, pp. 26–33, Feb. 1999.

[303]   B. G. Haskell et al. "Image and video coding emerging standards and beyond," *IEEE Trans. CSVT*, vol. 8, pp. 814–836, Nov. 1998.

[304]   T. Wiegand et al., "Long-term memory motion-compensated prediction," *IEEE Trans. CSVT*, vol. 9, pp. 70–84, Feb. 1999.

[305]   O. Al-Shaykh et al., "Video compression using matching pursuits," *IEEE Trans. CSVT*, vol. 9, pp. 123–143, Feb. 1999.

[306]   A. Ribas-Corbera et al., "Rate control in DCT video coding for low delay communications," *IEEE Trans. CSVT*, vol. 9, pp. 172–185, Feb. 1999.

[307]   G. Cote et al., "H.263+: Video coding at low bit rates," *IEEE Trans. CSVT*, vol. 8, pp. 849–866, Nov. 1998.

[308]   S. Wenger et al., "Error resilience support in H.263+," *IEEE Trans. CSVT*, vol. 8, pp. 867–877, Nov. 1998.

[309]   T. Mejer and K. N. Ngan, "Automatic segmentation of moving objects for video object plane generation," *IEEE Trans. CSVT*, vol. 8, pp. 525–538, Sept. 1998.

[310]   A. A. Alatan et al., "Image sequence analysis for emerging interactive multimedia services—the European COST211 framework," *IEEE Trans. CSVT*, vol. 8, pp. 802–813, Nov. 1998.

[311]   A. Kaup, "Object-based texture coding of moving video in MPEG-4," *IEEE Trans. CSVT*, vol. 9, pp. 5–15, Feb. 1999.

[312]   R. Stasinski and J. Konrad, "A new class of fast shape-adaptive orthogonal transforms and their application to region-based image compression," *IEEE Trans. CSVT*, vol. 9, pp. 16–34, Feb. 1999.

[313]   A. Vetro, H. Sun, and Y. Wang, "MPEG-4 rate control for multiple video objects," *IEEE Trans. CSVT*, vol. 9, pp. 186–199, Feb. 1999.

[314]   Y. He, I. Ahmed, and M. L. Liou, "A software based MPEG-4 video encoder using parallel processing," *IEEE Trans. CSVT*, vol. 9, pp. 909–920, Nov. 1998.

[315]   S.-F. Chang et al., "Content-based video search engine," *IEEE Trans. CSVT*, vol. 8, pp. 602–615, Sept. 1998.

CHAPTER 6: SOME ISSUES INVOLVED IN ASYNCHRONOUS TRANSFER OF VIDEO

[316] D. P. Heyman et al., "Statistical analysis and simulation of video tele-conference traffic in ATM networks," *IEEE Trans. CSVT*, vol. 2, pp. 49–59, March 1992.

[317] D. Reininger et al., "Variable bit rate MPEG video: characteristics, modeling and multiplexing," *Proc. ITC-13*, Elsevier, pp. 295–306, 1994.

[318] R. M. Rodriguez-Dagnino et al., "Prediction of bit rate sequences of encoded video signals," *IEEE J. Selected Areas in Comm.*, vol. 9, pp. 305–314, April 1991.

[319] A. Ortega et al., "Rate constraints for video transmission over ATM networks based on joint source/network criteria," *Annals des Tele-communications*, vol. 50, pp. 603–616, 1995.

[320] M. R. Pickering and J. F. Arnold, "A perceptually efficient VBR rate control algorithm," *IEEE Trans. Image Processing*, vol. 3, pp. 527–531, Sept. 1994.

[321] D. M. Cohen and D. P. Heyman, "Performance modeling of video teleconferencing in ATM networks," *IEEE Trans. CSVT*, vol. 3, pp. 408–420, Dec. 1993.

[322] A. Elwalid et al., "Fundamental results on the performance of ATM multiplexers with applications to video teleconferencing," *ACM Performance Evaluation Review*, vol. 23, pp. 86–97, May 1995.

[323] A. Elwalid et al., "Fundamental bounds and approximations for ATM multiplexers with applications to video teleconferencing," *IEEE J. Selected Areas in Comm.*, vol. 13, pp. 1004–1016, Aug. 1995.

[324] M. R. Frater et al., "A new statistical model for traffic generated by VBR coders for television on the broadband ISDN," *IEEE Trans. CSVT*, vol. 4, pp. 521–526, Dec. 1994.

[325] R. Grunenfelder et al., "Characterization of video codecs as autoregressive moving average processes and related queuing system performance," *IEEE J. Selected Areas in Comm.*, vol. 9, pp. 284–293, April 1991.

[326] B. Jabbari et al., "Statistical characterization and block-based modeling of motion-adaptive coded video," *IEEE Trans. CSVT*, vol. 3, pp. 199–207, June 1993.

[327] Y. Feng, H. Mehrpour, and R. T. Lo, "Statistical multiplexing schemes for MPEG video sources," *Proc. IEEE ICCS/ISPACS'96*, pp. 1501–1505, Singapore, Nov. 1996.

[328]   D. M. Lucantoni et al., "Methods for performance evaluating VBR video traffic models," *IEEE/ACM Trans. Networking*, vol. 2, pp. 176–180, April 1994.

[329]   D. L. McLaren and D. T. Nguyen, "Variable bit-rate source modeling of ATM - based video services," *Signal Processing: Image Comm.*, vol. 4, pp. 233–244, June 1992.

[330]   O. Rose and M. R. Frater, "A comparison of models for VBR video traffic sources in B-ISDN," *Proc. IFIP TC6 Int. Conf. on Broadband Communications*, North Holland, pp. 275–287, Paris, France, 1994.

[331]   C. Shim et al., "Modeling and call admission control algorithm of variable bit rate video in ATM networks," *IEEE J. Selected Areas in Comm.*, vol. 12, pp. 332–344, Feb. 1994.

[332]   P. Skelly et al., "A histogram-based model for video traffic behavior in ATM multiplexer," *IEEE/ACM Trans. Networking*, vol. 1, pp. 446–459, Aug. 1993.

[333]   J. Beran et al., "Long-range dependence in variable bit rate video traffic," *IEEE Trans. Comm.*, vol. 43, pp. 1566–1579, Feb./March/April 1995.

[334]   M. W. Garret and W. Willinger, "Analysis, modeling and generation of self-similar VBR video traffic," *ACM Computer Comm. Review*, vol. 24, pp. 269–280, Oct. 1994.

[335]   N. G. Duffield et al., "Predictive quality of service for traffic with long-range fluctuations," *IEEE ICC*, pp. 473–477, Seattle, WA, June 1995.

[336]   H. Heeke, "A traffic-control algorithm for ATM networks," *IEEE Trans. CSVT*, vol. 3, pp. 182–189, June 1993.

[337]   S. Chong et al., "Predictive dynamic bandwidth allocation for efficient transport of real-time VBR video over ATM," *IEEE J. Selected Areas in Comm.*, vol. 13, pp. 12–23, Jan. 1995.

[338]   M. Grossglanser et al., "RCBR: A simple and efficient service for multiple time-scale traffic," *ACM Computer Comm. Review*, vol. 25, pp. 219–230, Oct. 1995.

[339]   C. T. Chien and A. Wong, "A self-governing rate buffer control strategy for pseudoconstant bit rate video coding," *IEEE Trans. Image Processing*, vol. 2, pp. 50–59, Jan. 1993.

[340]   G. Keesman et al., "Bit-rate control for MPEG encoders," *Signal Processing: Image Comm.*, vol. 6, pp. 545–560, Feb. 1995.

[341]   W. S. Rhee, Y. Y. An, and H. S. Park, "Bandwidth management and allocation for the ABR service in ATM networks," *Proc. IEEE ICCS/ISPACS*, pp. 482–486, Singapore, Nov. 1996.

[342] A. Ortega et al., "Optimal trellis-based buffered compression and fast approximation," *IEEE Trans. Image Processing*, vol. 3, pp. 26–39, Jan. 1994.

[343] J. Zdepski et al., "Statistically based buffer control policies for constant rate transmission of compressed digital video," *IEEE Trans. Comm.*, vol. 39, pp. 947–957, June 1991.

[344] G. Niestegge, "The leaky-bucket policing method in the ATM network," *Intl. J. of Digital and Analog Comm. Systems*, vol. 3, pp. 187–197, April–June, 1990.

[345] E. P. Rathgeb, "Policing of realistic VBR video traffic in an ATM network," *Int. J. of Digital and Analog Comm. Systems*, vol. 6, pp. 213–226, Dec. 1993.

[346] S. S. Lam et al., "An algorithm for lossless smoothing of MPEG video," *ACM Computer Comm. Review*, vol. 24, pp. 281–294, Oct. 1994.

[347] T. Ott et al., "A scheme for smoothing delay-sensitive traffic offered to ATM networks," *Proc. IEEE INFOCOM*, pp. 776–785, Florence, Italy, May 1992.

[348] J. C. Bolot et al., "Scalable feedback control for multicast video distribution in the Internet," *ACM Computer Comm. Review*, vol. 24, pp. 58–67, Oct. 1994.

[349] H. Kanakie et al., "An adaptive congestion control scheme for real-time packet video transport," *ACM Computer Comm. Review*, vol. 23, pp. 20–31, Oct. 1993.

[350] J. Kurose, "Open issues and challenges in providing quality of service guarantees in high-speed networks," *ACM Computer Comm. Review*, vol. 23, pp. 6–15, Jan. 1993.

[351] J. W. Roberts, "Variable-bit rate traffic control in B-ISDN," *IEEE Comm. Magazine*, vol. 29, pp. 50–56, Sept. 1991.

[352] G. M. Woodruff and R. Kositpaiboon, "Multimedia traffic management principles for guaranteed ATM network performance," *IEEE J. Selected Areas in Comm.*, vol. 8, pp. 437–446, April 1990.

[353] G. Karlsson, *Asynchronous transfer of video,* SICS Research Report R95:14, Sweden, 1997.

[354] D. D. Clark et al., "Supporting real-time applications in an integrated service packet network: architecture and mechanism," *ACM Computer Comm. Review*, vol. 22, pp. 14–26, Oct. 1992.

[355] E. W. Knightly et al., "Fundamental limits and tradeoffs of providing deterministic guarantees to VBR video traffic," *ACM Performance Evaluation Review*, vol. 23, pp. 98–107, May 1995.

[356]   R. Cruz, "A calculus for network delay, part 1: Network elements in iso-
        lation," *IEEE Trans. Inform. Theory*, vol. 37, pp. 114–131, Jan. 1991.

[357]   S. J. Golestani, "A stop-and-go queuing framework for congestion
        management," *ACM Computer Comm. Review*, vol. 20, pp. 8–18,
        Sept. 1990.

[358]   A. K. Parekh and R. G. Gallagher, "A generalized processor sharing
        approach to flow control in integrated services networks: the single-
        node case," *Journal of High-Speed Networks*, vol. 1, pp. 344–357, June
        1993.

[359]   H. Zhang, "Service disciplines for guaranteed performance service in
        packet-switched networks," *Proc. IEEE*, vol. 83, pp. 1374–1396, Oct. 1995.

[360]   Y. C. Bolot, "End-to-end packet delay and loss behavior in the inter-
        net," *ACM Computer Comm. Review*, vol. 23, pp. 289–298, Oct. 1993.

[361]   E. Ayanoglu et al., "Performance improvement in broadband net-
        works using forward error correction for lost packet recovery," *Jour-
        nal of High-Speed Networks*, vol. pp. 287–303, June 1993.

[362]   N. F. Maxemchuk, "Dispersity routing in high-speed networks," *Com-
        puter Networks and ISDN Systems*, vol. 25, pp. 645–662, Jan. 1993.

[363]   S. Jamin et al., "A measurement-based admission control algorithm
        for integrated services packet network," *ACM Computer Comm.
        Review*, vol. 25, pp. 2–13, Oct. 1995.

[364]   S. Abe and T. Sormiya, "A traffic control method for service quality
        assurance in an ATM network," *IEEE J. Selected Areas in Comm.*,
        vol. 12, pp. 322–331, Feb. 1994.

[365]   D. Reininger et al., "Statistical multiplexing of VBR MPEG com-
        pressed video on ATM networks," *Proc. IEEE INFOCOM*, vol. 3, pp.
        919–926, San Francisco, CA, March 1993.

[366]   M. Krunz, R. Sass, and H. Hughes, "Statistical characteristics and
        multiplexing of MPEG streams," *Proc. IEEE INFOCOM*, pp. 455–462,
        April 1995.

[367]   M. R. Ismail et al., "Modeling prioritized MPEG video using TES and
        a frame spreading strategy for transmission in ATM networks," *Proc.
        IEEE INFOCOM*, pp. 762–770, April 1995.

[368]   N. Shroff and M. Schwartz, "Video modeling within networks using
        deterministic smoothing at the source," *Proc. IEEE INFOCOM*, vol.
        1, pp. 342–349, 1994.

[369]   P. Skelly, S. Dixit, and M. Schwartz, "A histogram-based model for video
        traffic behavior in an ATM network mode with an application to conges-
        tion control," *Proc. IEEE INFOCOM*, Florence, Italy, May 1992.

[370] D. L. Mils, "Improved algorithms for synchronizing computer network clocks," *IEEE/ACM Trans. Networking*, vol. 3, pp. 245–254, June 1995.

[371] R. P. Singh et al., "Jitter and clock recovery for periodic traffic in broadband packet networks," *IEEE Trans. Comm.*, vol. 42, pp. 2189–2196, May 1994.

[372] J. M. Simmons and R. G. Gallagher, "Design of error detection scheme for class C service in ATM," *IEEE/ACM Trans. Networking*, vol. 2, pp. 80–88, Feb. 1994.

[373] ITU-T SG XVIII, *Performance evaluation results on cell loss in ATM networks*, Doc. 1047, Nov. 1990.

[374] N. Ohta and T. Kitami, "Simulation study of the cell discard process and the effect of cell loss compensation in ATM networks," *Trans. IEICE*, vol. E-73, pp. 1704–1711, Oct. 1990.

[375] ITU-TS SGXV WPXV/I, *Cell loss experiment specifications*, Expert Group for ATM Video Coding, Document AVC-205, Jan. 1992.

[376] D. Habibi, S. Gabrielsson, and V. Ghoddonski, "A traffic shaping algorithm for MPEG video at the user-network interface," *IEEE ICCS/ISPACS*, pp. 1497–1500, 1996.

[377] G. Karlson, *Asynchronous transfer of video*, Swedish Institute of Computer Science (SICS), Research Report R95:14, Kist, Sweden, 1995.

[378] G. Karlson, "ATM adaptation for video," *Proc. Sixth Int. Workshop on Packet Video*, Portland, OR, pp. E.3.1–5, Sept. 1994.

[379] ISO/IEC 13818-2, *Generic coding of moving pictures and associated audio information—Video*, 1992.

[380] G. A. Coffey, "Video over ATM networks," 1997. [Online], Available WWW: http://www.cis.ohio-state.edu/~jain/cis788-97/video_over_atm/index.htm.

[381] M. Wada, "Selective recovery of video packet loss using error concealment," *IEEE J. Selected Areas in Comm.*, vol. 7, pp. 207–214, June 1989.

[382] M. Ghanbary and V. Sferidis, "Cell-loss concealment in ATM networks," *IEEE Trans. CSVT*, vol. 3, pp. 238–247, June 1993.

[383] M. Ghanbary and C. Hughes, "Packing coded video signals into ATM cells," *IEEE/ACM Trans. Networking*, vol. 1, pp. 505–508, Oct. 1993.

[384] Q. Zhu, Y. Wang, and L. Shaw, "Coding and cell loss recovery in DCT based packet video," *IEEE Trans. CSVT*, vol. 3, pp. 248–258, June 1993.

[385]   A. S. Tom, C. L. Yeh, and F. Chu, "Packet video for cell loss protection using deinterleaving and scrambling," *IEEE ICASSP*, pp. 2857–2860, Toronto, Canada, May 1991.

[386]   Y. Wang, Q. Zhu, and L. Shaw, "Maximally smooth image recovery in transform coding," *IEEE Trans. Comm.*, vol. 41, pp. 1544–1551, Oct. 1993.

[387]   Y. Wang and Q. Zhu, "Signal loss recovery in DCT-based image and video coders," *Proc. SPIE Conf. on Visual Communications and Image Processing*, pp. 667–678, Boston, MA, Nov. 1991.

[388]   H. Sun and J. Zdepski, "Adaptive error concealment algorithm for MPEG compressed video," *Proc. SPIE Conf. on Visual Communications and Image Processing*, pp. 814–824, Boston, MA, Nov. 1992.

[389]   W. Kwok and H. Sun, "Multidirectional interpolation for spatial error concealment," *IEEE Trans. Consumer Electronics*, vol. 3, pp. 455–460, Aug. 1993.

[390]   H. Sun and W. Kwok, "Concealment of damaged block transform coded images using projections onto convex sets," *IEEE Trans. Image Processing*, vol. 4, pp. 470–477, April 1995.

[391]   P. Salama et al., "Error concealment techniques for encoded video streams," *Proc. IEEE ICIP*, vol. 1, pp. 9–12, Washington, DC, Oct. 1995.

[392]   P. J. Burt and E. H. Adelson, "The Laplacian pyramid compact image coder," *IEEE Trans. Comm.*, vol. 31, pp. 532–540, April 1983.

[393]   J. Lee and B. W. Dickinson, "Temporally adaptive motion interpolation exploiting temporal masking in visual perception," *IEEE Trans. Image Processing*, vol. 3, pp. 513–526, Sept. 1994.

[394]   ATM Forum, *Traffic management specification 4.0*, ATM Forum/95-0013 R10, Feb. 1996.

[395]   ITU-T SG13 *Recommendation I.371*, Geneva, Switzerland, July 1995.

[396]   W.-S. Rhee and H.-S. Park, "A study on traffic control for the ABR service in ATM networks," *INTERWORKING*, Oct. 1996.

[397]   J. Zhang et al., "MPEG-2 video services for wireless ATM networks," *IEEE J. Selected Areas in Comm.*, vol. 15, pp. 119–128, Jan. 1997.

[398]   E. Ayanouglu et al., "Forward error control for MPEG-2 video transport in a wireless ATM LAN," *IEEE ICIP*, vol. 2, pp. 833–836, Lausanne, Switzerland, 1996.

[399]   J. Deane, *WATM PHY requirements*, ATM Forum /96-0785, June 1996.

[400]   D. Raychaudhury and N. Wilson, "ATM based transport architecture for multiservices wireless personal communication network," *IEEE J. Selected Areas in Comm.*, vol. 12, pp. 1401–1414, Oct. 1994.

[401]   K. Duantl, *Location management for mobile networks*, ATM Forum / 97-0087, Feb. 1997.

[402]   G. Bautz, *Addressing in wireless ATM networks*, ATM Forum /97-0322, April 1997.

[403]   J. Deane, *WATM MAC requirements*, ATM Forum /96-0786, June 1996.

[404]   A. Dinesh and M. Moh, "An efficient traffic control scheme for integrated voice, video and data over ATM networks: Explicit allowed rate algorithm," *(EARA) ICCCN*, 1997.

[405]   F. Guillemin and J. W. Roberts, "Jitter and bandwidth enforcement," *IEEE GLOBECOM*, vol. 1, pp. 261–265, 1991.

[406]   C. G. Kang and H. H. Tan, "Queuing analysis of explicit priority assignment partial buffer sharing schemes for ATM networks," *IEEE INFOCOM*, pp. 810–819, 1993.

[407]   L. Kleinrock, "The latency / bandwidth tradeoff in gigabit networks," *IEEE Comm. Magazine*, vol. 30, pp. 36–40, April 1992.

[408]   X. Lin et al., "Tight upper bounds for cell loss probabilities in ATM multiplexers and required bandwidth estimation," *ICCCN*, 1997.

[409]   Y. Nishibe, K. Kuwabara, and T. Suda, "Distributed channel allocation in ATM networks," *IEEE GLOBECOM*, vol. 1, pp. 417–423, 1993.

[410]   O. Rose and M. R. Frater, "Impact of MPEG video traffic on an ATM multiplexer, high performance networking VI," edited by R. Puigjaner, Chapman and Hall, pp. 157–168, 1995.

[411]   S. Bhagvat, D. Tipper, and A. Mahapatra, "Comparative evaluation of output buffer management schemes in ATM networks," *IEEE ICC*, vol. 2, pp. 1174–1178, 1994.

[412]   J. Cansey and H. Kim, "Comparison of buffer allocation schemes in ATM switches: Complete sharing, partial sharing and dedicated allocation," *IEEE ICC*, vol. 2, pp. 1164–1168, 1994.

[413]   R. Chipalkatti, J. F. Kurose, and D. Towsl, "Scheduling policies for real-time and non-real-time traffic in a statistical multiplexer," *IEEE INFOCOM*, pp. 774–783, 1989.

[414]   H. Kroner et al., "Priority management in ATM switching nodes," *IEEE J. Selected Areas in Comm.*, vol. 9, pp. 418–427, March 1991.

[415]   Y. Lai and Y. Lin, "Performance analysis of rate-based congestion control scheme and choice of high and low thresholds," *ICCCN*, 1997.

[416]   A. S. Tanenbaum, *Computer networks*, Third Edition, Englewood Cliffs, NJ: Prentice Hall, 1996.

[417]   L. Tassiulas and Y. Hung, "Optimal buffer control during congestion in an ATM network node," *Proc. IEEE INFOCOM*, pp. 1059–1066, 1993.

[418] L. Trajkovic and S. Halfin, "Buffer requirements in ATM networks with leaky buckets," *IEEE ICC*, vol. 3, pp. 1616–1620, 1994.

[419] J. Walrand and P. Varaiya, *High performance communication networks*, San Francisco, CA: Morgan Kaufmann, 1996.

[420] P. Yegani, M. Krunz, and H. Hughes, "Congestion control schemes in prioritized ATM networks," *IEEE ICC*, vol. 2, pp. 1169–1173, 1994.

CHAPTER 7: ASYNCHRONOUS TRANSFER OF VIDEO IN THE INTERNET

[421] B. M. Leiner et al., *A brief history of the Internet*, [Online], Available WWW: http://www.isoc.org/ internethistory, Feb. 1997.

[422] D. Kristula, *The history of the Internet*, [Online], Available WWW: http://www.davesite.com/ webstation.nethistory, March 1997.

[423] B. Goode, "Scanning the special issue on global information infrastructure," *Proc. IEEE*, vol. 85, pp. 1883–1886, Dec. 1997.

[424] G. Sackett and C. Metz, "ATM and multiprotocol networking," *Computer Communications*, 1997.

[425] S. Keshav et al., "An empirical evaluation of virtual circuit holding time policies in IP-over-ATM networks," *IEEE J. Selected Areas in Comm.*, vol. 13, pp. 1371–1382, Oct. 1995.

[426] J. Croworoft et al., "The global internet," *IEEE J. Selected Areas in Comm.*, vol. 13, pp. 1366–1370, Oct. 1995.

[427] M. Decina and V. Trecordi, "Convergence of telecommunications and computing to networking models for integrated services and applications," *Proc. IEEE*, vol. 85, pp. 1887–1914, Dec. 1997.

[428] I. Postel, *Internet control message protocol*, Internet Engineering Task Force, RFC792, Sept. 1981.

[429] I. Postel, *User datagram protocol*, Internet Engineering Task Force, RFC768, Aug. 1980.

[430] I. Postel, *Transmission control protocol*, Internet Engineering Task Force, RFC793, Sept. 1981.

[431] I. Postel, *Simple mail transfer protocol (SMTP)*, Internet Engineering Task Force, RFC821, Aug. 1982.

[432] P. Mockapertis, *Domain names—Concept and facilities*, Internet Engineering Task Force, RFC1034, Nov. 1987.

[433] H. Schulzrinne, "World Wide Web: Whence, whither, what next," *IEEE Network Magazine*, vol. 10, pp. 10–17, March/April 1996.

[434] T. Berners-Lee, R. Fielding, and H. Nielsen, *Hypertext transfer protocol HTTP 1.0*, Internet Engineering Task Force, RFC1945, May 1996.

[435] T. Berners-Lee and D. Connolly, *Hypertext markup language 2.0*, Internet Engineering Task Force, RFC1866, Nov. 1995.

[436] J. D. Case et al., *A simple network management protocol (SNMP)*, Internet Engineering Task Force, RFC1157, May 1990.

[437] J. Case et al., *Introduction to version 2 of the Internet standard network management framework*, Internet Engineering Task Force, RFC1441, May 1993.

[438] I. Dalgic and F. A. Tobagi, "Performance evaluation of ATM networks carrying constant and variable bit rate video traffic," *IEEE J. Selected Areas in Comm.*, vol. 15, pp. 1115–1131, June 1997.

[439] International Telecommunications Union, ITU-T *Recommendation E.164, Numbering plan for ISDN*, 1991.

[440] M. W. Garret, "A service architecture for ATM: From applications to scheduling," *IEEE Network Magazine*, vol. 10, pp. 6–14, May/June 1996.

[441] P. Newman, T. Lyon, and G. Minshell, "Flow labeled IP: A connectionless approach to ATM," *IEEE INFOCOM*, pp. 1251–1260, San Francisco, CA, March 1996.

[442] P. Newman et al., "IP switching and gigabit routers," *IEEE Comm. Magazine*, vol. 35, pp. 64–69, Jan. 1997.

[443] Y. Rekhter et al., Internet Engineering Task Force, RFC2105, Feb. 1997.

[444] P. Braden, D. Clark, and S. Shenker, *Integrated services in the Internet architecture: An overview*, Internet Engineering Task Force, RFC1633, June 1994.

[445] I. Wakeman et al., "Implementing real time packet forwarding policies using streams," in *Proc. Usenix Conf.*, New Orleans, LA, pp. 71–82, Jan. 1995.

[446] S. Deering, *Multicast routing*, Ph.D. dissertation, Stanford University, Stanford, CA, 1988.

[447] P. White and J. Crowcroft, "The integrated services in the Internet: State of the art," in *Proc. IEEE*, vol. 85, pp. 1934–1946, Dec. 1997.

[448] R. Braden et al., *Resource reservation protocol (RSVP) Version1: Functional specification*, Internet Engineering Task Force, Aug. 1996. [Online], Available WWW: http://www.ietf.org/html.charters/intserv.charter.html

[449] R. Braden et al., *The use of RSVP with IETF integrated services*, Internet Engineering Task Force.[Online]ftp://ds.internic.net/internet_drafts/draft_ietf_intserv_rsvp_use_00.txt

[450] J. Wroclawski, *Specification of the controlled-load network element service*, Internet Engineering Task Force, Internet draft. [Online] ftp://ds.internic.net/internet_drafts/draft_ietf_intserv_ctrl_load_svc_03.txt

[451] S. Shenker, C. Partridge, and R. Guerin, *Specification of guaranteed quality of service*, [Online] ftp://ds.internic.net/internet_drafts/ draft_ietf_intserv_guaranteed_svc_06.txt

[452] A. Parekh and R. Gallagher, "A generalized processor sharing approach to flow control—The single node case," *IEEE/ACM Trans. Networking*, vol. 3, pp. 344–357, June 1993.

[453] ISO/IEC JTC1/SC29/WG11 N2615, *Architectural considerations for carriage of MPEG-4 over IP networks*, Dec. 1998.

[454] IETF, Internet Draft, *RTP payload format for MPEG-4 Elementary Streams*, ietf-avt-rtp-mpeg4-00.txt, 1998.

[455] IETF RFC 1889, *RTP: A transport protocol for real-time applications*, Jan. 1996.

[456] IETF Internet Draft, *The role of DMIF in support of RTP MPEG-4 payloads.*

CHAPTER 8: QUALITY OF SERVICE FOR PACKET VIDEO OVER ATM NETWORKS

[457] ISO/IEC 13818, Draft International Standard: *Generic coding of moving pictures and associated audio*, Part 2 Video, 1993.

[458] B. D. Choi et al., "Priority queue with two state Markov modulated arrivals," *IEEE ICC*, pp. 1055–1059, Dallas, TX, June 1996.

[459] A. R. Reibman and A. W. Berger, "On VBR video teleconferencing over ATM networks," *IEEE GLOBECOM*, pp. 314–319, Dec. 1992.

[460] K. Joseph and D. Reininger, "Service traffic smoothing for VBR video encoders," *Proc. Int. Workshop on Packet Video*, pp. G1.1–G1.4, 1994.

[461] E. P. Rathgeb, "Modeling and performance comparisons of policing mechanisms for ATM networks," *IEEE J. Selected Areas in Comm.*, vol. 9, pp. 325–344, Apr. 1991.

[462] A. R. Reibman and B. G. Haskell, "Constraints of variable bit rate video for ATM networks," *IEEE Trans. CSVT*, vol. 2, pp. 361–372, Dec. 1992.

[463] M. Butto, E. Cavallero, and A. Tonietti, "Effectiveness of the leaky bucket policing mechanism in ATM networks," *IEEE J. Selected Areas in Comm.*, vol. 9, pp. 335–342, April 1991.

[464] S. C. Liew and Ch. Tse, "Video aggregation: adapting video traffic for transport over broadband networks by integrated data compression and statistical multiplexing," *IEEE J. Selected Areas in Comm.*, vol. 14, pp. 1123–1137, Aug. 1996.

[465] S. Jordan and H. Jiang, "Connection establishment in high-speed networks," *IEEE J. Selected Areas in Comm.*, vol. 13, pp. 1150–1161, Sept. 1995.

[466] ITU-T Recommendation I.371, *Traffic control and congestion control in BISDN*, July 1995.

[467] The ATM Forum, *Traffic management specification version 3.0*, June 1995.

[468] J. V. Nielsen et al., "VLSI implementation of a fairness ATM buffer system," *IEEE ICC*, pp. 681–686, Dallas, TX, June 1996.

[469] R. Roden and J. Kenny, "Available bit rate (ABR) service in ATM networks," *Proc. 13th UK Teletraffic Symposium*, pp. 13/1–13/8, 1996.

[470] D. J. Wright, "Assessment of alternative transport options for video distribution and retrieval over ATM in residential broadband," *IEEE Comm. Magazine*, vol. 35, pp. 78–87, Dec. 1997.

[471] N. Ohta, *Packet video: modeling and signal processing*, Norwood, MA: Artech House, 1994.

[472] R. Coellco and S. Tohme, "Video coding mechanism to predict video traffic in ATM networks," *IEEE GLOBECOM*, pp. 447–450, 1993.

[473] Ch. B. Lee, K. B. Ha, and R. H. Pane, "Computation of effective bandwidth of aggregated VBR MPEG video traffic in ATM networks using the modified equivalent capacity," *IEEE ICC*, pp. 626–631, Dallas, TX, June 1996.

[474] J. Enssle, "Modeling and statistical multiplexing of VBR MPEG compressed video in ATM networks," *Proc. 4th Open Workshop on High Speed Networks*, pp. 59–67, Brest, France, Sept. 1994.

[475] D. P. Heyman, A. Tabatabai, and T. V. Lakshman, "Statistical analysis and simulation study of video teleconference traffic in ATM networks," *IEEE Trans. CSVT*, vol. 2, pp. 49–59, March 1992.

[476] F. Yegenogly, B. Jabary, and Y. Q. Zhang, "Motion-classified autoregressive modeling of variable bit rate video," *IEEE Trans. CSVT*, vol. 3, pp. 42–53, Feb. 1993.

[477] A. Aparone et al., "Statistical models for video packet communications," *Digital Signal Processing*, Elsevier, pp. 654–659, 1991.

[478] Melamed et al., "TES-based traffic modeling for performance evaluation of integrated networks," *Proc. INFOCOM*, pp. 75–84, Florence, Italy, 1992.

[479] J. Mata, C. Pagan, and S. Salient, "Multiplexing and resource alloca-
       tion of VBR MPEG video traffic on ATM networks," *IEEE ICC*, pp.
       1401–1405, Dallas, June 1996.

[480] M. Hamidi, J. W. Roberts, and P. Rolin, "Rate control for VBR video
       coders in broad-band networks," *IEEE J. Selected Areas in Comm.*,
       vol. 15, pp. 1040–1051, Aug. 1997.

[481] R. Steinmetz and K. Nahrstedt, *Multimedia computing, communica-
       tions and applications*, Englewood Cliffs, NJ: Prentice-Hall, 1995.

[482] D. E. McDysand and D. L. Spohn, *ATM theory and applications*, New
       York, NY: McGraw-Hill, 1995.

[483] H. Ji, "Resource allocation and pricing in ATM networks," *Proc. 30th
       Conf. on Information Science and Systems*, Princeton, NJ, March
       1996.

[484] F. Z. S. Lin and J. R. Zee, "A real time distributed routing and admis-
       sion control algorithm for ATM networks," *Proc. IEEE INFOCOM*,
       pp. 792–801, 1993.

[485] ITU-T Recommendation I.356, B-ISDN *ATM layer cell transfer per-
       formance*, Geneva, Switzerland, Nov. 1993.

[486] F. Guillemin, C. Levert, and C. Rosenborg, "Cell conformance testing
       with respect to the peak cell rate in ATM networks," *Computer Net-
       works and ISDN Systems*, vol. 27, pp. 703–725, March 1995.

[487] C. J. Gallego and R. Grunenfelder, "Testing and measurement prob-
       lems in ATM networks," *IEEE ICC*, pp. 653–657, Dallas, TX, June
       1996.

[488] M. Ghanbari and J. Azari, "Effect of bit rate variation of the base
       layer on the performance of two-layer video codecs," *IEEE Trans.
       CSVT*, vol. 4, pp. 8–17, Feb. 1994.

[489] C. Gao and J. S. Meditch, "Two-layer video coding and priority statis-
       tical multiplexing over ATM networks," *IEEE ICC*, pp. 127–136, Dal-
       las, TX, June 1996.

[490] H. Saito, "Call admission control in an ATM network using upper
       bound on cell loss probability," *IEEE Trans. Comm.*, vol. 40, pp.
       1512–1521, Sept. 1992.

[491] K. Y. Siu and H. Y. Tzeng, "Adaptive proportional rate control for
       ABR service in ATM networks," *IEEE 14th Annual Intl. Phoenix
       Conf. Comp. and Comm.*, 1995.

[492] C. Nikolau, "An architecture for real-time multimedia communica-
       tion systems," *IEEE J. Selected Areas in Comm.*, vol. 8, pp. 391–400,
       Apr. 1990.

[493] J. Tarner, "New directions in communications (or which way to the information age?)," *IEEE Comm. Magazine*, vol. 24, pp. 8–15, Oct. 1986.

[494] S. Jai and K. Kitawaki, "Effects of cell loss on picture quality in ATM networks," *Elect. and Comm. in Japan*, part. 1, vol. 75, pp. 30–41, 1992.

[495] M. Goldstein et al., "Cell loss effects on perceived audio/video quality and quality of service," *Proc. of Sixth Int. Workshop on Packet Video*, pp. 13.1–4, Portland, OR, Sept. 1994.

[496] C. J. Hughes et al., "Modeling and subjective assessment of cell discard in ATM video," *IEEE Trans. Image Processing*, vol. 3, pp. 212–222, April 1994.

[497] N. B. Seitz et al., "User-oriented measures of telecommunication quality," *IEEE Comm. Magazine*, vol. 32, pp. 56–66, Jan. 1994.

CHAPTER 9: VIDEO IN MULTIMEDIA COMMUNICATIONS

[498] B. Furth, "Multimedia systems: An overview," *IEEE Multimedia Magazine*, vol. 1, pp. 47–59, Spring 1994.

[499] M. Blather and R. Deneburg (eds.), *Multimedia interface design*, Reading, MA: Addison-Wesley, 1991.

[500] The ATM Forum, *Audiovisual multimedia services: video on demand specification 1.1*, af-saa-0049.001, March 1997.

[501] M. J. Riler and J. E. G. Richardson, *Digital video communications*, Boston, MA: Artech House, 1997.

[502] H. V. Todd and J. S. Meditch, "Encapsulation protocols for MPEG video in ATM networks," *IEEE INFOCOM*, vol. 3, pp. 1072–1079, 1996.

[503] L. C. Wolf, C. Griwodz, and R. Steinmetz, "Multimedia communication," *Proc. IEEE*, vol. 85, pp. 1915–1933, Dec. 1997.

[504] S. Shenker et al., "Pricing in computer networks: Reshaping the research agenda," *ACM Comp. Comm. Rev.*, pp. 19–43, April 1996.

[505] O. Schelen and S. Pink, "Sharing resources through advance reservation agents," *Proc. Intl. Workshop on Quality of Service*, pp. 265–276, New York, NY: May 1997.

[506] L. C. Wolf, *Resource management for distributed multimedia systems*, Boston, MA, Kluwer Academic, 1996.

[507] L. C. Wolf and R. Steinmetz, "Concepts for resource reservation in advance," *J. Multimedia Tools Application*, Special issue on "The state of the art in multimedia computing," vol. 4, pp. 255–278, May 1997.

[508] S. Shenker and J. Wroclawski, *Network element service specification template*, Internet Engineering Task Force, RFC 2216, Sept. 1997.

[509] S. Shenker, C. Partridge, and R. Guerin, *Specification of guaranteed quality of service*, Internet Engineering Task Force, RFC 2212, Sept. 1997.

[510] J. Wroclawski, *Specification of the controlled-load network element service*, Internet Engineering Task Force, RFC 2211, Sept. 1997.

APPENDIX B: ATSC DIGITAL TV STANDARD TRANSPORT PACKET STREAM

[511] E. Petajan, "The HDTV grand alliance system," *Proc. IEEE*, vol. 83, pp. 1094–1105, July 1995.

[512] Advanced Television Systems Committee, Doc. A/53, *ATSC Digital Television Standard*, Sept. 1995.

[513] Advanced Television Systems Committee, Doc. A/54, *Guide to the use of the ATSC Digital Television Standard*, Oct. 1995.

[514] Advanced Television Systems Committee, Doc. A/52, *ATSC Digital Audio Compression Standard*, Sept. 1995.

[515] European Telecommunications Standards Institute, *ETS300 421 DVB-Satellite, ETS300 429 DVB-Cable, ETS300 744 DVB-Terrestrial*.

[516] *Grand Alliance HDTV System Specification*, ver.2.0, Dec. 1994.

APPENDIX C: MULTIMEDIA AND STANDARDIZATION

[517] K. Asatani and S. Nogami, "Trends in the standardization of telecommunications on GII, multimedia, and other network technologies and services," *IEEE Comm. Magazine*, vol. 34, pp. 32–46, June 1996.

[518] T. Ebrahimi and M.Kunt, "Visual data compression for multimedia applications," *Proc. IEEE*, vol. 86, pp. 1109–1125, June 1998.

LATE ADDITIONS

[LA1] J. D. Gibson et al., *Digital compression for multimedia: principles and standards*, San Francisco, CA: Morgan Kaufmann, 1998.

[LA2] W. Ciciora, D. Lauge, and J. Farmer, *Advanced cable television technology*, San Francisco, CA: Morgan Kaufmann, 1998.

[LA3] J. Wilberg, *Codesign for real-time video application*, Hingham, MA: Kluwer Academic, 1998.

[LA4] B. Fox, "Digital TV comes down to earth," *IEEE Spectrum*, vol. 35, pp. 23–29, Oct. 1998.

[LA5]   P. Dambacher, *Digital terrestrial television broadcasting*, Berlin, Germany: Springer, 1998.

[LA6]   U. Reimers, *Digital video broadcasting*, Berlin, Germany: Springer, 1998.

[LA7]   Special issue on "Segmentation, description, and retrieval of video content," *IEEE Trans. CSVT*, vol. 8, pp. 521–696, Sept. 1998.

[LA8]   Special issue on, "Representation and Coding of images and video I," *IEEE Trans. CSVT*, vol. 8, pp. 797–920, Nov. 1998. Part II, vol. 9, pp. 1–199, Feb. 1999.

[LA9]   R. de Bruin and J. Smith, *Digital video broadcasting: technology, standards and regulators*, Boston, MA: Artech House, 1999.

[LA10] L. J. Nelson, "Image compression technology: For the decade ahead, wavelet soars," *Advanced Imaging*, vol. 14, pp. 10–12, April 1999.

[LA11] Special issue on synthetic/natural hybrid video coding, *IEEE Trans. CSVT*, vol. 9, pp. 205–400, March 1999.

[LA12] A. Puri and T. Chen, *Advances in multimedia: standards, systems and networks*, New York, NY: Marcel Dekker, 1999.

[LA13] R. Koenen, "MPEG-4 multimedia for our time," *IEEE Spectrum*, vol. 36, pp. 26–33, Feb. 1999.

[LA14] *IEEE Transactions on Multimedia*, vol. 1, pp. 1–114, March 1999.

Index

About the Authors

K. R. RAO

K. R. Rao received his Ph.D. in electrical engineering from The University of New Mexico, Albuquerque, in 1966. Since 1966, he has been with the University of Texas at Arlington, where he is currently a professor of electrical engineering. He, along with two other researchers, introduced the Discrete Cosine Transform in 1975, which has since become very popular in digital signal processing. He is the co-author of *Orthogonal Transforms for Digital Signal Processing* (Springer-Verlag, 1975), *Fast Transforms: Analyses and Applications* (Academic Press, 1982), *Discrete Cosine Transform-Algorithms, Advantages, Applications* (Academic Press, 1990), and *Techniques and Standards for Image/Video/Audio Coding* (Prentice Hall, 1996). In addition, he has edited *Discrete Transforms and Their Applications* (Van Nostrand Reinhold, 1985) and co-edited *Teleconferencing* (Van Nostrand Reinhold, 1985). Some of his books have been translated into Japanese, Chinese and Russian. He has conducted workshops/tutorials on video/audio coding/standards worldwide. He has published extensively in peer-reviewed journals and has been a consultant to industry, research institutes, and academia.

ZORAN S. BOJKOVIC

Dr. Zoran S. Bojkovic is Professor and Chief of the Postal and Communication Department in the Faculty of Transport and Traffic Engineering, at the University of Belgrade, Yugoslavia. He received his B.S., M.S., and Ph.D. (1978) degrees in electrical engineering from the University of Belgrade. He has taught many courses in electrical technology, telecommunication systems and networks planning, design, control, and maintenance, image processing, and image compression. He has been a visiting professor at Stanford University (1986), the University of Texas at Arlington (1993, 1997), Hsinghua University in Beijing, China (1996), Northern Jiatong University, Institute of Information Science, Beijing (1998), and at universities in Poland, Greece, and Romania. Prof. Bojkovic is the author of 15 books and has published more than 260 papers in international books, journals, and conference proceedings. He is also an active reviewer and a member of the scientific committee of numerous journals and conferences, and serves as chairman for international conferences, symposiums, and workshops. He has conducted and participated in many communication, scientific, and industrial projects. His current interests are in the areas of image, video, and speech coding and compression, and image processing with applications in Broadband Integrated Services Digital Networks. He is also an active researcher in multimedia communications.